Glasgow The Uneasy Peace

GLASGOW
THE UNEASY PEACE

Religious tension
in modern Scotland

Tom Gallagher

Manchester University Press

Published by
Manchester University Press
Oxford Road, Manchester M13 9PL, U.K.
27 South Main Street, Wolfeboro, NH 03894-2069, U.S.A.

British Library cataloguing in publication data
Gallagher, Tom, *1954—*
   Glasgow: The uneasy peace: religious tension
   in modern Scotland
   1. Irish—Scotland—History—20th century   2. Scotland—Emigration and
   immigration—History—20th century   3. Ireland—Emigration and immigration
   —History—20th century   4. Scotland—Religious life and customs—I. Title
   305.8'9162'0411   DA 774.4.17

Library of Congress cataloging in publication data
Gallagher, Tom, 1954—
   Glasgow: The uneasy peace
   Bibliography: p. 357.
   Includes index.
   1. Glasgow (Strathclyde)—Church history   2. Irish—Scotland—Glasgow
   (Strathclyde)   3. Glasgow (Strathclyde)—Ethnic relations.   I. Title.
   BR788.G58G35   1987   941.4'43082   87-11049

ISBN 0-7190-2396-3 *hardback*

Printed and bound in Great Britain by
Anchor Brendon Ltd, Tiptree, Essex
Typeset by Hems & Co., Cypress House, Turners Lane, Gillingham, Dorset

Contents

Abbreviations

AOH	Ancient Order of Hibernians
CDS	*Catholic Directory for Scotland*
CPGB	Communist Party of Great Britain
EIS	Educational Institute of Scotland
GAA	Glasgow Archdiocesan Archives
GH	*Glasgow Herald*
GO	*Glasgow Observer*
GP	General Practitioner
NI	Northern Ireland
PRO	Public Record Office
RC	Roman Catholic
SCO	*Scottish Catholic Observer*
SNP	Scottish National Party
SRO	Scottish Record Office
TESS	*Times Education Supplement for Scotland*

Acknowledgements

Material and information for this book were gathered from a wide variety of sources. An award from the British Academy's Research Fund in 1981 helped me to get the project under way and the bulk of the research and the drafting of chapters were completed thanks to a personal award (No. G0023 2038) from the Economic and Social Research Council in 1983. I am grateful to each of these bodies for their backing at key moments, for without it, it is difficult to see how the book could have been assembled in its present form except over a considerably longer time-scale. Thanks is also due to my head of department, Professor James O'Connell, who offered me both breathing space and his own personal encouragement to pursue my research in a facet of inter-ethnic relations that he is keenly interested in. I just hope that the backing he extended to me is in some way validated by the end result.

Newspapers were a particularly rich source of information, especially for the earlier chapters, and my debt to *The Glasgow Observer* (today *The Scottish Catholic Observer*) is clear from the number of times it is cited in the notes. It and other west-of-Scotland newspapers, such as *Forward*, were studied in the Glasgow Room of the Mitchell Library in Glasgow, and I should like to thank Joseph Fisher and many other staff in this marvellous research centre for the assistance they extended to me over the years. Mr Fisher, in particular, took a keen interest in my work, pointing me in the direction of interesting material I might otherwise not have located. To Mrs Manchester of the former Bailie Library, Pat Woods of Parkhead Library, Glasgow, the Rev Mark Dilworth, OSB, Keeper of the Scottish Catholic Archives, Audrey Canning of the Scottish Communist Party Library, John Horton of Bradford University's J. B. Priestley Library and Nora Marshall of that library's inter-library loan section, thanks are also due for their real help with this project. I should also acknowledge the help of staff at the following institutions and libraries: the National Library of Scotland, Edinburgh Public Library, and the Scottish Record Office, all located in Edinburgh; the Public Record Office, the British Newspaper Library, and the British Library in London; the Linen Hall Library and the Public Record Office of Northern Ireland in Belfast; the National Library of Ireland, Trinity College Library, the Manuscript Room of University College Dublin, each in the Irish capital; and finally the Archive Department of

Strathclyde Regional Council, the Catholic Press Office, the Glasgow Archdiocesan Archives, and the libraries of the Universities of Strathclyde and Glasgow.

Journalists who helped me by offering information, giving me access to cuttings files, and providing me with the opportunity to try out my findings in the form of newspaper articles, include James Seaton of *The Scotsman*, Tom Shields and James Freeman of *The Glasgow Herald* and a trio of past editors of *The Glasgow Observer* and *The Irish Weekly*'s Scottish edition: Pat Bolan, Michael Fallon, and William Murphy gave me real encouragement at different moments and I hope that I have benefited from their advice and accumulated experience in Scottish Catholic journalism.

Professor Christopher Smout offered valuable advice and pointed out inaccuracies, oversights, and elisions for which I am grateful. Dr John McCaffrey and Ian and Gill Bayne commented on parts of the first draft and I appreciate the time and trouble they have taken on my behalf. Without Ian and Gill's encouragement and stimulating advice this book would be considerably duller, especially in the later sections. Dr John Durkan's often witty accounts of fifty years of change and resistance to change in the west-of-Scotland Catholic world were both entertaining and extremely helpful for offering a human and historical perspective that I could never acquire. Although I only met him once, James Darragh proved extremely helpful in providing me with material about the lay Catholic movement in the west of Scotland from the 1930s to the 1950s. He may consider that I have bitten off more than I can chew, but I remain indebted to him for bringing highly relevant but obscure material to my notice and for patiently fielding my sometimes naive questions. Bill Murray in Australia was a valued correspondent and I benefited from the discussions I had with him, Ian Wood, Bob Purdie, Steve Bruce, and Graham Walker. The bi-annual Lipman Seminar which Bob Purdie and Austen Morgan have staged in Ireland gave me an opportunity to compare Glasgow with Belfast and Liverpool in the very congenial surroundings of Townley Hall, Co. Meath. Graham Walker and the late Jim Fyfe of the Scottish press corps made the 1984 Lipman Seminar a very fruitful and enjoyable one in terms of discussion and stimulation for further research.

Perhaps the most important source of information for the book has been a series of (usually taped) interviews with over seventy people who had information and views to impart about the changing nature of community relations in the west of Scotland. It is a testimony to the more relaxed atmosphere in Glasgow during the first half of the 1980s and the willingness of people across the religious, political and social spectrum to talk about what previously had been a taboo subject, that only three of the many people I approached in the course of this research failed to respond or declined to see me. However, some of the people I interviewed and who helped me wish to remain anonymous. I am nevertheless grateful for the time and assistance they were able to spare me. Those whom I would like to thank publicly are listed in the bibliographical section on page 000; some among their number were particularly co-operative and I hope none of them will object to being singled out for special thanks here. They virtually span the entire spectrum of community life in Scotland as well informed readers can confirm from the following list of names: Hugh Brown, MP, David Bryce, Fr Bernard Canning, Tom Carberry, the Rev. James Currie, the Rev. Donald Macdonald, McDonald Morris, W. J. McKechin, J. G. MacLean, Peter Mullen, and Fr Anthony Ross, OP.

My debt to those who corresponded with me by letter should also be acknowledged. They include Bernard Aspinwall, Lawrence Daly, Tom Kirkwood of Corpach, the late Archie Lamont, Graeme Purves, Charles Smith of Edinburgh, and William Spiers.

By seeking to monitor community relations and the emergence of the Catholic community through the different lenses of electoral politics, religious friction and later dialogue, education, employment practices, and Northern Ireland's impact on Scotland, I may have left a number of hostages to fortune. I have no doubt that more probing and complete studies remain to be carried out into specific aspects of Protestant–Catholic relations, sometimes too briefly scrutinised here.

The aim has been to provide a balanced assessment of an issue that remains a sensitive one in the life of contemporary Scotland and which has not been examined in this degree of detail hitherto. Errors and imperfections will be found within the pages of the book, given its experimental nature; I take full responsibility for them although it ought to be pointed out that I have endeavoured not to give needless offence to any person mentioned, living or dead.

If *Glasgow: The Uneasy Peace* stimulates further research it will be ample reward for turning over a stone which has remained undisturbed for too long. My interest in Glasgow's rich and tumultous religious heritage will hopefully remain undiminished once the book comes before the public. If, on reading it, there is any reader who would like to raise any issue treated in the book in the light of local knowledge or personal experience, I can be contacted at the School of Peace Studies, University of Bradford, Bradford, West Yorkshire BD7 1DP.   T. G.

September 1986

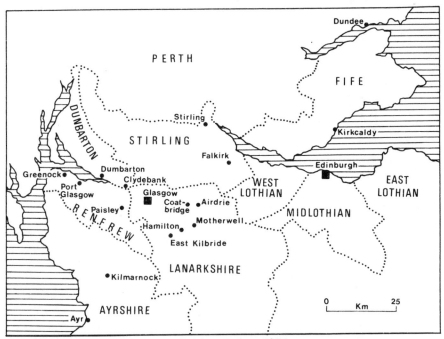

Central Scotland: administrative divisions before 1974

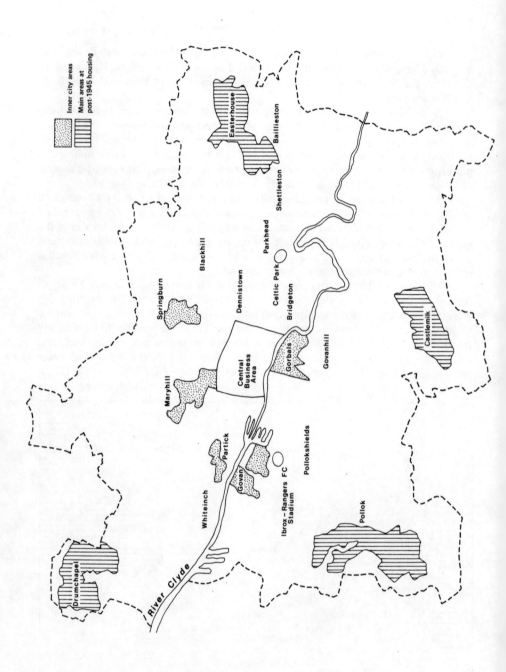

Inner city areas

Main areas at post-1945 housing

Easterhouse

Baillieston

Shettleston

Parkhead

Blackhill

Celtic Park

Dennistown

Springburn

Bridgeton

Castlemilk

Gorbals

Central Business Area

Govanhill

Maryhill

Partick

Pollokshields

Whiteinch

Govan

Ibrox – Rangers FC Stadium

Pollok

River Clyde

Drumchapel

The City of Glasgow

Introduction

The view that the Northern Ireland conflict is a horrible aberration quite at variance with traditions and practices in the larger neighbouring island can be immediately dispelled on attending any football match between two Glasgow rivals- Rangers and Celtic, known collectively as the 'Old Firm'. The enmity and hysteria sometimes on display at Old Firm matches can serve as a timely reminder of just how thin the crust of civilisation is. Here regular battles have been fought out between the supporters of a dead Dutch Protestant king (William of Orange) and a live continental priest (the Pope) for generations. The terms 'Catholic' and 'Protestant' are important symbols of solidarity which many Celtic and Rangers fans respectively choose to identify with. But their allegiance to these symbols is tribal rather than doctrinal and there is usually little that is Christian or spiritual about it.

The Old Firm phenomenon shows that Northern Ireland most certainly does not have a total monopoly of the sectarian religious tension to be found in these islands. It also demonstrates that one corner of Britain exists where large numbers of people both understand and identify with the rival national causes which are at the root of the warfare in Ulster. The rival flags of Protestant Ulster and Nationalist Ireland-the Red Hand and the Tricolour- are held aloft as battle emblems at Old Firm matches with Scotland's saltire flag usually nowhere in sight. Feelings are quickly aroused sometimes to the level of hysteria by the singing of Orange and nationalist songs imported from Ireland. Outside the ground propaganda from Ulster in the form of newspapers, badges, pennants, and stickers is often on sale; when feelings are running high in Belfast, collections are often taken for 'the cause' in pubs near the Old Firm stadia and generous donations made in the flush of victory.

It is appropriate that Scotland is the one remaining part of Britain where the religious divisions underlying the Ulster conflict continue to be something of a live issue. In its present form the conflict originated with the arrival of Scottish and English settlers who had been recruited by King James I early in the seventeenth century to maintain a Protestant bridgehead in Ulster, then the part of Ireland putting up the greatest resistance to English rule. Ulster was almost a Scottish colony in the seventeenth century, but settlers and natives refused to make common cause; in an era of savage religious warfare they belonged in opposite Christian camps: conflict over land and property as well as faith ensured that suspicion and enmity characterised ordinary social relations in Ulster long after religious peace gradually returned to the rest of Europe.

Very early in the nineteenth century immigrants from the northern counties of Ireland were drawn to Scotland by the industrial revolution. The reserve army of labour which made Glasgow the 'Second City of the Empire' largely came from this source. But the immigrants brought their quarrels and rivalries with them and economic rivalry between workers competing to sell their labour breathed new life into old disputes.

Among the immigrants the Protestant Irish were in a clear minority but they felt far more at home in Scotland than the more numerous Catholic Irish, since they were familiar with Scottish customs and institutions, shared the Protestant faith and were, in many cases, returning to the land of their forefathers. These ties of kinship enabled local workers and Protestant immigrants to display solidarity with one another. They made common cause against the Catholic immigrant Irish, who threatened working-class living standards by swamping the labour market and selling their labour at low rates. Since the Protestant immigrants were already mobilised against the Catholic threat at home, their partisan symbols, and institutions—principally the Orange Order—were adopted by all those workers keen to distinguish themselves from the despised Catholic Irish. Racial, cultural or religious criteria such as membership of the Orange Order or the freemasons, the adoption of a 'respectable' lifestyle, and worship at a particular church, were used to underline the difference and regulate entry into skilled trades. Catholics formed the marginal or unskilled proletariat and in Glasgow and Belfast they comprised similar proportions of the population roughly between one-quarter and one-third overall.

Neither city thus became a melting pot where workers could put aside their pre-industrial differences. But Glasgow avoided the complete religious polarisation which gripped Belfast and, above all, its working-class citizens by the middle of the nineteenth century. The west of Scotland showed itself to be more than a cultural extension of Ulster, being part of a national entity which had preserved its own distinct traditions, institutions, and ways of reconciling internal differences.

Orangeism was a dangerous but never absolutely dominant force in the skilled working class, Irish nationalist sympathies did not altogether prevent Catholics identifying with their adopted city. In a drastically overcrowded Glasgow, informal mechanisms of restraint emerged which prevented the city from being engulfed in sectarian warfare. While still holding fast to their hatreds, rival Orange and Green factions stepped back from the brink more often than in Belfast, and the soccer rivalry which emerged at the start of this century may have been a useful tension-releasing valve—two rival working-class communities were able to assert their identity through sporting champions who had the fortunes of their own people on their shoulders.

In time the working class acquired radical traditions and a level of class-consciousness which had brought the term 'Red Clydeside' into being by the 1920s. Visitors to Glasgow, struck by the militancy of workers then, could be excused for being puzzled by the survival of another form of assertiveness which stressed the religious symbols that divided workers. They got little enlightenment from local commentators, who viewed religious bigotry as a subject to be avoided and who were reluctant to draw attention to the fact that a very large proportion of the population of Scotland's largest city was in fact Irish by birth or extraction. Examination of local internecine tension was also discouraged by the fear that sectarian hotheads might draw encouragement from publicity. As a result reliable information about the strength of Orange and Green antagonisms on Clydeside—and just what fuelled them—became hard to come by.

Instead impressionistic reporting and stereotyping by visiting journalists after a particularly violent Old Firm match could often give a distorted impression of the nature and scale of relgious discord, especially to non-Scots. After decades of such reporting, Cliff Hanley, a Glasgow novelist, commented in 1981 that it would not surprise him if the English had 'fantasies of Catholics and Protestants slugging it out in every street from the east end to the west end, day and night' after hearing reports of fresh Old Firm violence. In the same year the usually reliable BBC World Service compounded the problem in a news bulletin on 15 February when it referred to 'Glasgow, a city notorious for its bigotry'.

Glasgow's contradictory image as a city of primitive religious passions simultaneously wedded to the ideals of socialism, a doctrine which relegates religion to a lowly plane and stresses the brotherhood of man, seemed a subject overdue for examination by 1981, the year in which I first began tentatively exploring the religious itch that is still capable of causing acute discomfort in the west of Scotland. It is for readers to make up their own minds whether childhood and adolescence spent in Glasgow, followed by fourteen years spent studying and teaching at universities in the north of England, has provided me with the right mix of detachment, insight and local experience to chart the ebb and flow of religious misunderstanding and conflict in Scotland. Glasgow is the primary focus of the book but its sweep extends over the whole of urban Scotland from the west to the east coast because a number of important local variations in Protestant–Catholic relations exist which make it unwise to generalise about the whole of central Lowland Scotland on the basis of what is the norm in its largest city.

A sense of religious difference remains that is sometimes shown in quite subtle ways in nearly every part of Scotland where Irish immigration ceased to make the locality a homogeneous one in religious terms. This was only really made clear to me on moving across the border to northern England. Here its cities and manufacturing towns also witnessed heavy Irish settlement at exactly the same moment as in Scotland, giving rise, in the case of the Lancashire cotton towns and the port of Liverpool, to much sharper friction than anything witnessed in Scotland even when relations between host and newcomer fell to their lowest point. Yet, by the 1980s, religious rivalry had long ceased to be an issue of importance in any of the chief English reception centres for the Irish and, even in Liverpool, where arguably such rivalry polarised the city until after 1945, it has been overtaken by other preoccupations.

This book explains what it is besides geographical proximity that allows the west of Scotland to have more in common with divided Ulster than any other part of the mainland has. It examines how two distinct religious communities grew up in Scotland's industrial heyday which inhabited different social and psychological worlds even though they lived in close proximity to one another.

Considerable attention is given to the Catholic community, since it was the catalyst whose existence produced a hostile reaction from Protestant Scotland which lasted in one form or another for well over a century. Moreover, the Catholic community (up till quite recently) has been neglected by those who have commented on the Scottish condition, despite its numerical size, or alternatively has been subject to misrepresentation or crude stereotyping by observers who felt that it was enough to acknowledge its existence without enquiring too closely about its role in Scottish life. From a predominantly working-class Catholic community engaged in an often grim struggle for exist-ence, there was little attempt to make up for the silence of the rest of society by attempting to carve out an identity or define a role in Scottish or British life.

Until quite recently many Catholics felt rootless, almost strangers in their own land. They were not really Irish, since the great majority were neither born nor reared there; neither were they British, since their Irish ancestry gave them a built-in hostility to that identity; nor were they yet Scottish, since the Scots were still confused about their own identity and were not always ready to acknowledge that Catholics of Hibernian extraction were full members of the Scottish nation. With such avenues blocked off Scottish Catholics drew a strong sense of identity from their religous faith, and significantly it was their religion and not their ethnic Irish identity which defined the community, both in its own eyes and to the rest of society, certainly by the end of the First World War.

Throughout the book the role of the Catholic Church in first of all laying down spiritual and psychological markers for a disorientated people trying to adjust to a strange environment, and later creating an alternative institutional structure of schools and lay institutions to which the descendants of the first wave of immigrants might relate, is stressed. An explanation for the decision of the leaders of the Catholic community to embark on a path of 'separate development' from the rest of society is found in the sharp economic, religious, and ethnic gulf which placed it outside mainstream Scottish society. The book seeks to identify what were the pressure points which gave rise to tension and division in society and how and why these altered down the years. It examines the effect a number of influential institutions and social forces had on community relations, ranging from the chief religious groupings and affiliates such as the Orange Order, to the state at local and national level, and the political parties. The manner in which some of these bodies interacted, especially at sensitive moments, helped to offset complete religious polarisation, but it is less easy to see why some sources of friction have dried up (in the ecclesiastical and party political context, for instance) while others, in the sporting context and in the field of state education, have renewed themselves down the generations.

The 1930s were in many ways the most testing period for community relations in Scotland, since they witnessed the worst outbreaks of religious strife; the manner in which the complete polarisation of Scottish society was avoided then is examined and particular attention is given to the social and economic changes of the subsequent decades which may have helped to prevent a reoccurrence of street conflict in the 1970s and 1980s. Community relations in these two decades are closely monitored, and why Scotland has enjoyed domestic peace and improving community relations in the shadow of the Ulster conflict is one of the key questions posed.

The rise and decline of acute religious tension in Glasgow turns out in many ways to have been a lively and eventful story but I have tried to resist the temptation of over-dramatising it for the sake of the narrative. That would only distort it and frustrate one of the prime aims of the overall project: why *relative* harmony and the emergence of peaceful coexistence in the midst of very tangible community disagreements? What have been the chief factors that have encouraged assimilation and reduced the feeling of 'us and them'?

It was to remind me of the need to remain low-key, especially when discussing religious issues, that the lower-case has been used in the main body of the text whenever the words 'protestant' and 'catholic' appear (other than in specific titles). These emotive religious terms occur so frequently that if they had been 'sign-lit' by capitals on every occasion it might have fostered the subconscious impression that religious identity or friction was a more determining feature of Scottish life than in the case in reality. I had no other motive in using such a device and I hope that no reader who identifies with any denomination coming under the heading 'protestant' or 'catholic' will take offence at my usage.

Chapter 1 **Protestant Scotland and the arrival of the Irish**

Immigrants from rural Ireland first began to arrive in Scotland in considerable numbers at the dawn of the nineteenth century. The industrial revolution was already gathering pace in lowland Scotland and, with it, a demand for low-cost labour needed to build the roads, canals and railways, and work in the mines, factories and mills that would transform the appearance of central Scotland in a few decades. With Lancashire in mind, Friedrich Engels claimed in 1843 that the industrial revolution would have been a much more gradual affair but for the human raw material provided by the immigrant Irish.[1] This may have been even more true of Scotland where, by 1851, 7·2% of the population was Irish compared with 2·9% in England and Wales.[2] But in no part of industrial Britain were the catholic Irish welcomed or esteemed, and they in turn showed no anxiety to correspond to the cutoms and routine of their adopted communities.

In Scotland it could have been predicted in advance that the encounter between host and newcomer would be traumatic for both parties. In previous centuries a sharp cultural and developmental gulf had opened up between Ireland and Scotland which had not previously existed when both had lain outside England's political orbit. The catalysts were the Reformation, the Act of Union of 1707, and the industrial revolution, starting around 1760.

Scotland enthusiastically adopted the new reformed faith, more hesitantly entered into political union with England, and became one of the first nations to industrialise, as Ireland remained faithful to Rome, locked in colonial subjugation to Britain, and economically destitute but politically unreconciled to the version of 'Pax Britannica' imposed upon it.

Of course, this broad generalisation needs to take into account developments in the north of Ireland where, in the seventeenth century, a British settler community took hold whose links with the west of

Scotland and with Lancashire, were bound to greatly complicate community relations in these two areas of heaviest immigration from Ireland. Otherwise Scotland moved closer to England even though it preserved important areas of autonomy through its legal, religious, and educational institutions, while Ireland drifted apart from the larger island, even though under absolute domination from London.

By the 1800s, when the first emigrant ships were docking at the Broomielaw in Glasgow, blood ties and a common heritage up to the end of the Middle Ages counted for little between the peoples of Scotland and Ireland. Bishop Gray explained to Henry Manning, the English prelate who visited Scotland in 1867, that there was little common ground between them:

> The Scotch are animated by a strong hereditary hatred of Catholicity. nor is the feeling of the country favourable to Irish settlers . . . The religion, the history, the character and habits of the two peoples show many elements not of difference only but antagonism.[3]

Manning spent a week in Scotland in order to draw up a report for the Vatican about strife within the church between Scottish and Irish clergy. Even the leadership of the church, drawn mainly from the Highlands, had been more than touched by the changes occurring in Scottish society so that it presented an alien face to many of the Irish. Acceptance of such conditioning may have been the price for its survival after the Reformation of the mid-sixteenth century.

The Scottish Reformation was so complete that, unlike other parts of northern Europe, no bloody civil war between protestants and catholic factions was necessary for the reformed faith to triumph. The old faith simply melted away except in the Gaelic-speaking West Highlands, some of the offshore Hebridean islands, and in Banffshire in the north-east. Scotland avoided the horrific carnage of the Thirty Years War fought in central Europe between 1618 and 1648 and persecution of roman catholics could not be described as systematic or savage. The only priest to be put to death in seventeenth century Scotland was St John Ogilvie SJ, who was executed at Glasgow cross in 1615.[4] Protestants were far more vindictive towards fellow protestants as the bloody persecution of the Covenanters in the 1680s by the temporarily ascendant Episcopalians (who subscribed to the Anglican communion) showed. This was not the first nor would it be the last time that family quarrels in the reformed Christian church diverted attention from the 'Menace of Rome'. Protestant fundamentalists and radicals would always be more animated by anti-elitism or by religious deviationism within their own ranks than by the survival of some thousands of Scottish catholics.[5] But their tiny church entered its most perilous phase in the year 1700 when the penal laws introduced throughout Great Britain and Ireland banned catholics from practising their faith, prohibited them from teaching even their own children, and risked them losing their property to their nearest protestant relatives.

Between 1680 and 1800 the number of catholics in Scotland may have dropped from 50,000 to 30,000.[6] Catholic attachment to the Jacobite cause, which was vanquished in the rebellions of 1715 and 1745, increased the pressure of the state on them and thousands of Highland catholics emigrated to north America in succeeding decades. But the penal laws were not applied as harshly as in Ireland; some powerful catholic nobles existed who were able to protect tenant farmers and labourers from the worst rigours of persecution; the eighteenth century Enlightenment glowed strongly in Scotland, one of its cornerstones being religious toleration; and the Highland clan society disintegrated so rapidly after 1745 that the penal laws were increasingly allowed to lapse.

A growing spirit of toleration was confirmed by the 1793 Relief Act which abolished the most punitive anti-catholic laws still on the statute books. By now the bishops and clergy of the Scottish mission (Rome relegated the catholic church in Scotland to missionary status between 1603 and 1878), were ready to accept the new Hanoverian order and indeed had lost the taint of Jacobitism more quickly than the Episcopalians.[7] George Hay, bishop of the lowland district, insisted that all clergy and laity pray for the Hanoverian monarch and, by the end of the eighteenth century, some Scottish priests were beginning to serve as chaplains in the British army.[8]

In the 1780s Scottish bishops were already making it clear to Rome that, although they desperately needed extra clergy, they would prefer not to have Irish priests, some of whom were willing to sanction resistance to British domination.[9] They remembered the anti-catholic riot in Edinburgh during 1779 and the 'No Popery' scare of 1788, in which 12,000 Glaswegians vowed to suppress idolatory and managed to block a relief bill.[10] One nineteenth century historian claimed that in the 1790s, when Glasgow had no more than thirty-nine catholics, there were forty-three anti-catholic societies.[11]

Such hostility stemmed from a more general fear of Jacobitism in lowland Scotland. Any revival of Prince Charles Edward Stewart's cause would, it was feared, jeopardise the new-won prosperity of industrial Scotland and perhaps encourage a French invasion. So potential adherents of the pretender's cause were scarcely esteemed and the hostile atmosphere delayed by fourteen years a relief bill already law in Ireland and England by 1779.[12]

So the 1770s and 1780s demonstrated how deeply anti-catholicism was embedded in the popular culture of Scotland. However, the death of the pretender in 1788 and the manner in which the French revolution produced an unlikely alliance between Britain and the Vatican broke down much upper-class religious prejudice in Britain. The exchequer even paid a grant to catholic clergy from 1798 to 1804, since the revolutionary upheavals in Europe had closed off their main sources of financial support.[13]

A sign of local harmony emerged from Glasgow in 1817 when Kirkman Finlay, the city's MP, sponsored a Catholic Schools Society along with several other city businessmen. Its object, the creation of a catholic school for the city's mounting catholic population, was achieved soon after. St Andrew's parish, the first in the city, had already been created in 1792 and, in 1816, a landmark in the history of the catholic community was reached with the opening of St Andrew's cathedral in Clyde street.

But when Sir James Mackintosh, the rector of Glasgow university, made a favourable reference to the new cathedral, he was howled down by the students.[14] Toleration still had a long way to go and it could not simply be legislated into existence. This was demonstrated in 1829 with the stormy passage of the Catholic Emancipation Act which allowed catholics to be elected to parliament. Edinburgh's legal and academic establishment publicly supported the act, Sir Walter Scott signed their petition, and the charismatic Church of Scotland minister, Thomas Chalmers, placed his influence and oratory behind it. But if allowed to express their opinion in a referendum, the majority of Scots would probably have voted no and the opposition intensified as one moved east to west and nearer to Glasgow.[15] By a large majority, the General Session of Glasgow (comprising ministers and elders of the Church of Scotland) rejected the act as did Glasgow university students. The town council voted against, although by a narrow majority, and the *Glasgow Herald* was hostile.[16]

Ordinary Glaswegians displayed particular hostility to the act for social as well as religious reasons. Workers and artisans were acutely aware how rapidly the city's Irish community was growing and what the consequences might be for their livelihoods:

> the lower orders in the west of Scotland were very naturally ever ready to do anything which, in their opinion, would press and keep back the Irish Catholics who pour in upon them almost with every tide, coming to compete with them successfully in all their occupations, and thereby materially lowering the rate of wages.[17]

Irish immigration to Scotland was not a new phenomenon; indeed population movements across the North channel, the narrow waterway which separates the south-west tip of Scotland from the Ulster coast, had been relatively frequent across the broad sweep of recorded history. But the character and extent of Irish immigration began to change abruptly in the first quarter of the nineteenth century.

Hitherto immigrants had been mainly seasonal agricultural labourers who were often only temporary visitors hardly visible to most of the Scottish population. But a new type of immigrant appeared after 1775 when the Scottish canals began to be dug. They stayed for longer periods, some settled permanently in Scotland, and their growing numbers led to friction with indigenous Scottish labourers. They collided with Highland migrants for whom it had been hoped the building of the canals would relieve some of the acute distress in the north.[18] In many cases, both groups of workers shared the Gaelic tongue and belonged to similar rural societies but this common cultural heritage counted for little in the hectic and often violent struggle for jobs.

Few if any Irishmen settled in the Scottish countryside where work was usually only seasonal and which many Scots were themselves quitting for the towns. Many labourers needed to send money to dependents at home and often the reward for farm work was payment in kind.[19] So, like the immigrant Irish elsewhere, those in Scotland increasingly flocked to the populated centres. Before the close of the eighteenth century, they were already clearly visible in Glasgow. In 1805, when Andrew Scott came to the city, where he found himself the only priest, he had 450 parishioners but, in less than five years, the Irish had swelled the numbers to well over 3,000.[20] In a few years, the whole map of Scottish catholicism was to be changed. By 1822, there were an estimated twelve hundred catholics in Glenlivet, a Highland stronghold of the faith, compared to 15,000 in Glasgow,[21] by 1851, the Irish made up 7·2% of the Scottish population and 18·2% of that of the largest city, Glasgow.

There were separate emigration routes from different parts of Ireland to Britain. Most of those reaching Scotland took the northern route from Ulster and north Connacht.[22] The passage money to Scotland was becoming cheaper due to new innovations in, and the growth of, transportation so that it could fall within the reach of even the very poor. Not all the nineteenth century immigrants chose to settle down permanently in Scotland, otherwise they would have made an even greater demographic impact. The more enterprising, and those with fewest dependants often used Scotland as a convenient jumping-off point until they could gather together enough cash to embark on the voyage across the Atlantic. The less energetic and the poorest tended to stay put where they dominated the ranks of the casual and unskilled labour force.

Unlike later wages of migration, religion only lightly touched the first arrivals once in Glasgow and was not a major bone of contention with their hosts. Many lost their faith through 'a total submersion in the common culture of poverty'.[23] By the 1840s, there were only half-a-dozen Scottish clergy to cope with the 70,000 Irish immigrants who were pouring into the west of Scotland as famine raged in Ireland— when over one hundred priests, preferably from the same society as the immigrants, would have been needed. In 1847, three of those Scottish priests, one in Greenock and two in Paisley, died of typhus fever while ministering to destitute refugees in flight from mass starvation at home.[24] It has been reckoned that when Irish priests did begin to arrive, it was thirty years too late and wholesale apostasy had already taken place.[25]

Concentrated on the bottom rungs of the occupational ladder and huddled into their cramped quarters in the chief urban centres, the Irish constituted 'the most abject part of the population, prepared to tolerate a lower standard of life than all but the very poorest' of the workforce.[26] Many were unable to survive the very painful transition from a rough and simple peasant society to the far more brutal and alien industrial environment and they succumbed to disease, under-nourishment, or alcohol. The average life expectancy in Glasgow during the 1840s was thirty which is lower than in most big cities of the Third World today. On average, Scots drank five times as much spirits as the English so this shared weakness did not make the Irish nearly as conspicuous as they were in other centres of the diaspora where their fondness for alcohol became a key element of their stereo-type.[27] But nevertheless the Irish were despised and feared because of their poverty and alien character and respected nineteenth century opinion moulders like Matthew Arnold and Thomas Carlyle did not hesitate to describe the Irish influx as a social disaster for Victorian Britain.

The priest was the only authority to whom Irish labourers readily showed any deference and he was *the* central figure in immigrant neighbourhoods.[28] Often he was the only man of education and stand-ing in what were uprooted peasant communities and the last point of orientation with their old way of life.[29] But in Scotland, this was not as true as in other parts of industrial Britain, at least before 1850. Irish priests were not welcomed by the Scottish church which feared being colonised outright by the much larger church in Ireland. Alexander Cameron, bishop of the lowland distrist from 1805 to 1825, at the very time of maximum transition, was even reluctant to accept any sons of immigrants to train at the single Scottish seminary.[30] Scottish priests complained of the superstitious practices indulged in by the Irish and could be exasperated by the inconsistency of parishioners whose devotion could be disfigured by recourse to drink or to brawl-ing.[31] This was unstable behaviour which Scottish clergymen more readily ascribed to the Irish national temperament than to the upheavals occasioned by migration to a strange and uncongenial new homeland.

In their turn, the Irish sometimes felt that Scottish catholics were little different from protestants. Their clergy disliked the continental-style devotions, the religious images, and the elaborate ceremonial, all things the Irish cherished.[32] Immigrants did not readily forget the ways of the 'oul country' and would not be ready for many years to contemplate assimilation with even fellow Scottish catholics.

In 1823, a Glasgow Catholic Association, composed entirely of Irishmen, was formed which identified itself with what were the first stirrings of political nationalism at home and with the more traditional hostility to landlords. From his pulpit, Bishop Scott condemned disloyalty, and support for Irish secret societies, and he told his congregation that they were ignorant, dirty, and uncouth, mention being made of the forms of animal life which he saw infesting their persons.[33] William McGowan, the chief force behind the new association, was dismised from his teaching post and it folded. The association's plans to establish a catholic newspaper and library came to grief, more because of the economic weakness of the Irish than because of clerical displeasure. Although it would be a long time before they could have their own institutional outlets, many of the Irish in Glasgow were inflamed by the behaviour of the bishop and his co-adjutor John Murdoch who succeeded him in 1846. The animosity between the Irish and their Scottish clergy of the 1820s and 1830s spread to later waves of immigrants and would produce a full-scale crisis in the church during the 1860s.

The polarisation of the catholic church in Scotland on straight ethnic lines demonstrated how completely out of step the immigrants were with the outlook and values of the host society. But the initial cause of friction between immigrants and the local population tended more often to be economic rather than religious. Working-class solidarity was not a strong enough impulse to bring Irish and Scottish wage labourers together even though, during the 1830s and 1840s, they were already toiling in close proximity at a time when radical movements like the Chartists enjoyed a mass following in Britain. Even before the famine of the mid-1840s, frequent calls were made to restrict Irish immigration. In 1834, Dr Muir, a Presbyterian minister in Glasgow, declared that 'it would be advantageous were such immigration stopped because it would prevent the growth of Popery in the west of Scotland, which is the fruitful mother of all evils that at present afflict Ireland'.[34] This call received the loudest endorsement in working-class communities but not for the reason outlined by Dr Muir.

It was the Irishman's readiness to toil longer, harder, and for less remuneration which elicted the bitterest response from Scottish and

English workers. Coming from a rural society where money often did not have much meaning, the Irish undoubtedly helped to depress real wages and conditions by working longer for lower rates of pay. In Scotland, this was particularly true of the Lanarkshire coalfields, south-east of Glasgow, where antagonism between Scottish and Irish workers was possibly at its worst in the nineteenth century. During 1854, miners in Airdrie struck to expel the Irish from the coalfields.[35] As late as the 1880s, Keir Hardie could complain about the Irish collier who had 'a big shovel, a strong back and a weak brain', came straight from 'a peat bog or a tattie field' and produced 'coal enough for a man and a half'.[36]

Coal owners and iron masters did not hesitate to import Irish workers (and Highlanders) so as to break strikes. In 1831, Irish labour was used to break a strike in Coatbridge which became an important immigrant centre rivalling the adjacent and mainly indigenous mining town of Airdrie.[37] Well into the nineteenth century, plenty of Irish were to be found in those parts of the Scottish coalfields where non-union labour predominated.[38] In the 1850s and 1860s, the truck system, whereby employees were paid in tokens that could be exchanged for goods in company shops, flourished in the Scottish mines and iron works, even though condemned by act of parliament. The MP James Baird (1803-76), owner of the Gartsherrie coal mines and iron works in Lanarkshire, was twice prosecuted under the truck act in the 1860s.[39] Sometimes employers sponsored sectarian infighting by recruiting an Irish workforce composed of rival protestant and catholic ('Orange' and 'Green') segments and then setting them down in the same locality.[40] As a parliamentary candidate for Falkirk in 1851, Baird included anti-catholic statements in his manifesto even though he had sent agents to Ireland in order to recruit a workforce from among rural catholics.[41]

In Glasgow, with its high ratio of skilled jobs, there was less economic friction since the poorly educated immigrants, totally lacking local connections, simply could not compete for them. Instead they dominated the unskilled labour market in the city finding work as casual construction or dock labourers, coal heavers, and as sweated labour in textiles, and in the chemical and dyeing works which were polluting the city by the middle of the century; here men, and especially women, toiled in truly appalling conditions.[42]

Nineteenth century Glasgow was second only to Liverpool as a reception-centre for Irish immigrants and, to this day, the communal tensions which unite the two in many minds, are seen as taking identical forms. But, in practice, surface similarities give way to a more complex picture. Nineteenth century Liverpool was a mercantile and commercial port rather than an industrial centre. The occupational structure of the city included a far higher percentage of unskilled manual, and part-time jobs for which the Irish *were* in a position to compete. So, to a greater degree than in Glasgow, sectarian friction stemmed from economic competition and was of a more intense and unpleasant kind.

But Scotland had its own mini-Liverpools. Down the river Clyde in Greenock and in the adjacent town of Port Glasgow, the labour market was far more fluid than in the nearby metropolis of Glasgow. Here catholic and protestant workers from Ireland worked in uneasy proximity in the sugar refineries and on the dockside quays. Economic competiton was fierce and spilled over into communal disorders, especially in the 1850s. Some employers in Greenock favoured the Irish because they were more adaptable than Scottish workers.[43] In Lanarkshire, the Irish secured work in the textile mills, from which they had been barred in the north of England, because of the reluctance of Scots to be drawn into the factory system on terms that the Irish accepted far more willingly;[44] Sir Walter Scott was impressed by the industry of the Irish labourers who worked on his estate and spoke up for them.[45] Because of their economic value, British politicians ignored requests that immigrants from Ireland be denied entry to Britain.[46]

But it would be wrong to portray the Irish as empty-headed automatans who were like clay in the hands of whosoever employed them. No uniform pattern emerges because the industrial revolution was a very complex process to which workers responded in different ways even within specific regions. Where the Irish left behind casual open-air labour and became part of the factory workforce, they were affected by the class consciousness which grew up in the enclosed world of the factory. In 1836, employers who gave evidence before the select committee on the Irish poor, testified that Irish workers were more prone to rebellion and insubordination than English workers. The Irish were 'the talkers and ringleaders on all occasions', the 'most difficult to handle', having a 'command of words' by which they often misled English workers.[47]

Even the historian of the nineteenth century Lanarkshire miners was to conclude that the evidence is contradictory regarding Irish attitudes to strikes and combinations.[48] D. F. Macdonald has suggested that although the labour surplus created by the immigrants was a real barrier to successful trade-unionism, 'the Irish actually took a prominent part in labour disturbances', at least by the mid-nineteenth century.[49] But the hope of Engels, expressed in the 1840s, that 'the . . . mixture of the more facile, excitable, fiery Irish temperament with the stable, reasoning, persevering English must, in the long-run be productive only of good for both' was a highly optimistic one for the time and might have been rash if it was specifically addressed to the Scottish situation.[50]

If economic friction had been the only major source of division, community relations would have begun to steadily improve, perhaps even in the lifetimes of the first and second generation Irish resident in industrial Scotland. However, the gulf between the Irish and nearly every section of the host population was more of a cultural one which made it difficult for misunderstandings and social antagonisms to be breached. A whole bundle of distinguishing characteristics—race and accent, religion, occupation, residence, and politics—set the catholic Irish portion of Glasgow's population apart from the rest.[51] Prejudice towards them came not just from traditional religious or political foes but was endemic throughout society. In 1847, when the anti-catholic journal, *The Witness*, associated roman catholicism with dependance and indigence, and protestantism with vitality and progress, it was merely repeating a widely-held Victorian nostrum.[52] Some years later, the *Glasgow Herald* reacted bitterly against the starving Irish, much preferring that they choose north America as a permanent home, while pointing to the potential benefits for Britain in the recent famine:

> The Irish family grows on the other side of the Atlantic, and grows so prosperous that we could almost hope that the whole of their disconnected connections who have been left behind, will shortly follow them . . . If the country continues to be thinned, as we believe it will be by the deportation of families left behind, we may yet have the power, so much desiderated, of establishing a British population in Ireland and rendering real the Union of the United Kingdom.[53]

Even in the unlikely pages of the census report for Scotland, strong hostility towards the Irish presence could be found. That for 1871 included the following passage: 'as yet the body of those Irish do not seem to have improved by their residence among us and it is quite certain that the native Scot who has associated with them, has most certainly deteriorated'.[54]

In order to make themselves acceptable in Victorian Scotland, the Irish would have needed to make themselves invisible.[55] Perhaps their most conspicuous distinguishing feature was their religion; certainly in Scotland it may have been the one which most delayed integration into the host society. Looking at Britain as a whole, it is not difficult to see why. The Victorian Age was one where much of the world was seen and understood in religious terms even by those who did not regularly practice a faith. This was no less true for the immigrants, (however they might fail to reach Victorian norms in other respects), but it made no difference since their religion was regarded as a menace to protestant Britain and its liberties. The 1643 Westminster Confession of Faith was still a cornerstone of Scottish and English protestantism. It called the Pope that 'anti-Christ, that man of sin, and son of perdition'. It rejected the catholic belief in transubstantiation, i.e. that Christ was present body and blood in the Eucharist, and it affirmed that there are only two sacraments—baptism and communion—as against the seven proclaimed by roman catholicism.[56] Since magistrates were no longer empowered by law to root out these blasphemies and heresies, the most dedicated protectors of the reformed tradition in nineteenth century Britain propagated these articles of faith more zealously than at any time since the seventeenth century. Indeed, until 1861, teachers were still legally compelled to swear an oath that they would uphold the Westminster Confession of Faith.[57]

Note how the language protestants used to each other, never mind towards papists, could be deeply intolerant. When the Church of Scotland was split in two as a result of the Great Disruption of 1843, the churches of the established faith were soon being dubbed 'synagogues of Satan' by the disruptionists or Free Kirkers who were 'traducers of the Mother Kirk' to those who remained within the Church of Scotland.[58] So the invective reserved for roman catholics was bound to be even more scalding. The supremacy claimed by Rome over the whole of the Christian church was angrily rejected by the national or voluntary protestant churches of Britain. During the 1860s, the Vatican in Rome responded to the loss of political influence in the Italian peninsula by re-affirming its claim for spiritual leadership over world Christianity, as *the* one true faith. The Doctrine of the Syllabus of Errors of 1864 condemned liberalism and socialism and was followed by the declaration of papal infallibility in 1870. Its effect on protestant sensibilities can be imagined when even a liberal reformer like Gladstone was finally driven to conclude that roman catholicism and modern civilization were incompatible;[59] he judged well the temper of the times; within two months, 145,000 copies of Gladstone's pamphlet 'Vaticanism' were sold in Britain.[60]

'Popery' was the broad term coined for Roman pretensions but it came to have an impact beyond its narrow literal meaning. An elaborate mosaic of theological, moral, political, economic, and even sexual attitudes lay behind popular anti-catholicism. In patriarchal Victorian society, the priest was depicted as a subversive agent who was a menace to the family on account of his ability to undercut the role of the father and husband and gain sway over his womenfolk.[61] He was viewed as most dangerous in the confessional box and the frenzy that anti-catholic propaganda about the function of confessionals produced, especially in Lancashire starting in the 1830s, showed how raw a nerve Rome's enemies were touching here. Thirty years later, this craze was followed by a new one about convents and the belief that protestant girls were lured into them against their will, forcibly converted, or used as sweated labour in convent laundries. A clamour for convents to be inspected annually just like prisons or lunatic asylums, grew steadily and was not just confined to marginal or uneducated groups. In 1870, some 800 members of the Glasgow stock exchange signed a petition calling for convent inspection.[62]

The intolerance of the host society could sometimes be mirrored, if not matched, by a similar response from the leaders of the immigrant community whereby any contact or discourse with Scottish protestants was thoroughly forbidden. In 1867, the extremist *Glasgow Free Press* brought the turbulent Fr Lavelle to Glasgow, where he endorsed the use of force to throw off British rule in Ireland.[63] Earlier, a correspondent in this newspaper of the immigrant community warned of the danger of association with protestant Scotsmen: [they] 'will poison and corrupt our hearts, they will, by degrees, make us cold and indifferent about our religion and duty to God'.[64]

The community preserved its separate identity because it was a form of psychological protection. Priests and other community leaders encouraged what amounted to voluntary segregation in all the big areas of Irish settlement and in many of the smaller ones where the conditions existed for a distinct enclave community. The Irish side of the ghetto frontier may even have been patrolled more vigorously from the inside than the outside. The preservation of the faith and the need strangers in a strange land had for a distinct community that might resist the economic and social pressures which made the Irish a highly marginal and mobile group in Scottish society, were strong incentives. The growing number of Irish priests in the west of Scotland after the 1850s reinforced the distinctiveness of the immigrant community. Many, though by no means all, were chiefly interested in events at home and, as late as the 1930s, there was one who boasted that during his twenty-one years in Scotland, he had never looked at any paper other than the *Cork Examiner*.[65]

But priests from a Scottish or continental background could be just as insistent about preserving an enclave insulated from the surrounding society through encouraging their congregation to focus all their free time on devotional and social activities centred on the parish.[66] It was from the immigrant community that the funds were largely scraped together for the impressive gothic churches, elaborately decorated inside, which usually provided such a striking contrast to the mean dwellings in the rest of the neighbourhood. These handsome churches were the nerve-centre of the community and elicited reluctant admiration from some protestants relieved to find that the results of the Irish influx were not all degradation and decay. But often such manifestations of catholic revival were viewed with barely concealed hostility by less tolerant Victorians.

'No Popery' crossed the barriers of class, district, and denomination and drew in adherents from the most respectable to the most abject corners of British society. A number of events in the middle decade of the nineteenth century demonstrated just how potent a force it was.

In 1845, opponents of Popery had a field-day when Peel's government tripled the size of its annual grant to the senior Irish catholic college at Maynooth and put it on the consolidated fund, thereby removing it from the list of estimates that came under annual discussion. The award was fifty years old, dated from the confiscation of church funds by the French revolutionaries, and was early recognition that the church of Rome might be a stabilising element in Irish society. Yet it led to Gladstone's resignation from the government and Macauley's loss of his Edinburgh seat has been attributed to his support for the measure.[67]

But it was the restoration of the English roman catholic hierarchy in 1850 that produced the strongest backlash from protestant fundamentalists. This was dubbed 'papal aggression' because of the triumphant manner in which it was announced by Wiseman, the new archbishop of Westminster. Even the Whigs led by Russell, the prime minister, were prompted by the chauvinist mood of the country to slam Rome's impertinence. Rioting broke out in Liverpool and Birkenhead and in the cotton towns of south-east Lancashire. In early November 1850, an anxious *Manchester Guardian* declared:

> There is such a tumult of alarm and indignation as has scarcely been known since the fitting out of the Spanish Armada . . . It is felt by all well-constituted minds that this present fifth of November must turn out either a GORDON riot or a massacre of SAINT BARTHOLOMEW.[68]

It took some years for the uproar to fully subside and in 1854 Gladstone claimed that 'we have a parliament which, were the measure of 1829 not law at the moment, would, I think, probably refuse to make it law'.[69]

Scotland was not directly affected by the restoration of English catholic bishops but the clamour was loud enough, particularly in areas of dense Irish settlement. Indeed it was at the start of the 1850s that colourful anti-catholic preachers began first to create an impact. Many were from protestant Ulster and some were even lapsed roman catholics who had been converted by evangelical preachers in Ireland known as 'soupers' during or after the famine.[70] They were early vaudeville artists who mimicked the more mysterious aspects of the catholic religion, denounced 'Popery and Priestcraft' in extravagant terms and sometimes were supplemented by allegedly renegade priests or nuns who alternately titilated or shocked the audience with a gamut of religious horror stories. When communal tensions were high, the rodomontades of these itinerant preachers could result in violence, sometimes of a serious kind. This was the case in Greenock during 1851 and 1852 when John Sayers Orr, known as the 'Angel Gabriel', whipped up disturbances against the local catholic community which lasted on and off for well over a year. Homes were wrecked including that of the local priest, the catholic church was attacked, and in the inflamed atmosphere, many immigrants were dismissed from their jobs.[71] Peace returned only when the 'Angel Gabriel' took his anti-catholic crusade to the USA but, when he reappeared in Greenock in 1855, there was more unrest, a catholic school was wrecked, and the militia had to be called in to restore order.

In Scotland and Lancashire, religious agitators tended to concentrate on small towns rather than the larger centres (unlike their conterparts of the 1930s). In these smaller communities, on the lower reaches of the Clyde or in Lanarkshire, there was often a greater degree of residential segregation on ethnic lines because of the much sharper economic rivalry that had taken place in earlier decades. Religious polarisation was therefore greater and the local authorities, drawn mainly from the host community, tended to permit agitators to speak who, in bigger cities like Glasgow or Liverpool, would have been moved on or restrained.

Occasionally, local elites would bestow their approval on anti-catholic preachers, thus boosting their credibility. In 1851, the Provost of Perth welcomed one such preacher, a genuine ex-priest Alessandro Gavazzi from Italy, with a public dinner.[72] Two years before, James Begg, a leading Free Church minister in Edinburgh, took up Patrick McMenemy who had arrived in the city claiming to be a Presbyterian minister, to have been a catholic priest, and to hold an American doctorate. Begg made him an elder of his congregation and won for him the backing of the Free Church Presbytery in Edinburgh. But McMenemy was a charlatan who embezzled church contributions.[73] Begg remained loyal after his church dismissed McMenemy, whose final downfall occurred in 1855 when he was arrested for brawling in a Liverpool brothel.[74]

Mainstream Scottish protestants took their own initiative in the crusade against religious error. In 1850, the Scottish Reformation Society was founded for this purpose from within the Free Church of Scotland. Its periodical, *The Bulwark* survives to this day and, by the time its second edition had appeared in 1851, it had a circulation of 30,000 and was being published simultaneously in Edinburgh, London, and Dublin.[75] Six Free Church ministers were on the editorial board and its editor was James Begg who was probably even better known for his bestselling *Handbook of Popery*.[76] It was not long before the Church of Scotland riposted with its Scottish Protestant Society, founded in 1854, with the Edinburgh lawyer and church elder, John

Hope, as its secretary.

Hope was a philanthropist and anti-drink campaigner who, in 1851, received a great shock when an early and intimate friend became a catholic convert.[77] This caused him to diversify his interests and many years later in 1890, not long before his death, he endowed a trust, much of whose funds were to be applied to 'the dissemination of knowledge regarding the anti-scriptural nature of Popery, in arousing people to a sense of the evils of Popery, in efforts towards the conversion of Roman Catholics'.[78]

Sincere protestants like Hope were deeply alarmed that the catholic church was rapidly ceasing to be the church of the immigrant poor and that it was attacking the well-born and the successful in growing numbers. Following the conversion of Henry Newman in 1845, over 500 Anglican clergymen followed in his path during the rest of the century. They were accompanied by some 400 members of the nobility, a hundred generals and admirals, 250 lawyers and physicians, along with more ordinary converts who averaged 10,000 a year.[79] By 1914, there were some thirty million roman catholics in the British Empire and their numbers were increasing.

Defections were not as steep or as alarming in Scotland where the Oxford Movement associated with Newman in the 1840s, never really caught on and where presbyterianism, in all its forms, was deemed to be more immune from roman catholic contagion than anglicanism. For instance, it was only in 1900 that two Church of Scotland clergy-men, Henry Grey Graham and Robert Charleson, became the first ministers to defect to Rome since the Reformation. But earlier, a number of grave shocks had been administered to protestant opinion; at the beginning of the 1850s, *The Witness*, edited by the gifted zealot Hugh Miller raged when four members of the Scottish nobility became converts.[80] In a leader entitled 'The Four Ducal Perverts', he exclaimed: 'Because a meddling priest captures four "silly women", does he think therefore that he drags at his chariot wheels, the entire Scottish nation?'[81] Well-known converts included the grand-daughter of Sir Walter Scott,[82] Robert Monteith, the son of a Glasgow Lord Provost and heir to a notable industrial fortune, who became influential in Rome,[83] and the headmaster of Fettes College, a top Scottish school, whose son William Heard became, in 1959, the first Scottish cardinal to be created by Rome since the Reformation.[84]

These spectacular nineteenth century gains for what had been a despised minority sect caused immense panic and bewilderment in Britain. In England, a campaign against rituals in the Anglican church such as the use of incense, the offertory, or the wearing of a surplice, was fueled by these dramatic conversions. To low church clergymen, 'ritualists' were crypto-papists and, even beyond the Victorian Age,

ritualism led to the mass picketing of churches and violent confronta-
tions in Liverpool and bills designed to outlaw it were introduced
into parliament.

In the Scottish boarder town of Kelso, in 1856, a newly-built
catholic church endowed by the convert James Hope-Scott was
'attacked by a Protestant mob, set fire to and burned to the ground,
with the school-house and dwelling-house adjoining'.[85] Priests were
sometimes assaulted in public during tense periods. In 1850, the redoubtable Michael Condon was seriously beaten up at Hamilton in
Lanarkshire 'by an Orange gang to whom the sight of a "Papist" priest
was too much'.[86] It has been alleged that Fr Jeremiah Coakley had to
leave East Lothian in 1861 because he had compelled the local
authorities to put a stop to an Orange march in Bo'ness,[87] thus placing
his life in danger from enraged local Orangemen.

The larger urban centres tended to be more peaceful than smaller
densely-populated communities. In Glasgow during 1860 and 1861,
the swift intervention of the local constabulary prevented serious
violence in Bridgegate, one of the oldest districts of the city, then
mainly populated by catholic immigrants. A Free Kirk church was
built in Bridgegate in order to convert the 'heathen' to 'a proper system
of Christian belief'. When the minister, Mr McColl, had a stone pulpit
built outside the church from which he preached, rival crowds gathered.
On one Sunday, 40,000 people had gathered in the narrow streets,
including many Orangemen from Paisley and outlying towns where this
anti-catholic body was then at its strongest and it took a huge
contingent of police to disperse the crowds. Sheriff Alison, their
commander, commented in his memoirs that 'one trifling incident
would have lighted up a conflagration, but happily it did not occur',
and the law was successfully utilised to restrain Rev McColl.[88]

Even amidst the acrid atmosphere which much of lowland Scotland
presented in the middle years of the last century, there were some
signs of mutual regard. Thomas Chalmers (1780–1847), the best-known
evangelical preacher in nineteenth century Scotland refrained from
making anti-catholic statements even though giving in to popular
prejudice would no doubt have enhanced his reputation, at least in the
short-term. Instead he backed catholic emancipation, made provisions
for the catholic poor in his social work activities in Glasgow and
preached sermons for religious tolerance in Ulster as well as in
Scotland.[89] Chalmers was among those who welcomed the Irish priest
Theobald Mathew when he came to Glasgow in August 1842 to preach
total abstinence; in fact he received a tremendous welcome from
protestants and catholics alike, brought together by a common concern
about drunkenness.[90] Very occasionally, personal encounters smoothed
the path of reconciliation. For instance, in Hamilton, the Free Church

minister in 1851 preached a sermon appealing for the revival of the spirit of Cromwell to combat catholicism. Shortly afterwards, the neighbouring priest, Fr Michael Condon helped to save the manse (the home of a Presbyterian minister), when a chimney fire threatened to spread. After this contact, Condon recorded in his diary how 'the sword of the Puritan was no longer appealed to'.[91]

Throughout the nineteenth century, *The Scotsman* newspaper in Edinburgh was a rare beacon of sanity and moderation in its views on the Irish in Scotland. It frequently refuted the more extravagant or spiteful claims of their religious detractors and was prepared to highlight virtues among them such as the chastity of their womenfolk even in the most reduced circumstances or their low illegitimacy rate when compared with the native Scottish figure.[92] *The Scotsman* also broke new ground by appointing a roman catholic, Charles Cooper to be its editor in 1876. A Unionist and an Englishman, he was hardly a representative catholic but he held the job for the next thirty years and broke down prejudice against catholics in public life. During the 1880s, Canon Edward Hannan of St Patrick's, Cowgate, was even elected deputy chairman of the Edinburgh school board and his new parochial hall was opened by the city's Lord Provost, both indications that catholics were viewed with rather less hostility in Scotland's capital than elsewhere, perhaps due to their smaller numbers.[93]

The 1880s also saw the election of the first roman catholic MP in Scotland. Donald MacFarlane was the Liberal member for Argyllshire from 1885 to 1886 and from 1892 to 1895. Religious prejudice undoubtedly played some part in the two defeats he suffered but it is also noteworthy that none of the well-known spokesmen for militant protestantism in the House of Commons, such as Richard Spooner, John Plumptrie, George Whalley, and Henry Drummond, represented Scottish seats. Indeed Lord Aberdeen, a Presbyterian and a Scot was a moderating influence on religous questions when he was prime minister in the tense period from 1852 to 1855.[94]

Although anti-catholicism acquired its longest-lease of life on the British mainland in Scotland, it would be wrong to assume that the most concentrated inter-ethnic strife occurred here. Lancashire in fact witnessed the sharpest collision between Irish immigrants and British workers, in the period between 1848 and 1870. Since it is important to place the Scottish situation in a comparative framework and not view it completely in isolation, the situation in Lancashire is discussed below.

During the nineteenth century Lancashire was the chief destination of immigrants quitting backward and exploited Ireland for industrial Britain. A steady stream of new arrivals turned into a human torrent during the famine of the mid-1840s. 300,000 people arrived in

Liverpool during the first half of 1847 alone.[95] Many moved on but plenty stayed so that, by 1851, 23% of the city's population was Irish-born, making up an estimated 33% of the working-class.[96] In no other British city would the Irish make up such a large proportion of the population. Uneducated, penniless, many not knowing English and some disease-ridden, they were an alien and unwelcome force which strained the city's facilities to breaking-point and brought it many social problems. As will be seen, prejudice towards not only them but their offspring was to colour the life of the city into the next century.

Irish immigration to the west of Scotland was more gradual. The famine did not overwhelm the amenities or living space of Glasgow in quite the same way as in Liverpool. The province of Ulster, always the chief source of Irish immigration to Scotland, had been spared the worst effects of the famine. Also, the industrial economy of central Scotland was at the peak of expansion and was able to absorb large amounts of cheap unskilled labour. So, compared with Liverpool, the backlash against the Irish from the established community was slower in making itself felt.

Indeed, the first sectarian riot had taken place in Liverpool as long ago as 1819.[97] It occurred during the first annual parade of the Orange Order which had just been introduced to the city. Founded in 1795, at Loughall in the Ulster county of Armagh, it had derived its impetus from fierce competition for scarce land between protestant and catholic farmers. So, at its birth, as in many of its later phases, its chief rationale was to represent a defence against catholic economic pressures rather than to be a strictly religious organisation. But in Ulster itself, the Order rapidly outgrew its initial purpose as a rural defence force and Orangeism came increasingly to stand for the maintenance of British power in Ireland and the defence of the protestant constitution and liberties established by the Glorious Revolution of 1688 when their hero, King William of Orange, ascended the British throne. This victory for limited monarchy and the reformed faith was clinched by the defeat of the catholic King James II at the Battle of the Boyne in Ireland on 12 July 1690. It is this date which Orangemen in different parts of Britain and Ireland have celebrated each 12 of July down to the present day (although in Scotland Orange marches take place on the previous weekend to enable Scottish Orangemen to travel to Ulster for the 12th, where it is a public holiday).

Despite its origins in Irish rural agitation, Orangeism proved suitable for export because it blended well with certain ideals and prejudices that were widely shared in nineteenth century Britain. The first lodge there was founded in 1798 by magistrates and ex-soldiers in Manchester which remained the centre of the movement until the 1830s. It was mainly a lower middle-class body patronised by the military, Anglican clergymen, Tory politicians, and lawyers and publicans. Despite the Order's perceived self-image as a bulwark of protestant liberty and British democracy, it was a reactionary institution which was a centre of opposition to the 1832 Reform Act and to the radical aims of the Chartists. The fears of moderates in the establishment that it might become a rallying-point for counter-revolutionary forces opposed even to limited democracy, were strong enough for its patron, the Duke of Cumberland reluctantly to order its dissolution in 1836. But the arrival in numbers of the catholic Irish and widespread unease about roman catholic activities at the start of the 1850s, provided the groundswell for a significant revival, not merely confined to its previous strongholds. This time around, Orangeism appealed to a much broader band of the population. While its leaders were still often drawn from local notables, the Order made greater headway among working people by its consistent support for factory and trade-union legislation and for social reform. The decline of labour conditions in the wake of mass Irish immigration enabled the Order to make anti-catholic and anti-immigrant prejudice compatible with the wide economic concerns of a much larger spectrum of working people.[98] Even ex-Chartists were attracted to the Orange Order, whose traditional links with the Tory Party were also revived. But through the vehicle of the Orange Order, it was a far less oligarchical brand of Toryism that began to emerge in industrial Lancashire in the 1860s, one which identified with local interests, defended working-class rights against Liberal employers, and played upon the religious prejudices and patriotic feelings of the common man.

Orangeism was even more adept at sparking off religious unrest. Probably the worst trouble occurred at the end of the 1860s, just as the franchise was being extended to part of the working-class for the first time. Anti-Irish prejudice had been revived by the Fenian bombings of 1867, the first expression of Irish terrorism in an urban context and by Gladstone's bill of 1869 to disestablish the Anglican church in Ireland (the Church of Ireland). During the election campaign of 1868, Tory speakers in working-class districts insisted that Irish church disestablishment would lead, in no time, to catholic supremacy in England and the abolition of the protestant monarchy.[99] Into this volatile atmosphere, stepped the firebrand preacher William Murphy who arrived in Lancashire in early 1868 after storming through the Midlands. Having been born and baptised a roman catholic in Co. Limerick, Ireland, he had been converted to protestantism and by the age of eighteen he was a scripture reader for the Irish society, an evangelical protestant society.[100] In England, Murphy's carefully stage-managed anti-catholic lectures whipped up large audiences into a state of frenzy and excitement. As he wound his way through the cotton towns of south-east Lancashire in 1868, a whirlwind of destruction was left in his wake. Immense damage was done to property, human relations, and even lives in the most serious bout of religious rioting seen in nineteenth century Britain.[101] His extremely provocative performances drew thousands to indoor meetings who were not only from the lower reaches of society. The evidence shows that many of the rioters who later wrecked catholic chapels or attacked the local Irish quarter, were drawn from 'a wide spectrum of working-class occupations, many of them respectable'.[102]

Because of his threat to publc order, Murphy was kept out of Liverpool and Glasgow by the city authorities there and a career in which he proved to be the most dangerous of all the raving anti-catholic fanatics was cut short by his death in 1872 at the hands of Irish miners in Workington.[103] But his presence had revealed the depth of anti-Irish prejudice in industrial communities and the extent to which these could be played upon. Both the immediate and longer-term beneficiaries of religious and ethnic polarisation were the Tories who captured most of Lancashire in 1868. Gladstone lost the seat of South-West Lancashire and was 'kicked out of the county for not being a Protestant'. In many working-class districts, the real issue in the election was 'whether you will have a Pope or a queen'. In a letter from Queen Victoria, written not long after she had talked to Disraeli about the impending election, she set out just how his party proposed to trade on the religious and anti-Irish prejudices of newly enfranchised skilled workers:

> He thinks that Mr Gladstone has mistaken the spirit of the times and the temper of the country. The abhorrence of Popery, the dread of Ritualism, and the hatred of the Irish have long been smouldering in the mind of the nation. They will seize, Mr Disraeli thinks, the opportunity long sighed for and now offered, to vent their accumulated passions . . .
>
> In the Boroughs, there will be revived, with feverish earnestness, the no Popery cry; in the counties, the clergy and gentry will rally round the sacred and time honoured principle of Church and State.[104]

Well into the 1880s, it remained the case in Lancashire that 'the greater the proportion of Irish immigrants, the larger the tendency to vote Conservative'.[105] This was not nearly as true of the west of Scotland where Orangeism and populist Toryism revived around the same time as in Lancashire but without being able to influence voting habits, at least until much later.

Until the end of the 1850s, Orange activity had been confined to the smaller industrial communities of Lanarkshire and Renfrewshire. Glasgow did not possess an Orange lodge until 1860.[106] The founding of a lodge almost coincided with a controversy which erupted in the city when the Irish sponsored recruits for the Papal volunteers in Italy who were fighting against Garibaldi, in whose army several Glasgow men served.[107] Garibaldi was a hero to many working-class men and the action of the Irish both deeply offended them and was not quickly forgotten. In the 1860s, there was a warm reception in Glasgow for European speakers who condemned catholic absolutism. The Hungarian patriot, Louis Kossuth, made several speaking tours of Scotland and in a second one during the 1860s, he talked explicitly about the evils of catholicism.[108] So 'No Popery' could be linked with European liberalism as well as with working-class rights and, in Scotland, it attracted some ex-Chartists but to a lesser degree than in Lancashire.

Undoubtedly, a more potent reason for Orange progress in the west of Scotland was the proximity of Ulster, the birth-place and chief stronghold of Orangeism. Clydeside shipyard workers who had earlier gone to Belfast to teach workers how to build iron ships were returning to Glasgow at the end of the 1850s, just as the upturn was starting.[109] Belfast's shipyard workers were the most intensely Orange section of that city's proletariat and, by the 1870s, the same thing was being said about shipyard workers living in the Partick and Springburn districts of Glasgow.

Orange prospects were aided most of all by the presence of a large and energetic Ulster protestant community in Glasgow.[110] Ulster protestants made up 1/4 of all the Irish in Glasgow by the 1860s and they were also well established in Liverpool.[111] Many had prospered and close personal and social ties were forged with the citizens of Glasgow, whose religion and ancestry they shared, unlike the catholic Irish. But the Ulster protestants retained their specific identity and were well-organised in religious and other societies.[112] In its turn, this cohesiveness helped to spread Orangeism which, more than any church, kept alive links with the homeland. The Ulster-born Robert Gault was the first clergyman to encourage the Order in Glasgow. He was super-intendent of the Free Church Anti-Popish Mission in the city and, at the end of the 1860s, he was a regular speaker at Orange meetings.[113]

The boom period for recuitment in Glasgow was the 1870s. Whereas in 1868 only 600 had turned out for the 12th of July procession, 10,000 were taking part in the 1870s and, by 1878, it was estimated that there were a hundred lodges in the city with a total membership of fourteen to fifteen thousand.[114] In 1876, the rather loose organisational framework was greatly strengthened when the two separate Orange associations which had hitherto existed in Scotland, amalgamated to create the Loyal Orange Institution of Scotland. Its first Grand Master was an Edinburgh advocate, Chalmers Izett Paton.[115] But there was, as yet, little scope for Orangeism to intervene effectively in Scottish politics which had been dominated by the Liberal Party from 1832 onwards. Political conditions differed from Lancashire and indeed Ulster, although many of the same sectarian tensions existed in the west of Scotland that gave Orangemen cause to hope that the popular Tory cause could be advanced in the future.

In the 1870s, Orangemen were already making some headway in one specific area of Glasgow politics. When, following the creation of a state system of education in 1870, elections for local boards became customary, Orange candidates did well. Harry Alfred Long, the main exponent of 'No Popery' in Glasgow, topped the poll in the first election, held in 1873 and, with the exception of one contest, topped the poll right up to 1901.[116] Like so many agitators who made anti-catholicism their passport to fame in cities like Glasgow and Liverpool, Long was an outsider. He was born in 1826 in Cambridge and only came to Scotland in 1847.[117] He was an Episcopalian and, from premises in the Saltmarket district, he carried out social work, feeding and clothing the poor, while devoting his main effort to grappling with religious error. Long resembled the better-known James Begg of the Free Church who combined a concern with social reform, especially in housing, with a violent disdain for roman catholicism. Long once stated openly that 'I, for my part, could not shake hands with the Pope, I could only punch his head'.[118] He was so effective in mobilising an Orange vote in the city that, by 1881, he was vice-president of the Glasgow Conservative Association. The revival of Toryism in Glasgow indeed coincided with the rise of Orangeism but the relationship between these two bastions of tradition was tense and there was always a reluctance to admit Orange leaders into the inner circles of the party. Adhesion to the slogan of Church, Crown, and Empire was not sufficient to dispel antagonism between the plebeian Orangemen and more respectable Glasgow Tories, who were often reluctant to appear on Orange platforms or attend Orange social events. Tory managers preferred to woo moderate Liberals and usually, it was only when this course was not available that Orangeism was embraced.[119]

The Orange Order was all-protestant by statute and the Tories in Glasgow would be the same in practice until well into the twentieth century. These sharp religious distinctions ran through many other areas of Victorian life as immigrants often discovered if they tried to better themselves or collided with, or else became dependant on, the state. 'No Irish Need Apply' was a common warning in the employment columns of the press or on the walls of economic concerns looking for extra hands. Even well-disposed citizens often wished to keep contacts with the Irish down to a minimum as the remeniscences of a Glaswegian recalling life in the Calton district during the 1880s, graphically convey:

> The less we had to do with them the better. Their religion was not our religion, which was the best; and their customs were different from ours, as was their speech. Doubtless there were good folk among them, but the unruly

and turbulent ones showed us what we might become if we did not keep to our own people.[120]

Inevitably, the reluctance of most citizens to treat the Irish as part of the mainstream community was reflected in their treatment at the hands of the authorities. There was little love lost between the police and the Irish in Victorian Scotland. The police, backed up by the courts, regarded the denizens of the Irish quarter as unruly, anti-social, and worth watching carefully, while Irish apologists, like John Denvir, felt that the police approach towards the Irish was often one of straight victimisation.[121] Certainly they figured in Victorian crime statistics much more prominently than any other specific grouping which was a cause of great complaint in mainstream society. But, if broken down, the offences committed by immigrants often appear to have been of a comparatively minor kind—drunkenness, petty theft, vagrancy, and crimes committed against the person in mitigating circumstances.[122] Writing in 1904, Denvir offered an example of the type of offence which boosted the gaol statistics:

> A 'basket girl' or hawker might be sent to gaol, not having the money to pay the fine for simply 'obstructing' the pathway trying to sell her fish, or apples, or oranges. Nay, the same hawker might fall into the hands of the police a second or third time and be classified each time as a separate and distinct criminal in the year's returns.[123]

It is not just the Irish case which demonstrates how police tend to have tunnel vision in relation to specific minorities who may stand out owing to their appearance, customs, or place of residence. Sometimes, when the Irish were in need of police assistance, it was withheld or only offered grudgingly. This was shown during communal disturbances when Irish people or their property was under attack. *The Glasgow Herald* of 24 July 1835, when reporting an anti-catholic riot in Airdrie, wrote that 'the crowd seemed to have the tacit support of the local authorities. When the crowd attacked the home of a Protestant by mistake, the head of the Airdrie police merely pointed out the error to them but made no effort to dissuade them. One of the burgh magistrates was also reported to be in the midst of the mob'.[124]

During similar violence in Greenock, in 1852, when armed mobs were patrolling the streets and catholic property was being attacked, the offenders received very lenient treatment from the local bench. A man who attempted to take the life of a catholic policeman with pistol and dagger, received a sentence of only sixty days. Finally, in January 1853, with violence continuing, the government intervened, to suspend the magistrates and the town clerk, and appoint in their place a stipendiary magistrate.[125]

The press often characterised the Irish in racialist and demeaning terms which did little to improve their image. In *The Irish in Modern Scotland*, James Handley culled the following illustrations at random from the news columns of the *North British Daily Mail*:

Yesterday at the Central Police Court, an ape-faced small-headed Irishman . . .

An impudent Irish ruffian . . .

A middle-aged, malicious-looking Irishman . . .

Pat O'Shannon, a startled-looking Irish tailor, with a cruel Tipperary visage . . .

Ann Brady or Brogan, a wicked-looking daughter of the Green Isle . . .[126]

Unvarnished hostility like this had a vital effect in prolonging the negative image of the Irish in Scottish society, long after the chaos and dislocation produced by the mass influx of immigrants in the 1840s and 1850s had subsided. A perusal of Glasgow newspapers up to the outbreak of World War I showed that more than in other parts of Britain, they tended to portray the Irish in cartoons as ape-like creatures with simian features, thus stressing the racial gulf between host and newcomer which was, in fact, less true of the west of Scotland than of Saxon England.

Although titans in their own country, priests did not always fare much better than their congregations in the wider society. In 1897, when Fr John Murphy, the parish priest of St Aloysius in Springburn, Glasgow struck with his cane, a boy who had spat at him, the boy and his companions took him to court where he was found guilty of assault, even though one of the youths admitted in the witness box that it was the custom of the fellows to spit and throw stones at catholic priests as they walked by.[127] Often priests found they were barred from entering the workhouse to provide religious comfort and instruction for catholic children. The Greenock authorities, particularly inflexible on this score, were much criticised by *The Scotsman* for their policies towards catholic children in their care during the early 1870s.[128] Many of the middle-class guardians who administered the poor law locally, possessed strong religious opinions that made them hostile to catholics. The catholic church frequently complained in the 1860s and 1870s about local poor law boards in which catholic children were taught the protestant catechism, refused permission to attend Mass on Sundays, and boarded out to protestant families.[129]

In Greenock, the guardians insisted that orphans should be brought up according to the religion of the majority of ratepayers. During 1862, the board of supervisors in the town, responding to a petition presented by catholic clergymen, alleged that 'experience had taught the Board that children boarded to roman catholic families were brought up to be perfect pests to society'.[130] Finally, in 1870, catholics appealed to parliament for redress and, in that year, Fr Bernard Tracey, later the first roman catholic elected to a school board in Scotland, submitted a report to the House of Commons on the proselytism of catholic children in the care of local authorities.[131] Conditions gradually improved but, in the 1880s, the catholic *Glasgow Observer* was campaigning against the destitute children institute known as the Quarrier homes which had been founded in 1876 by William Quarrier. A leader in the paper on 20 June 1885, made the following accusation against the Quarrier homes: 'that in the city of Glasgow, and within the short space of twelve months, 800 destitute Catholic children should be shamelessly bribed to become Protestants and then transported to Canada and other places beyond the seas'.[132]

Even bodies like the trade unions which, in the twentieth century, contained many leading activists from the catholic community, were for a long time, hostile to Irish immigration. In the nineteenth century, only certain craft trades were unionised in Britain. The Irish who dominated the unskilled labour market in Glasgow were not organised and in the second half of the nineteenth century, the outlook of many Glasgow trade unionists towards them was 'racist'.[133] An example of prevailing attitudes among Scottish workers comes from Aberdeen where, in 1881, the trades council, listened to delegates complaining that 'in great measure, the chief obstacle to any material or satisfactory improvements in the conditions of the people of Ireland lay in certain natural defects incident to their race'.[134] Where, as in Liverpool, some Irish workers were organised, they had their own bodies so, for instance, the coal-heavers in the city had two rival societies.

Progress began to be made in the docks when two Ulstermen, Edward McHugh and Richard McGhee began to build up the non-sectarian National Union of Dock Labourers in Liverpool and Glasgow after 1889.[135] Even the strife-torn Lanarkshire coalfield witnessed growing co-operations between miners of different faiths in the 1870s and 1880s. Alexander McDonald (1821–81), their leader up to his death, worked hard to heal sectarian divisions and made no anti-catholic utterances.[136] The emergence of Keir Hardie, a Lanarkshire miner, as the founder and leader of the British Labour Party before 1914, demonstrated that class consciousness among the miners had not been entirely drowned by the religious battles of previous generations. But even those early Labour pioneers, striving to bury the differences which made workers weak and powerless, sometimes echoed anti-catholic sentiments. When the militant protestant John Kensit was killed at Birkenhead in 1902, J. Bruce Glasier (1859–1920) wrote in his diary: 'I esteem him as a martyr. He had real enthusiasm and courage as an agitator and was I think a good man. I feel honest sympathy with his anti-Romanist crusade';[137] Glasier's friend, Ramsay Macdonald shared his hostility to catholicism according to one historian[138] and the biographer of Ernest Bevin has revealed that 'the very sight of priests upset him'.[139]

Finding religious intolerance and sectarian hate in many areas of nineteenth century Scottish life, the immigrants preferred to remain expatriate Irish rather than strive to make common cause with the Scots in their midst.[140] There were occasional exceptions, like Patrick O'Hare, the first roman catholic councillor in Glasgow, who refused to buy shares in Glasgow Celtic after it was founded in 1888, for fear that a football team from the Glasgow catholic community, would only create further divisiveness.[141]

In a few centres of Irish settlement, such divisiveness was surprisingly absent. Dundee is probably the best example. In 1851, 18·9% of its population was Irish born, a higher proportion than Glasgow's and one only surpassed in Britain by Liverpool. Yet there were remarkably few reports of serious inter-communal strife in the town during the nineteenth century and the Orange Order never took root.[142] The historian of the Irish in Dundee thinks that an explanation for the lack of friction may lie in the type of Irish immigrant drawn to the city, which was different from elsewhere. According to the 1871 census, there were twice as many women as men among the immigrants resident in Dundee, which can immediately be contrasted with the immigrant strongholds in the west of Scotland where there were more adult males than females.[143] It was probably easier for women to be absorbed into the local population since they were not likely to share to the same degree as Irishmen, the political and cultural preoccupations with 'the oul country' which could antagonise part of the host society.

Dundee's prosperity rested on jute mills that mainly employed female labour which explains the unusual gender ratio of immigrants. It was a fast-expanding town throughout the nineteenth century, drawing in Highlanders and people from the east coast, so the Irish may not have stood out nearly as much as elsewhere. Unlike Clydeside, Dundee was not a magnet for Ulster protestants, so the element which introduced organised anti-catholicism into Liverpool, and the west of Scotland, was absent; minus its Orange foe, Irish nationalism was correspondingly weaker in Dundee and its catholic workers began to be attracted to radical politics earlier than in the west. 1906 saw Dundee elect one of Scotland's first two Labour MPs, although the city's Irish nationalist movement had opposed Labour. More importantly, the jute workers were unionised before the First World War, which made the Irish in Dundee one of the first parts of the immigrant community in Scotland fully to participate in the trade union movement.

But, even in Dundee, it has been reckoned that the children of unmixed Irish blood were more Irish than their forebears, so insulated were they by religion, poor education, and their humble social status from the rest of the population.[144] At first glance, integration and upward mobility ought to have occurred at a faster rate in Scotland, given that it possessed a more egalitarian and democratic political culture than England. The Irish and the Scots both shared an absence of deference to local artistocracy and a dislike of landlordism. These and other features of Scottish life, such as the widespread system of education, the relatively democratic structures of the protestant churches, and belief in the freedom of the individual as justified by his essential rationality, and widespread support for the extension of the franchise were encapsulated by the phrase 'Scottish democracy'.[145] The outright domination by the Liberal Party of Scottish politics between the 1st Reform Act of 1832 and the 3rd of 1884 has been ascribed to the vitality of *Scottish democracy*. But the Irish, and their Scottish–Irish offspring, were unable to take advantage of the philosophy of equal opportunity upon which Scottish democracy was based.[146] They resisted intermarriage with protestants, kept their own enclave identity, and were the only religious denomination to educate their children in their own schools. The widespread hostility of the host community to their presence must also only have encouraged the tendency, common initially in all immigrant groups, to remain locked in isolation. Such isolation was imposed as well as voluntary and it constrained the Irish in Britain far more than it did those who settled in north America or Australasia.

Anti-Irish prejudice had a longer lease of life in Scotland than in other countries of the Irish diaspora and the immigrants were more isolated from the host society than elsewhere, but nevertheless, the *violent* backlash against the Irish was not as extreme in Scotland as in some other places. There was no equivalent of the Know Nothing movement, which turned anti-Irish sentiment into a strong political force on the north-eastern seaboard of the USA during the early 1850s. Scotland was spared the savage inter-communal violence which flared up sporadically in Liverpool during the eighty years after the great famine. Irish immigration and its attendant social consequences also affected the *politics* of lowland Scotland to a lesser extent than for instance the eastern United States or Liverpool.

Why then was anti-Irish hostility pressed into a number of deep but narrow channels which only rarely burst their banks to swamp society as a whole? A number of tentative explanations can be offered:

1. High immigration occurred just at the time when the face of Scotland was being altered more rapidly than at any other moment in the nation's history. So, at a time of maximum transition and great economic upheaval, the influx of the Irish was far less traumatic and

dislocating than it would have been at other moments. Allied to this, the economy was buoyant in the 1840s and 1850s and able to absorb the extra numbers; in fact there was a demand for unskilled labour which could not be met from the local population and which prompted some Scottish capitalists to actually send their agents to Ireland in order to recruit labour for their expanding concerns.

2. Scotland already had an immigration culture that had grown up because her cultivated land, in recent centuries, had not been productive enough to sustain the settled population. This tradition may have made the arrival of the newcomers slightly less intolerable than otherwise might have been the case; the expansion of the British empire at the time of the Irish diaspora may also have acted to dampen down unrest in Scotland since it must have removed a number of energetic and restless people who might have fomented inter-communal strife if they had chosen to remain in Scotland.

3. The Irish were also pouring into Scotland just at the time when north British values seemed to be replacing Scottish ones as important symbols of identity. So although they were despised for their religious allegiances or lowly status, they were not treated as scapegoats by a nationalistic bourgeoisie as was already beginning to happen to their counterparts in the multi-national empires at the opposite end of Europe. Strangely enough, it was the third or fourth generation of Irish, more accurately described as the 'Scoto-Irish' who, in the 1920s and 1930s were victimised for their 'unScottishness' but this was a shortlived phenomenon that will be examined later in chapter 4.

4. One of the upheavals which Scottish society was already experiencing as the Irish arrived was the civil war within the Presbyterian church which was known as the Church of Scotland by virtue of being the established faith of the country. In 1843, the year of the 'Great Disruption', the Church of Scotland split over the question of church patronage—whether a minister should be appointed by the elders of the congregation or whether local landowners should have an important say as permitted by the 1712 Patronage Act. In reality, this dispute went further than religious practice and was, in part a contest for primacy between church and state and, in part, a class conflict between the new lower middle-class and the pre-industrial establishment which hoped to retain influence in the matter of church appointments. Anyway, the Great Disruption produced the greatest fissure in Scottish society and culture of the nineteenth century.[147]

Presbyterians were more preoccupied with their own internal schisms and rival church-building programmes to spare energy for properly combatting 'the menace of Rome'. Of the few who could spare the energy, the best known was Dr James Begg, a minister of the breakaway Free Presbyterian Church. He was based at Newington in

Edinburgh, a prosperious district which was not a centre of immigration. Other anti-catholics were located in similar districts. This may have been purely coincidental or it may have been that congregations in sensitive areas with a strong Irish presence, were sometimes uneasy about appointing a minister ready to indulge his anti-catholic views in public.

Far from leading to a decline in Presbyterianism, the 1843 split resulted in the expansion of two rival churches and demonstrated the vitality of the reformed tradition even in the midst of great social change. The protestant faith had a greater, if declining hold, over the masses than in industrial Lancashire, and so there was not the same degree of panic about working-class irreligion or the spread of catholicism. The fact that Presbyterianism in all its forms was more immune to roman catholicism than Anglicanism was, also made the religious environment more secure. There were fewer defectors to Rome and most Scottish protestants had no reason to doubt Queen Victoria's belief that 'the Scottish Church is the real and true stronghold of Protestantism'.[148]

5. Papal interference and Jesuit intriguing in international and British politics, which was staple fare in English anti-catholicism, did not loom so large north of the border, possibly because Scotland no longer possessed a state of its own. A test of protestant feelings came when the Scottish catholic hierarchy was restored in 1878. Remembering the backlash which had greeted this development in England after the catholic hierarchy there had been restored in 1850, the British government, through its agents in Rome, had been lobbying against a Scottish restoration throughout the 1860s, for fear of 'the disastrous effect in Scotland'.[149] But when the first act of the new pope, Leo XIII was to restore the hierarchy on 13 March 1878 after a gap of 275 years, it passed off relatively peacefully despite the recent collapse of a major Glasgow bank which had resulted in thousands of workers losing their jobs.

In the closing decades of the nineteenth century, only one Church of Scotland minister attempted to rival the Anglican priests who openly encouraged anti-catholic feeling among their English congregations. This was Joseph Primmer (1842–1914) who was minister in a small colliery village outside Dunfermline in Fife after 1876. As a young man, he had come under the influence of John Hope. Later, as a minister, Primmer embarked upon a colourful career of pope-baiting which took him to Rome for a six-week visit in 1895. Twice he attempted to enter the Vatican but he was prevented by the papal guards and he wrote up his experiences in a book which ran into several editions. But he was most famous for his summer speaking tours, known as conventicles, a name borrowed from the seventeenth century

Covenanters. From 1890 to 1903, he toured Scotland each summer, defending the reformed faith and excoriating Roman error.[150] Sometimes these meetings were disorderly as in Paisley and Coatbridge during 1896.[151] But Primmer was a relatively isolated figure who had no great following inside his own church which, in 1899, rebuked him at its annual General Assembly.[152] Nevertheless, Primmer was a fine speaker and the 632 meetings he held, the total attendance at which, he estimated to have been 2,830,000, must have had some success in propagating firmly held anti-catholic beliefs, especially to the growing numbers of common folk who were not regular church-goers.[153] John Paton, ruefully reflected in his memoirs that they could prove to be stiff competition for socialists in Glasgow and he has left a vivid description of the pastors who made Bridgeton Cross, in the east end of Glasgow, a centre of fierce propaganda against roman catholicism in the years before 1914:

> Orange propaganda was conducted in the main by a number of 'pastors' who were without academic qualifications, but had a crudely effective platform skill based on a great command of abusive language . . . With powerful voices, they related at great length and with circumstantial detail, juicy and stimulating stories of the immorality that was supposed to occur in nunneries and monasteries. Occasionally they'd make the flesh creep by a lurid account of the alleged finding of dozens of skeletons of illigitimate children in one of these places.
>
> All this was extremely popular with Orangemen and other Protestants who loved their religion raw and bloody. The 'pastors' were literally 'witch-doctors', who performed the ritual dance on the platform; the necklet and teeth and the grinning mask were replaced by the shabby tall-hat and the frock-coat which was their uniform; the ceremonial chant was duplicated by the ranting sing-song of their rhetoric: the effect was entirely the same—the tribesmen were worked up into a frenzy of blood-lust.
>
> Several nights a week, and always on Sundays, there would be a huge gathering at the Cross, round one of these 'pastors'.[154]

In Liverpool, one such demagogue, Pastor George Wise, triggered off serious rioting in the city in 1903 and 1909. Glasgow may have escaped communal violence on the same scale due to the determination of the city's authorities to keep provocative sectarian displays in check.[155] Factional marches were closely supervised and in the counties of Renfrewshire, Ayrshire, and Lanarkshire, Orange marches were actually banned between 1857 and 1867 following serious rioting. In 1859, the sheriff of Ayrshire appealed to the coal and ironmasters of that county to use their influence to dissuade workmen from participating in Orange processions but he received no assistance and finally complained in exasperation:

If they showed half the alacrity to defend the public against the outrages of those men, that they exhibit when they *demand* the civil and military authorities to protect them against those men on strike, we should probably never hear more of an Orange procession.[156]

Quite often, senior law encorcement officers had experience in Ireland which could stand them in good stead in Scotland. For instance, J. V. Stephenson, the chief constable of Glasgow from 1903 to 1922 had acquired his police experience in the Royal Irish Constabulary:

He joined the RIC in 1884 ... and he saw plenty of lively work in the politically disturbed areas of Cork and Donegal. In ... 1890, he was transferred to Belfast, and he successively had charge of three of the important divisions there ... His busy years in Belfast were 1892–3 and 1898 when serious riots had to be handled.[157]

The self-restraint of opposing factions may have made the policeman's lot easier in Glasgow than in Liverpool or Belfast. The leaders of Orange and Irish factions in Glasgow often emphasised in their followers the need for discipline. When trouble did arise it was not unknown for apologies to be offered to the offended community.[158] Such informal mechanisms were probably essential for disastrous collisions between rival protagonists to be avoided; such restraint may have been simple commonsense in a city where, by 1914, some 700,000 people lived in its three central square miles, the densest concentration of people anywhere in Europe.[159] The absence of space produced appalling social conditions but it also discouraged complete residential segregation on an ethnic or religious basis. So Glasgow avoided much of the polarisation which in Belfast and Liverpool stemmed from the creation of rival religious ghettoes. No districts were completely inhabited by members of one denomination and even Irish strongholds like the Calton, High Street, Bridgegate, the Gorbals, and Cowcaddens were partly mixed. These factors acted as an important safety-valve preventing a total collision between hosts and newcomers. But a feeling of common identity eluded the two religious and cultural groupings making up the population of the west of Scotland. They would first have to see out the nineteenth century before it became apparent to significant numbers that their similarities might outweigh their differences.

Notes

1 Erich Strauss, *Irish Nationalism and British Democracy*, Methuen, London, 1951, p. 123.
2 Gerry Charles Gunnin, *John Wheatley, Catholic Socialism, and Irish Labour in the west of Scotland*, Ph.D. thesis, University of Chicago, 1973, p. 23.
3 Memoranda for Archbishop Manning drawn up by Bishop Gray, quoted by J. F. McCaffrey, 'Roman Catholics in Scotland in

the nineteenth and twentieth centuries', *Records of the Scottish Church History Society*, 21, 2, 1983, pp. 283-4.

4 John Cooney, *Scotland and the Papacy*, Paul Harris, Edinburgh, 1982, p. 10.

5 Owen Dudley Edwards, 'Scots and the Pope', *Irish Times*, 26 February 1983.

6 James Darragh, 'Catholic population of Scotland in the twentieth century', *Glasgow Observer and Scottish Catholic Herald, Scottish Survey*, 1878-1955, p. 11.

7 A. L. Drummond and J. Bulloch, *The Church in Victorian Scotland, 1843-1874*, St Andrew Press, Edinburgh, 1974, p. 71; Christine Johnson, *Developments in the Roman Catholic Church in Scotland*, John Donald, Edinburgh, 1983, p. 71.

8 Cooney, *Scotland and the Papacy*, p. 14.

9 Drummond and Bulloch, *The Church in Victorian Scotland*, p. 71.

10 Cooney, p. 10.

11 Colm Brogan, *The Glasgow Story*, Muller, London, 1954, p. 183.

12 Johnson, *Developments in the Roman Catholic Church*, p. 18.

13 Cooney, p. 13.

14 Brogan, *The Glasgow Story*, p. 184.

15 Ian A. Muirhead, 'Catholic emancipation: Scottish reactions in 1829', *Innes Review*, 24, 1, 1973, p. 41.

16 Muirhead, pp. 26-8.

17 Sir M. S. Stewart, quoted in Muirhead, p. 31.

18 Owen Dudley Edwards, 'The Irish in Scotland', in David Daiches (ed.), *A Companion to Scottish Culture*, Edward Arnold, London, 1981, p. 183.

19 Colm Brogan, 'Catholics in changing social conditions', *Glasgow Observer and Scottish Catholic Herald, Scottish Survey*, p. 4.

20 V. A. McClelland, 'The Irish clergy and Archbishop Manning's apostolic visitation of the western district of Scotland, 1867', *Catholic Historical Review*, LIII, 1, 1967, p. 3.

21 Johnson, p. 136.

22 M. A. G. O'Tuathaigh, 'The Irish in nineteenth-century Britain: problems of integration', in *Transactions of the Royal Historical Society*, 5th series, 31, 1981, p. 152.

23 Sheridan Gilley, 'English attitudes to the Irish in England, 1780-1900', *Immigrants, Hosts, and Minorities in British Society*, (ed.) C. Lunn, Dawson, Folkestone, 1978, pp. 92-3.

24 Johnson, p. 139.

25 McClelland, 'The Irish clergy', p. 2.

26 Neville Kirk, 'Ethnicity, class and popular Toryism, 1850-70', C. Lunn, Dawson, Folkestone, 1980, p. 69.

27 Edwards, 'The Irish in Scotland', p. 185.

28 E. P. Thompson, *The Making of the English Working Class*, Pelican edition, London, 1968, p. 479.

29 Neville Kirk, *Class and Fragmentation: some Aspects of Working-class Life in North-east Cheshire and South-east Lancashire*, Ph.D. thesis, University of Pittsburgh, 1974, p. 262.

30 Johnson, p. 137.

31 McClelland, 'The Irish clergy', p. 2.

32 McClelland, 'The Irish clergy', p. 2.

33 McClelland, 'The Irish clergy', p. 4.

34 Quoted in Muirhead, p. 32.

35 See Gordon M. Wilson, *Alexander McDonald, Leader fo the Miners*, Aberdeen University Press, 1982, pp. 122, 168.

36 Quoted by David Howell, *British Workers and the Independent Labour Party, 1886-1906*, Manchester University Press, Manchester, 1983, p. 142.

37 Alan B. Campbell, *The Lanarkshire Miners, a Social History of their Trade Unions, 1775-1874*, John Donald, Edinburgh, 1979, p. 181.

38 A. Campbell, p. 237.

39 James E. Handley, *The Irish in Modern Scotland*, Cork University Press, 1947, p. 138.

40 Sydney and Olive Checkland, *Industry and Ethos, Scotland 1832-1914*, Edward Arnold, London, 1984, pp. 88, 94.

41 Handley, p. 138.

42 Handley, pp. 130-4.

43 R. D. Lobban, 'The Irish community in Greenock in the nineteenth century', *Irish Geography*,

vi, 1971, pp. 273-4.

44 E. H. Hunt, *British Labour History, 1815-1914*, Weidenfeld & Nicolson, London, 1981, p. 165.

45 Letter from Sir Walter Scott to Maria Edgeworth, 4 February 1829, quoted in John Gibson Lockhart, *The Life of Sir Walter Scott*, Constable, Edinburgh, 1903, p. 261.

46 E. Strauss, *Irish Nationalism*, p. 123.

47 N. Kirk, thesis, p. 279.

48 A. Campbell, *The Lanarkshire Miners*, p. 194.

49 D. F. Macdonald, *Scotland's Shifting Population, 1770-1850*, Glasgow, 1957, p. 83, quoted in Campbell, p. 194.

50 Engels, quoted in Kirk, thesis, p. 279.

51 I. G. C. Hutchinson, *Politics and Society in Mid-Victorian Glasgow, 1846-86*, Ph.D. thesis, University of Edinburgh, 1974, p. 475.

52 *The Witness*, 25 January 1847, quoted by Handley, p. 25.

53 *The Glasgow Herald* (hereafter *GH*) 7 July 1851, quoted by Handley, p. 32.

54 E. P. M. Wollaston, *The Irish Nationalist Movement in Great Britain, 1886-1908*, MA thesis, King's College London, 1958, p. 1.

55 William Walker, *Juteopolis: Dundee and its Textile Workers, 1885-1923*, Scottish Academic Press, Edinburgh, 1979, p. 171.

56 Cooney, *Scotland and the Papacy*, p. 10.

57 Checkland, *Industry and Ethos*, p. 112.

58 James G. Kellas, *Modern Scotland, the National since 1870*, Pall Mall, London, 1968, p. 56.

59 McCaffrey, 'Roman Catholics in Scotland', p. 291; E. R. Norman, *Anti-Catholicism in Victorian England*, Allen & Unwin, London, 1968, p. 21.

60 Lytton Strachey, *Five Victorians*, reprint Society edition, London, 1942, pp. 417-8.

61 G. F. A. Best, 'Popular Protestantism in Victorian Britain', in *Ideas and Institutions in Victorian Britain*, R. Robson (ed.), Bell, London, 1967, p. 134.

62 Handley, p. 121.

63 Hutchinson, thesis, p. 479.

64 *Glasgow Free Press*, 2 January 1864.

65 Anthony Ross, OP, 'Development of the Scottish Catholic community, 1878-1978', *Modern Scottish Catholicism, 1878-1978*, David McRoberts (ed.), Burns, Glasgow, 1979, p. 41.

66 McCaffrey, 'Roman Catholicism in Scotland', p. 277.

67 Handley, p. 107; but other reasons for his defeat are advanced in W. Ferguson's *Scotland: 1689 to the Present*, Oliver & Boyd, Edinburgh, 1968, p. 323. Macauley regained his Edinburgh seat in 1852.

68 Kirk, thesis, p. 291.

69 Quoted by G. I. T. Machin, *Politics and the Churches in Great Britain, 1832 to 1868*, Clarendon Press, Oxford, 1977, p. 255.

70 Patrick Joyce, *Work, Society and Politics, the Culture of the Factory in later Victorian England*, Harvester, Brighton, 1980, p. 259.

71 Handley, pp. 95-6.

72 Handley, p. 98.

73 Drummond and Bulloch, *The Church in Victorian Scotland*, pp. 73-4.

74 Machin, *Politics and the Churches*, p. 253.

75 Norman, *Anti-Catholicism*, p. 65; Handley, p. 99.

76 Machine, *Politics and Churches*, p. 254.

77 David Jamie, *John Hope, Philanthropist and Reformer*, Eliot, Edinburgh, 1900, p. 251.

78 Jamie, *John Hope*, p. 531.

79 See Anthony C. Rhodes, *The Power of Rome in the Twentieth Century, the Vatican in the Age of Liberal Democracies, 1873-1922*, Sidgwick & Jackson, London, 1983, p. 164.

80 Handley, p. 108.

81 Handley, p. 108.

82 George Scott-Moncrieff, *The Mirror and the Cross, Scotland and the Catholic Faith*, Burns & Oates, London, 1960, p. 146.

83 See Bernard Aspinwall, 'David Urquhart, Robert Monteith and the Catholic Church: a search for justice and peace', *The Innes Review*, 31, 2, 1980, pp. 57-70.

84 *Catholic Directory for Scotland*,

1971 (hereafter referred to as CDS), obituary of William Cardinal Heard, p. 360.

85 Machin, *Politics and the Churches*, p. 254.

86 Bernard J. Canning, *Irish-born Secular Priests in Scotland, 1829–1879*, Bookmag, Inverness, 1979, p. 50.

87 Canning, p. 43.

88 See Sir Archibald Alison, *Some Account of my Life and Writings*, Blackwood, Edinburgh and London, 1883, II, pp. 292–6.

89 J. F. McCaffrey, *Scottish Catholic Observer*, 29 October 1982.

90 Anthony Ross, 'Development . . .', p. 40.

91 McCaffrey, 'Roman Catholicism in Scotland', pp. 289–90.

92 Handley, *The Irish in Modern Scotland*, p. 111.

93 Canning, *Irish-born Secular Priests*, p. 134.

94 Machin, *Politics and the Churches*, p. 261.

95 Frank Neal, 'The roots of violence', *Tablet*, 1 May 1982.

96 Neal, 'The roots'.

97 Neal, 'The roots'.

98 Kirk, thesis, p. 366.

99 See R. W. Greenall, 'Popular Conservatism in Salford, 1868–86', *Northern History*, 9, 1974, pp. 131–2.

100 W. L. Arnstein, 'The Murphy riots: a Victorian dilemma', *Victorian Studies*, 19, 1975, p. 52.

101 See Machin, p. 371, and Arnstein, 'The Murphy riots', *passim*.

102 Kirk, thesis, p. 345.

103 H. J. Hanham, *Elections and Party Management*, Longmans, London, 1959, p. 306.

104 Letters of Queen Victoria, 2nd series, I, 517–18, quoted in Hanham, p. 214.

105 Henry Pelling, *Social Geography of British Elections, 1885–1910*, Macmillan, London, 1967, p. 284.

106 Hutchinson, thesis, p. 387.

107 Hutchinson, thesis, pp. 486–7.

108 Hutchinson, thesis, p. 399.

109 Hutchinson, thesis, p. 395.

110 Hugh McLeod, *Religion and the Working Class in Nineteenth Century Britain*, Macmillan, London, 1984, p. 38.

111 Hutchinson, thesis, pp. 476–7.

112 McLeod, p. 31.

113 Hutchinson, thesis, p. 396.

114 Hutchinson, thesis, p. 388.

115 *Orange Torch*, February 1979.

116 *Bailie*, 25 March 1896; Hutchinson, thesis, p. 403.

117 *Bailie*, 25 March 1896.

118 James M. Roxburgh, *The School Board of Glasgow, 1873–1919*, B.Litt. thesis, University of Glasgow, 1968, p. 12.

119 Hutchinson, thesis, p. 390.

120 Quoted by Hutchinson, thesis, pp. 485–6.

121 John Denvir, *Glasgow Observer*, 19 March 1904 (hereafter referred to as *GO*).

122 See E. H. Hunt, *British Labour History, 1815–1914*, Weidenfeld & Nicolson, London, 1981, pp. 162–3.

123 Denvir, *GO*, 19 March 1904.

124 Campbell, *The Lanarkshire Miners*, p. 202.

125 Handley, *The Irish in Modern Scotland*, p. 96.

126 Handley, p. 108.

127 *GO*, 17 July 1897.

128 Handley, p. 251.

129 Handley, pp. 250–3.

130 Handley, p. 252.

131 Bernard J. Canning, *Adventure in Faith, St. Ninian's, Gourock, 1880–1980*, Burns, Glasgow, 1980, p. 19.

132 Handley, p. 258.

133 Checkland, *Industry and Ethos*, p. 90.

134 James G. Kellas, *The Liberal Party in Scotland, 1885–1895*, Ph.D, University College, London, 1961, p. 366.

135 See Eric Taplin, 'Irish leaders and the Liverpool dockers: Richard McGhee and Edward McHugh', *North West Labour History Society*, 9, 1983–4, pp. 36–44.

136 Wilson, *Alexander McDonald*, pp. 122, 168.

137 Diaries of J. Bruce Glasier, 8 October 1902, in the possession of Liverpool University Library.

138 R. K. Middlemas, *The Clydesiders: a Left-wing Struggle for Parliamentary Power*, Hutchinson, London, 1965, p. 110.

139 James Downey, 'Bevin and British history', *Irish Times*, 14 January 1984.

140 See Compton Mackenzie, *Catholicism and Scotland*, Routledge, London, 1936, p. 185.
141 Interview with Dr Patrick Connolly (grandson), 29 April 1984.
142 William Walker, 'Irish immigrants in Scotland: their priests, politics, and parochial life', *Historical Journal*, xv, 4, 1972, p. 655.
143 Walker, *Juteopolis*, p. 121.
144 Walker, *Juteopolis*, p. 115.
145 Kellas, thesis, pp. 26, 365; Joan Smith, 'Labour tradition in Glasgow and Liverpool', *History Workshop*, 17, spring 1984, p. 34.
146 Kellas, thesis, pp. 365-6.
147 Checkland, *Industry and Ethos*, p. 75.
148 Kellas, thesis, p. 204.
149 V. A. McClelland, 'A hierarchy for Scotland, 1868-1878', *Catholic Historical Review*, 56, 1970, p. 483.
150 See J. Boyd Primmer, *Life and Work of Jacob Primmer, Minister of the Church of Scotland*, Bishop, Edinburgh, 1916, p. 261.
151 Primmer, p. 271.
152 Primmer, p. 200.
153 Primmer, p. 271.
154 John Paton, *Proletarian Pilgrimage*, Routledge, London, 1935, p. 270.
155 McCaffrey, 'Roman Catholicism in Scotland', p. 291.
156 Quoted in Campbell, *The Lanarkshire Miners*, p. 224.
157 *Bailie*, 11 January 1920.
158 Hutchinson, thesis, p. 394.
159 Checkland, *Industry and Ethos*, p. 185.

Chapter 2 **Strangers in a strange land: the immigrant Irish community**

The sheer isolation and weakness of the Irish in Scottish society meant that they were despised rather than actively feared by those sections of the population who felt their presence to be uncomfortable. Even in those manual occupations where they were becoming strongly entrenched such as mining, they were unable to establish a commanding presence, so the reaction of indigenous workers was not as antagonistic as it might otherwise have been. But through their homogeneity and concentration in largely separate neighbourhoods, a distinct identity was being forged that would place the Irish at variance with different aspects of Scottish life. Second or third generation Irish who were counted as Scottish in the census returns, often retained the attitudes and traditions of their Irish parents or grandparents, even if outwardly, these heirs of the original settlers, seemed to have adopted the speech and ways of west central Scotland.

The survival of a double identity among the descendants of the immigrants caused confusion and could be exploited for partisan ends. Even well-meaning observers talked about 'the Irish in Scotland' well into the twentieth century when already, by the last quarter of the nineteenth century, a clear majority of west of Scotland catholics were Scottish-born; to more sophisticated commentators, in the 1920s and 1930s, such as the Scottish Nationalists Oliver Brown and Hugh McDiarmid, they had graduated to being the 'Scoto-Irish'. But these were the decades when Tory, ultra-protestant, and Nationalist zealots, identifying continued Irish immigration as the chief symptom of Scottish decline, demanded repatriation and sought to underline the gravity of the problem by indiscriminately branding the bulk of Glasgow's catholics as 'the Irish'.

As they slowly became upwardly mobile, the grandsons or great-grandsons of immigrants were only now beginning to compete with native Scots for remunerative jobs and opportunities. In the religious sphere, this phenomenon was first witnessed back in the 1850s and 1860s and the degree of friction it gave rise to must have seemed like an alarming portent for the future.

Until the 1850s the mainly Highland leadership of the church had been reluctant to accept Irish priests out of fear that their arrival might only reinforce the enclave identity of the immigrant communities and could possibly result in an Irish takeover bid for the small and vulnerable Scottish church where, by the 1850s, the Irish far out-numbered the indigenous membership. But the shrinking catholic areas of the Highlands could not meet the desperate shortage of priests and Ireland was the only source near at hand. Here, after the famine of the 1840s, there was a comfortable surplus: the number of priests and nuns rose steadily as the population declined.[1]

By 1867 twenty of the 106 clergy in the western district of Scotland were Irish.[2] Their arrival gave encouragement to those behind *The Glasgow Free Press*, which was the weekly paper of the Irish in the west of Scotland from 1851 to 1868 (when it folded on being condemned by Rome). This paper projected a bellicose form of Irish nationalism and it did not hesitate to fan discord among those immigrants out of sympathy with the methods and precepts of Bishop Murdoch and his Scots clergy. Many of the priests destined for the Scottish mission had trained at All Hallows College, Dublin and some had come under the influence of a member of the teaching staff, Dr Richard O'Brien, the founder of the Catholic Young Men's Society. Dr O'Brien was an ardent Irish nationalist 'who had the gift of inspiring young people'.[3] By 1858 one bishop was already complaining that, through the influence of these priests, immigrant sons who had been accepted as candidates for the priesthood in the Scottish seminary, were being subject to nationalist indoctrination.[4]

Archbishop Manning of Westminster, on his visit to the troubled western region in 1867, found a deep divergence between the two sets of clergy operating in the Glasgow area:

> I must add that the unhappy discord between the Irish and the Scottish clergy is fostered by the national character and behaviour of the Scots. The reserve of the Scots does not react sympathetically to the Irish temperament and the clergy of Scotland, being in their home territory, have held themselves aloof as if affronted by the Irish invasion. The active, expansive, zealous, and sometimes more heated than calm temperament of the Irish clergy has given some annoyance to the less active and perhaps less zealous Scottish clergy.[5]

Besides their shared nationality, the Irish clergy struck a chord with immigrant congregations because of their greater readiness to become involved with them outside the church. Here they differed from the

Scots clergy who 'wished to keep a basic organisation going without committing themselves to extensive debts. The basic provision of a mass centre and the sacraments was as much as they would envisage.'[6]

John McCaffrey, the writer of these words, detected a feeling among the Scottish clergy that the immigrants were only temporary visitors and that they would emigrate again before long,[7] which may explain their reluctance to engage in long-term pastoral work. Given such an outlook, it is not surprising that the tight-knit Highland bishops and clergy showed no eagerness to promote Irish clergy (by 1867, only one Irish priest was in charge of a parish).[8] Established missions were given to Scottish priests and the more difficult task of building up new ones to Irish priests who were better equipped to deal with their fellow countrymen.[9] Eventually, discontent about the lack of recognition for their labours burst into the open in January 1864 when twenty-two priests in the western district sent a memorial to their bishop setting out ten grievances, the most important of which were that: new bishops are always Scottish; appointments to missions are not made by merit and that priests are removed arbitrarily; the laity have no say in managing institutions like reformatories or orphanages which are mismanaged due to excessive clerical control; collections made annually in churches are kept secret as are the debts incurred in building churches, even though congregations are responsible for these; and no clergyman was ever furnished with a copy of the statutes of the mission.

Three of the signatories, headed by Michael Condon, the secretary, sent the memorial to Rome without consulting the others, thus laying complaints about their bishop before his ecclesiastical superiors.[10] The letter was also published by *The Free Press*, proof of liaison between some of the priests and this vitriolic paper. Meanwhile, Scottish clergy responded by presenting an address of loyalty and sympathy to the ailing Bishop Murdoch who died in 1865. He was succeeded by his co-adjutor John Gray but, in 1866, an Irishman James Lynch, rector of the Irish college in Paris was appointed, in turn, co-adjutor to Bishop Gray with the right of succession. This second appointment was secured largely by the influence of Archbishop Paul Cullen of Dublin and it struck deep unease in the minds of Scottish clergy who feared that their church was on the verge of being turned into a mere extension of the Irish church, something which would surely 'lose them any standing they might have in the eyes of their Protestant neighbours . . . undermining their long-term hopes for the conversion of their countrymen'.[11]

For Cullen was already using his considerably influence in the Vatican to promote close associates, friends, and even relatives to bishoprics in different parts of the English-speaking world. Monsignor David McRoberts is not the only observer to have compared his ecclesiastical imperialism with the contemporary political imperialism of Victorian

England.[12]

Alarmed by news of the polarisation in Scotland, Rome despatched Archbishop Manning to Scotland in 1867 to report on the situation as a neutral observer. As the already quoted extract from his report shows, Manning was prepared to be critical of the Scots past behaviour and present attitudes but he deprecated those Irish priests who, along with *The Free Press*, wished to preserve a separate Irish identity in a self-imposed ghetto, resisting all contact with national life. 'One cannot conceive anything more fatal to the Church in Scotland', Manning wrote, 'than to present it in the guise of the religion of the Irish and so put it in direct opposition not only to the fanatical Protestant opinions of the Scots, but in opposition also to the Catholic Hierarchy and the faithful of Scotland.'[13] In the USA, Irish insensitivity eventually led to a secessionist Polish church in the late nineteenth century, while Manning was mindful of the possible repercussions in England; in 1869, he wrote that 'the Glasgow affair may teach us a lesson. Unless we are firm, we shall have a demand for an Irish bishop in Liverpool some day.'[14]

Manning had been a genuine honest broker who, in his own diocese of Westminster, established excellent relations with the London Irish and, unlike most other English Catholics, became a supporter of Irish home rule, meeting frequently in the House of Commons with Irish MPs. His detachment stemmed from the fact that he was a convert who did not possess the hidebound attitudes of the 'recusants', or old English catholics who had survived down the centuries through preserving a studied anonymity and demonstrating an unswerving loyalty to the English state and who were psychologically ill-equipped to welcome the Irish or tolerate their enthusiasms. Manning was relieved to find that in fact those priests 'of the Irish race born in Scotland are for the most part at one with the Scottish clergy', and he saw their role as that of intermediary between the two quarrelling parties. The transfer of Monsignor Lynch to Ireland was recommended by Manning who declared in the most important passage of his report that 'I remain completely convinced that the only adequate remedy for the very serious troubles of the present and the great dangers of the future is to be found in the division of Scotland into dioceses and in the restoration of the hierarchy'.[15]

H. J. Hanham has characterised the religious discord within the church as 'one of the earliest struggles of Scottish nationalism against domination from outside'.[16] Such a bold pronouncement would carry more weight if the Scottish clergy had been to the fore in demanding a restored hierarchy. But this very conservative group of men, drawn from the same localities and not a few related to each other, were not enthusiastic about the idea and 'felt that the future lay in holding fast to the old arrangements'.[17] But Manning's formula was endorsed by the Vatican and the way ahead was cleared by the appointment as bishop of the western district in 1869 of a patrician Englishman from Yorkshire, Charles Eyre (1817-1902). Suffering worsening health, Bishop Gray had resigned and his ill-matched co-adjutor was transferred to Ireland. Lord Bute, the chief catholic layman in Scotland and the spokesman of the catholic aristocracy, also favoured Scotland becoming a complete unit of the catholic church once again and he lent his authority to the idea. Bute *was* an early Scottish home ruler who wrote in 1881 that 'if the Irish could manage their own affairs . . . I don't see why they shouldn't [have home rule] . . . but my impression is that they are incapable. No one would say the same thing about us'.[18]

Much politicking attended the restoration of the hierarchy before it was accomplished in 1878. Bute ensured that the Scottish island his title derived from was placed in the diocese of Argyll and the Isles and not Glasgow. Edinburgh, and not Glasgow, was chosen as the metropolitan see or chief archdiocese. Lord Bute would have preferred St Andrews, the centre richest in ecclesiastical traditions but it only had two dozen catholics.[19] Although Manning, in his report, had assumed that Glasgow would have acquired metropolitan rank because it was the greatest centre of catholic population as well as Scotland's largest city,[20] it was rejected, possibly because the troubles of the previous decade and the unassimilated nature of its catholic faithful gave it an alien and discordant image. But care was taken to make Glasgow an archdiocese, directly subject to the Holy See and not to the province of St Andrews and Edinburgh, under whose authority lay the other dioceses of Aberdeen, Argyll and the Isles, Dunkeld, and Galloway.[21] An arm of the Vatican bureaucracy, the Congregation for the Propagation of the Faith, known as Propaganda for short, continued to have overall charge of Scottish church affairs until 1908. In 1883, Propaganda had ruled that it was not yet appropriate to set up parishes in Scotland and it was not until 1946 that Rome felt the Scottish church to be financially sound enough for the network of missions to be replaced by fully fledged parishes[22] (however, in practice, they were already known as *parishes*, the term used here).

Charles Eyre, Glasgow's first archbishop, was determined to erase the city's unruly ecclesiastical image and conformity became the watchword of his episcopate. He was a centraliser who distrusted new ideas and it is interesting to note that during his time, few religious orders moved into Glasgow where they might have encouraged a degree of pluralism and diversity in church affairs, given their relative autonomy, that might have even rubbed off on ordinary catholics.[23] But Eyre was an energetic and skilful administrator who pressed ahead with much needed expansion. In 1874, he founded a seminary, St Peter's college, at Patrickhill, to train priests for the new archdiocese. This was not the only project into which he put part of his own fortune (in this cawe £40,000) and other benefactors, such as Lord Bute were similarly generous with endowments.[24] In his twenty-four years as Glasgow's first post-Reformation archbishop, the number of clergy rose from 134 in 1878 to 234 in 1902; the number of parishes increased from sixty to eighty-four and a total of forty-four new chapels and chapel-schools were built; in 1869, the number of baptisms was 8,519; in 1900 they totalled 13,414 and over the same period the catholic population increased by around 100,000.[25]

The Victorian philosopher Thomas Carlyle scoffed at these signs of growth and consolidation. 'Popery can build new chapels. Let them. Popery cannot come back, any more than paganism can.'[26] In 1847, the anti-catholic paper, *The Witness* had mocked at the types emerging from one of these new chapels in Edinburgh: 'the Protestantism of the Kingdom possesses no such congregation—no such array of looped and windowed raggedness, or where hard-handed and not unremunerative labour may be seen, bearing with it so unabashed to the place of Sabbath worship the soil and stain of its week-day occupation'.[27]

It would be many decades before Rome's detractors faced up to the fact that the catholic church's identification with the poor was a source of strength rather than weakness. Increasingly the protestant churches were losing what contact and influence with the humblest groups of citizens that they may once have possessed, vacating the field for the roman church to claim that *it* was the real church of the urban poor. Certainly, catholic priests were the only clergy in Scotland to live on the standards of the nineteenth century working-classes.[28] They easily assumed the leadership of catholic parishes because they were close-knit and uniform in character, with so many of the inhabitants not only sharing the same faith, race, and political outlook, but also sometimes coming from the one locality and, as Handley says, 'held in unity through the difficulty of mixing freely with the native population'.[29]

Such cohesiveness was particularly marked in the smaller mining communities, such as Baillieston, on the northern outskirts of Glasgow. Here Fr Peter Terken, a Dutch priest, became in the words of socialist politician Patrick Dollan 'an excellent leader and organiser' during the thirty-five years he built up St Bridget's parish from 1879 to 1914. Fr Terken 'tamed and refined the wild men of Donegal and Connaught'. They contributed 'a full day's pay to the church at Easter and Christmas plus one shilling a month for every wage earner in each household . . . The names of subscribers and defaulters were read at Mass once a month . . . To be a defaulter was the biggest shame of all. He never made an appeal for funds in vain'.[30]

Probably a measure of authority was needed to establish respect and order in catholic parishes created in what were new frontier towns such as Coatbridge or mushrooming cities like Glasgow and Dundee. Priests drawn from Ireland established a relationship which had been entirely natural between priests and unlettered peasants in rural Ireland. All the moneys of the congregation passed into their hands without need to render an account. They dominated unquestioningly the numerous lay societies concerned with charitable, spiritual or recreational matters which began to flourish in catholic parishes in the 1880s and which, so often, met in the local church hall. Sometimes the brusque and outspoken manner of a parish priest might occasion personal resentment. Clergy preferred an unquestioning and docile congregation. In 1893, a priest chastised those who 'think that they can teach the world. . . and are wiser than the chaplain; and in their vanity, anxious to manifest their imaginary experience they oppose him, not lawfully and reverentially, but unbecomingly . . .'[31] These remarks appeared in a Catholic Young Men's Society paper given to members in 1893. In 1949, they were thought sufficiently apt to be reissued in the centenary brochure of the Scottish CYMS, which shows how, in one respect, time had stood still in catholic parishes.

One early example of a priest demonstrating his authority as the community supervisor in a non-religious matter came from Dundee in 1862 where a group of Irishmen were thwarted in their effort to establish reading-rooms in the city in order to combat 'the moral degredation of their fellow-countrymen' who 'were capable of higher culture than midnight brawling'.[32] One of them wrote to the local press about their difficulties:

> And why do they condemn our reading rooms? Simply because they are not under their immediate control—because the promoters did not ask their liberty—because the books, newspapers etc, are not under their immediate censorship—and because they are of a secular and educational tendency.[33]

This was an early and isolated expression of lay independence. Clerics had to tread more carefully when the Irish Home Rule movement began to grow in Britain during the 1870s. When the centenary of Daniel O'Connell's birth fell in 1875, they were still strong enough to dictate the nature of the commemoration, emphasising the social and religious benefits of his political activity to the exclusion of his nationalist concerns.[34] But the early Home Rulers staged a rival match on the day of the clergy's procession, an early sign that separate Irish and catholic preoccupations were a source of tension within the immigrant neighbourhoods.

In discussing the autocratic ways of Victorian clergy, it is worth remembering that the authority of bishops over their priests was often exercised in an arbitrary manner. Archbishop Eyre, along with Robert Monteith, the convert who became a leading Scottish layman in the nineteenth century, were strong advocates of papal infallibility. Later, Scottish bishops were to the fore in condemning the work of progressive theologians prepared to derive some insights from modern thought. In 1907, Pope Pius X condemned this trend as the heresy of Modernism and Bishop Turner of Galloway cried out in alarm that 'the spirit of Modernism is especially antagonistic to that principle [of authority in religion] and one of its primary aims is to abolish all authority in religion'.[35] From 1910, newly ordained priests in Scotland had to take an anti-Modernist oath. Such outspoken hostility to new ideas was also found in other national hierarchies in these islands and it may account for the anti-intellectualism which had such a profound effect on the Scottish church up to and beyond even the 2nd Vatican Council of the 1960s.

Strong willed churchmen, emphasising ritual and devotion and having little time for independent thought, blended well with the ethos of the immigrant communities. Acutely aware of how bleak and hazardous life could be, they yearned for certainty which was provided by many through their religious conviction. Even those who were indifferent towards attending mass and taking the sacraments, seldom lost their emotional loyalty to the catholic church and the key dates of the life cycle (birth, marriage, death), were seldom commemorated without the church's involvement.[36] Many indifferent catholics could be just as hostile as firm adherents to mixed marriage or even to accepting charity from protestant institutions.[37]

Throughout the areas of densest settlement, the Irish adamantly refused to follow the most effective route to assimilation which was intermarriage. Family and neighbourhood pressures and the implacable hostility of the priest were strong deterrents. These were reinforced by the Vatican's 1908 Ne Temere decree which made the conditions for marriage with a non-catholic even more rigorous than before, all combining to keep the community catholic and Irish in outlook.

The most detailed research on nineteenth century catholic marriage patterns in Scotland has been made in Greenock, a classic area of Irish settlement. Irish catholic migrants were joined in the town by protestant Irish and Highlanders. Throughout the second half of the nineteenth century, the catholic Irish had the greatest degree of inter-group marriage. In 1851, some 80% of the Irish men and women in Greenock had found partners from amongst their own number while, in 1891, the percentage figure was 72·4.[38]

The insularity and clannishness of the Irish in Scotland is well captured in a story that was serialised in weekly parts in the catholic

Glasgow Observer between 23 October 1915 and 6 May 1916. It concerns the difficulties of young Hannah Purcell, newly arrived in the city from County Cavan. The story has no literary pretensions but it was skilfully written in that it gives a convincing portrait of how the metropolis must have seemed to many members of the Irish community, even those long resident in the city, and of the dangers and temptations therein.

The story has a number of twists but generally it traces the fortunes of Hannah after she leaves good employment as a maid in the West End because of finding herself too far from a catholic church. Obtaining another job in a city centre warehouse, she receives the attentions of her superior Mr Pendleton, the cashier. 'I don't like him', says Nelly Morrison, Hannah's friend and workmate. 'He is called Mr Pendleton but I'm sure that's not his real name, for he is a kind of Polish Jew, one of those oily, sneaking kind of people you can never understand.'[39]

This type of anti-semitic remark was not confined to the catholic tabloids of the day but it shows how the prevailing antagonism to the Jews current over so much of Europe could be transmitted easily to the Irish.

Curiosity about life beyond the tight-knit community and desire to improve the mind were also frowned upon or quietly mocked:

> 'I was only once in the galleries', Hannah replied, 'and I did not like them: too grand, not simple enough to be understood by common people like me. Everything you saw was intended . . . to show how superior the producers of the things you saw were to ordinary mortals.'
>
> 'Fr Joyce told me to be very careful as to which picturehouse I go to, should I wish to go to any . . .'
>
> 'You certainly take a great heed of what the priest says.'
>
> 'Certainly we do. They always speak for our good, especially when people have no other guide in a large city like Glasgow . . . we Irish people love our priest in a way that the Scotch and other people cannot quite understand.'
>
> 'Yes, Hannah, I know that. I have met many Catholic girls and they all seemed—well, afraid of the priest, even those girls who were not good Catholics.'[40]

Fr Joyce, although a Glaswegian, fails to identify with his native city.

> *Hannah.* 'I don't think you could ever look at Glasgow as your home in quite the same way as the Irish look upon our country.'
>
> 'I think you are right, Hannah. Somehow or other, although I have been born and reared in this town, I don't think I would feel much regret at the prospect of never coming back.'[41]

Hannah, of course, comes into contact with protestants but the anonymous writer makes allowance for the fact that their attitude towards catholics can vary. On the one hand there is the Morrison family with whom she lodges:

> James Morrison staunch and consistent . . . was one of those intelligent Scotchmen . . . who were able to see through the trickery practised on credulous people in order to procure money. 'No, no, lassie,' he said to Nelly [his daughter] on one occasion when she asked permission to go to a 'No Popery' lecture. 'If the Pope is wrong, God will be the judge. We have got the pure Gospel in the Bible and anybody that goes into the conduct of others instead of going to the Word, is no true preacher of the Gospel. No, lassie, don't go to such places. If you want the truth you will find it here,' and he draws over an old Bible which lay on the table . . .[42]

But at her work Hannah had to contend with a different manner of Protestant:

> Andrew Petrie was a religious crank who attended revivalist meetings, Bible classes, etc, and had the usual strong desire to show a Papist all the enormities of Roman Catholicism . . . He would argue religion for hours if anyone was foolish enough to engage him. Of course, he had voluminous quantities of 'No Popery' literature which he had vainly endeavoured to get Hannah to look at. She knew enough of Catholic doctrine to enable her to give a good account of herself when debating with the pertinacious Scotchman. Indeed, as far as she was aware, she was the only Catholic in the place, except for John Boyle, the doorkeeper.[43]

Hannah actually goes to hear Sarah McGrath, 'the escaped nun', at the City Hall but is unimpressed. The drama instead centres around Pendleton who is 'fascinated by her beauty'. He has her promoted so that she will be working with him. He asks her to visit him for some late work at his lodgings in the YMCA. When she resists his advances, he falsely charges her with embezzlement but, before a tragedy occurs, he is unmasked as a crook operating under an assumed name. The story ends with Hannah marrying Maurice O'Neill, an up-and-coming young catholic who takes her to a nice suburban home, while her friend Nelly becomes a convert, so as to marry Terence Boyle, the son of the doorkeeper at the warehouse.

Although their literary merit may be neglegible, such stories provide a very useful insight into the outlook of ordinary Glasgow catholics and the way they viewed the outside world and their immediate surroundings. The story-line may jar in places and characters may come over as mere caricatures but the stories were composed in such a way as to provide maximum authenticity in the minds of the paper's readers who could not have been expected to follow them over six months if they did not respond to their own instincts and emotions.

'An Irish Girl In Glasgow' reveals a deep distrust of the surroundings in which most of the Irish in Scotland had spent *all* their lives, certainly by the time the story was serialised in 1915-16. Industrialisation and immersion in an unfamiliar culture made the Irish huddle together for security in all the centres of the nineteenth century diaspora but, in Scotland, there may have been additional special features which encouraged such introversion. A strong Scottish identity existed in the nineteenth century but it contained little that the Irish could draw inspiration from. As the immigrants became more politicised—behind the cause of nationalism in their former homeland—the rather synthetic Scottishness which had been usurped and even recast, by the royal family, the British army, and the English music hall, held little appeal. Without being aware of his words, many Home Rulers took their cue from Parnell whose opinion of the Scots is enshrined in the remark that 'Scotland has ceased to be a nation'.[44] Much later, in the 1930s, the novelist Compton Mackenzie spelled out their feeling of alienation from Scotland in possibly exaggerated terms, not long after he had become a catholic convert:

> The Irish who settled in Scotland settled in a country which seemed to them, to have surrendered what they had never surrendered—nationhood . . . They were not willing to suffer a comparable loss of status, and finding where they penetrated little peculiarly Scottish left except religious intolerance and sectarian hate, they preferred to remain expatriate Irish.[45]

In the nineteenth century, it was difficult to preserve an Irish identity if one embarked upon the odyssey of self-improvement that was part of 'Scottish Democracy'. One who managed it was Patrick O'Hare, the first catholic elected to Glasgow town council. O'Hare graduated to the licensing trade from the Lanarkshire steelworks and he brought up his family in the lower middle-class suburb of Dennistoun. They were probably the first catholic family in a locality which would put militant anti-catholics into the council during the 1930s. Patrick O'Hare's grandson recalls that his own father and uncle had to fight their way to school at St Mungo's academy practically every day.[46] Against this background, it may have been easier for rising catholics to quietly drop their religion completely if they made the transition out of the immigrant neighbourhood. Nineteenth century Dundee provided a few examples of elected councillors who did just that.[47] *Boyhood of a Priest*, by an anonymous Dundee clergyman, refers caustically to a fictitious 'Lord Provost O'Donnell', who was a 'notorious turncoat':

> He had come over with the rest of them during the Hard Times and, having got on, pitched his neighbourhood and joined up with the genteel Freemasonry and Town Councillors. When a man appeared in a public house with a new collar and tie, he would be warned that he would be walking in the footsteps of Lord Provost O'Donnell. If a Catholic householder took leave

of his sense of humour so far as to put a nameplate on his door, the neighbours would . . . say, 'Lord Provost O'Donnell'.[48]

Such aversion to self-improvement except within prescribed limits is also a constant theme in 'An Irish Girl in Glasgow'. If a community norm is being expressed here, it is plainly not sufficient to place the entire blame for the immobility of catholics onto the shoulders of the dominant community. Irishmen who became 'turncoats' got on faster than those who kept the faith because, outside the enclave, it was far easier to adopt the individualistic approach to life that was a prerequisite for material advancement in and beyond the Victorian era—probably the best-known nineteenth-century Scottish lapsed catholic was the Edinburgh-born novelist and creator of Sherlock Holmes, Arthur Conan Doyle (1859–1930).

Once the infrastructure of the church·in urban Scotland began to take shape, priests sought to control the 'leakage' which was a topic of concern in the catholic press and pulpits right down to the 1930s. Some priests, such as Bernard Tracey (1832–1912) gained a reputation for combatting proselytism, which was viewed as a particularly serious threat when catholic children were taken into private or state institutions.[49] Evangelical protestant missionaries had comparatively little success in detaching catholics from their faith.[50] Instead mixed marriages were viewed increasingly as a source of danger as the boundaries of the ghetto began to grow more elastic at the turn of the century. It is interesting that the best-known Scottish catholics in the Communist Party, William Gallacher (1884–1966) and Harry McShane (1892–   ) were both products of mixed marriages where their catholic fathers had gone out of the enclave to find marriage partners in the wider community.

To counteract the external influences which weakened the solidarity of the catholic community, church leaders, from about 1885 onwards, began to create a wide variety of organisations which were designed to absorb the energies and take up the leisure time of parishioners young and old. These bodies had distinct religious, recreational, charitable and social functions and in a parish where each of them was in place, it was felt that catholics had no need to go further afield to look for companionship or to use up their leisure time. By the turn of the century, catholics lived in 'a self-enclosed social world in which the Church had duplicated every movement of Protestant and secular social service and charity'.[51]

The proliferation of catholic associations came after the successful efforts of evangelical protestants to provide a religious dimension to ordinary life. The Young Men's Christian Association (1841) and the Boys Brigade (1883) were both founded in Scotland and immigrant associations seeking to keep the links with Ireland evergreen, were already in existence; these included the Gaelic Athletic Association which spread over much of the west of Scotland after the 1890s, to a lesser extent the Gaelic League, dedicated to the restoration of the Irish language, and numerous other associations devoted to the cultivation of Irish music and song, Irish debating and literary clubs, and informal and formal countrymen's association. St Patrick's Day, 17 March usually saw the annual climax of their activities and was the most important day in the calendar for most catholic immigrants. In Scotland, one distinctive Irish body, the Ancient Order of Hibernians fell foul of the religious authorities and came under a ban in 1899. While acting as a charitable institution for its members, it fell under episcopal disapproval because it was alleged also to be a secret society pursuing political ends and, under the ban, sacraments and the privileges of the church were withheld from the membership.[52]

But usually the competition between Irish and catholic associations was amicable, many possessed overlapping memberships, and they often collaborated for specific events. The best-known of the new religious groups was the Catholic Truth Society founded by the Bishop of Salford in 1885. It contributed to the education of catholics in all things pertaining to their faith and also sought to provide answers for or refute the calumnies of non-catholics interested in the faith as the titles of just a few of its pamphlets make clear: 'Does the Pope Claim to be God?' 'What Catholics Do Not Believe', 'Why in Latin?' etc.[53] The CTS was backed up by religious associations such as the Sacred Heart and the Legion of Mary organised on a parish or parochial basis and known as confraternities. Their membership provided the dedicated worshippers who attended extra catholic services, such as the Rosary, Sunday Benediction, weekly evening devotions, and the Stations of the Cross.

Charitable associations tended to be older given the duration and scale of the appalling social problems they sought to reduce. The Society of St Vincent de Paul is the best-known one and is still in existence today. It came to Scotland in 1845 and was run on authoritarian lines. Each parish unit was known as a conference and the president of a conference was appointed for life without any recourse to elections. The local priest acted as its spiritual director and, at meetings of different parochial bodies, it was rare for a priest not to be in attendance.[54]

However, elections did occur in the Catholic Young Men's Society, which was an association open to all catholic men in the parish and has been described by one member as an early working man's club.[55] The CYMS was directed by a chaplain who was usually one of the local priests. It had three fundamental rules, Monthly Communion, the

Chaplain's Veto, and No Party Politics.[56] In St Mary's, Leith as in so many Scottish parishes, the CYMS was a focal-point for the men of the parish and it enjoyed its greatest influence in the decades before 1914. The parish was a self-contained entity in Leith with the school and church together in one unit and the CYMS meetings in the basement of the school. Here there was a billiards room, six tables, and a card room.[57] The priest was the dominant force and the rules barring political talk and laying down monthly communion were scrupulously enforced, leading one historian, himself a catholic, to describe catholic social organisations such as these as 'inimical to free expression and suspicious of spontaneity'.[58]

The CYMS branch at the main catholic parish in Edinburgh, St Patrick's, Cowgate was particularly well-organised under the direction of an energetic Limerick priest, Canon Edward Hannan (1836-91). From St Patrick's CYMS, Canon Hannan founded Hibernian football club in 1875 and became its first manager.[59] For the first sixteen years of its existence, its constitution laid down that its players had to be practising catholics. Because of this Hibs was recently dubbed as 'the first sectarian team in Scotland'.[60] The charge may not be an entirely fair one since the ruling may well have been enforced as much to keep out nominal or lapsed catholics as to bar protestants. Clergy were deeply alarmed by the 'leakage' of catholics in the 1870s but, by the time Hibs dropped its catholics-only clause in 1893, this fear had subsided to a large extent.

In Glasgow, Celtic FC emerged from similar origins but over a decade later in 1887. It was founded by Brother Walfrid, a member of the Marist religious order, as a charitable organisation to raise money for free dinners, clothing, and other relief for the poor of the east end of Glasgow in the parishes of St Mary's, St Andrew's, and St Alphonsus.[61] The fear that protestant soup-kitchens might tempt young catholics into apostasy and that they might drift away from their faith through meeting protestants in their place of employment or leisure, also motivated him.[62] But Celtic opened its doors to all-comers and in 1897 moved away from its charitable origins when it became a limited liability company. However, its new shareholders were largely drawn from the immigrant community and a perusal of the early membership of its committees and later board of directors gives a good indication of who were the rising figures in the community: John Glass, a joiner-builder did much to get Celtic off the ground in its earliest years; the Shaughnessy's were prominent in law and the priesthood; the McKillop's were big restauranteurs in Glasgow; and John McLaughlin was a publican from Hamilton.[63] Indeed, all but one of the first seven-man board of directors was a publican.

Members of the drink trade had been instrumental in forcing the changes which turned Celtic into a professional club. They were opposed by the *Glasgow Observer* (weekly paper of the immigrants after 1884) and its redoubtable editor, Charles Diamond, whose ally was the League of the Cross, the church temperance organisation. Archbishop Manning had founded the League in 1873; Canon Hannan in Edinburgh had already anticipated it in 1872 by founding his own parish temperance association which gained a membership of 4,000.[64] But the League of the Cross did not spread to the west of Scotland till the late 1880s. Thanks to Archbishop Eyre's firm backing, it took off and by 1892, the archdiocese had 128 branches and 30,000 members.[65] Many of these branches provided games rooms in which the main pastimes were billiards, dominoes, cards, and draughts. Usually located on church property, they were intended to act as counter-attractions to public-houses, shebeens, and street gambling. However, the nature of the games rooms became a cause of concern and, in 1903, bookmakers and others involved in the gambling business were prohibited from joining the League in Glasgow. In 1913, one resident of the Gorbals complained of the noise emanating from the League's rooms at St Andrew's cathedral just over the Clyde. The church, the correspondent stated, was teaching young men gambling.[66]

Protestant temperance societies placed a greater emphasis on moral reform rather than mere substitutes.[67] This may explain their greater longevity. The Band of Hope survived after 1918 while the League of the Cross collapsed, apparently due to its failure to recruit among younger catholics. Beforehand, co-operation with protestant temperance bodies had not been encouraged. After the 1850s, temperance bodies were providing much of the impetus for anti-catholicism in the city. Evangelical preachers like Harry Alfred Long fought both Popery and drink and linked the two.[68] His missionary work in the east-end of Glasgow initially attracted greater support from protestant employers than from protestant clergymen but by the 1880s, he had created a strong proletarian evangelical movement which he placed at the service of the Tory party in elections.[69]

Drink produced tensions in catholic homes and was a source of discord between the leaders of the immigrant community as already noted. This is hardly surprising, for the licensing trade was one of the chief avenues of advancement for catholics since entry could be secured with very little capital.[70] And often publicans were generous benefactors to the church. Edwin Scrymgeour, the veteran prohibition campaigner in Dundee and the city's MP from 1922 to 1931, drew attention in 1912 to the inconsistency of the catholic church on this:

> The powerful hold that drink retains upon all the churches is clearly shown . . . by the Dundee and District Catholic Year Book for 1912. In this are to be found among the various agencies at work 'Leagues of the Cross', 'Total

Abstinence Leagues', 'Holy Angels Guilds' . . . Yet alongside . . . are numerous advertisements seeking to lure the faithful into the 'Bee', 'Harp', and other institutions for the distribution of . . . whisky.[71]

The clergy were not noted for encouraging sturdier enterprises such as co-operatives or savings associations which might have meant that, over time, rather fewer enterprising catholics graduated to 'trades that ministered to the weaknesses of mankind'.[72] Once more, Canon Hannan of Edinburgh was exceptional in that he enrolled 1,500 into a Penny Savings Bank.[73] But an Irish co-operative society in Lanarkshire, where there was the density of numbers for it to be feasible, failed to get off the ground. In northern Italy and other parts of Europe such as Bavaria and the Low countries, priests were encouraging catholic co-operatives and savings societies at this time.[74] But, in urban Scotland, there was no educated professional elite and very few skilled artisans who could have provided the initial impetus for such schemes. The catholic population was overwhelmingly proletarian and only a few priests may have had the expertise or the inclination to get such ventures off the ground.

Until well into the twentieth century, the absence of good educational facilities and the opportunities to use them, was a prime factor inhibiting even the brightest working-class catholics from becoming the masters and mistresses of their own destinies. Before 1870, when much of education was under denominational control, the hardpressed catholic clergy simply lacked the resources to provide the same standard and range of education as the protestant schools which were themselves coming under increasing criticism for their inadequacy. Catholic education was very rudimentary, school buildings were of inferior standard, and the meagre resources at hand were barely able to provide the three 'R's and religious instruction to a minority of catholic children.

In Glasgow, catholic schools such as St Aloysius and St Mungo's, which would enjoy prestige in times to come as institutions turning out well-educated young adults, had been built by 1870 but it is a revealing comment on their limitations that the emerging middle-class in the immigrant community preferred to send their children elsewhere. John Maguire, the first archbishop of Glasgow to emerge from the local community was a pawnbroker's son who went to Stonyhurst, the Jesuit college in Lancashire. So did John McLaughlin, one of the prime movers behind the rise of Celtic.

In 1872 the Scotch Education Act transformed a sluggish scene and new school boards took over the church schools, making attendance at school compulsory from five to thirteen years.[75] Guarantees offered to the Presbyterian churches about religious education were sufficiently reassuring for them to transfer their schools to the new school boards. But the catholic authorities chose to remain outside the state system, thus failing to benefit from the expansion in education provision which the state now oversaw. The church was not satisfied with the type of religious instruction provided in public schools, its main reason for going it alone in 1872. Fearing wholesale proselytism and viewing the classroom as a vital forum, alongside the church and the home, for ensuring that children had a catholic upbringing, the church wished to provide its own management. It was adamant about its desire to appoint and control the teaching staff, determine the provision of future schools, and oversee the running of existing ones. Compromise with the framers of the 1872 act was plainly impossible and a settlement which would give catholics the financial benefits of the public system along with a degree of autonomy that would be the envy of catholic leaders outside Scotland, only came about in 1918. Meanwhile catholic school costs could not be charged on the local school rates and it was only when they had been built and equipped that some aid could be claimed on a direct grant basis from the Scotch education department.[76]

Sometimes rich catholic benefactors came to the rescue of school managers totally bereft of the cash needed to provide a new school or maintain or improve an existing one. But they were mainly dependent on the voluntary efforts of local congregations. 'Charity' sermons by well-known preachers and charity balls and concerts were typical methods of raising funds and, once each quarter, wage-earners were urged to donate a day's wages but the most lucrative method tended to be the holding of bazaars in town halls.[77] Such endeavours enabled the roll in Scottish catholic schools to rise from 47,000 in 1883 to 85,000 in 1908.[78]

One source claims that the school was often built before the church in new parishes[79] but complaints arose in some areas, Dundee, for instance, about the inertia of the Scottish clergy in providing schools for immigrant children.[80] Where the Church could not meet the need, catholic pupils could be forced into board schools. In some of these schools located in working-class areas of Glasgow, catholic pupils even predominated.[81] There was plenty of scope for mis-understanding here and, in 1885, the Irish National League, then the chief political voice of the immigrants, protested about a local school requiring a daily singing of God Save The Queen from its mainly catholic pupils.[82]

Catholic luminaries payed close attention to state schools and not just for the above reason. Catholic ratepayers were required to pay rates for the support of these schools, which was a longstanding source of grievance. James Handley claims that between 1872 and 1914, one estimation places the contribution of the catholic section of the population towards board schools at £1,500,000 or one-sixth of the total.[83]

Local education boards were elected bodies and, from the outset, the church decided to participate in these triennial contests through the Catholic Union, which was its spokesman on political affairs. The Catholic Union did not contest local or parliamentary elections but senior priests as well as approved lay catholics were regularly elected to school boards throughout industrial Scotland. By the 1900s, it became the practice in Glasgow that, of the fifteen board members, three were from the Catholic Union, three were Labour, three independent, and the rest were provided by the Presbyterian churches.[84] In these contests, the church put on show the influence it wielded in tight-knit communities by regularly inducing a higher turnout than any of the other participants. But there was scope for friction with the Irish National League, and much later the Labour Party who felt that they had prior claims over the voting loyalties of working-class catholics. In Liverpool, where the Home Rule movement was stronger than anywhere else in Britain, a confrontation between the church and the local political machine occurred in 1892 when Bishop Whiteside placed an English Unionist on the list of catholic candidates for the school board elections. Viewing this as a declaration of war, the Home Rulers put up three of their own candidates, each of whom was elected and secured the defeat of all six of the bishop's.[85]

In Glasgow, relations with ward politicians could be tense if priests urged the congregation to make their political choice on a question of reigious significance like education rather than Ireland. But there was never a conflict on the Liverpool scale perhaps because of the presence of Charles Byrne, who was a member of the school and education boards from 1900 to 1922. Byrne was born in 1856 in remote Banffshire, a stronghold of old Scottish catholicism, the son of Patrick Byrne, so in his own person he managed to personify the native and immigrant strands of catholicism. As honorary secretary, he was the senior figure in the Catholic Union from 1885 to 1915 and he maintained cordial relations with the Home Rule association.

The school board is also significant due to it being the first elected body on which representatives of the Glasgow Irish were to be found. However, catholic education languised while the national system expanded. After prejudice and discrimination, educational backwardness must be counted as a prime reason why catholics coming on to the labour market were unable to compete for jobs and opportunities on equal terms with other young Glaswegians until the 1950s and 1960s at the very earliest.

In 1895 a catholic teacher training college run by the Notre Dame sisters, was established at Dowanhill, Glasgow but this was not destined to be one of the supporting pillars for a future middle-class. It was a female college, many of whose graduates would remain single since marriage and attendant child rearing would have taken them out of teaching. They earned far less than state teachers and a revealing statistic shows that, before 1918, the minority of make catholic teachers (one-fifth of the total), earned in a week, half of what a steelworker could expect to earn in a day.[86] So teaching was not a prestigious calling in the catholic community and within the denominational system, teachers were a compliant group who, compared to present-day catholic teachers, possessed very few rights and were at the mercy of the clergy and their appointed supervisors.

William Haddow, one of the early socialist members of the school board in Glasgow, recalled interceding with Archbishop Maguire when a teacher was sacked for joining the Independent Labour Party by the local priest who was 'King of the Castle'. As Haddow wrote, 'to be dismissed from one school was to be dismissed from the teaching profession, such was the power the religious authorities had over teachers they employed'.[87] Luckily for the lady in question, the Archbishop exercised leniency after receiving a deputation from the Catholic Socialist Society which persuaded him that the ILP was not an irreligious organisation and could not be since the teacher was a faithful and practising catholic.[88] A few years later, in 1912, teachers went unrepresented on the Catholic Education Council for Scotland which was then negotiating with the government for a fairer educational settlement. The membership is a useful guide to who were the leading roman catholics in Scotland before 1914 and it was dominated by army officers and landowners from the catholic aristocracy, and by some members of the professions mainly drawn from Glasgow.[89]

Glasgow was much slower than Liverpool and other centres of Irish immigration such as the USA and Australia in producing thriving businessmen and respected civic leaders. By 1900, 'it would have been possible to accommodate in a third-class carriage all the Catholic men who occupied positions of public prominence or trust'.[90] In catholic education, there was just no equivalent of a school like Allen Glen's fonded in 1853 to provide an education shaped by pure and applied science, technology, and craftsmanship.[91] Thus in a city whose prosperity was disproportionately based on heavy engineering and manufacturing industry, the sons and grandsons of Irish immigrants were automatically excluded from entering the areas of the local economy which conveyed prestige and acceptability.

In the USA, the openness of society and the faster rate of expansion enabled the Irish to surmount discrimination and social disadvantage far more quickly than in Britain. Their anti-British and non-royalist instincts made them feel far more at home in America than the Irish felt in Glasgow or Liverpool. They had a head start over other European migrants to the New World since they did not need to discard any remote language or culture so as to become acceptable in the eyes of the host community; 'their "intermediate ethnic status" between Yankees and continental Europeans gave them the role of imposing social control as priests, policemen, political leaders and trade union bosses'.[92]

In Glasgow, fewer young immigrants broke out of the syndrome whereby they remained in overcrowded, inner-city neighbourhoods, holding down unskilled jobs that were poorly paid and at risk in times of depression, marrying within their own community, and passing down the same tradition to the next generation. In 1896, P. de Rousier, a French observer of the Irish in Glasgow wrote:

> The Irish in Glasgow are not usually very amenable to the influence of environment and find it difficult to acquire the habits of self-respect and persevering energy . . . The Highlanders are more easily aroused to ambition, and to the desire to better themselves, and they become modified by contact with those influences which were lacking in the solitude of their mountain or island houses . . . The Irish generally remain mere labourers, as do their children after them.[93]

Perhaps a closer glance at the situation would have shown P. Rousier that Highlanders had far fewer obstacles to overcome than the Irish, further handicapped as they were by misunderstanding and prejudice, some of it, admittedly, of their own making. But even in Liverpool, where hostility to the Irish was far more marked, if the city's political history and propensity to riot is anything to go by, the immigrants made far quicker progress than in Glasgow. John Denvir applauded them for their skills as dealers and traders which led him to believe that 'under the fostering care of a native government, ours would develop into a great commercial people'.[94]

More prosaically, the same claim was made in Glasgow in relation to the success of Celtic. At its half-yearly committee meeting in 1891, a member pointed to the club as 'proof of the ability of Irishmen to manage any concern in which they took an interest: in the club rested the fair name of their nationality'.[95]

In a community corresponding to 250,000 people in 1880, there were only six catholics studying at Glasgow university, five in medicine and one in law.[96] Only in 1884 was it possible for a stable catholic immigrant paper to be launched. This was the pugnacious and well-designed *Glasgow Observer*. In its twentieth anniversary special edition, it mentioned that, by common consent, the most prominent catholic layman in the city was not a son of Erin, but Mr James Brand KCSG, a building contractor—and a convert.[97]

But already by the 1880s, a two-tier community was taking shape among the Glasgow Irish. Enterprising figures started out as hawkers, or second-hand dealers, for which little capital was needed. From this, they might move on to own pawnshops, lodging houses, public houses, betting shops, eating houses, or grocery shops, catering for the needs as well as the comforts and weaknesses of their own community. Later these tradespeople could think of sending their children to university, by which time they would have moved out of the immigrant neighbour-hood, even if much of their livelihood still derived from it. If they entered the professions, their children were likely to sever many more of their links with the community; a factory owner like John Barry, who came to Edinburgh's port of Leith in 1850 from Newry, County Armagh had founded a paper mill which stayed in the family for well over a century, had hardly any counterpart in the west of Scotland.[98]

Very occasionally, an energetic priest could create the right pre-conditions for greater endeavour. This seems to have been the case in the parish of St Bridget's comprising the mining village of Baillieston. Fr Terken the local priest, placed a high value on education and had the strength of personality to enforce his belief in temperance. He was a formative influence on Patrick Dollan, the first member of his com-munity to be elected to a prestigious civil office when he became Glasgow's Lord Provost in 1938.[99] John Wheatley, Labour's first minister of health, also grew up in the parish as did Tommy McGhee, later Provost of Clydebank who blotted his copybook by entering the licensing trade. Fr Terken doubled as the teacher and six of his pupils became shopkeepers in Glasgow, which is a striking incidence of upward mobility for such a small community.[100]

But it took another generation before the enterprising products of the immigrant community began to make a mark on local politics. This was already happening in Liverpool by 1876, the year in which the first Home Ruler was elected to the city council.[101] In 1877, another four followed and the same trend was noticeable somewhat later in Manchester. It has a smaller Irish community than either Liverpool or Glasgow but it had an Irish nationalist councillor by 1889, Daniel McCabe, who later became the city's mayor and was knighted.[102]

In Glasgow, by 1883, the 300-strong Jewish community had a councillor, but the Glasgow Irish, numbering many thousands more, had none. The first Home Ruler on the council was John Ferguson, a *protestant* Ulsterman, who was elected for Calton in 1893. This fact alone indicates that immigrant politics had their own distinct rhythm and could contradict some of the stereotypes attached to the Irish in Britain and their politics.

Strong political feelings first became evident in the west of Scotland immigrant communities at the start of the 1870s. Here, as in other British centres of Irish settlement, Irishmen were chiefly concerned with events back home, a preoccupation that, in many cases was passed on to sons and grandsons who were destined never to set foot in Ireland. In November 1871, a Glasgow branch of the Irish national movement, then known as the Home Government Association, was formed and the leader, Isaac Butt MP was on hand to deliver the inaugural address. In the next forty years, this association would go through several name changes but the Home Government branch would always be one of the strongest in Britain. After 1880, the Home Rule movement was known as the Irish National League and between 1883 and 1890 the number of British branches rose from fifty-two to 630 and the registered membership from 4,000 to over 40,000.[103]

But these advances occurred only after a slow start. It was only in 1872 that Glasgow Home Rulers achieved a breakthrough by turning 17 March, St Patrick's Day into a symbolic political one as well as an occasion for religious and social celebrations.[104] This was all the more creditable since the most senior Home Ruler could not be described as a typical member of the exile community.

John Ferguson was born in 1837 and came to Glasgow in 1860. His interest in nationalist politics was only kindled after he left Ireland. Entering the publishing business, he rose to become a partner in the firm Ferguson and Cameron, and a fairly wealthy man by the standards of the day.[105] Ferguson chaired nearly every Irish meeting of importance in the west of Scotland from 1873 up to his death in 1906.[106] His solid financial background meant that he was able to devote more time to politics than almost anybody else in the Irish community and he represented stability at the top of a movement which had a highly mobile rank-and-file.[107] Ferguson was influential in Ireland as well as the west of Scotland and he could easily have claimed a seat in the Irish Parliamentary Party which, after 1890, had many British-based Irishmen representing Irish constituencies, but he preferred to remain in Glasgow. His religion may have placed him in an awkward position when questions like religious education or denominational schools intruded into the nationalist debate but he was a discreet person whose conciliatory talents came to be highly valued in a community where political feuding and factionalism regularly threatened the equilibrium of the Home Rule movement. Like the Irish leaders Butt and Parnell, his religion could turn out to be an asset since it enabled nationalists to argue that Home Rule was an aspiration that had exponents among the descendants of settlers as well as among the native Gaels.

Political consciousness among the immigrants was stirring as the infighting within the church began to subside. Archbishop Eyre opted for a policy of coexistence between the native and immigrant traditions in his church. Later, the Home Rule movement simply grew too large for the bishops of England or Scotland to isolate it or turn it into a clerical tool. So, in 1885, a Catholic Union was set up by the church in Glasgow (a development repeated elsewhere) in order to promote catholic interests in specific areas of political life, particularly in education. Relations with the Irish Natonal League usually were cordial. Both were organised on a parish basis and sometimes joint meetings of their local committees occurred. By tacit agreement, school board elections were left to the Catholic Union and local and parliamentary elections to the league.[108]

Through its different stages, catholic priests could always be found playing a role in the home rule movement or in its cultural adjuncts. In 1875, it was the formidable Michael Condon who addressed the political rally in Glasgow commemorating the centenary of Daniel O'Connell's birth, even though the church had appealed to the Irish community to join *its* non-political rally; other well-known nationalist priests included John Danaher (1821–86) and John O'Dea (1877–1934) who, during his short stay in a Lanarkshire parish from 1901 to 1904, did much to stimulate the Gaelic League, concerned with reviving the Irish language, and the Gaelic Athletic Association, created in 1884 to foster traditional Irish games.[109] The priest espousing the Home Rule cause with the greatest zeal may have been John Murphy (1857–1913). As the assistant priest in the parish of St John's in the Gorbals area of Glasgow during the early 1880s, he was prepared to defy openly his religious superiors on this political question. In 1882, he even ran for the school board with only the backing of the league, as a gesture of protest at the fact that Scottish clergy and laity alike had monopolised the catholic ticket since 1875.[110] Fr Murphy was elected ahead of the three official church nominees, one of whom was defeated. Interestingly, Murphy was not silenced or removed by Eyre and was given his own parish in 1886.[111]

But in Edinburgh, during that year, an open clash occurred over politics when George Angus, an Oxford-educated Scottish convert secured the dismissal of the president of the CYMS in the city for having publicly welcomed T. D. Sullivan, a released Irish prisoner.[112] Certain of Fr Angus's clerical colleagues were in attendance and such divergences even within the church help explain why a confessional party on the European model did not get off the ground in central Scotland (even though it could be said to exist in embryo in the education elections which demonstrated that, under the system of proportional representation which applied, Scottish catholics were gathered together in sufficient density to make it viable).

In Scotland, there was no equivalent of Cardinal Manning (1808–92), archbishop of Westminster from 1865 to 1892. He recognised that the achievement of Irish self-determination should be the first concern of immigrant catholics in the sphere of politics, taking precedence even over education.[113] When Manning supported the Land League which was using militant measures in the early 1880s to press for land reform in Ireland. English catholics rebuked him. One, in a letter to the *Times*, wrote that 'the public regard a man of profound piety and zeal like the archbishop of Westminster as our public spokesman but we . . . are not bound to approve him politically. Perhaps the less English Catholics as such have to do with politics, but especially Irish politics, the better.'[114]

Thus, in Britain, there was tension not only between immigrant and native catholics but between recusants or old catholics (who had survived persecution through cultivation of anonymity and support for the political *status quo*) and converts who could be zealous in proclamation of their new faith, but were rarely as strongly hibernophile as Manning, the Anglican parson who became archbishop of Westminster.[115]

Later, some English catholics backed by their bishops, discarded their apoliticism to advocate support for the Conservative Party because it backed denominational education and had no secularists in its ranks, unlike the Liberal Party.[116] Such calls met with an angry response from immigrant leaders; in the first general election of 1910, when the parties were running neck-and-neck, and a Liberal victory held out the prospect of Home Rule, John Redmond, leader of the Irish Parliamentary Party, angrily denounced his English co-religionists at a speech in Manchester:

> The English Catholics have always been the most bitter enemies of Ireland. Why, I do not know unless it be their jealousy of the race which has maintained the faith against persecution . . . We fought their battles, we emancipated them in spite of themselves . . . But . . . not even the Orangemen in Belfast today are more bitter opponents of the cause of Irish freedom than are the average English Catholics.[117]

Scotland usually avoided such rancour in electoral politics since its native catholics were fewer in number than they were in England and they resided far from the main centres of population. But, in Glasgow, internal feuding between the two largest branches of the city's Home Rule movement often proved a regular distraction. The Home Government branch and the William O'Brien branch were locked in fierce rivalry over many years, which events like the divorce scandal leading to the downfall of the Irish leader Parnell in 1890 only helped intensify. The Home Government branch often managed to send a bigger delegation to the annual convention of the League than any other branch in Britain which gave it a preponderance in immigration affairs.[118] Many of its leading members, such as the brothers Hugh and

Arthur Murphy during the 1890s, were prominent in the drink trade which enabled the Home Government branch to contribute handsomely to the fighting funds of the Irish Parliamentary Party.[119]

A complicating element was added by the energetic Charles Diamond (1858–1934) who, in 1885, took over the *Glasgow Observer*, which would be the principal newspaper of the Irish in Scotland for the next half-century. Diamond used his paper and the numerous local editions in different parts of urban Scotland to promote strong temperance views and it was not long before he was attacking the Home Government branch for its links with the drink trade.[120] Time did not heal this quarrel and, in 1903, the Home Government branch launched the *Glasgow Star* in order to compete against the *Glasgow Observer*. At the local elections of that year, it even campaigned against Mitchel Quin, the editor of the *Observer*, who was a candidate in the Cowcaddens ward.[121] Such infighting may have been responsible for the delay in getting a Home Ruler elected to the council, since a break-through only occurred in 1893 with John Ferguson's election. Then, and afterwards, the Glasgow Home Rulers had no pretensions of municipal power, unlike the Liverpool movement. At its peak, it had 17,000 members, between 1892 and 1895, it shared the running of the city with the Liberals and, after 1900, it superseded them as the city's second biggest party.[122] Gradually, the league in Liverpool turned into a local party in its own right rather than a British outpost of Irish nationalism. Local politics sustained the party far more than events or issues relating to Ireland, and immersion in local government affairs enabled it to establish a great measure of independence from the Irish Parliamentary Party.

But the political leadership in Glasgow also had its own distinct style and could strike up novel alliances as well as squabble and argue. Starting in 1881, Michael Davitt, the radical Home Ruler, took up the land question in Glasgow, advocating nationalisation and a taxation of land values. Davitt was then orchestrating a struggle against absentee landlordism in Ireland which came to be known as the 'Land War' and the West Highlands of Scotland would witness a mini-version of this great agrarian conflict later in the 1880s, so at least on this issue there was common ground between two sets of immigrants in Glasgow who were otherwise kept apart by religion and nationality.

Parnell addressed Highland societies in 1881, at a meeting in the city hall, Glasgow when there was much concern about evictions in the Isle of Skye.[123] The Irish National League in Glasgow donated £1,000 to be used for the prevention of Scottish evictions and, in 1885, one of the five Crofters or Land League candidates elected to parliament was D. H. MacFarlane, a Scottish roman catholic who had previously sat for an Irish constituency.

John Murdoch, a veteran Highland campaigner and early Scottish Nationalist supported Irish self-determination and sought to revive cultural links between Scotland and Ireland based on the threatened rural Celtic cultures of both countries.[124] He was offered an Irish constituency in 1881 but he chose to retire from politics. Six years later, Davitt was offered a Highland seat after making a tour of the noth-west of Scotland in which he was particularly well-received.[125] G. B. Clark, Land League MP for Caithness also had a longstanding commitment to Irish nationalism and, as a member of the Social Democratic Federation, he toured Ireland in the 1880s. Their shared radicalism made it possible for Clark and Davitt to co-operate fruit-fully. On a broader scale, such involvements dented the isolation of the Glasgow Irish, chimed in with the traditional anti-landlord views of the Scottish working-class and produced greater understanding between the Irish and that large section of the city's proletariat that was of Highland descent.[126]

The social dimension of the nationalist struggle produced tensions within the Home Rule movement both in Ireland and Britain. Partial success in the 1880s, made Parnell, the Irish nationalist leader, increasingly autocratic and in 1884 he publicly criticised Davitt's belief in land nationalisation as a hollow alternative to undisputed peasant ownership once the great estates were broken up.[127] In 1888, he was not helping Davitt's efforts to build up support for home rule within the working-class in Britain with the following statement:

> I would not tolerate, if I were at the head of a government, such bodies as trade-unions. They are opposed to individual liberties and should be kept down as Bismarck keeps them under in Germany . . . Whatever has to be done for the protection of the working-classes . . . should be the duty of the government.[128]

Earlier, in 1885, Parnell's call to the British Home Rulers to campaign for the return of a Conservative government rather than support the Liberals, produced dismay in Glasgow and many other immigrant centres. It may have shown the Liberals that Irish support was not automatically their's but the movement in Britain was weakened as (to a much greater extent) it was in 1890 with the political downfall of Parnell after he had been cited in a divorce case. In Ireland, the movement split although it held together better in Scotland and, once the divisions began to mend, a new organisation emerged in 1898 known as the United Irish League (UIL) which continued in existence until after the First World War.

The downfall of an autocratic leader seemed to be the right moment to demand a more democratic movement. At its Newcastle convention in 1891, the Glasgow branches were to the fore in demanding a radical re-shaping of the league. For once, even Charles Diamond and the Home Government branch buried their differences to campaign together on this issue. Frustration had been building up in the 1880s over the tight control exercised by the Irish Parliamentary Party which appointed full-time organisers without consulting the branches and, in 1886, had prevented John Ferguson chairing the St Patrick's Day rally in Glasgow because of his support for the radical views of Michael Davitt.[129] The main demand in 1891 was for a democratic executive, half of whose members were to be elected by the local branches, half by the parliamentary party.[130] Its defeat produced disillusionment among the radical members of the league and, in years to come, helped swing some of them towards the left and away from exile politics.

But the league was able to mobilise the bulk of votes in strongly immigrant neighbourhoods right up until the First World War. Its support was usually placed at the disposal of the Liberal party which introduced Home Rule bills into parliament in 1886, 1892, and 1912. But this alliance was a marriage of convenience rather than a genuine partnership. League policy demanded that 'the Irish vote should not be committed to any British party, Tory, Liberal, or Labour, but directed where the interests of Ireland demanded such action'.[131] Relations were often tense between local Liberal associations and the league in areas like the west of Scotland where, after 1886, the Liberals undoubtedly lost votes for espousing Home Rule. Sometimes they calculated that it was tactically shrewder to put up a candidate who was lukewarm or even hostile to Irish self-determination. When this happened, the league did not vacate the field but instead would direct its vote to the Tory or Labour side in order to secure the downfall of the Liberal. An extreme case occurred in 1900 when the local branch of the UIL in the Blackfriars division of Glasgow fell out with the defending Liberal and placarded the constituency with emerald green posters in favour of Andrew Bonar Law, the Tory, who won and later was to loom large in the demonology of Irish nationalism.[132]

The Irish vote in Britain was a solid and highly disciplined one which the branches delivered according to the instructions of the head of the Irish Parliamentary Party, who was not concerned with British domestic issues but with completing Ireland's national struggle.[133] In the west of Scotland, the UIL had a tendency of exaggerating its local strength. In the 1880s, when even relations with the Liberals were uneasy, the League had threatened to put up its own candidates in selected parliamentary seats. But the Irish in Glasgow were simply not that densely concentrated to accomplish the return of a Home Ruler which Liverpool had brought off in 1886 with the return of T. P. O'Connor, who held the Scotland division of the city for the next forty-three years.

Other factors prevented the immigrant community from moulding the politics of its adopted city. It is worth remembering that many Irishmen came from the north-west, from Ulster and north Connacht which were far calmer politically than other areas. A strong nationalist awareness would not be a distinguishing feature of the catholic minority in Ulster until after the creation of the Northern Ireland state in 1921, so it is likely that immigrants to Scotland were not unaffected by their relatively apolitical home background. The relatively high level of illiteracy also posed problems and organisers claimed that some Irish electors spoiled their ballots rather than run the risk of victimisation by revealing their preference to the polling clerk.[134]

Even more to the point, a high degree of residential mobility and the failure to meet property qualifications, kept many Irishmen off the voting rolls.[135] Despite the Third Reform Act of 1884, the consequence was that some 40% of adult males were still unenfranchised by 1911.[136] While progressively extending the franchise the Liberals had placed handicaps in the way of those least likely to be 'respectable or independent' in the working-class. The Irish were strongly to the fore in the relevant categories: those with insecure employment who had to move house frequently, who could not always pay their rates, or who were lodgers who faced difficulty over voter registration. 'Respectability rather than humanity was the criterion for the vote'.[137] This attitude fueled the tension between Liberal Party managers and the Irish who were locked in an uneasy political alliance where partners desired differing political ends: reliance on Irish support proved insufferable for many of the Liberals who broke away from their own party in 1886 and it would lead later on to Irish defections from the home rule movement in Britain.

The weakness of the Irish vote in Glasgow probably diminished militant feeling on the Orange side of local politics and so indirectly may have been a stabilising factor in community relations. But it is worth noting that there was a greater level of enfranchisement in the small and remoter mining communities in Lanarkshire.[138] Here the Irish had securer employment, were far less migratory and, according to John Denvir, were 'much better off . . . than in Glasgow, Edinburgh, Greenock, Paisley, or Dundee'.[139] The Home Rule movement flourished in the Lanarkshire mining areas and Coatbridge, which in the 1890s boasted the largest branch in Britain, and was able in one year to donate more funds to the league's treasury than almost any of the great cities.[140]

The leader of the league in Coatbridge was Dr Charles O'Neill (1844-1918) who, after Ferguson, was 'probably the outstanding figure in the movement in Scotland'.[141] A native of Armagh and one of the earliest catholics to graduate from Glasgow university, he established his medical practice in Coatbridge, became head of the league there, and eventually was MP for South Armagh from 1909 to 1918. He was not the only member of the immigrant community in Scotland to be returned to Westminster. William McKillop (1860–1909), a successful Glasgow restauranteur, was MP for North Sligo from 1906 to 1909.[142] Patrick O'Hare (1847–1917) was MP for North Monaghan from 1906 to 1907 (when ill-health forced him to retire), having been returned as a Glasgow councillor in 1897 as a Labour reformist. He can be compared with the freethinking Ulster protestant, friend of Davitt, and trade union organiser Richard McGhee (1851–1930) who was Irish Nationalist MP for North Louth from 1896 to 1900 and for Mid-Tyrone from 1910 to 1918.[143] Liverpool provided no less than eight members of the Irish Parliamentary Party and Manchester's Irish leader, Daniel Boyle (1859–1925) was MP for North Mayo from 1910 to 1918. Evidently the party leadership had a partiality for Irishmen who had distinguished themselves abroad. Local constituency associations, subject to factionalism, could often unite around a reputable outsider far better than around a local aspirant while in Britain, the elevation of an immigrant from Coatbridge, Liverpool, or Glasgow was a handy device to still criticism about the heavy-handed way in which the UIL was controlled from London.

After 1905, with the foundation of Sinn Fein, a completely separatist movement wanting to take Ireland right outside the British orbit, nationalists dissatisfied with the moderation or opportunism of the league had an alternative movement with which to identify. In 1908, a branch of Sinn Fein was formed in Glasgow, the year in which its leader Arthur Griffith visited the city.[144] Patrick Pearse, another separatist, then still better known for his work in the Gaelic League, had visited Glasgow in 1903 to speak about the restoration of the language.[145] But Sinn Fein posed little threat to the league and although its visitors might be revered in years to come, they got a far less warm reception than Joseph Devlin, the leading home ruler in Belfast, who was a very popular figure in the Glasgow Irish community from the turn of the century onwards.[146]

Devlin may have felt very much at home in Glasgow. There, as in his native Belfast, the Home Rule movement was permanently in opposition but the strength of antagonistic bodies like the Orange Order encouraged those living in the Irish catholic neighbourhoods of both cities to close ranks and relegate their differences. Communal solidarity may have been at its strongest in 1886 when the Irish question seemed to turn politics in Glasgow completely upside down.

The 1886 crisis over Irish home rule was a sudden one and its political impact could not easily have been foreseen. In the previous fifty years, the Liberals had completely dominated Scottish politics;

in Glasgow, Toryism was so weak that forty years elapsed before the party won a seat there in 1874. But the egalitarian impulses which gave rise to the term 'Scottish Democracy' co-existed uneasily with the imperial and military roles so many Scots were undertaking in the high-noon of Victorian expansion. The Scottish political consensus finally collapsed in 1886, apparently as a direct result of Prime Minister William Gladstone's Irish Home Rule Bill.[147] But other longer-term issues contributed to the gaping split in the Liberal Party which had suddenly opened up. Disputes between radicals and moderates over the pace of reform and especially over the proposed disestablishment of the Church of Scotland were vital contributory factors. Gladstone so alienated both camps in this religious dispute that some of their leading members joined forces against him; radicals, like the former Chartist Duncan McLaren, found themselves lining up with the old guard in the new formation called the Liberal Unionist Party that quickly emerged. In the general election held later in 1886, the Tories only made two gains in the whole of Scotland but seventeen Liberal Unionists were returned, the Liberals losing two-thirds of their seats in the west of Scotland.

The fact that Gladstone offered Scotland nothing at all in his first Home Rule bill also accounted for defections. Without this strife-torn background, the 1886 bill might have created far less havoc for Scottish Liberalism but there is no doubt that on its own, the Irish question had a massive political impact on Glasgow in that year. From hindsight, some of the reasons may seem spurious or exaggerated but the 1886 debate was not carried out in a calm atmosphere. Here are some of the decisive elements that explain the degree of opposition to Irish Home Rule to be found at various levels of society: Glasgow's geographical proximity to Ulster and the existence of a large Ulster protestant community there; the feeling that any change in the status of Ireland would leave the undefended coastline of the west of Scotland vulnerable to foreign invasion; the linked concern that Ireland's departure from the British orbit would weaken imperial unity and thus jeopardise Scottish trade with the empire.[148]

Scotland, like the rest of the capitalist world, was in the midst of a severe recession during the first Home Rule crisis, which may explain why its local impact was far greater than during the second Home Rule crisis of 1912-14 which coincided with a period of economic prosperity. The collapse of the Irish economy was predicted in 1886 if Gladstone's bill was passed. Unskilled workers, many of whom had been enfranchised by the third Reform Act of 1884, were persuaded to believe that mass Irish immigration to the west of Scotland would follow and threaten their livelihood.[149] But the political drama rarely spilled over into major communal violence on the streets of Glasgow. This was despite the activities of the Irish Loyal and Patriotic Union which, along with the Scottish Protestant Alliance, was using anti-catholic propaganda to rally support for the Unionist cause in 1886. These tactics brought a rebuke from the editor of the *Scotsman*, Charles Cooper, himself a catholic though also a Unionist, who must have been apprehensive on hearing the publicly expressed view of his press colleague James Henderson, owner of the *Belfast Newsletter* that 'if we can stir up the religious feeling in Scotland, we have won the battle'.[150] Ultimately these Anglo-Irish troubleshooters of 1886 were more pleased with their propaganda work in England than in Scotland and complained of 'the great hold Gladstone had over the Scottish mind', especially in the east, where the Liberals held firm.[151]

The more serious second Home Rule crisis of 1912–14, when protestant Ulster was turned into an armed camp so as to resist the measure, had surprisingly little impact in the west of Scotland. In 1910, F. E. Smith had described the issue as 'a dead quarrel for which neither the country nor the Unionist party cares a damn outside of Ulster and Liverpool'.[152] Afterwards the response from Scotland for a Unionist *jihad* was distinctly feeble. In October 1912, only 8,000 turned out in Glasgow for Carson, the Ulster leader, compared with the 150,000 who at 7.00 a.m. on a Sunday morning had awaited his arrival at the Liverpool pier head a few days earlier.[153] In the two elections of 1910, most Glasgow workers had been swayed by the peers versus people arguments of Liberal speakers and had voted enthusiastically for reform of the House of Lords and an assault on aristocratic privilege.[154] It meant little that Andrew Bonar Law, party leader and Tory champion of Ulster resistance was a Glasgow industrialist.[155] When he lost his Manchester seat in December 1910, it was to Liverpool and not to his native city that he turned for a replacement.

Liverpool responded so emphatically to the Ulster drama not so much for the issue at stake but because it mirrored its own municipal quarrels and enabled the rival Tory and Irish machines to reinforce the communal allegiances that made Liverpool politics so different from those anywhere else in England. Much of the worst sectarian violence occurred there when the Irish question was in abeyance and was fuelled by the nature of the labour market which encouraged intense competition among workers for short-term jobs. Two communities grew up that were segregated from each other residentially and politically. To a much greater extent than in nearby Manchester or Salford where community relations steadily improved after 1880, the Tory party turned the manipulation of the protestant working-class and its communal allegiances into a veritable art-form. 'Tory Democracy' which stressed some of the rights as well as the duties of labour along with devotion to Church, Crown, and Empire, was the recipe for virtual one-party rule from the 1880s onwards. The 'parson and squire' type of Toryism, commonplace elsewhere, was quite redundant on Merseyside. Here the party was run by a succession of Tammany-style bosses, the greatest of whom was the brewer Archibald Salvidge who controlled Liverpool Toryism from the 1890s down till his death in 1928. Salvidge's base was the Workingman's Conservative Association which, like the Orange Order in Ulster, united the political and leisure activities of its working-class membership and was confined to protestants. With the Irish Home Rulers presenting the main opposition on the council after 1900, religious sectarianism was openly fanned to keep the working-class Tory vote intact. Protestant militants made the Church discipline bill a live issue in Tory ranks in the Edwardian age. It aimed to out-law ritualism, the collective name for the adoption of some Anglican clergymen of ceremonies, vestments, and practices which allegedly symbolised catholic beliefs.[156]

Salvidge would defy old-fashioned Tory notables unhappy with the Liverpool model, for many years to come. In many ways, the radical conservative movement he built up in Liverpool anticipated fascism and in key respects was alien from mainstream English Conservatism.[157] Salvidge was a rather bogus figure, married to a roman catholic and financially insolvent by the end of his life.[158] F. E. Smith, later Lord Birkenhead, a lower middle-class *protege* of Salvidge who used Liverpool as a launching-pad to national politics, could confidently tell a Liverpool election audience in 1906 that 'my Protestantism is not of recent growth' when in fact he was an unbeliever.[159]

In nineteenth century Glasgow there were relatively few adventurers or machine bosses to give elections in the city a colourful edge. So volatile were protestant politics in the city often compared with Glasgow that the Liverpool Tories even faced an electoral challenge from a religious party that was strongly entrenched in a number of districts. This was the National Protestant Electoral Federation of Pastor George Wise (1857-1916) which survived for over sixty years under Wise, and his successor H. D. Longbottom (1886-1962), when it was known as the Liverpool Protestant Party. Wise came from Bermondsey in London and did not set foot in Liverpool till he was over thirty (he can be compared with Harry Alfred Long in Glasgow, another outsider) but he was one of the few protestant crusaders successfully to make the transition from preaching to politics. He exemplified how important territoriality was in the ordinary social relations of Liverpool in the early 1900s by holding provocative meet-ings and processions in an area where the catholic bishop's residence, two convents, and three churches were sited. Assertions he made about how priests 'lived with harlots' and 'got the poor to feed their bastards' incited disorder and he was gaoled for two months in 1903. In 1909, 100,000 people accompanied him to the prison gates when he received another four-months sentence for refusing to halt provocative parades.[160] Fierce rioting in that year, over rival religious processions, led to hundreds of families fleeting the district in which they were a religious minority and put back what religious progress there had been in previous decades.

In the past, the Liverpool Tories had been able to control the aggressive Anglican clergymen who had adopted chauvinist positions on many of the issues which had a vital bearing on community relations. But the dissenters who superseded them after 1900 were less pliable and, as for Wise, he was a law-unto-himself. In 1903, his newly founded party won three seats and he sat as a councillor until 1906, when he was debarred from recontesting his seat because, in the meantime, he had become an ordained minister.[161] The historian Sir Charles Petrie (son of the Tory leader on Liverpool city council at the turn of the century), described Wise as that 'combination of Uriah Heep and Titus Oates'.[162] His party's rapid progress was eventually halted by internecine disputes but Wise still accomplished the transition from itinerant preacher to regular minister of a dissenting congregation. His Protestant Reformed Church was big enough to organise a whole range of activities before 1914, from education classes to womens groups and social outings.[163] But it was chiefly by whipping up sectarian feelings, by incendiary statements, and provocative assemblies that Wise made his bid for fame in the 1900s and, in the process, postponed the day when Liverpool's sectarian divisions could be broken down.

Wise had his emulators in Glasgow, such as the itinerant preacher Samuel Boal who, around 1908, mingled his denunciations of catholicism with attacks on socialism.[164] Socialists speaking in the Bridgeton district were barracked by Orangemen but the trouble spread to other areas and, in Partick, a lorry used by the ILP municipal candidate as a platform was drenched with petrol and set alight. But Glasgow was a poor imitation of Liverpool in most respects. The one noteworthy riot in the 1900s after the annual 12 July celebrations of the Orangemen, never threatened to assume Liverpool proportions; the Glasgow WMCA was a broken reed compared to Salvidge's powerful movement.[165] But serious incidents occurred in the Lanarkshire steel town of Motherwell in the summer of 1909 when Henry Grey Graham, catholic priest and ex-Presbyterian minister, made a public exposition of the catholic faith at a series of twelve indoor meetings. In response, the anti-catholic Hope Trust despatched two of its lecturers to the town, who were later convicted and bound over to keep the peace, and on 8 July a pitched battle occurred in Motherwell between rival factions.[166] Grey Graham's biographer relates that 'the agitation of the ranters ensured that they [the talks] would not be repeated':

> Perhaps he was naive and insensitive in thinking that a former minister of the kirk would win a peaceable hearing on such a subject. The local Catholic clergy had been doubtful about the enterprise from the beginning. They shared the old catholic feeling, a legacy from the penal days, that it was better to let sleeping dogs lie. Their caution was an honourable scar, but to the convert it looked like a self-inflicted wound of timidity.[167]

The annoyance displayed by protestant preachers and groups like the Orange Order whenever catholics ventured boldly out of the ghetto probably only served to reinforce their solidarity and bring waverers into line. Ordinary catholics could also be unduly touchy about religious matters in the political sphere. When, in 1879, a young trade unionist called Keir Hardie innocently compared Alexander McDonald, the miner's leader, with the great Martin Luther, he was immediately heckled by the catholic miners in his Lanarkshire audience. Events like the execution of the archbishop of Paris by the communards in 1870, and the great battles between church and state in Italy, Germany, and France made many pious catholics willing to listen to the warnings of their priests about sacrilegious ideas drifting across from the continent. Many of the priests who had come to the Scottish mission from Ireland hailed from comfortably-off parishes in the southern grassland counties of Limerick and Cork, some came from garrison towns and were the sons of tailors andboot-makers,[168] so they were inherently conservative in their social outlook and were ready to denounce radicalism in whatever guise it might appear. It is doubtful if any priest availed of the language used by the *Glasgow Observer* which, just before the appearance of Leo XIII's encyclical *Rerum Novarum* in 1891, issued its own attack on socialism and its alleged danger to the faith of catholics:

> It means a nation of paramours, bastards, and profligates. It is Manichaeism, Montanism, Waldensianism, Mormonism, and Divorce Court Protestantism rolled into one.[169]

But, even as early as 1891, Charles Diamond's papers were prepared to make a distinction between the strongly anti-clerical Socialist parties operating on the continent and the Labour movement in Britain, which in years to come, this press baron would identify himself with.[170] Already, he occasionally instructed his local editors to back left-wing candidates in local elections if a Liberal was not in the field or was lukewarm towards home rule. Even in Parnell's time, the Irish National League in Glasgow was prepared to endorse radicals. In 1885, John

Ferguson ignored Parnell's directive to back Tory candidates and campaigned for Shaw Maxwell, a land nationalisation candidate in Glasgow.[171] In 1888, he backed Keir Hardie who was standing as a working-class radical in the Mid-Lanark by-election.[172] Hardie only obtained 617 votes but the contest was a watershed which led to the creation of the Scottish Labour Party, the direct progenitor of the Labour Party. The new party included dissenters from official Liberalism such as the Scottish laird, R. B. Cunninghame-Graham, returned for North West Lanarkshire in 1886 as a Scottish Land League candidate, John Murdoch, and G. B. Clark MP, Crofters leader, Shaw Maxwell, Hardie, and John Ferguson and another fellow Ulster protestant resident in Scotland, Robert Smillie, the miners leader from Larkhall. The SLP was a response to the crisis of Scottish Liberalism induced by the 1886 split rather than the result of a socialist groundswell, and after a poor electoral showing, it was absorbed into the newly-created Independent Labour Party in 1895.[173] By then, Hardie had drifted apart from Ferguson and Davitt and they would not be reconciled until shortly before the 1906 general election.[174] But in outline the SLP had been a foretaste of the coalition of forces that would make up the Labour Party in Scotland after its decisive electoral breakthrough of 1922.

Ferguson was the midwife whose assistance at this long-drawn-out birth was crucial. He survived in league politics thanks to the faithful support of the powerful Home Government branch which had a strong labour orientation. Hugh Murphy, its president up till his death in 1903, was a member of the Glasgow Trades Council and a supporter of the Independent Labour Party, a sign that old animosities between the Irish and the trade union movement in Glasgow were breaking down.[175] Davitt may have done more than anybody else to break down old suspicions. He was particularly popular in Scottish radical circles and, in 1912, the Glasgow left-wing weekly *Forward* gave him the accolade of 'the greatest Irishman of the last fifty years'.[176]

Patrick O'Hare, on the council from 1897 to 1906, also built bridges between the two communities. Earlier, as a member of the parochial board, he had gained the appelation of 'Watchdog of the Poor' because of the interest he showed in the system of granting poor relief. Having been elected for Springburn, a district with a strong Orange presence, he was twice re-elected without opposition. But he did not play down his commitment to his own community:

> His tenderness is always in evidence, especially on the bench where his leaning is invariably to the side of mercy. Let the prisoner at the bar and his antecedents be what they may, the prisoner inevitably gets the benefit of the doubt where any doubt there is.[177]

Patrick O'Hare's descendants continued his tradition of service and his two grandsons, Eugene and Patrick Connolly won the affection of several generations of residents in the Gorbals and Govanhill areas of Glasgow, where they had a medical practice for forty years up to the 1980s.

Unlike O'Hare and Ferguson, some radical politicians largely put their Irish connections to one side as they undertook political careers. Relatively few examples came from the Glasgow Irish community because of its watertight character but one is Patrick Curran, born in Glasgow in 1860 who, by 1907, had moved to Tyneside where as Pete Curran, he was MP for Jarrow until 1910. James Sexton (1856-1938), born in Newcastle of Irish stock, and a dockworkers leader on Mersey-side after 1890, so departed from his roots that when, as Labour MP for St Helens from 1918 to 1931, he described Bonar-Law (high in Irish nationalist demonology), as 'the most broadminded and trans-parently honest opponent I have ever known'.[178] James O'Grady (1866-1934), from the small Bristol Irish community, also discarded his Irish connections on entering politics as Labour MP for Leeds East and Leeds North-East from 1906 to 1924.

Despite early pioneers like Ferguson and O'Hare, one commentator James Kellas has asserted that 'it was the attitude of the Irish working-class which prevented the emergence of a strong Labour movement in Scotland until Irish Home Rule was achieved'.[179] The Irish question, in other words, was a diversion and an irritant which replaced a working-class consciousness with a nationalist one and triggered off sectarian quarrels in the working-class.[180] There might be some truth in this argument but, going by the lacklustre growth of socialism in areas of Britain where emigration or the Irish issue did not count, one might just as easily conclude that, minus Ireland and its troubles, the end result would not have been a faster socialist breakthrough but instead a more stable and entrenched Liberal party.

Without the Irish question, it is hardly likely that so many un-skilled workers would have got involved in politics. Handley described the Home Government branch of the league as 'the parliament of the Irish people in Glasgow' where 'Sunday after Sunday its large hall was crowded with eager listeners to the debates'.[181] It should not be forgotten that arguably the two best-known *revolutionary* socialists in these islands, James Larkin (1876-1947) and James Connolly (1868-1916), emerged respectively from the Liverpool and Edinburgh Irish communities, where their early political awareness was germinated by the importance of the Irish question. Both were leaders of unskilled workers in Ireland, Britain, and north America. Larkin became a champion of revolutionary syndicalism, in 1913 fought the 'Great Dublin Lock-Out' with employers out to smash the Irish Transport and General Workers Union and, after a long interval in the USA, became a radical trade union leader in the new Irish state.[182] Connolly sought to combine his militant socialism with a commitment to Irish self-determination which led him to the General Post Office, the headquarters of the 1916 Easter Rising in Dublin and to instant canonisation as one of the martyred founders of the Irish Republic.

Connolly's memory is preserved by small knots of activists in the Glasgow area who give backing to Irish republicanism but his name is just a blur even to those Celtic football supporters who recite the song 'James Connolly, the Irish Rebel', at Parkhead while having no idea that he was Edinburgh-born. Even more forgotten is John Wheatley (1869–1930), unfairly so, since more than any other specific individual, he was responsible for pushing the descendants of Irish immigrants in a leftward direction and for making Glasgow by 1922 a strong Labour city. Since Wheatley's background and early life have been thoroughly explored elsewhere, a brief biographical outline will suffice here.[183] Irish-born, he was reared in the mining village of Baillieston, near Glasgow, and was one of a number of young intelligent members of the Irish community to come under the influence of local priest Peter Terken. At the age of twelve, he was already working underground in the pits but, after attending evening classes in Glasgow, he was able to find alternative employment in local shops and licensed premises, although he himself would be a lifelong abstainer from alcohol. Along with his younger brother Patrick, he set up his own small grocery business when in his mid-twenties and he was active in Irish Home Rule politics, first joining the Baillieston branch of the league, then led by the tailor, Denis Brogan, head of a talented family which would make its mark in different walks of life.[184] In 1898, two years after moving to Shettleston, in the east-end of Glasgow, he became president of the Patrick Sarsfield branch of the UIL; on stepping down in 1903, it had become the fourth largest in Scotland and he had won a proven reputation for fund-raising and organising ability.

Wheatley was one of the radical Home Rulers unhappy with the lack of democracy inside the movement and drawn increasingly to labour politics. Early in 1906, he derived great encouragement from the success of the Labour Party in capturing Blackfriars, its first Glasgow seat whose large Irish electorate generally heeded the advice of the Home Government branch to vote for the winner George Barnes. Later that year, Wheatley publicly declared himself to be a socialist and formed the Catholic Socialist Society along with his brother Patrick, his lifelong collaborator.

The aim of the CSS was to win catholic workers over to the Labour Party by demonstrating that belief in socialism and adherence to catholicism were not incompatible. Wheatley was to remain a committed catholic, one who had turned leftwards from the belief that 'capitalism and what it did to people was a destroyer of faith', and it was from the standpoint of radical Christianity and not Marxism that he was to justify his socialism.[185] Even so, he was soon embroiled in controversy with local clergy who automatically viewed socialism as anti-Christian and may also have regarded Wheatley's new departure as a challenge to their sway in the Glasgow catholic community.

The *Glasgow Observer* was the stage for the debate between John Wheatley and his religious detractors that went on intermittently right up until 1910. Charles Diamond knew Wheatley since he had worked for the paper up until 1906. A militant catholic, nevertheless he knew that British socialism was not generally anti-clerical and he even published articles by Wheatley. The latter was also fortunate in that Archbishop Maguire, Eyre's successor, was a socially conscious prelate who, in a number of speeches, had displayed enthusiasm for the cause of organised labour.[186] He never endorsed Wheatley in public, but he refused to accede to the wishes of those priests who wanted him to be condemned for contravening the papal encyclical *Rerum Novarum*.

Wheatley emerged unscathed from his jousts with hostile clerics where a lesser figure, in a more hostile climate, might well have been crushed by the weight of church hostility. Possibly the trickiest moment for him came in 1912 when Andrew O'Brien, the outspoken parish priest in his own parish of St Mark's Carntyne, denounced him from the pulpit. That evening, a threatening mob gathered outside his home and burned his effigy, but Wheatley outfaced the mob by standing at his front door, and calmly puffed his pipe with a cool courage that was long remembered.[187] He may have escaped the more general wrath of the clergy owing to the long sway of Home Rule politics which may already have predisposed some of them to welcome the advent of a more locally-rooted cause—even though the bulk would have preferred a less radical one to be the agent that weaned catholics away from Irish preoccupations. Wheatley's achievement has been expertly summed up in the following way:

> As far as can be seen, this is the only instance in Europe of a formal Catholic socialist movement emerging from within Catholic ranks and not being condemned but, in fact, tacitly accepted by the ecclesiastical authorities.[188]

Before 1914, the CSS held speaking tours and debates in order to convince catholic voters that socialism could be embraced from a clear-cut ethical standpoint. One of the most dramatic encounters took place one Sunday afternoon in November 1909 when 2,000 men and women assembled in Glasgow's Pavilion Theatre to hear Wheatley debate the question, 'Should Catholics Support Socialism' with the writer Hilaire Belloc, a favourite on the catholic lecture circuit.[189] Belloc was unexpectedly worsted in this encounter by the local speaker who was acquiring impressive dialectical skills which would be demonstrated even more effectively once he entered parliament. But it is hard to gauge the overall influence of the CSS, since no general election was held between 1910 and 1918, by which time it was being wound up. Its influence within the broad catholic proletariat, as opposed to the smaller group of skilled catholic workers whose ties with the immigrant neighbourhood were not as strong, is liable to be exaggerated. But Wheatley was elected to Lanarkshire county council in 1909 and to Glasgow town council in 1912; by now he was financially secure, since a small publishing business, Hoxton and Walsh, which he and his brother had launched in 1906 was prospering, and by 1921 would have an annual turnover of £21,000.[190]

Wheatley was on his way to becoming a socialist entrepreneur before 1914 as he was creating a strong local power-base as a member of the Independent Labour Party (ILP); it was affiliated to the British body and, to all intents and purposes, *was* the Labour Party in Scotland since it was only after 1918 that it began to set up branches of its own. He concentrated on health and housing issues and, by denouncing local abuses, he increased his credibility in the catholic community which felt these as much as any group. Within the ILP, he found a secure perch; since anti-clericalism was largely absent, he was not the only exponent of radical Christianity to shine in its ranks. The ILP supported Irish Home Rule and during the 1913 transport dispute in Ireland known as the 'Great Dublin Lock-Out', *Forward*, the Glasgow ILP paper was able to raise over £3,000 for the families of the victimised workers.[191] Liverpool scarcely matched this degree of solidarity even though Larkin, the workers leader hailed from the port.

On Merseyside, Labour politics failed to act as a bridge linking the divided working-class and it was only in 1911 that a functioning Labour group emerged on the council. In 1907 Labour had come near to capturing Liverpool Kirkdale at a by-election but, in the event, it would have to wait until the 1920s before capturing any one of Liverpool's twelve seats. The Tory steamroller was unstoppable and it was a bitter Ramsay McDonald who remarked to Archibald Salvidge at the 1907 count:

> It is astonishing how in Liverpool, whatever the issue appears to be at the start, you always manage to mobilise the full force of Orangeism. We will never do any good here until that power is broken.[192]

In Glasgow, radicals who wished to break down strictly communal allegiances and replace them with a more universal kind had more space in which to operate. Orangemen and Irish nationlists did not occupy centre-stage, instead it was the Liberal Party; attacks from the right in the 1880s showed that its hold on the working-class was not absolute, and the loyalties of one group, the Irish in Glasgow, were highly conditional.

Before the Labour Party entered into its political inheritance, personal as well as political events showed that the city was emerging out of the nineteenth century world. In 1912, the marriage in Glasgow of Patrick Dollan to Agnes Moir was a good case in point. Her father was an Orangeman while Dollan came from an archetypal immigrant background in the Lanarkshire coalfields. The early socialist movement had brought them together and for others it created a new environment where ancient prejudices and misunderstandings could be breached. Sometimes ethnic differences spilled over into its ranks but in Glasgow, at least, the left had a forum where a feeling of common humanity posed a strong challenge to sectarian identities. So, by 1914, with Ulster seemingly about to plunge into a sectarian civil war and Liverpool divided against itself, Glasgow and the west of Scotland generally presented a more hopeful picture, although once the guns on the western front fell silent, it would become speedily apparent that the city's sectarian ghosts had not been completely exoricsed.

Notes

1 Sheridan Gilley, 'The Roman Catholic Church and the nineteenth-century Irish diaspora', *Journal of Ecclesiastical History*, 35, 2, 1984, p. 193.

2 James Walsh, 'Archbishop Manning's visitation of the western district of Scotland in 1867', *Innes Review*, 18, 1, 1967, p. 15.

3 David McRoberts, 'The restoration of the Scottish Catholic hierarchy in 1878', *Modern Scottish Catholicism, 1878-1978*, David McRoberts (ed.), Burns, Glasgow, 1979, p. 11.

4 McRoberts, p. 11.

5 Archbishop Manning, 2 December 1867, quoted in Walsh, p. 15.

6 McCaffrey, 'Roman Catholicism in Scotland', p. 287.

7 McCaffrcy, p. 283.

8 Hutchinson, thesis, p. 478.

9 McCaffrey, p. 279.

10 McClelland, 'The Irish clergy', p. 12.

11 McCaffrey, p. 278.

12 McRoberts, p. 15.

13 Manning, quoted in Walsh, p. 14.

14 McRoberts, p. 20.

15 Manning, quoted in Walsh, p. 17.

16 H. J. Hanham, *Scottish Nationalism*, Harvard University Press, Cambridge, Mass., 1969, p. 20.

17 McCaffrey, p. 283.

18 Lord Bute to Lord Rosebery, 3 November 1881. Rosebery Papers, National Library of Scotland, quoted in Hanham, p. 85.

19 McClelland, 'A hierarchy for Scotland', p. 490.

20 McClelland, p. 490.

21 James Darragh, 'The hierarchy of Scotland', *CDS*, 1982, Burns, Glasgow, 1982, p. 39.

22 Cooney, *Scotland and the Papacy*, pp. 47, 50.

23 I am grateful to Dr John Durkan for this view.

24 Cooney, p. 74.

25 Cooney, p. 47; David McRoberts, 'The archdiocese of Glasgow', *Glasgow Observer and Scottish Catholic Herald, Scottish Survey*.

26 *Scottish Catholic Observer*, 5 March 1965.

27 *The Witness*, 25 January 1847, quoted in Handley, *The Irish and Modern Scotland*, p. 25.

28 Drummond and Bulloch, *The Church in Victorian Scotland*, p. 74.
29 Handley, p. 223.
30 Sir Patrick Dollan, 'Memories of fifty years', *Mercat Cross*, August 1953, p. 40.
31 Catholic Young Men's Society, *Centenary Celebrations*, Glasgow, 1949, quoted in Walker, *Juteopolis*, pp. 133-4.
32 Walker, *Juteopolis*, p. 125.
33 Walker, *Juteopolis*, p. 125.
34 Hutchinson, thesis, p. 481.
35 Cooney, *Scotland and the Papacy*, p. 61.
36 O'Tuathaigh, 'The Irish in nineteenth century Britain', p. 166.
37 McLeod, *Religion and the Working Class*, p. 39.
38 Lobban, 'The Irish community in Greenock', p. 279.
39 *GO*, 23 October 1915.
40 *GO*, 30 October 1915.
41 *GO*, 30 October 1915.
42 *GO*, 18 December 1915.
43 *GO*, 11 December 1915.
44 Quoted in James Hunter, 'The Gaelic connection: the Highlands, Ireland and nationalism, 1873-1922', *Scottish Historical Review*, 54, 1975, p. 187.
45 Mackenzie, *Catholicism and Scotland*, p. 185.
46 Interview with Dr Patrick Connolly, 29 April 1984.
47 This book is examined by Walker, *Juteopolis*, p. 140.
48 Walker, *Juteopolis*, p. 140.
49 Canning, *Irish-born Secular Priests*, pp. 170-1.
50 O'Tuathaigh, 'The Irish in nineteenth century Britain', p. 166.
51 Sheridan Gilley, 'Catholics and socialists in Glasgow, 1906-12', in *Hosts, Immigrants and Minorities in British Society*, (ed.), C. Lunn, Dawson, Folkestone, 1980, p. 165.
52 Handley, *The Irish in Modern Scotland*, p. 283.
53 John Lynch, 'Catholic lay societies, 1878-1956', *Glasgow Observer and Scottish Catholic Herald, Scottish Survey*, p. xxi.
54 Walker, 'Irish immigrants in Scotland', pp. 658-9.
55 Interview with John McLaughlin, 21 August 1984.
56 Walker, 'Irish immigrants in Scotland', p. 658.
57 Interview with John McLaughlin.
58 Walker, 'Irish immigrants in Scotland', p. 659.
59 Canning, *Irish-born Secular Priests*, p. 135.
60 Bill Murray, *The Old Firm, Sectarianism, Sport, and Society in Scotland*, John Donald, Edinburgh, 1984, p. 19.
61 Murray, pp. 17-8.
62 Murray, p. 60.
63 Murray, p. 68.
64 Canning, *Irish-born Secular Priests*, p. 135.
65 C. G. Brown, *Religion and the Development of an Urban Society: Glasgow, 1780-1914*, Ph.D. thesis, University of Glasgow, 1981, p. 166.
66 Brown, thesis, p. 169.
67 Brown, thesis, p. 166.
68 Brown, thesis, pp. 323-4.
69 Brown, thesis, p. 324.
70 Walker, *Juteopolis*, p. 120.
71 Walker, *Juteopolis*, p. 120.
72 John Denvir, *The Irish in Britain, from the Earliest Times to the Fall and Death of Parnell*, Kegan Paul, London 1892, p. 451.
73 Canning, *Irish-born Secular Priests*, p. 107.
74 Norman Stone, *Europe Transformed, 1878-1919*, Fontana, Glasgow, 1983, p. 92.
75 Checkland, *Industry and Ethos*, pp. 112-3.
76 Ian Wood, 'Irish immigrants and Scottish radicalism, 1880-1906', *Essays in Scottish Labour History*, (ed.), Ian McDougall, John Donald, Edinburgh, 1979, p. 74.
77 Handley, *The Irish in Modern Scotland*, p. 74.
78 Handley, p. 236.
79 McRoberts, 'The archdiocese of Glasgow'.
80 Walker, *Juteopolis*, p. 127.
81 Wood, 'Irish immigrants and Scottish radicalism', p. 74.
82 Wood, p. 74.
83 Handley, *The Irish in Modern Scotland*, p. 237.
84 James Kellas, *Modern Scotland, the Nation since 1870*, Pall Mall, London, 1968, p. 57.
85 Bernard J. O'Connor, *The Irish*

Nationalist Party in Liverpool, 1873-1922, MA thesis, University of Liverpool, 1971, p. 88.

86 Brogan, 'Catholics in changing social conditions', p. iv.

87 William Martin Haddow, *My Seventy Years*, Robert Gibson, Glasgow, 1943, p. 82.

88 Haddow, p. 82.

89 See Brother Kenneth, 'The Education (Scotland) Act, 1918, in the making', *Innes Review*, 19, 2, 1968, pp. 95-6.

90 Hugh G. McEwan, *Bishop Grey Graham, 1874-1959, an Essay on his Life and Times*, Burns, Glasgow, 1973, p. 93.

91 Drummond and Bulloch, *The Church in Victorian Scotland*, pp. 100-1.

92 Gilley, 'The Roman Catholic Church', pp. 204-5.

93 Quoted in Hutchinson, thesis, pp. 483-4.

94 Denvir, *The Irish in Britain*, p. 437.

95 Murray, *The Old Firm*, p. 68.

96 McRoberts, 'The archdiocese of Glasgow'.

97 *GO*, 19 March 1904.

98 *Centenary Brochure of John Barry & Sons Ltd*, Mackenzie & Storrie, Leith, 1951; interview with T. C. Barry, Dirleton, East Lothian, 5 July 1984.

99 Sir Patrick Dollan, 'The Pat Dollan story', *Sunday Mail*, 15 September 1957.

100 Sir Patrick Dollan, 'Memories of fifty years', *Mercat Cross*, October 1953, p. 110.

101 Bernard O'Connor, 'Irish nationalism in Liverpool, 1873-1923', *Eire-Ireland*, 10, 1, 1975, p. 26.

102 E. P. M. Wollaston, *The Irish Nationalist Movement in Great Britain, 1886-1908*, M.A. thesis, King's College, London, 1958, p. 27.

103 Handley, *The Irish in modern Scotland*, p. 280.

104 Hutchinson, thesis, p. 488.

105 Wollaston, thesis, pp. 21-2; T. W. Moody, 'Michael Davitt and the British labour movement, 1882-1906', *Transactions of the Royal Historical Society*, 5th series, 3, 1953, pp. 61-7.

106 Handley, *The Irish in Modern Scotland*, p. 270.

107 Hutchinson, thesis, p. 488.

108 Wollaston, thesis, p. 20.

109 Canning, *Irish-born Secular Priests*, p. 293.

110 Hutchinson, thesis, p. 482.

111 Canning, p. 225.

112 Handley, p. 279.

113 John Hickey, *Urban Catholics*, Geoffrey Chapman, London, 1967, p. 149.

114 Quoted in Georgina Putnam McEntee, *The Social Catholic Movement in Great Britain*, Macmillan, London, 1927, p. 59.

115 Hugh Trevor-Roper, 'From Guy Fawkes to the Pope', *Daily Telegraph*, 28 April 1982; O'Tuathaigh, 'The Irish in nineteenth-century Britain', p. 169.

116 Wollaston, thesis, p. 4.

117 *Manchester Guardian*, 19 January 1910, quoted in E. D. Steele, 'The Irish presence in the north of England, 1850-1914', *Northern History*, 12, 1976, pp. 239-40.

118 Handley, p. 284.

119 Wollaston, thesis, p. 22; Handley, p. 284.

120 Handley, p. 284.

121 Handley, p. 288.

122 O'Connor, thesis, p. 250.

123 D. W. Crowley, 'The Crofters' Party, 1885-1892', *Scottish Historical Review*, 35, 1956, p. 112.

124 Hunter, 'The Gaelic connection', pp. 184-5.

125 Hunter, pp. 187-8.

126 Tom Gallagher, 'A tale of two cities: communal strife in Glasgow and Liverpool before 1914', in *The Irish in the Victorian City*, (ed.), Sheridan Gilley Croom Helm, London 1985.

127 Moody, 'Michael Davitt and the British labour movement', p. 62.

128 Moody, p. 68.

129 Wood, 'Irish immigrants and Scottish radicalism', pp. 71-2.

130 Wood, p. 73.

131 A. G. Hepburn, 'Political and industrial relationships', *Glasgow Observer and Scottish Catholic Herald, Scottish Survey, 1878-1955*, p. xv.

132 Wood, p. 81.

133 Wollaston, thesis, p. 3.

134 Howell, *British Workers and the*

Independent Labour Party, p. 141.

135 J. B. Russell, *Vital Statistics of the City of Glasgow*, (3 parts, Glasgow, 1886), quoted by John McCaffrey, 'The Irish vote in Glasgow in the later nineteenh century, a preliminary survey', *Innes Review*, 21, 1, 1970, pp. 32–3.

136 T. C. Smout, *A Century of the Scottish People, 1830–1950*, Collins, London, 1986, p. 246.

137 Smout, *A Century of the Scottish People*, p. 247.

138 Handley, *The Irish in Modern Scotland*, p. 141.

139 Denvir, *The Irish in Britain*, p. 446.

140 Denvir, p. 447.

141 Wollaston, thesis, p. 23.

142 Wollaston, thesis, p. 24; Murray, *The Old Firm*, pp. 68, 73.

143 Taplin, 'Irish leaders', pp. 37–8; Moody, 'Michael Davitt', p. 67.

144 Handley, *The Irish in Modern Scotland*, p. 291.

145 Handley, p. 291.

146 Handley, p. 287.

147 The impact of the 1886 split in Glasgow is exhausticely dealt with in Kellas, thesis, and Hutchinson, thesis.

148 See Howell, *British Workers and the Independent Labour Party*, p. 143 and Kellas, thesis, pp. 42–3.

149 Howell, p. 43.

150 Quoted in D. C. Savage, *The General Election of 1886 in Great Britain and Ireland*, Ph.D. thesis, King's College, London, 1958, p. 42.

151 Savage, thesis, pp. 483–4.

152 Quoted in P. J. Waller, *Democracy and Sectarianism, a Political and Social History of Liverpool, 1868–1939*, Liverpool University Press, Liverpool, 1981, p. 249.

153 O'Connor, thesis, p. 111.

154 Joan Smith, 'Labour tradition in Glasgow and Liverpool', *History Workshop*, 17, spring 1984, p. 45.

155 Bonar Law had strong Ulster family connections as well as personal ties with Canada. These probably intensified his hardline over Home Rule. If these linkages had not intruded into his Glasgow background, it is possible that this low-key and colourless politician would not have displayed such extremism before World War I. Perhaps a useful comparison might be made with Campbell-Bannerman, the Glasgow businessman who supported Home Rule and was Liberal Prime Minister from 1906 to 1908.

156 G. I. T. Machin, 'The last Victorian anti-ritualist campaign, 1895–1906', *Victorian Studies*, 25, 3, 1982, p. 277.

157 An historian who sees Liverpool Toryism as a precursor of fascism is Norman Stone. See *Europe Transformed*, p. 127.

158 Waller, *Democracy and Sectarianism*, pp. 179, 313. But Salvidge pledged that 'no Roman Catholic priest had ever crossed the threshold of his door'.

159 John Campbell, *F. E. Smith, Lord Birkenhead*, Jonathan Cape, London, 1984, p. 125.

160 Waller, *Democracy and Sectarianism*, p. 240.

161 Waller, p. 209.

162 Quoted by Waller, p. 313.

163 R. S. W. Davies, 'The Liverpool Labour Party and the Liverpool working class, 1900–39', *North West Labour History Society*, 6, 1979–80, p. 10.

164 Paton, *Proletarian Pilgrimage*, p. 171; Smith, 'Labour tradition', p. 54.

165 D. Urwin, 'The development of the Conservative Party organization in Scotland until 1912', *Scottish Historical Review*, 44, 2, 1965, p. 106.

166 Hugh G. McEwan, *Bishop Grey Graham, 1874–1959, an Essay on his Life and Times*, Burns, Glasgow, 1973, pp. 95–6, 148.

167 McEwan, p. 97.

168 Interview with Bishop Joseph Devine, Glasgow, 26 August 1981.

169 *GO*, 17 January 1891.

170 Wood, 'Irish immigrants and Scottish radicalism', p. 88.

171 Howell, *British Workers*, p. 141; Moody, p. 64.

172 James G. Kellas, 'The Mid-Lanark by-election (1888) and the Scottish Labour Party (1888–1894)', *Parliamentary Affairs*, 18, 1964–65, pp. 321–4.

173 Howell, *British Workers*, p. 146.

174 Moody, 'Michael Davitt', pp. 71,

73, 74; Kellas, 'Mid-Lanark by-election', pp. 324-5.

175 See Keith Harding, *The Irish Issue in the British Labour Movement*, Ph.D. thesis, University of Sussex, 1984, p. 19.

176 *Forward*, 20 April 1912, quoted in Harding, thesis, p. 24.

177 *The Bailie*, 4 January 1905.

178 James Sexton, *Sir James Sexton, Agitator*, Faber, London, 1936, p. 287.

179 Kellas, thesis, p. 297.

180 Tom Gallagher, 'Scottish Catholics and the British left, 1918-39', *Innes Review*, 34, 1, 1983, p. 17.

181 Handley, p. 276.

182 See Emmet Larkin, *James Larkin, Irish Labour Leader*, Routledge, London, 1965. James Connolly's early life in Scotland is dealt with to varying degrees in the following works: Ruth Dudley Edwards, *James Connolly*, Gill & Macmillan, Dublin, 1982; Owen Dudley Edwards, *James Connolly, the Mind of an Activist*, Gill & Macmillan, Dublin, 1971; and Desmond Greaves, *The Life and Times of James Connolly*, Lawrence & Wishart, London, 1961.

183 Among other works there is Sheridan Gilley, 'Catholics and socialists in Glasgow, 1906-12', in *Hosts, Immigrants, and Minorities in British Society*, (ed.), C. Lunn,

Dawson, Folkestone, 1980, pp. 160-200; Ian Wood, 'John Wheatley, the Irish, and the labour movement in Scotland', *Innes Review*, 21, 1980, pp. 71-86; Gerry Charles Gunnin, *John Wheatley, Catholic Socialism and Irish Labour in the West of Scotland*, Ph.D. thesis, University of Chicago, 1973; Samuel Cooper, *John Wheatley, a Study in Labour History*, Ph.D. thesis, University of Glasgow, 1973; Bob Purdie, *Outside the Chapel Door: the Glasgow Catholic Socialist Society*, History diploma, Ruskin College, Oxford, 1975.

184 Dollan, *Mercat Cross*, July 1953, p. 8.

185 Wood, 'John Wheatley', p. 73.

186 Gilley, 'Catholics and socialists', pp. 164-5, 184-5.

187 Ian Wood, 'John Wheatley', *Scottish Labour Leaders, 1918-39, a biographical Dictionary*, (ed.), William Knox, Mainstream, Edinburgh, 1984, p. 277.

188 McCaffrey, 'Roman Catholicism in Scotland', p. 293.

189 Gunnin, thesis, p. 1.

190 Wood, *Scottish Labour Leaders*, p. 275.

191 Smith, 'Labour tradition', p. 43.

192 Stanley Salvidge, *Salvidge of Liverpool*, Hodder & Stoughton, London, 1934, p. 90.

Chapter 3 Community in transition: Ireland, the rise of labour and the church resurgent

It is probably fair to say that the First World War was the first major event in the history of its chosen homeland that the immigrant community in Scotland heavily participated in. Its location in the unskilled working-class of a country which had always made a disproportionate contribution of men to the British army ensured a favourable response to the post-1914 recruiting drive from the Irish in Scotland. Their religious leaders, such as the archbishops of Glasgow and Edinburgh, blessed and approved the war against Germany in unequivocal terms.[1] So did Charles Diamond, fiery editor of the *Glasgow Observer*, at least in the earlier stages. The influence he wielded in a community whose manpower was valued by the British authorities, saved him from prosecution after he made a pointed reference to the royal family's German ancestry. The Home Office wanted him prosecuted, but the cabinet felt that the maintenance of 'Roman Catholic co-operation was more important'.[2]

The death-columns on the back page of the *Observer* were well filled with the names of first and second generation immigrant Irish volunteers killed on the western front and elsewhere.[3] By the end of the war, six soldiers hailing from the catholic community in Glasgow had been decorated with the Victoria Cross.[4] Shared war comradeship held out the promise that religious barriers would be far less relevant for those whose narrow horizons had been expanded by participation in gruesome trench warfare. But in the midst of war, the Irish crisis was revived when news trickled across from Ireland of a separatist uprising that had broken out in Dublin on Easter Monday 1916. The Easter Rising was condemned by nationalist opinion in Ireland and in immigrant circles in Britain. It was widely viewed as an insane enterprise that had placed in jeopardy the peaceful realisation of Irish Home Rule after the war. Charles Diamond was particularly damning in his condemnation:

> The Irish people . . . will not manifest the slightest sympathy or approval with the madly criminal action of the pro-German plotters who resorted to insurrection in Dublin. Since the acceptance of the Irish people at large of the Home Rule Act, the vast mass of Irishmen everywhere are, and will hold themselves, rigidly loyal to the Empire with which they have concluded an act of partnership . . . With the action of the Dublin revolters, then, we can have no sort of complicity or even tolerance. Their action . . . was needless, foolish, wicked, and unjustifiable. Irish nationalists will . . . condemn it as unpatriotic folly: rash, blind, headlong, stupid and wrong.[5]

Even after the initial shock had subsided, he almost seemed to justify the court-martial sentences which were shortly to be passed upon the rising's leaders: 'their doom is just. They got, or will get, no more than they gave. They shed blood and took life recklessly.'[6]

But the mood in Ireland and its satellite communities across the world changed rapidly when the British took out and shot the 1916 leaders. Rebels and fanatics were transformed into heroes and martyrs, a metamorphosis that was fully reflected in the columns of the *Glasgow Observer* and its numerous local editions. Charles Diamond pilloried the British war cabinet before bestowing the status of martyr on a few isolated separatists, and he went on to lend his backing to Sinn Fein, the separatist party which, by the general election of 1918 had displaced the Home Rule Party as the main spokesman for nationalist Ireland.

The rapid change of mood and political behaviour in Ireland was reinforced by the wartime emergency. War has proved to be a catalyst for political change in many societies and its impact may have been even greater among the immigrant Irish in places like Scotland where— unlike Ireland—conscription was in force by 1916 and the economy was almost wholly geared to wartime production. Even before the catalyst of the Dublin rebellion, the political domination of the United Irish League was no longer being taken for granted. In 1915, with its political machine lying dormant, Diamond's papers declared that the time was at hand for the UIL to disband and make way for the Labour Party.[7] Following the Easter Rising, the Ancient Order of Hibernians emerged as a political rival to the UIL in the Irish nationalist camp. Local immigrant leaders, some with a record of ignoring UIL directives, gathered together in this friendly society which for many proved to be a stepping stone into the Labour Party. Thus, in 1918, the Irish political machine was in some disarray when a snap general election, the first in eight years was called by Lloyd George. The endorsement of T. P. O'Connor, the Liverpool MP and leader of the UIL (hitherto a guarantee of victory for Liberal MPs standing in constituencies with a large Irish presence), proved worthless in 1918, since, outside his own city the organisation existed increasingly only on paper. But the beneficiary was not the Labour Party but the ruling coalition Unionists (the alliance of Tories and Lloyd George Liberals) who won a landslide victory in the atmosphere of patriotic fervour in which the election was held.

As might be expected, the immigrant Irish were more immune than most from appeals to jingoism, but their voting strength was dissipated by a number of factors: firstly, the sorry state of the movement which had harvested the Irish vote in previous decades meant that essential tasks like keeping the electoral registers up to date had been neglected; this was doubly unfortunate since, with women able to vote for the first time in 1918, the potential immigrant electorate had greatly increased. Without being taken in hand by the UIL machine, it is quite possible that many of those immigrants on the electoral register abstained in the absence of any strong directives being issued in their areas; it is also worth remembering that many of those of military age were abroad in the forces and thus had no vote to cast.[8]

The writer of 'Catholic Socialist Society' notes in *Forward* commented in September 1918 that 'there are many cross-currents in the local Irish movement at the moment'.[9] At least one part of the Irish local machine did mobilise on behalf of the Labour Party and, in the seat of Glasgow Shettleston, John Wheatley failed to be elected by a bare seventy-four votes. As the political crisis in Ireland spilled over into outright warfare between the British forces and Sinn Fein's military arm, the Irish Republican Army, ties between the left and the immigrant population were strengthened. Wheatley found it easier to preach socialism to them now that it was widely known that the Edinburgh-born James Connolly, one of the leaders of the 1916 rebellion, had been a lifelong socialist.[10] But Connolly's commitment to a completely separate Irish republican state was not shared by Wheatley and there were a number of stormy debates about Ireland at the weekly forums of the Catholic Socialist Society both before and after the 1916 rising.

Nevertheless, the Labour Party in Glasgow was vocal in its criticism of British policy in Ireland, even though it had to be careful not to alienate protestant skilled workers who identified with their strongly unionist counterparts in Belfast. Tom Johnston, the editor of *Forward*, persistently lobbied Arthur Henderson, the Labour Party leader who was in the war cabinet, for the release of Irish socialists imprisoned in 1916.[11] In 1919, Wheatley spoke at the May Day demonstration in Glasgow, along with Countess Markiewicz of Sinn Fein, an occasion in which the Irish tricolour was carried in the crowd of 100,000 and the Irish national anthem, 'The Soldier's Song' was sung along with The Red Flag.[12] At the Scottish conference of the Independent Labour Party (the ILP: which *was* the Labour Party in Scotland till the early 1930s) in 1920, the Irish Republic was recognised, but the vote was surprisingly narrow (268 to 207), indicating that many had deep reservations about complete Irish separation. Lukewarm support for the gathering Irish struggle from sections of the ILP may have been a contributory cause of the emergence of an 'Irish Labour Party' at the end of 1918, centred on the railway suburb of Springburn in Glasgow. Its place of birth might not have been entirely fortuitous. Back in 1909, a strongly worded attack on the role of the Spanish catholic church in the execution of the free-thinker, Francisco Ferrer, had split the Springburn branch of the ILP and led to the withdrawal of its catholic immigrant members.[13] This shortlived party collaborated with the ILP in holding a 'Hands off Ireland' conference followed by a successful demonstration in the autumn of 1919, but the existence of rival Labour Parties showed how the Irish question caused strains on the Glasgow left.[14] Earlier, break-away parties in Clydeside and Tyneside had applied to join the Irish Labour Party in Dublin only to be rebuffed and told to work through the British Labour movement.[15] This was also the message of the *Glasgow Observer* which accused those behind the 'Irish Labour Party' of 'wire-pulling and self-seeking':

> The Irish and Catholic people of Great Britain are citizens of England, Scotland, and Wales . . . We say to Irish workers that the best way to get their share of public positions is to join the Labour Party. They will be chosen in accordance with their capacity, ability, and character.
>
> Of course prejudice may exist here and there.
>
> But the way to break that down is not to accentuate nationalist or religious difference . . . Join the Labour Party and vote Labour every time.[16]

Diamond himself had been a Labour candidate at Peckham in 1918. Five of the ten roman catholics standing for Labour at that election actually fought west of Scotland seats. They included Owen Coyle in Coatbridge, later to be given a long term of imprisonment for his Sinn Fein activities, and D. J. Mitchel Quin (1866–1940), managing editor of the *Observer* who stood against Bonar-Law, the Tory leader, in Glasgow Central. The paper even backed the candidacy in Glasgow Gorbals of the Scottish marxist revolutionary, John Maclean (1879–1923), not long after he had been appointed Soviet consul in Glasgow by Lenin.[17] Despite the *Observer*'s backing for the imprisoned Maclean, the sitting member George Barnes was able to retain the seat even though he had been disowned by the Labour Party for remaining in the war cabinet. The voting behaviour of the seat with the strongest immigrant presence in Scotland showed the extent to which the community was in a state of flux.

John Maclean went on to endorse the Irish struggle against British rule at public meetings which he even dared to hold in strong Orange areas like Port Glasgow and Motherwell.[18] Both he and Connolly had been born to Gaelic-speaking parents and they made separate attempts to reconcile socialism with the nationalism of their respective countries.[19] Maclean was sufficiently influenced by the Irish struggle and the impact it had on the Irish in Scotland to press the case for a Scottish Communist Party rather than take his place in a British revolutionary movement;[20] in August 1920, he wrote a pamphlet, *Ireland's Tragedy, Scotland's Disgrace*, of which 20,000 were sold in a few months.

Maclean was ultimately a disappointed man because the Irish movement failed to give rise to a movement for a Scottish Marxist Republic and he gained few recruits from the Irish community. Nevertheless, many of the Irish on Clydeside found themselves caught up in the Irish war of independence and, after a slow start, made a substantial contribution to the achievement of self-government in 1922. Things got moving in 1919 when Sean O'Sheehan was sent from Dublin to build up a solidarity movement in Scotland. Within a year, the number of Sinn Fein clubs rose from twenty to eighty, 'income increased forty times and membership eightyfold'.[21] Michael Collins, leader of the IRA, appointed a Glasgow organiser Joe Vise who set about creating a military wing in Scotland. Having found the Irish Volunteers (a Sinn Fein militia) to be 'in a lamentable state' with 'A' company composed 'of a good many undesirables' he got to work and by September 1919 a battalion of the IRA, comprising eight companies, existed in the city.[22] By September 1920, the Procurator Fiscal estimated that the size of the IRA in the Glasgow area had risen to 3,000 men: 'they have no rifles but the police have now obtained information . . . that they are in possession of numerous revolvers which have been picked up here and elsewhere'.[23] The chief constable of Paisley reported how the mood of the Irish in his locality had greatly changed in recent years: 'at the outbreak of war, the young men of the Catholic religion in Paisley enlisted in greater proportion than the rest of Paisley's inhabitants; they were apparently loyal but their attitude has changed since the Dublin rebellion'.[24]

Some precautions had to be taken against the sabotage of power stations and oil pipelines. In London, Sir Basil Thomson, head of the Special Branch, kept a close watch on the situation in Clydeside because it was also a source of major industrial unrest. He looked for collusion between local Sinn Feiners and militant trade unionists so as to confirm his belief that a revolutionary conspiracy was being put together on Clydeside in 1920, but his evidence was flimsy.[25] Most Sinn Feiners were to be found in unskilled occupations that were not particularly militant. No evidence has emerged that Michael Collins in Dublin sought to foment industrial unrest in Glasgow, so as to overextend the British. The Republican leadership had allotted a different and more crucial role to the Irish in Scotland: they were to provide money and military supplies to keep the war effort going back home and safe houses for IRA men on the run from British or Irish gaols.

In the words of Andrew Allan, a Glasgow IRA man interviewed in 1969, 'our job was to raise money and obtain guns which were then smuggled to Ireland'.[26] By 1921, almost every Scottish town with a sizeable Irish presence had its own IRA company that was required to send a regular quota of revolvers, ammunition, and rifles to head-quarters in Glasgow; from quarries, coal pits, and shale mines powder and gelignite was obtained; eight successful raids were carried out on Clyde shipyards engaged in munition works; a gunboat being over-hauled at Finnieston dockyard was raided, the skeleton crew surprised, and small arms taken.[27] Many ex-servicemen belonged to the IRA while women supporters, such as Julia Foy, the owner of a second-hand-clothes shop in Glasgow acted as couriers or provided safe houses; men were trained for service in Ireland and, on two occasions, high-ranking IRA officers crossed to Scotland to 'review the troops' on remote moorlands.[28]

Local police forces mounted a close watch on Sinn Fein, but their most sensitive operations eluded their gaze and they were unable to penetrate the organisation, a great obstacle being the fact that so few policemen came from the immigrant communities. In December 1920, the Chief Constable of Lanarkshire recommended that Sinn Fein be suppressed, but the Scottish Office commented that 'there seems nothing here on which we can take action'.[29] Months previously, the Procurator Fiscal's Office had commented realistically that 'so far there has been no outbreak of disorders on the part of Sinn Feiners and, so far as I can judge, this state of matters is likely to continue as long as they are not interfered with'.[30]

Given its vital function, the last thing the Irish solidarity move-ment in Scotland wished to do was draw attention to itself. There was relatively little *political* agitation on the Irish question in Scotland compared with other parts of Britain, beyond occasional speaking tours by Sinn Feiners from Ireland. Scotland remained outside the main solidarity organisation, the Irish Self-determination League founded in Manchester on 30 March 1919. It carried out propaganda among the English public by highlighting the misdeeds of the Black and Tans and doing educational work among the Irish in English cities where, by the beginning of 1922, it had 294 branches and over 20,000 members, but a search of the papers of its founder Art O'Brien has found no example of activity in Scotland.[31] The strategists behind the Republican campaign in Ireland may have concluded that propaganda was wasted in Scotland which was far from the seat of power and where the local population, with their instinctive concern for the catholics of the north of Ireland, did not have open minds on the Irish question like a large part of the English public; or it may have been due to personality clashes, long a bane of solidarity movements in Britain.

Only in the final stages of the Irish War of Independence were the repeated injunctions from Dublin for caution in the securing and transport of arms, disregarded. On 4 May 1921, just weeks before a cease-fire was declared in Ireland, a van carrying a Sinn Fein prisoner through Glasgow was ambushed in a rescue bid which left a detective lying dead.[32] Homes of well-known Sinn Fein sympathisers were raided and some thirty-four people were arrested and charged. They included Patrick McRory, a twenty-five-year-old priest from Co. Tyrone in Ulster who was attached to St Mary's parish in Calton. He was held in custody for eleven weeks before charges of conspiracy were dropped against him and most of the others. Thousands of his parishioners packed Abercromby Street in tense vigil on the night of his arrest and in joyful welcome when he was once more restored to them.[33] Police records in the Scottish Office show that a number of priests were under surveillance at this time.[34] Recently it has been claimed that when on the run from Lincoln gaol, in 1919, de Valera sheltered in the Presbytery of St John's church in the Gorbals,[35] but no priests were prominent in Sinn Fein in Scotland.

By the end of 1919, Charles Diamond's intemperate pen had finally landed him in severe difficulties after his papers, *The Catholic Herald* and the *Glasgow Observer*, and their thirty-four local editions carried an article by him on 27 December entitled 'Killing No Murder'. It was prompted by a recent attempt on the life of Field Marshal Lord French, Viceroy of Ireland. French, he wrote, represented 'foreign rule, physical force, tyranny, and brutality' and the Irish had the moral right to sweep him and their other oppressors into the sea.[36] On 9 January 1920, Diamond was arrested and, at his trial in March, the Attorney General argued that passages in the article were 'a calculated and deliberate incitement . . . to make a further, and this time successful, attempt upon the Viceroy'.[37] At his trial he was found guilty of incitement to violence and imprisoned for six months. Later, in June 1920, the entire Scottish catholic hierarchy petitioned the Home Secretary for Diamond's release (one among their number, the Bishop of Galloway was his brother-in-law). Leaving aside the humanitarian motive (he was over sixty), they may have done so because, for all his invective, he was a convinced assimilationist, unaware of further need for Irish political organisation in Britain, now that the island was on the last lap towards some degree of freedom.

Diamond's relations with Scottish churchmen were generally good (Henry Grey Graham, bishop-auxiliary of St Andrews and

Edinburgh once described this learned tyro as the best theologian among the laity in Scotland),[38] but those with Cardinal Francis Bourne, head of the English hierarchy turned acrid over Ireland. Bourne's reluctance to condemn British methods in Ireland, which a number of leading protestant churchmen had already done, drew bitter comments from the pages of his newspapers as did the support of English catholic landowners in politics for the British presence in Ireland. This had been displayed before the war when the Duke of Norfolk, the premier catholic peer, presented a golden sword to Sir Edward Carson at a monster rally against home rule in Blenheim Palace and again in 1921 when Lord Edmund Talbot agreed to become the last viceroy of Ireland.[39] The same divisions did not affect Scotland since roman catholic aristocrats were not as numerous and it would be some decades before they assumed roles in public life.

Like a *deus ex machina*, a religious champion ready to speak up for British and Irish catholics opposed to British policy in Ireland suddenly emerged in 1920 with the arrival in Britain, under extraordinary circumstances, of Archbishop Daniel Mannix (1864–1963) of Melbourne. Mannix was one of the few prelates anywhere to publicly endorse the actions as well as the cause of his fellow countrymen who had taken up arms against British rule. He had first gained the reputation of being a turbulent priest in Australia where he successfully mobilised opposition against the proposed introduction of conscription which was defeated in two stormy referendums. Hughes, the Australian prime minister branded Mannix a public enemy and persuaded fellow Welshman Lloyd George to ban him from his native Ireland. Accordingly, two British warships intercepted his ship in August 1920 and deposited him at Penzance rather than allow him to land in Ireland where it was feared that his eloquence would raise the populace to new levels of defiance.

In Britain, Mannix soon clashed with Cardinal Bourne, contrasting his silence with that of his predecessor Cardinal Manning, who is claimed to have said that 'if I were an Irishman, I should never have lived to be 80 years of age, for I should have been shot or hanged as a rebel'.[40] Mannix was barred from visiting every British city outside London with a sizeable Irish community, but in February 1921, he carried out a highly effective three-week tour of Scotland at the suggestion of Sean O'Sheehan, Sinn Fein's man there.[41] He stayed at Nazareth House, Edinburgh, the guest of Bishop Grey Graham and received many delegations from the Irish community. Unable to enter Glasgow, he spoke at a vast open-air rally in Whiflet, ten miles away, attended by over 50,000 people and, according to one of his biographers, Mannix remarked to the throng that 'the British government prevented me from going to Glasgow; obviously it was unable to prevent Glasgow from coming to me'.[42] Other huge meetings were held at Dalmuir, Kilmarnock, Dumbarton, and Cowdenbeath, the final one taking place in Winston Churchill's constituency of Dundee. Mannix reviewed a procession ten miles in length and his electrifying presence may well have contributed to Churchill's defeat in 1922, the Irish in the city having previously been his most loyal supporters.[43]

Afterwards, the Irish leader de Valera emphasised just how important a role nationally minded immigrants in Scotland had played in Ireland's bid for freedom, 'The financial contribution to the Irish struggle from among the Scottish communities was in excess of funds from any other country, including Ireland.'[44] But the events of the Anglo-Irish war remain a forgotten chapter in the story of the Irish in Scotland largely due to what happened after the 1921 ceasefire with Britain. A peace treaty was agreed which fell short of an outright Irish Republic but gave Ireland far more autonomy than it would have enjoyed under home rule. Even though the treaty contained the signature of Michael Collins, the lengendary head of the Republican movement's military wing, the IRA, it produced dissension in Dublin and soon cries of sell-out were heard. In January 1922, William Gallacher, a Paisley-born lapsed catholic now on the executive of the British Communist Party was sent to Dublin where his advice to Cathal Brugha that the compromisers needed to be taken out and shot was tactfully listened to but ignored.[45] However, the mood in Ireland grew more embittered as Sinn Fein split into Republicans and Free Staters (i.e. those who endorsed the treaty from which emerged the Irish Free State), and full-scale civil war broke out in June 1922.

Among the Irish in Scotland, as indeed in the rest of Britain, news that the movement had split over the new state's constitutional relationship with Britain was greeted with sadness and dismay. In and around Glasgow, there was far more anxiety about the plight of Ulster roman catholics in the newly formed state of Northern Ireland, which remained linked to Britain while enjoying internal self-government. Controlled by the local Unionist Party, and comprising six of the nine counties of the province of Ulster (so that protestants were left in a permanent two-thirds majority), the *partition* of Ireland (even though deemed a temporary expedient until the cooling of passions allowed nationalists and unionists on the island to be reconciled) was a far more emotive issue on Clydeside. Ulster was close by, the bulk of the Irish hailed from there, and many still had deep family links through which they learned about the rough treatment meted out to roman catholics who attempted to challenge the new status quo.

Nevertheless, it was not long before the divisions in Ireland were duplicated inside the solidarity movement in Britain. A report from the chief constable of Dundee to Scotland Yard about 'Sinn Feiners,

Communists etc.' and dated 5 May 1922 makes this clear:

> I have to inform you that the Sinn Fein Clubs in Dundee are divided on the
> question of Collins or de Valera. At a meeting of the Sinn Feiners held in the
> Masonic Hall recently for the purpose of deciding whether an invitation
> should be sent to Collins asking him to address meetings in Dundee, it was
> quite apparent that a serious division had arisen in the ranks.[46]

A majority of active Sinn Feiners in Scotland seem to have gone
with the Republicans just as Art O'Brien's Irish Self-determination
League, taking up the rest of Britain, sided with de Valera by a narrow
majority. But many sympathisers must have dropped out, baffled by
the origins of the split and not willing to be drawn into what became a
savage internecine conflict that lasted till April 1923. Certainly Sinn
Fein in Glasgow was much depleted, but it was allocated the vital role
by the Republicans of providing military supplies for the rebel army.
Joseph Robinson, who had been Officer Commanding, the Scottish
Battalion of the IRA, was made director of purchases for Britain, and
placed in charge of the IRA publicity department with Seamus Reader
as his deputy in these posts. Glasgow seems to have been the headquarters of the IRA's propaganda machine after the rebels were forced
out of Dublin early in the civil war. The director of Republican propaganda, P. J. Little, later to be Irish minister of posts and telegraphs
in the 1940s, set up his headquarters in the city where newspapers like
Eire were printed and smuggled across the Irish Sea. Joseph Robinson
also claimed that a column of men had been sent to fight in Ireland,
'equipped and financed by sympathisers in Scotland';[47] three Scots
with Glasgow addresses were actually seized following the storming of
Republican headquarters in Dublin at the Four Courts building in
June 1922; the Free State side also attracted Scottish volunteers:
with Michael Collins when he was ambushed and killed in August 1922
was his driver John McPeake who was from Lanarkshire.[48]

The intelligence services and the police in Scotland had a much
clearer picture of who was who in Sinn Fein circles by the time of the
civil war. This was largely due to the Free State government in Dublin
sending them detailed information gathered by its own agents who
were anxious to sever the Glasgow connection as a source of aid to its
enemies. In the papers of Ernie O'Malley, a leading Irish Republican,
there is a detailed list of the main activists in Glasgow who, in early
1923, were still busy supporting the Republicans in Ireland even as
military defeat began to stare them in the face. The main names are
printed here:

> Mrs Moran, 10 Robinson Street, Glasgow. Acts as despatch and Ammunition
> carrier from Glasgow to Ireland.
> Mrs Pidgie Dougan, 23 Bank Street, Hillhead. Engaged to Joseph Robinson.

Acts as Despatch and Ammunition carrier from Scotland to Ireland.

Miss Nelson, 4 Washington Street, Anderston. Acts as Despatch and Ammunition carrier from Scotland to Ireland.

Miss Mollie Duffie, 4 Washington Street. Acts as Despatch and Ammunition carrier from Scotland to Ireland.

Joseph Browne, 4 Clyde Terrace, Glasgow. Is said to be new O/C Glasgow. Now organiser for Sinn Fein clubs.

Matthew Coleman, 38 East Side, Kirkintilloch, active organiser for [Art] O'Brien's association [ISDL].

Fr McRory, St Mary's chapel house—not dangerous.

Miss Padden or Patton, c/o Murray, 56 Crown Street, Glasgow. Purchasing agent for Irregulars.

Liam Travers, lecturer at Sinn Fein meetings, thought to work at Paisley's Tailors and Outfitters, Jamaica Street, Glasgow.

Messrs Kirkwood & Co, 127 Stockwell Street, Glasgow. Printers of the 'Republic of Ireland'. Also printed 'Reply to the Bishops Pastoral'.

James Hickey, 492 Gallowgate, Glasgow, supplied Robinson with large quantities of arms, authorised salesman.

Seamus Reader is in charge of four murder columns in Glasgow.[49] In Gresham Hotel during the [Easter] Rising, was arrested, released.

H. W. Hutchinson, 4 Arundel Drive, Langside, Glasgow, does printing work for the Irregulars.[50]

From the above list, it is worth making the following points: a large number of women were engaged in solidarity work and their importance can be gauged from the fact that four were placed at the top of the list; not all of the activists had Irish names and some were Glasgow small businessmen who provided their services either for financial reasons or, more likely, out of sympathy with Republican aims; other names were listed, many of the addresses being in the north of the city in districts like Maryhill and even Partick which did not have strong natinalist Irish associations and where they may have hoped to avoid the attentions of the police. However, with their former Irish comrades in league with the British authorities this was a formidable task and, on 11 March 1923, the police used the information received from Dublin to arrest thirty-seven people in Scotland, twenty-eight from Glasgow, five from Lanarkshire, one from Dumbartonshire, two from West Lothian, and one from Dundee.[51] A further seventy-three Irish activists were detained in England and all 110 were handed over to the Free State forces who interned them in Mountjoy gaol, Dublin. There was a wave of protest from Labour Party branches (copies of their letters being found in the file on 'Irish disturbances' in the Scottish Record Office), and questions in parliament from James Maxton and others. Consistently stressed was the fact that many of those deported to Ireland were in fact of English and Scottish birth, a few possessing no Irish ancestry at all. After a few months, they were all released by which time the Irish civil war had ended in victory for the Free Staters. In October 1923, a total of £17,000 was awarded to the Scottish deportees, the highest award going to H. W. Hutchinson, a printer with offices in Bath Street, Glasgow who had been Treasurer of the Republican movement there.[52]

The enmity which plunged the Republican movement into fratricidal conflict did not unduly polarise the immigrant communities in the west of Scotland who just did not relish getting involved. This was no thanks to Charles Diamond who produced many highly charged editorials during the civil war. Even before its outbreak, he responded to the news that a woman deputy had stood up in the Irish parliament to declare that the majority had no rights if they were in the wrong with the words that 'the only answer to this insanity which is criminal and lawless, is a whiff of grapeshot'.[53] Later, he branded de Valera as 'a hybrid Spaniard of alleged Jewish extraction'[54] and for a number of years he waged a vendetta against the leader of the Irish Self-determination League, Art O'Brien, virtually accusing him of mis-appropriating ISDL funds and getting young Irishmen into trouble.[55] In 1926, Diamond was finally taken to court by O'Brien for impugning his character and forced to pay damages and costs.[56] For those who sought to keep Irish political movements alive in Britain rather than follow an integrationist course, he showed no quarter, but it is ironic that Diamond's own influence in the Irish community greatly diminished, once his goal had been realised and Ireland was at last relegated to the sidelines.

Even before the dramatic events of 1922-23, much evidence points to the Irish in Britain showing a willingness to throw aside their absorption in enclave politics connected with the situation in Ireland. There is no doubt that the Irish civil war greatly hastened this process of disengagement. The spectacle of Irishman killing Irishman greatly weakened Irish political and cultural movements in many British cities where these activities had reached a high pitch only a short time before. The Gaelic League all but died away in Glasgow where under the patronage of people like Denis Brogan (1856-1934), a self-made Donegal tailor with a successful shop in the centre of the city, it had enjoyed impressive growth.[57] Brogan produced a famous family whose sons made their mark in academia, teaching, and journalism, but interestingly none showed any enthusiasm for Irish topics such as the restoration of Gaelic. By their generation, the immigrant communities were at last sinking deeper roots in their chosen homeland and less and less looking over their shoulders to Ireland, so that 1922 may be a appropriate point at which to discard the word 'immigrant' as a term of identification for the Glasgow Irish. Of course, Irish political movements continued to exist, but largely in the shadows, and even the

Gaelic League revived in time. In 1928, six branches of Fianna Fail, the newly formed populist republican party that would dominate Irish politics for the next half-century, were founded in Glasgow.[58] They emerged out of the old Sinn Fein movement and one continued to remain in being down to the 1960s, the only party branch to be found outside Ireland.[59]

Unlike the old Irish Home Rule party, those parties in the new Irish state did not encourage offshoots in Britain which made the transfer of allegiances to a party whose priorities the Irish understood to be social reform and the end of economic injustice, a far less protracted process.

The dropping of Ireland from the British political agenda after 1922 had a salutory effect on community relations. There was now one less issue to engender misunderstanding between workers with different religious and national allegiances in Scotland. A sign of the times was the election of two roman catholic miners to parliament as Labour MPs in 1922. Joseph Sullivan (1866-1935) North Lanark and Hugh Murnin (1861-1932) Stirling and Falkirk, representing mining seats where the workforce had in the past been too bitterly divided to use their numerical strength to return one of their own leaders to parliament. But it has to be said that the Labour Party was extremely fortunate that Ulster had remained aloof from the warfare which had engulfed much of the rest of the island. Hundreds died in Belfast street-fighting during 1921-22, but if these sectarian pogroms had been supplemented by direct confrontation between the unionist north and the nationalist south, then it is quite likely that protestant sympathisers on Clydeside would have been able to organise a movement of solidarity with even more teeth than that which emerged from the catholic community. A split Republican movement may therefore have prevented a bloody showdown, not just in Ulster but possibly also in Scotland and Liverpool, while enabling the Unionist state to consolidate itself.

But as Labour made inroads elsewhere, working-class wards near the Glasgow shipyards, where there was regular contact with Belfast, remained staunchly Tory. In 1920, Labour was heavily defeated in Patrick and Whiteinch which *Forward* described as 'a noted stronghold of Carsonism', where 'at election time the primitive passions of the people are easily roused into violent opposition to Labour'.[60] In 1923, Hugh Ferguson, the candidate of an ephemeral Orange and Protestant Party was actually returned to parliament for Motherwell. This party was formed in protest at the fact that the Tories had associated themselves with the 1921 Irish peace treaty, but Ferguson took the Tory whip in parliament. An ex-soldier, scrap metal dealer, and member of the Plymouth Brethren sect, he called in parliament for another Cromwell to get to work in Ireland,[61] but he was only there a year before being rejected by the electors of Motherwell in favour of Rev. James Barr for the Labour Party.

In some parts of Scotland, sectarianism intruded into politics even without the stimulus of the Irish question. This was clearly seen in 1918 when Colonel A. C. Stirling lost the seat of West Perthshire which he had won for the Coalition Unionists at a 1917 by-election. Despite coming from a landed family with an illustrious military record, he was the only member of the government party to lose his seat in Scotland where it recorded sweeping gains, an outcome which the *Glasgow Observer* did not hesitate to ascribe to his catholic religion.[62]

In at least one major respect, Scotland generated a form of communal friction that was peculiar to itself and could not be said to be an importation from Ulster. This was the fierce rivalry between the respective followers of Glasgow's principal soccer teams Rangers and Celtic. Supporters drew upon their respective protestant and catholic allegiances to give a sharper edge to their rivalry than almost anywhere else in the footballing world. The two teams had become locked in competition as the era of mass spectator sport dawned around 1900. It was becoming a well-established pattern for many British industrial cities to provide two rival teams before which other local sides paled and the competition was friendly enough until after the First World War. Rangers, although drawing its support from the overwhelmingly protestant craft workers who lived and worked not far from its ground at Ibrox in the west of the city, signed players from other denominations as Celtic has always done. But, after the First World War, the team's players came to be drawn from one religion in a city where almost one-third of the inhabitants were roman catholic.

Rivalry took an increasingly ugly turn in the shadow of the escalating crisis in Ireland between 1912 and 1922. The arrival from Belfast of protestant shipyard workers in 1912 to build a new yard near Ibrox at a time when feelings in their community was running dangerously high over Irish Home Rule, possibly aggravated matters.[63] The war, and the depression which threw members of the aristocracy of labour onto the dole as some better-educated catholics began to compete for more skilled jobs in the labour market, cannot have helped. Through its shareholders and directors, Rangers had close ties with the freemasons and, in a time of uncertainty and shrinking economic horizons, it is not to be wandered at that such a powerful social institution, by its signing policy, emulated the protestant-only recruitment policy long associated with the freemasons in skilled industry. The masonic lodge drew craft workers, foremen, and white-collar staff under its protective umbrella. Catholics were banned from joining on pain of excommunication by their church. Some viewed it as a devilish cult, but it encouraged religious observance among skilled workers, thus reinforcing the protestant identity of skilled workers on Clydeside. One historian has estimated that one in ten adult male Scots had been enrolled into the freemasons by the 1920s.[64] By drawing masters and men together, it impeded the rise of class consciousness, although it should not be forgotten that the severe industrial unrest on Clydeside between 1915 and 1919 mainly involved skilled workers anxious to protect their differentials.

On the continent, freemasonry was associated with secularism, anti-clericalism, and radical politics but, in Britain, it was far more conventional and many joined to gain advancement in their place of work. Catholics readily viewed the masonic lodge as the places where jobs and promotions were decided and in the 1920s and 1930s, any catholics who were thwarted in their bid to get on in the world needed only to point the finger at the shadowy freemasons to be believed by their fellows.

One of the primary reasons why the Labour Party in the 1920s became so attractive to nearly all sectors of the catholic community in the west of Scotland was the hope that, by its reforming efforts, the social scales would be redressed a little more in their favour. Although social amelioration would prove a slow process for the descendants of immigrants, their commitment to the Labour Party remained un-dimmed in decades to come. Of course, a number of hurdles had to be surmounted before the catholic minority could be regarded as loyal supporters of the party of the emancipated working-class. Everything did not just fall into place after Ireland was removed as an issue from local and national politics.

Even before the 1921 peace treaty, the ILP was faced with the problem of how to respond to the Home Rule politicians who wished to preserve their local influence by operating inside the umbrella of the Labour Party. At a time when the party was moving leftwards under the influence of the war, the Russian revolution, and a gathering depression, the socialist credentials of the local political brokers who had previously controlled much of the Irish vote in inner-city wards seemed extremely flimsy. Even the commitment to genuine participatory democracy of the publicans, traders, and members of the professions who had been to the fore in the UIL, was not always self-evident. Some in the ILP were fearful that they would seek to practice their Tammany Hall style methods in their new home and thus subvert its noble socialist purpose. That the fear was not entirely groundless was confirmed by the experience of Liverpool, the chief city stronghold of the UIL. Here, during the 1920s, it was the still vigorous home rule machine which absorbed the Labour Party rather than the other way round.[65] For some decades, the machine had been engrossed in municipal politics and being autonomous from the larger partner at Westminster, it was able to survive the drastic political realignment occurring in Ireland. As a result, the Labour Party in the city became identified with back-room politics and with advancing the interests of the catholic church.[66] It failed to become a rallying-point for those forces wishing to replace the city's ethnic politics with something corresponding to the pattern already emerging in other English cities that had experienced heavy Irish immigration. More than once, party headquarters in London had to intervene to sort out bitter wrangles between Irish godfathers and left-wingers battling to create a more orthodox party, the ultimate beneficiaries being the Tories who retained the support of enough protestant workers to remain in power till 1955.

Glasgow was probably the British city which stood the greatest chance of taking the Liverpool road by institutionalising ghetto religious politics. However, while the draft of events on Merseyside had an inexorable quality to them in keeping with the port's reputation for confrontation politics, political behaviour on Clydeside usually has been more restrained, despite a turbulent image in other respects. Home rulers did not make a wholesale grab for power in the Glasgow labour movement and had to contend with entrenched competition even in their own electoral bailiwicks. Thanks to the pioneering work of John Wheatley and his lieutenants in the Catholic Socialist Society, there was already a definite socialist presence in a number of immigrant neighbourhoods even before the home rule machine began to splinter. ILP branches were not divided on religious grounds because of the absence of complete residential segregation in Glasgow, so immigrants who got involved were able to put behind them the enclave mentality associated with home rule politics. Activists from a Glasgow Irish back-ground were rewarded for their enthusiasm and commitment and, indeed, the Labour movement was practically the first 'secular' body where they made their mark. Many immigrants must have drawn encouragement from the rise of John Wheatley, returned to parliament in 1922 and a member of the cabinet two years later, and from the emergence of his *protégé* Patrick Dollan, who masterminded the 1922 electoral campaign which saw ten of Glasgow's fourteen parliamentary seats fall to Labour.

After 1920, none of the ex-Home Rulers who transferred to the Labour Party received a parliamentary nomination and in immigrant strongholds like Glasgow Gorbals, George Buchanan, a non-catholic brought up in the district was elected in 1922 with little difficulty. Some did get on the city council from 1920 onwards, but their path was not a smooth one. At the 1920 municipal elections, two members of the licensing trade and a lawyer who were unable to get Labour nominations, stood in strongly immigrant wards and won. William T. Docherty was elected for Cowcaddens along with John McGuire in

Calton, and Thomas O'Hare in Provan.[67] Their links with, or support for, the licensing trade estranged them from the ILP which, at its Scottish conference in 1920, voted by forty-seven to fifteen in support of prohibition. Many of the leading socialists in Glasgow, such as Wheatley, Tom Johnston, and William Gallacher were abstainers from drink. The ILP's hardline opposition to drink stemmed from the widely held belief that it was a destroyer of working-class lives and a primary cause of slums, ill-health, and poverty.[68]

In order not to jeopardise its electoral hopes, the drink question was played down and prohibition quietly shelved by the ILP. The three 'Unofficial Labour' candidates of 1920 were accorded the party whip, O'Hare and Docherty going on to hold senior positions in the city administration.[69] For McGuire in Calton, acceptance was a more gradual process: he was still described as an 'Independent' in 1923, an 'Independent Socialist' in 1926 and only when he stood for the last time in 1929 was he granted the full Labour nomination.[70] In 1921, five more candidates, whose Ancient Order of Hibernians membership was stressed by the hostile *Glasgow Herald*, were returned to the council.[71] Most were official Labour candidates as was John Cruden, the former treasurer of the local UIL who was elected for Calton in 1922. Thereafter the entry into the upper ranks of the Labour Party of home rulers tailed off. Little evidence has been found to suggest that they formed themselves into a caucus to shape party policies on the council (of course the incentive to do so was slight since the party was in opposition until the 1930s). Nor were they able to establish complete dominance over the party machine even in strongly Irish wards like Gorbals or Hutchesontown where candidates obviously not from the home rule stable were nominated and elected; occasionally calls were heard for a 'Catholic Labour Party', but by the 1920s, Glasgow's working-class catholics were not as removed from the rest of society (at least in their political behaviour) to make this an attractive proposition even for those who fitted uneasily into the new local order.

The Labour movement came to terms with the ethnic bosses of the immigrant districts in ways described above, but the power of these Irish community leaders has been overstressed, not least in Iain McLean's *The Legend of Red Clydeside*. Politically, it is an over-simplification to say that the catholics were 'bound together by the bar, the pulpit, and an "ethnic" press'.[72] If more attention had been paid to the Catholic Socialist Society (and to the backing for radical politics from Irish community leaders in the Home Government branch of the UIL before 1914), he might have found significant divergences from the Tammany Hall stereotype in the behaviour of Irish voters and activists. Of especial importance is the fact that many immigrants only came on to the electoral rolls thanks to the 1918 Representation of the People Act, by which time the home rulers were in retreat. By now, they were just as likely to be receiving their first instructions in politics from the Labour Party as from any old-fashioned ethnic source.

The Labour Party could count itself lucky that the burning question of catholic education and who should pay for it, had largely been settled by the time it began to court working-class catholic votes. The 1918 Education (Scotland) Act removed nearly all of the burden for maintaining and financing catholic education from the religious authorities. It was one of the last important acts of the Liberal Party in Scotland, its architect being Robert Munro, Secretary of State for Scotland, who later became Lord Alness (1868-1955). Negotiations with the catholic authorities were protracted since many important issues were at stake. The passages dealing with catholic education were contained in Section 18 of the act which has been hailed as the Magna Carta of twentieth century Scottish catholicism. The relevant catholic authorities agreed that its schools could be transferred to the local authorities in return for certain safeguards about their religious character: only teachers acceptable 'in regard to religious faith and character' to the church authorities could be appointed; religious instruction was to be kept up at the same level as before; and priests were given full access to the schools where, on an unpaid basis, they could oversee religious instruction and worship.[73] Catholic schools thus became part of the state system and were known as *denominational schools.*

In no other predominantly protestant country did catholics enjoy such latitude in the educational sphere. The settlement was envied by clergy in England and Wales where, in large part, catholic schools continued to be funded by voluntary contributions. Today it is strange to think that Scottish bishops and relevant clergy had temporised over accepting it, even though it relieved them of a great financial and administrative burden.[74] The willingness of local authorities to administer Section 18 in an even-handed way had been doubted and it was only the intervention of the Vatican and Bishop William Brown (a convert whose grandfather had been Provost of Dundee), whom Rome had earlier appointed apostolic visitor to Scotland, which led to the proposed legislation being accepted.[75] In the archdiocese of Glasgow, a further decade would have to elapse before the act was fully implemented: catholic schools were only loaned to the education authority by their catholic trustees who were waiting to see how it would be implemented. New schools in large part continued to be built from church funds and it was only in 1928 that the smooth working of the new act convinced the trustees that they could be completely transferred to the local authorities.

As will be seen, the 1918 settlement produced a storm of protest from protestant spokesmen who complained about 'Rome on the Rates' and lobbied vociferously for the offending Section 18 of the act to be rescinded. The schools question breathed life into the No Popery movement to an alarming degree in the two subsequent decades and was responsible for giving it a legitimacy in Scotland which it had never previously enjoyed in modern times. It may now become clearer why the Labour Party was extremely fortunate that the tricky matter of bringing catholic education into the state system, under terms favourable to the church trustees, was not left for it to accomplish. If it had been, the balancing act of satisfying catholic voters and keeping in line protestant workers unsympathetic to the new arrangement, might have proved extremely difficult to bring off. Church pressure on the party could have split specific constituency parties and given an extended lease of life to ethnic politics, enabling the Tories to acquire working-class voters by a straight appeal to religion, and allowing catholic ward politicians to do likewise in their own bailiwicks.

In a way, the left was just as fortunate that there was a vacuum in the catholic church as it and catholic voters were drawing closer together. From the First World War onwards, Glasgow and St Andrews and Edinburgh, the two largest dioceses, were administered by ailing prelates who did not have the strength to perform many of their customary duties, never mind issue political instructions to their flock. When Archbishop Maguire of Glasgow died in 1920, Rome did not install a successor until 1922, the interregnum years being those in which the church could have made plenty of trouble for a Labour Party not yet able to take the support of ordinary catholics for granted. In Edinburgh, Bishop Henry Grey Graham was placed in effective charge of the archdiocese after 1917 but, as a convert, he may not have enjoyed the familiarity with his flock that would have enabled him to make *ex-cathedra* statements on politics and be listened to. In a hierarchical institution, it was only a minority of priests, such as the redoubtable Canon Andrew O'Brien of St Mark's, Shettleston or Canon Anthony Mullins of the Sacred Heart, Bridgeton, who had the confidence to make emphatic political statements to their flock without episcopal approval. In the west of Scotland, the Labour Party still did not need to come to terms with the Catholic Social Guild, being built up by Fr Leo O'Hea, ex-science master at Stonyhurst college; it encouraged catholic workers to engage in political and trade union activities motivated by a catholic perspective on social and economic questions.[76] By the end of the 1920s, its banner was visible at the May Day procession in Glasgow, but the CSG was largely absent from the scene at an earlier and more decisive stage in the political evolution of Glasgow catholics.

The lack of direction from the top in the Catholic church in

COMMUNITY IN TRANSITION 105

Scotland may be of more than a little relevance in seeking to explain why Charles Diamond promoted his political views with such vigour in newspapers which depended on church outlets for much of their sale. All his titles carried the 'Vote Labour' recommendation on the eve of the 1918 general election but, in Scotland, his backing for the left was even more full-blooded than elsewhere. Besides backing the Gorbals candidacy of the marxist John Maclean, he was the principal speaker at a large meeting held at the St Andrew's Hall Glasgow early in 1919 concerning recent industrial unrest that had gripped the city. With the radical James Maxton in the chair, he 'expressed the conviction that there would have been no serious breach of the peace but for the baton charges of the police'.[77] Not long before, he had denounced those seeking to take advantage of the relegation of the Irish question to launch a specifically catholic party in Britain:

> In our view at least, the Labour Party is not a party of revolution, of Bolshevism, or social destruction. And thousands of Roman Catholics in every part of the country have recorded their votes for Labour candidates because they believe that the party stands for *fairness all round*. That is the workers demand and that is the plain and invariable demand of the Roman Catholic Church.[78]

However, in 1920 Diamond backed those former UIL officials attempting comebacks by standing in Glasgow's council elections without lambasting Labour for denying them the nomination. Like many of the socialists, he despised their connections with the drink trade, but he was appeased by their refusal to fall in with T. P. O'Connor's spasmodic attempts till 1923 to keep alive a grassroots Irish lobby in British politics.[79] Thomas O'Hare, standing in Provan, was described as a 'Moderate', but rather confusingly, the *Observer* stated that 'his activities in the Labour interest on the Glasgow Education Authority merit for him the support of the Labour voters'.[80]

Despite flirting with the left, at no time did Diamond cross the Rubicon and fully espouse socialism. His close associate, the Glasgow physician, Thomas Colvin (1863–1941) echoed his own views when addressing the Glasgow University Catholic Students Sodality in 1919 which was fully covered by the *Observer*:

> Socialism is like morphia. Just as a small dose of morphia would to the patient good and a large dose kill him, so a small dose of socialism would to the state good but a large dose would undoubtedly kill it.[81]

Articles such as the one carried in the *Observer* on 14 April 1917 about 'Socialist "Sunday Schools" Their Atheistical Tendency and Effect' were a warning to his readers that there was a limit to the degree of support that they should give to the Labour Party. But no real storm clouds appeared on the horizon for several years to come. The Labour Party's backing for the 1918 educational settlement, despite the presence of secularists who would have preferred to see all children educated under the one roof, raised the party's standing in the eyes of the catholic press. Triennial elections for the education boards of Scotland's local authorities fell due in 1919 and provided another opportunity for co-operation between church interests and the forces of the left. Fought under proportional representation, they demonstrated the political influence clerics had over catholic voters, at least where education was concerned. The Catholic Union, composed of active laymen in each parish, made sure that a maximum number of catholics were enrolled on the electoral register and it campaigned for the return of senior clergy as well as respectable laymen, each of whom was nominated by the archbishop. Invariably, there was a much higher turnout of catholics than non-catholics and the discipline of the catholic vote gave the Catholic Union the appearance of an embryo political party. Indeed, persistent calls were heard in the 1920s and 1930s from some members out of sympathy with the Labour Party for the Catholic Union to contest municipal elections, but they were usually restrained by wiser elements only too aware that they could accomplish very little without proportional representation, which was only permitted in the educational contests so as to give the various religious interests a chance to representation.

In 1919 the church was to enjoy its best-ever results in any educational election. Catholics headed the poll in each of the seven Glasgow districts, except Partick and Hillhead, four of the victors being clergy, while in Dundee, catholics cam top in all three districts. The *Observer* gave its readers minute instructions about which order of preference candidates should be backed in and it urged that second preferences should go to Labour. Apparently it had no hesitation about viewing the result as a happy outcome for the Catholic–Labour entente:

> In all the burghs and particularly Glasgow and Dundee, the Catholic voters turned out magnificently . . . In some places it was estimated that 90% of the Catholic vote was polled whilst the total percentage of the electorate which voted was rarely above 30%.
>
> If the surplus of the Catholic votes went Labour last Friday, as we trust it will go Labour this Friday in the County areas, that step was taken not from a cynical form of gratitude which arises from a sense of favours to come, but from a desire of the Catholic electorate to stand by those who, in the past on the Scottish School Boards, have always invariably shown themselves to be the sturdy advocates of fairplay for Catholic Schools, and who in the future can be relied upon to adhere to that enlightened, tolerant, and equitable policy.[82]

The quixotic relationship between Diamond's papers and the mass working-class party of the British left continued to flourish up to and beyond the 1922 general election when the Labour Party made an impressive breakthrough in nearly all the industrial areas which had working-class communities of Irish descent. In a special article which appeared in *The Times* after the dramatic advance of the left in Glasgow, the swing to Labour by the Scoto-Irish was singled out as one of the keys that explained the scale of the victory.[83] The exact role of the *Observer* in this major political realignment is hard to judge since it is never easy to measure the impact of the press on political attitudes and voting behaviour. Iain McLean suspects that locally, the catholic press was more influential than *Forward*, the socialist weekly, because of its much higher circulation.[84] Thus its political line is worthy of examination but, interestingly, Diamond himself failed to get elected in 1922 when he stood for the Rotherhithe division of Stepney. where he lost by forty-six votes.

At the 1922 general election, Diamond's papers began to criticise 'pro-bolshevik' elements within the Labour Party but, strangely enough, he was relatively slow to direct his fire at the Communist Party of Great Britain itself. Communist candidates were still being sent questionnaires by churchmen keen to acquaint their parishioners with the views of candidates on questions deemed relevant to catholics when making up their minds how to vote. In Dundee, the *Observer* reported that William Gallacher, a Communist from a catholic background replied while Winston Churchill, the sitting MP gave no answer.[85] Gallacher did well while Churchill lost and in Motherwell a Communist was actually elected in a seat with one of the highest concentrations of catholics in Scotland.

Gradually it dawned on the church that the atheistic Communist Party of Great Britain (CPGB) was capable of drawing recruits from catholic workers, especially those caught up in industrial struggles in mining areas in Fife and, to a lesser degree in Lanarkshire. The CPGB had emerged from the Socialist Labour Party which had enjoyed adherents among the Irish on Clydeside according to a historian of the party.[86] Its principal founder had been James Connolly, while two of the early leaders of its better-known successor came from a Scoto-Irish background: Gallacher and Arthur McManus, the son of a Fenian, who was buried in Red Square, Moscow, following his death in 1927. Peter Kerrigan and Harry McShane were other front-rank members from the same background. 'Lenin became their Pope' according to ex-member Harry McShane.[87]

Once Scottish catholic workers transferred their loyalties to the materialist religion of communism, they often proved the most dogged and orthodox of members ready at all times to adjust to the latest twist in the party line emanating from Moscow.[88] John Campbell, secretary of the Catholic Union in Glasgow later claimed with a little hyperbole in 1951 that the Communist Party was dominated by renegade catholics and that fact had to be faced up to.[89] From 1923 onwards, catholics were instructed at every opportunity by clergy, the religious press, and the Catholic Union to have no truck with the CPGB or any communist front and it was only non-communist candidates whose views were canvassed on matters deemed relevant to catholics. Such hostility contributed to the failure of the party ever to win a single parliamentary or even municipal seat in Glasgow. In single-industry towns and villages, where the church's resources were weaker and where the class struggle made the economics of survival drown out the appeal of religious salvation, the battle between the pulpit and the party was less of a foregone conclusion as was shown by Willie Gallacher's election in 1935 for West Fife.[90]

Not only the Labour Party but the church was lucky in the timing of the 1918 settlement since it gave its lay activists the time to combat the Communist Party much of which would, otherwise, have been taken up in gathering funds to maintain a threadbare educational system. There is no guarantee that in the 1920s, parishioners would have been willing to dig as deeply into their pockets for catholic schools, given the slump and the introduction of new ideas into the community. The financial pressures which the priest imposed on his flock might even have produced dissension which communists could have tried to turn to their advantage.

Time would show that the extreme-left only had a distinct appeal for small sections of the catholic community at specific moments. Even in the midst of industrial turmoil, the power of the church could be vividly demonstrated as in the small Lanarkshire mining community of Carfin in the early 1920s. During a prolonged stoppage, striking miners erected a small grotto at the request of the local priest, Thomas Nimmo Taylor (1873–1963). Soon this bleak and ugly mining village became a place of pilgrimage for thousands of Scottish catholics.[91] Its appeal grew as the waters of the shrine, dedicated to Our Lady of the Rosary in 1922 were claimed to have miraculous properties. Over one-quarter of a million pilgrims visited Carfin in the summer of 1923.[92] This was a time of economic hardship, rapid political transition, and civil-war in Ireland; the uncertainty of the age made public expression of faith and devotion a source of reassurance that filled a psychological need for many catholics buffeted by harsh winds of circumstance.

Carfin's appeal was undiminished even when the authorities prohibited an open-air procession due to be held on Corpus Christi Sunday, 22 June 1924. At the behest of Hugh Ferguson, Orange MP for Motherwell, the police had activated legislation dating from the 'papal aggression' storm of 1850 which had rarely ever been used. The interference with the Carfin procession prompted Francis Blundell, the Tory MP for Ormskirk, and the member of an old Lancashire catholic family, to propose a private members bill designed to sweep away archaic laws prohibiting catholic religious processions and public ceremonies.[93] The Roman Catholic Relief Act passed into law in 1926 at a time when the image of the church in Scotland increasingly was becoming a devotional one. In Glasgow, Archbishop Donald Mackintosh was concerned not to provoke the traditional opponents of the church and religious events were usually held at discreet locations away from the city centre. Between the wars, Eucharistic Congresses were the customary means whereby catholics publicly proclaimed their faith; notwithstanding the size and the devotional commitment of the catholic population in Scotland's largest archdiocese, Glasgow never held one; however, the popular fury which erupted in Edinburgh, the venue of a Eucharistic Congress in June 1935, showed Mackintosh's caution to have been far from misplaced.[94]

Popular devotion was encouraged by organisations of Irish origin such as the Legion of Mary, begun by Frank Duff a civil-servant in Dublin, during the traumatic year of 1921.[95] The Legion of Mary grew rapidly in Scottish parishes which were not unaffected by the degree of religious fervour and organisation displayed by catholics in Belfast around this time. Excluded from effective political participation in the Northern Ireland state and subject to forms of discrimination which resulted in even greater hardship than before for ordinary catholics, the more active members of the community threw their energies into founding bodies such as the Pioneers Association of the Sacred Heart and the Apostolic Work Society.[96] These were developed to prevent community disintegration by encouraging the renunciation of alcohol and providing aid for the most deprived and vulnerable members of society. They had an impact in Glasgow, a city with similar social characteristics where catholics were a highly visible minority but not with their backs as pressed against the wall. In 1919, Glasgow was the birthplace of the Knights of St Columba, later to be the largest organisation of catholic laymen in Britain, which quickly found plenty of scope to perform a charitable and welfare role.[97] The objects of the Knights were to promote the moral, intellectual, and material welfare of its members, to provide for its widows and orphans, and to contribute to Catholic Action.[98] It was very much a sign of the times that the Knights displaced the Ancient Order of Hibernians, which had similar objects but in its heyday had been more 'Irish' than 'catholic' in its orientation.

In the 1930s the already long-established Catholic Young Men's Society (CYMS) was reinvigorated by Canon Joseph Daniel (1897–

1981), who probably did more than any other figure to reinforce the devotional character of Scottish catholicism by holding rallies, vast outdoor masses, and organising annual pilgrimages to Lourdes in the late 1930s, by which time there were direct sailings from the Clyde by the SS Athenia, via Dublin to the south of France.[99] These had a beneficial effect on catholic solidarity, but it was difficult to generate momentum from these large static gatherings that could spill over into other areas of the community. Canon Daniel's name was also linked with efforts to launch a movement of the lay Apostolate that would make the social environment more receptive to the message of Christ. However, this dedicated, energetic, but overbearing priest envisaged a movement firmly under clerical tutelage that had little intellectual content. Laymen must know their place, an attitude which even extended to the educational sphere. Here some priests reacted with barely concealed hostility to new catholic state secondary schools like Holyrood in Glasgow, opened in 1936. The reason? It was staffed by lay teachers, the tiny catholic secondary sector having hitherto been dominated by the religious orders.[100]

By 1939, one quarter of the CYMS branches were in Scotland with a total membership of 5,620.[101] A rare note of public criticism about the lack of direction in the movement had been expressed by an activist in the previous year:

> We are quite content to amble along year after year, following the same old routine being jerked into a brief sensibility occasionally by a rally, or a pilgrimage, or an annual dinner, preferably an annual dinner . . . We point with satisfaction to the number of lectures and meetings we have arranged during the year, to the number of protests we have lodged against this, that, or the other measure, to the number of social functions we have organised in an effort to stimulate friendly feeling among our people.
>
> Where is it getting us? Is it a step towards real lay action or have we made this undirected, undisciplined step an end in itself. Yes, I am afraid we must admit it, we are much more in love with Catholic activity than with Catholic Action.[102]

Such frank introspection only rarely crept into the catholic press or was noticeable in the statements of lay and clerical leaders. Instead the view was frequently expressed that the church had the answer for every type of problem confronting British society.[103] Self-doubt was a luxury the foot-soldiers of Christ could not afford. The catholic press was remarkably sensitive to what it perceived as insults directed at its faith. Headlines such as 'St Joan, An Insult to the Saint and a Travesty' or 'The Pope's Sister Not Living in Poverty, Daily Mail Story Rebutted' were not uncommon before 1939.[104] Before the era of ecumenism, other provocative headlines belittled other faiths such as the one in the

Observer on 17 July 1935: 'Luther as Father of Bolshevism: Sacrificed Human Personality to Material Individuality'. But mostly, the paper reflected the news and events of its own community to the exclusion of the outside world, with anniversaries, deaths, ordinations, visits, the schedule of bishops and priests, and international catholic news being given detailed coverage. Three headlines in the *Glasgow Observer* for 13 March 1937 were not untypical:

Catholic Violinist on Tour

Canon Hackett's 50 Years in Priesthood

Sensational Claim by Scottish Convert, Recovery from Incurable Complaint

Even after 1945 a strict adherence to orthodoxy and decorum was required in the pages of the newspaper. In a piece marking its centenary in 1985, a former editor recalled how:

It was said that glasses were painted out of the hands of photographs of bishops at receptions or longer shorts were painted on the legs of netball teams and that ecclesiastical permission had to be sought before a photograph of Catholic Scout chaplains of yesteryear could be published because they were not wearing dog-collars.[105]

Frequently the catholic press carried lengthy and intricate articles about church history and church teaching on a variety of religious and social issues. The demand for such knowledge in the 1930s should not be underestimated. The Catholic Truth Society, designed to give catholics and non-catholics a better understanding of church faith and practice, had been in existence since 1893 and was active throughout Scotland by the 1930s. Bookshops for the sale of CTS literature were opened and, in one year, a quarter of a million pamphlets were sold in Glasgow alone. The demand for religious literature enabled John S. Burns & Sons, a catholic publishing house, to be launched in 1926.[106] In 1936, one of the books published by Burns was a *Catechism of Social Questions* by Fr T. O'Kane, then a curate in Wishaw. It sold over 100,000 copies in its English edition as well as being translated into many foreign languages.[107]

Invariably, much of the energy of lay catholics was channelled into the safe areas examined above where the traditional unspoken authority of the clergy rarely came into question. This may explain why the self-organisation of catholics in their place of work was such a late development. Priests were not in a position to exercise supervisory role in factories and coalmines and it was largely the proselytising by communists in the early years of the Second World War which encouraged lay catholics to take the initiative themselves in forming the Catholic Workers Guild in Glasgow and the Association of Catholic

Trade Unionists in the east of Scotland (their role will be discussed in chapter 4).

The hierarchical structure of the church inhibited lay initiatives with a practical purpose and episcopal approval was not always a foregone conclusion. Caution was preferred over innovation which meant that much of the potential of the engaged laity (which as a proportion of the entire catholic community was high in Scotland compared to the rest of Britain and indeed much of catholic Europe), was not tapped to its fullest extent.

From the outset, the overriding priority of Donald Mackintosh, installed as archbishop of Glasgow in 1922, was to restore the depleted finances of the archdiocese. They had been allowed to run down, to the point of bankruptcy, during the previous decade when his predecessor had been prostrated for long periods by an illness of the nervous system. Previously rector of the Scots College in Rome, Mackintosh had been appointed because the Vatican had been impressed with his ability to raise funds in Scotland for the missions. He proved to be a capable and prudent administrator, but there had been a breakdown of communications somewhere along the lines since the real credit for the missionary drive belonged to Monsignor James Mullin who had previously been the favourite to step into the vacant Glasgow see.[108] Mackintosh went on to rapidly establish his authority in Glasgow by switching pieces on the clerical chessboard and removing some altogether. In 1922 he removed Canon William O'Brien (1860-1937), forty-one years at Holy Cross Chruch, Crosshill, from the Education Authority and replaced him with a layman, Mitchel Quin of the *Observer*, an authority on catholic education who had failed to win a seat in the recent election.[109] Around the same time, he retired the redoubtable Canon Andrew O'Brien of Shettleston when it came to his notice that he had used money from his church building fund to open a soup-kitchen for the needy of the parish; it was open to all irrespective of religion which won him the regard of the local Orange leader, King Lawson.[110]

Archbishop Mackintosh's official obituary notice was surprisingly frank about his personal traits. It left it open to doubt as to whether he was the most appropriate choice for an archdiocese like Glasgow:

> The new archbishop suffered from certain disadvantages. He had no personal experience of parochial work, and indeed was hardly familiar with Glasgow or the industrial towns of the neighbourhood. The necessary work of restoration and extension demanded an intimate knowledge of time and place and strong, good health . . .
>
> He set about the laborious, complicated, delicate work of centralising and systematising the finances of the Archdiocese, and this is likely to remain the greatest of his permanent achievements . . .

... a multitude of routine duties excessively taxed the strength of a man who was too devoted to shirk responsibility and perhaps too scrupulously conscientious to be very apt at delegating it ... He never sought the limelight and those who did not know him might consider him to be reserved and unapproachable ... In dealing with cant, abuse, and unworthy conduct he could be stern, and Donald Mackintosh's sternness was something to remember.[111]

Before long, Archbishop Mackintosh fell victim to heart disease and turned into an invalid for long periods so that, in the words of a successor, 'he grew rather out of touch with the problems of the arch-diocese'.[112] In the view of a well-informed catholic layman, a number of clerical 'godfathers' were able to wield considerable power in Glasgow down to the 1970s. They could make or break a bishop's plans by their willingness or unwillingness to raise money for him. A large number were Irish priests who headed 'great clans of priest relatives'—one priest having as many as twenty relatives (cousins and nephews) as priests in the diocese. It has been claimed that many Irish priests were slow in encouraging vocations to the priesthood among Scots-born boys in their parishes. Such boys sometimes never had their applications answered, but bishops accepted the situation because it meant that they could get Irish-trained priests 'free' at no cost to diocesan funds. The source for this information links the current acute shortage of vocations with the traditional lack of encouragement in many parishes for boys to try their vocations. Many of those Scots who did enter the priesthood preferred to join the religious orders. So pronounced was this trend that, by the 1950s, the British province of the Franciscans was estimated to be almost two-thirds Scots-born, mainly from Glasgow or Dundee.

It was a few dynamic figures in religious orders like the Jesuits or the Dominicans who very often provided the initial spur for move-ments of the laity whose objective went beyond affirming the faith and concerned giving a catholic focus to social and economic issues of the day. Diocesan priests, with the exception of figures like John McQuillan or P. J. Flood, avoided social involvements of this kind and their definition of parish work was often a narrow one mainly revolving around the spiritual welfare of parishioners and seeing that they fulfilled their religious duties. Provided the priest was not over-bearing or unduly zealous, there were few to complain about the emphasis placed on ritual and devotion.

By the 1920s, Scottish catholicism only possessed the glimmer of an intellectual or professional class which might have preferred a more rounded definition of the faith. Glasgow only possessed five catholic doctors in 1905, a situation that only came to be remedied after the war.[113] Prejudice in middle-class professions made it easier for those catholics who secured a full education to start their professional careers elsewhere unless they were servicing the needs of the catholic community as doctors or lawyers. The university-educated Scots catholic was more likely to make a name for himself outside Scotland; one such was the doctor from Cardross in Dumbartonshire who, as A. J. Cronin (1896–1981) became a bestselling author of popular fiction.[114] It was not until 1932 that a catholic from immigrant stock entered the Scottish Bar. This was John Wheatley who, as the nephew of the Socialist politician and businessman who was his namesake, belonged to one of the few catholic families in the west of Scotland with the private means to follow a course which, in 1974, saw him appointed Lord Justice Clerk, the top legal position in Scotland. Even as late as the 1950s and 1960s, there was a mass exodus of catholic graduates to seek jobs outside the west of Scotland. In some cases, their failure to find openings at home left bitter memories: one source points to three men, a senior civil servant, an ambassador, and a doctor 'all of whom spit bile at the mere mention of Scotland'.

In 1919 only 8·5% of the catholic school population benefitted from some form of post-elementary education, a figure that had risen to only 13·9% by 1939.[115] The prospects of catholics at university began to rise following the decision in 1924 that all catholic male teachers had to be graduates.[116] The 1918 Act greatly expanded that part of the catholic middle-class based on teaching. A few individual teachers, notably James Edmund Handley (Brother Clare), (1900–71), distinguished themselves as scholars despite having a demanding routine. Brother Clare came to St Mungo's Academy, Glasgow in 1926 and, as principal teacher in English, and later headmaster from 1944 to 1960, he still found the time to publish five important books, some of which illuminate the early history of the Irish in Scotland, and to obtain four academic degrees.[117] William Murphy of the *Glasgow Observer* was still able to recall how, after completing a busy working day, he would walk across Glasgow to the Mitchell Library to begin his academic labours, stopping on the way for a cup of tea and a chat at the paper's offices in Waterloo Street.[118] But he was a lonely exception to the rule: the emergent teaching profession was conspicuous by its absence from scholasticism, and public affairs (perhaps out of fear of alienating clerical superiors) and could have made far more of a mark in the catholic social movement.

Attendance at university did not greatly broaden the horizons of catholic students or take them out of a specifically catholic milieu. Many found themselves in an environment which they suspected of being at best apathetic and at worst hostile both towards their religious faith and national origins.[119] The catholic novelist George Friel was even dislodged as editor of the Glasgow student newspaper on account of his religion.[120] In 1931, when catholic students played a prominent role in the election of Compton Mackenzie, the Scottish Nationalist and author, as rector of Glasgow University, a whispering campaign about the impending catholic takeover of the party was started by its enemies which discouraged many catholic students from further participation in politics.[121]

It was not long before nearly all catholic students at Glasgow found their way to the Catholic chaplaincy. It had been opened in 1925 and, by 1930, almost 500 catholic students were studying at Glasgow. The first chaplain was William Eric Brown, a convert and former Glasgow history lecturer who influenced the views of a great number of catholic students in the 1920s and 1930s.[122] Another significant experience for many was membership of the University Distributist Club founded in 1930 and which celebrated fifty years of existence in 1980.[123] Distributism is the theory that personal freedom can only be safeguarded if there is widespread personal ownership of property. The theory was popularised by Hilaire Belloc and G. K. Chesterton, the best-known catholic intellectuals of the inter-war period, which helps to explain why its greatest appeal lay among younger aware catholics. *GK's Weekly*, the journal of the Distributist League, edited by Chesterton as its name suggests, attacked large concentrations of wealth, mass production, and money-lending. To combat the evils of industrialism, distributism urged the revival of small-scale family farming, small units of trade and industry, and the encouragement of the craftsman. Eric Gill brought to the movement a hatred of mass production and a love for the craftsman who could develop his personality through his work.

Distributism had a strong impact on Glasgow university catholics for a number of reasons. It blended with the papal encyclicals that addressed social questions and, in an industrial city stricken by the depression, it provided an attractive theoretical alternative to 'the rule of the machine' for students from a subordinate closed community unable to play a major role in the technological field, at least locally. Increasingly, the Distributist Club became more of a social club for young catholics preparing to be teachers, lawyers, or doctors which explains why it has outlived all the rest in Britain's universities. The entry in the *New Catholic Encyclopedia* claims that, although the distributist message helped make public opinion aware of the need for social reform, it hampered the political education of part of a generation of British catholics:

> The distributists attacked many real evils . . . but it must be recorded, too, that their distrust of central government and their hatred of party politics, diverted part of a generation of intelligent people into a dream-world and kept them out of politics and government.[124]

Distributism's early promotion of the 'Small Is Beautiful' concept encouraged a back to the land movement. Because it was a return to primitive agriculture in the midst of an agricultural, as well as, industrial, depression, few of those who went back were able to survive for long.[125] One Land Colony was established in 1931 at Symington in Lanarkshire by the Rev. Dr John McQuillan, a lecturer at St Peter's College, the catholic seminary, then in Bearsden. It had the backing of Archbishop Mackintosh, himself from a small farming background in the west Highlands. McQuillan promoted his rural vision in *Land For The People*, the quarterly journal of the Scottish Catholic Land Association, which he edited from 1931 until 1935 when it ceased to appear. He branded city life as 'inimical to religion and to every decent human impulse'.[126] The pattern of urban living was gradually corrupting town dwellers who were becoming inaccessible even to the most zealous priests: 'divine grace runs through many of them like a sieve', persons 'who live in the same street as the church absent themselves'.[127] This was 'the leakage', the loss of church membership, which was a favourite topic of conversation in the 1930s. Explanations were often found in the spread of communism or the lack of church resources, but McQuillan believed they were only contributory factors and that it was city life itself which encouraged mixed marriages, ignorance of religion, and non-frequentation of the sacraments. Because these problems were practically negligible in the countryside, he advocated its repopulation:

> Let us develop the country then. Multiply the parishes outside the town. Supply the countryside with priests and chapels. Many families would have left the towns long ago had there been but churches and schools in the country districts. Make Scots land Catholic and Scotland will become Catholic too. Meanwhile the cities can be left in ruin as inglorious memories of unhappy days.
> Delenda est Carthago.[128]

Glasgow for McQuillan was 'the second plague spot of the empire and he enlisted the now forgotten but evocative words of the Czech novelist, Karl Capek to drive home his image of 'the city of dreadful night':

> Oh Glasgow, city without beauty, city of noise and commerce, city of factories and wharves, harbour for wares of all kinds, what am I to say about you? Is there then any beauty in factories, docks and warehouses, cranes in the harbour, towers of steelworks, flocks of gasometers, chattering cartloads of goods, tall chimneys and thundering steam-hammers, structures of girders and iron buoys in the water, and mountains of coal?
> I, miserable sinner, think that all these things are very beautiful and picturesque and monumental, but the life which is born from this is neither beautiful or picturesque, but is deserted by the breath of God, crude and

grimy and sticky, noisy, reeking and oppressive, disorderly and burden-
some . . . and there sank on me the weariness of myriads and I fled, Oh
Glasgow, for I had no courage to behold and compare.[129]

Gradually, the enthusiasm McQuillan and the young men who
were being trained in practical farming brought to their rural experiment
was drained by the practical difficulties they encountered in a harsh
economic climate. Shortly before a breakdown in his health necessitated
his withdrawal from the scheme, *Land for the People* in September
1935 mentioned that numerous approaches to government departments
for help had been in vain. He was succeeded by a young Irish priest,
Fr John Crerand who succumbed to pneumonia in 1936 and two years
later the archdiocese decided to wind up the scheme.[130]

Although his vision of urban dereliction and the potential for rural
renewal may have been crudely simplistic, as a priest John McQuillan
was exceptional for his determination to test out his ideas in such a
challenging way. A thoughtful and widely read cleric who occasionally
wrote for the Church of Scotland journal, *The Scots Observer*, he
tended to avoid the crude anti-communism and belief in right-wing
solutions which passed from the lips of many catholic spokesmen as
the political situation at home and abroad grew darker in the 1930s.[131]
But as the Land Scheme encountered mounting problems, even he
expressed anti-democratic sentiments which shows the sheer prevalence
of authoritarian ideas inside and outside the church at this time:

> It has been suggested that there be abolished the House of Commons. As
> most people are now beginning to see, the government of the country would
> be carried on in the same way as before the abolition, but there would remain
> the distinct advantage, that there would be an enormous saving of money.
> The yearly salary of every deposed MP would be more than enough to enable
> a man to take over a small farm . . .[132]

Later he wrote:

> The Communist propaganda is itself daily becoming more intense. Its
> principles and atmosphere are spreading in government circles, and there
> seems some danger of panic legislation of a Communistic flavour, irrespective
> of the parties in office in the probable event of a second financial crisis.[133]

McQuillan's apocalyptic mood in the 1930s reflected the views of
less thoughtful priests and laymen who were prepared to lend support
to strong men or strong solutions for the problems of the age. As early
as 1923 a photograph appeared in the *Glasgow Observer* of Archbishop
Mackintosh surrounded by Italian Blackshirts blessing the flag of those
members of the Italian community in Glasgow marking Italy's national
day.[134] Later he adopted a prudent course in politics and, through the

Catholic Union, counselled support for the Labour Party unless its candidates were hostile to catholic social and political principles. But the *Glasgow Observer* was less discreet even when the vitriolic pen of Charles Diamond was silenced on his death in 1934. As will be seen, it gave unconditional backing to the Franco side of the Spanish civil war; in neighbouring Portugal, Dr Salazar, a backward-looking intellectual, already installed in power, was hailed as the finest upholder of roman catholic principles in politics. His active propaganda machine stressed his fidelity to the church, his scholarly image, and quiet lifestyle so as to build up Salazar's reputation in other parts of catholic Europe by presenting a 'dictator with a difference' who had answers for many of the problems afflicting European society. The *Observer* swallowed this view even more readily than most press organs, conveniently ignoring the fact that Salazar's was a repressive police state where workers already meagre living standards were being pressed down in order that the corporative state and its rich backers could accumulate capital for their own narrow projects. Hence such lavish headlines as 'Up-to-date medievalism, Portugal's Progress under Catholic Social Principles unique in Europe, a reluctant and loved dictator, he has restored confidence in a badly demoralised people';[135] or even more fancifully: 'Portugal is the Workers Utopia, They get a Raw Deal in the USSR.'[136]

Occasionally the *Observer* emulated the far-Right by singling out the Jews for criticism in a quite indiscriminate manner. A not untypical example was: 'The Jew is an odious and unscrupulous exploiter . . . the most intolerant on earth and the least amenable to social discipline.'[137] This form of crude Jew-baiting eased considerably with Diamond's passing and, by the late 1930s, the *Observer* was carrying reports of anti-semitic persecution in Germany in an unfavourable light. The head-line that appeared in 1938—'Cardinal Hinsley's Tribute to the Jews, they have been generous to Catholics'—was indicative of the change of mood in response to the reports of persecution emanating from Germany.[138] Already, the Scottish catholic, Malcolm Hay (1881-1962) was embarking on valuable work of reconciliation between catholics and jews which had a resonance far beyond Scotland.[139]

Until the Second World War, the main catholic voice on social, political, and moral questions was the Catholic Union whose object was 'the protection and advancement of Catholic interests in the public sphere'.[140] The Catholic Union operated in most parishes under the patronage of the archbishop. A 1935 communication set out the power of the archbishop: 'the Union comes into activity only when a Roman Catholic interest or issue is at stake, and it is to be clearly understood that no interest or issue may be put forward as a Catholic issue or interest without the express and formal approval of the Diocesan Authority'.[141]

After the 1921 Irish settlement, the role of the Catholic Union had expanded beyond the original one of ensuring that catholic voters placed their names on the electoral register. The Catholic Union still fought the triennial education elections, but catholic adherence to the Labour Party, the emergence of Communism, and the growing tendency of government to legislate on social and moral questions of concern to catholics, turned it into a more broadly-based pressure group keen to influence catholic popular opinion and demonstrate its strength to outside agencies hoping to enlist catholic support whether at the polls or elsewhere. More than anybody else, Glasgow solicitor John J. Campbell (1900–63) transformed the role of the Catholic Union in the inter-war period. He came from one of the early immigrant families who had made a mark not just in its own community. He was the grandson of William Rodgers, the first catholic councillor in Scotland.[142] His father played for Celtic and three of his brothers belonged to the legal profession besides himself.

John Campbell became secretary of the Catholic Union in 1929 following the replacement of the Education Authority by a non-elected Education committee. Much of its previous role had been taken up with mobilising the vote for the education elections but, under his energetic leadership, the Catholic Union struck out in other directions. As will be seen shortly, the 1930s were the chief period when the Catholic Union sought to influence catholic voters and make the views of political representatives on matters of importance to catholics known, by publishing questionnaires with their replies in the catholic press on the even of local and national elections. The Catholic Union also kept watch on film entertainment and in 1938 was involved in persistent efforts to prevent an international Anti-God Congress being held in London by the League of Militant Atheists. A Catholic Inquiry Bureau was attached to the Catholic Union which, during the gathering depression of the 1930s, had the difficult task of organising aid for deserving cases in the form of social assistance and legal advice.[143]

1935 was a high-point in the activities of the Catholic Union. As well as drawing up questionnaires for candidates in the general election of that year, the branches in Glasgow campaigned up and down the country for the holding of a public enquiry into political conditions in Northern Ireland. Concern about the treatment of the 500,000 strong catholic minority at the hands of the Unionist government was heightened by the eruption of sectarian rioting in the summer of 1935. The communal violence had followed quickly on the heels of inflammatory speeches by Unionist leaders and members of the Orange Order. John Campbell then swung into action, making frequent trips to Northern Ireland to see conditions at first hand, and to London to try and persuade the government to abandon the convention that it could not interfere in the internal affairs of Northern Ireland, now that it had its own parliament of government. He had the full backing of the archbishop of Edinburgh in whose city sectarian disturbances had also erupted that summer, and of the archbishop of Glasgow who wrote to every member of the English hierarchy requesting their support.[144] The support of catholic MPs at Westminster, most of whom were English Tories, was judged to be crucial if the Baldwin government was to pay any heed. By early 1936, Campbell had come to the dismal conclusion that co-religionist Tories were not interested and that even sections of the religious press felt the plight of catholics in Northern Ireland to be a dead issue.[145]

Tory catholic MPs stayed away from a meeting that was organised on Campbell's behalf by James Maxton MP in the House of Commons during 1936, but Nancy Astor, the anti-catholic Tory MP for Plymouth Drake, turned up, using 'abusive language' and behaving in 'a most unladylike manner'.[146] The campaign ultimately fizzled out, Campbell having received far more practical help from left-wing Glasgow MPs like Jimmy Maxton, John McGovern, and Neil Maclean than from likelier sources.[147] McGovern dined at Campbell's home even though this truculent politician was a lapsed catholic who crossed words with the church in the 1930s and was frequently denounced by the *Glasgow Observer*, a paper that campaigned against him when he first stood in the Shettleston seat in the 1930 by-election that followed the death of John Wheatley.[148] Informal contacts like these belied the public hostility that often existed between stormy petrels of the left like McGovern and the Catholic Union and would have come as a great surprise to many ordinary catholics.

The Catholic Union also roused ordinary co-religionists to the dangers of the modern age. It campaigned against artificial birth control and the sterilisation of mental defectives, a pamphlet being prepared in 1933 opposing a bill to legalise voluntary sterilisation. The boarding out of orphaned catholic children to protestant homes or state orphanages was also a very sensitive issue in the 1930s and it was always looking out for any examples. Bitterly fought court cases where the church sought to have orphaned children, one of whose parents was a roman catholic, placed in the care of co-religionists, were not unknown.[149] A current Scottish bishop, as a child, found himself at the centre of one such tug-of-war and Archbishop Mackintosh always insisted that the Catholic Union must never relax its vigilance over the fate of catholic orphans.

This was one way of stemming 'the leakage', the loss of church members. The fact that the leakage was such a source of concern when the church was actually retaining the loyalty of most of its flock highlighted the deep feelings of insecurity that existed in catholic circles during the 1920s and 1930s. The triumphalist tone of religious pronouncements from lay and clerical figures was often an attempt to mask this insecurity. Dr McQuillan was less complacent than most and, in 1930, he claimed that the church was losing more members through the leakage than it was gaining by conversions, and he put the undoubted rise in overall church membership down to the high catholic birth-rate.[150] Marriage with a partner from outside the catholic religion was identified as the main cause of this leakage and one that led on to such evils as the use of artificial methods of birth control and the espousal of communism.[151] But, on the whole, the church was more successful in the west of Scotland than elsewhere in enforcing the *Ne Temere* decree of the Vatican which, in 1907 effectively condemned 'mixed marriages'. The social isolation of the catholic community in central Scotland induced by occupational, cultural, and religious factors which kept it apart from the majority of Scots down to the 1960s, ensured that endogamy (marriage within the tribe) remained the absolute norm for years to come. But the church was not taking any chances: it would be decades before any priest even contemplated officiating at a wedding where one of the partners was a non-catholic who was not being received into the church. Any other tendency that might lead impressionably young catholics into dangerous paths was discouraged. In 1936, the *Observer* complied with a request from Archbishop Mackintosh that it should stop carrying cinema adverts, even though it was priests who were among the best patrons of the cinema hall.[152] A year earlier, the paper had carried a series on the best way to go about 'Courting' so as young catholics were not led astray.

Mixed marriage was the theme of 'Strong Wind', a play written by Fr Herbert Rogers (1903–73) under the pseudonym George Hyde. Possessing Scottish Nationalist sympathies, he was associated with the cultural revival of the 1930s and he drew inspiration for much of his writing from his own community. Ill-health forced him to move to California in 1949 but, his obituarist recalls that to him, 'Glasgow roman catholics were always a unique breed, witty, warm-hearted, pugnacious, intelligent, politically self-opinionated and that . . . Fr Herbert loved their ways'.[153]

However, their high-spiritedness went hand in hand with an essential religious deference and feeling of social isolation that may have impeded the emergence of promising writers confident enough to frankly depict life in their own community. Rather optimistically Christopher Murray Grieve (Hugh McDiarmid) thought that the blending of the romantic and visionary Irish with the materialist and logical Scots on Clydeside might knock some life into the sluggish literary scene in the west of Scotland. In 1926, he proclaimed that 'the so-called "Irish invasion" of Scotland' wad 'destined . . . to be the best thing that happened to it [Scotland] for over 200 years at least . . .'[154]

Few other Scottish nationalists of the day could find it in themselves to be as confident about the presence of the Clydeside Irish. However, there was previous little interaction between the two communities living in uneasy proximity for budding writers from either of them to be granted the perspective that would have enabled them to convey the realities of Glasgow life in fictional form. Frank examination of the city's communal divisions was for so long a taboo subject that most of the city's novelists (though not all of its poets) preferred to place them outside their work or only refer to them tangentially.

The most accomplished writer to depict the hardship and uncertainty of the immigrant community was the Donegal-born Patrick MacGill (1891–1963). Known as the 'navvy poet', his books portrayed not the second and third generation Scoto-Irish but the lives of the migrant workers who came to Scotland as 'tattie-hawkers' (potato gatherers) or building labourers until well into this century. A socialist early in his life, MacGill gave voice to the half-literate and sorely exploited fellow countrymen who took the 'Derry boat' to the west of Scotland, without lapsing into propaganda.[155] The autobiographical *Children of the Dead End* is an outstanding social document which charts the author's own early years. Dermid Flynn is sent off to the hiring fare at Strabane by parents ground down by the priest's tax and the landlord's rent. After brutalising farm work, he migrates to Scotland with the potato squad and becomes an itinerant navvy. Incidents involving sudden, violent death are recalled with chilling realism. Somehow Dermid develops a strong interest in literature and politics. He organises an unsuccessful strike and, disillusioned with the fear and apathy of his fellow workers, he moves to London where he pursued a brief career in journalism before returning to Glasgow where he discovers his childhood sweetheart in the most appalling circumstances.

The Rat-Pit is the sequel which traces the life of Norah Ryan, an unsophisticated Donegal girl who emigrates to Scotland after the death of her father in a fishing accident. There she has an illegitimate child fathered by a Scots farmer's son who spurs her. Unable to return to her own people, she is plunged into a nightmare existence in the hovels of Glasgow. Circumstances force her to stay at the Rat-Pit, a lodging house for destitute women, where drunkenness, brawling, and obscenity are normal behaviour. Near starvation and fearing for the life of her sick child, Norah is reduced to the ultimate degradation—prostitution— before being attacked by a gang of hooligans and left to die.[156]

Interest was briefly shown in the condition of the Irish 'tattie hawkers' following a fire in a Kirkintilloch 'bothy' (hut) which claimed the lives of ten of them on 16 September 1937. Soon after *The*

Glasgow Herald declared that the incident justified ending 'the importing of casual labour from beyond the North Channel'. Scottish workers, it said, would be less likely than friendless strangers from a land whose standards of comfort are lower than ours to accept unsuitable housing conditions'.[157]

An inquiry found that there was insufficient evidence to decide the cause of the fire but, many years later in 1982, the authorities began a new investigation when an elderly woman involved in a marital dispute passed on information that the fire was not accidental, but no action was taken by the Procurator Fiscal.[158] Apparently even these seasonal labourers living in remote agricultural districts were not able to escape the sectarian fury which badly affected urban Scotland in the 1930s.

Peadar O'Donnell, the Irish novelist and champion of the downtrodden peasant campaigned for an improvement in the conditions of the 'tattie hawkers' and he was appointed to a commission that the de Valera government appointed to see how their lot might be bettered.[159] Several Scottish-based priests took an interest in their welfare but in the past the church had failed to develop a mobile mission for itinerant workers, whether it be the labouring navvy or the potato pickers.[160] In *Moleskin Joe*, another of MacGill's powerful social novels, he describes a dedicated priest, Fr Nolan who follows his migrant flock round the country and is the antithesis of the grasping clergy who come in for even harsher criticism than the Scottish Presbyterian farmers for taking advantage of the workers' poverty and ignorance. An Irish bishop sought to prevent the publication of *The Rat-Pit* and MacGill's books passed most people by in Scotland until a revival of interest in the 1980s saw the best of them reissued in paperback.[161]

The suffering and exploitation which MacGill's grimy realistic novels described had encouraged the formation of the Catholic Socialist Society in 1906. Once it was absorbed into the Labour Party during the 1920s, the field was clear for the church itself to, cautiously at first, give a lead in mobilising those members of the flock, with strong social consciences who felt that more than charity was required to alleviate the misery of the times. In 1923 Dr P. J. Flood, a dynamic Coatbridge-born priest was appointed diocesan director of social studies and social action. From his base in the busy east end parish of the Sacred Heart, Bridgeton, he broke new ground by mobilising catholics who shared his social concern and by working alongside them in a democratic manner, oblivious of his priestly rank.[162] Dr Flood was a fine speaker but, his obituary notice in the Catholic Directory for Scotland enigmatically stated that, in 1929, 'his superiors felt that his health was being overtaxed trying to carry out the duties of a curate in a busy city mission, in addition to his work for the Arch-diocese, and he was transferred to the chaplaincy of Dalbeth'.[163] Later, he became chaplain to the Eric Gill community at High Wycombe before emigrating to Australia where he was secretary to Archbishop Mannix of Melbourne.

Too often, the effectiveness or even survival of lay catholic move-ments with a social or political purpose depended on a single driving force, such as Dr Flood or John J. Campbell of the Catholic Union. There also tended to be a good deal of overlap between groups like the Catholic Social Guild, the Distributists, the Catholic Union and, in the 1940s, the Catholic Workers Guild. The Catholic Social Guild had received an impetus from the setting up of a Catholic Workers College at Oxford in 1921. Its director, Fr Leo O'Hea was a popular speaker in Glasgow, where Frank Callaghan, a former member of the Catholic Socialist Society built up the CSG. However, its impact on the political behaviour and outlook of catholic workers was a faint one. Activists immersed themselves in catholic social teaching but often they 'were more interested in study for study's sake rather than as preparation for action'.[164] A catholic publication in the 1950s frankly exposed its weakness:

> The great difficulty of the young movement was to recruit into its ranks genuine horny-handed workers. The hot-heads and wild men of the working-class movement had had too long a lead with their doctrine of class hatred and their facile panacea of socialisation of everything within reason.[165]

Arguably more successful were the vocational guilds formed among catholic workers and professional men and women so that they could retain a catholic outlook in their work environment. Medical guilds among doctors and later nurses started to be formed before the First World War. Numerically, the largest guild was the Don Bosco Guild of Catholic Teachers formed in the 1930s. The guild movement also spread to manual workers in this decade thanks to the work of the religious orders, particularly the Jesuits and the Franciscans; Fr William d'Andria (1895–1977), a Jesuit who was science master at St Aloysius College, Glasgow, helped to set up the Transport Workers Guild in 1931 and would be an influential force in the catholic social movement for years to come.[166] Guilds were next formed among railwaymen, postal workers, and the police and, by the 1950s, miners, tele-communication workers, and catholic social workers had entered the guild movement, which was more advanced in Glasgow than anywhere else in the world.[167]

The spread of the guild movement meant that catholics in the workplace had a source other than their trade unions through which to debate and view industrial problems. Guilds were never in a position to supplant trade unions but they gave the church a base from which to combat communist influence in the workplace. Each guild had a chaplain, frequently a member of one of the religious orders. Without them, lay activists operating in these sensitive areas would not have received much clerical backing and might have encountered unexpected obstacles. Senior parish clergy could often be apathetic or even hostile to the catholic social movement because its religious character was not always apparent to them. Some were reluctant to see dedicated members of the laity become too assertive in case it brought their own role into question: the most appropriate model for the mobilisation of the laity was 'Catholic Action', which was centralised, Rome-inspired and hierarchically-controlled. The various lay movements active between the wars were frequently grouped under this title; Catholic Action was, by definition, lay participation in the hierarchy's work under the hierarchy's control.[168]

Scotland, and the rest of Britain, lacked the infrastructure—such as a catholic daily paper, or university, political party and trade union— that could have provided the inspiration for Catholic Action. But it was possible to achieve a surprising amount even in localities where catholics comprised a small minority of the population. The city of Edinburgh, where roman catholics made up less than 10% of the population, illustrated this point in the 1930s and 1940s. Here a bid was made to relate catholic principles to modern society and both laymen and priests were given more autonomy to organise a catholic social move-ment than elsewhere in Scotland. It is probably no coincidence that the Hibernian tradition, with its emphasis on devotional catholicism, was relatively weak and that between 1929 and 1950 a member of a religious order was Archbishop of St Andrews and Edinburgh. Andrew Joseph McDonald (1871-1950), former head abbot of the Benedictine monastery at Fort Augustus is now widely recognised as having been perhaps the most dynamic and outward-looking member of the catholic hierarchy in twentieth century Scotland. At a time when many in the church distrusted universities and the intelligentsia, he sent some of the most promising younger clergy to universities in England and abroad. There they studied sociology and other liberal arts subjects that might equip them for new responsibilities the church needed to face up to in a rapidly changing age.[169] Walter Glancy (1914-80) and the Irishman Patrick Quill (1914-84) were two priests who put some of his ideals into effect locally in the educational and social spheres after time at Cambridge.[170] He also placed the Dominicans in charge of the newly-opened Catholic Chaplaincy at Edinburgh University in 1931. One of their converts was a student, Anthony Ross, who entered the Dominican Order and, in the post-war years, became a public figure in Scotland, outspoken about social injustice, and an inspiration for many young people inside and outside the church, the students of Edinburgh University electing him as their rector in 1980.

In the 1930s Archbishop McDonald grew increasingly concerned about the rise of communism and he issued a whole series of episcopal homilies on the subject, warning of the implications for the future of mankind if this materialist and 'godless' social system gained a firm hold. He layed great store on prayer but, to counter communism, he felt that prayer and vigilance were not sufficient. Nor was there much point in blindly defending everything that communists condemned, because it had to be acknowledged that they rightly highlighted economic and social evils that could not be excused by any aware catholic. McDonald insisted that a just social order had to be promoted in order to undercut the appeal of communism among the poor and downtrodden. He was influenced by John Barry, a factory-owner in Leith who made a genuine attempt to implement papal social teaching by providing holidays with pay, regular bonuses, and good working conditions for his employees.[171]

Archbishop McDonald was a gregarious prelate and spellbinding orator: 'he really had a fantastic delivery, he could easily speak at 200 words a minute, and was the only man who could beat the shorthand writer of a newspaper'.[172] An informal man, he did not stand on ceremony and was no respecter of rank as Frank Sheed, the catholic publisher and lay activist recalled in his book *The Church and I*:

> I report from memory a conversation Archbishop McDonald had with Pope Pius XII. It went something like this:
>
> *Archbishop.* Would Your Holiness not agree that English-speaking Catholics are among the most devoted supporters of the papacy?
> *Pope.* Yes indeed.
> *Archbishop.* Would Your Holiness not also agree that the friendship of the English-speaking nations is of tremendous value to the church?
> *Pope.* Certainly.
> *Archbishop.* Then does not Your Holiness find it strange that no member of the Curia can speak English?
>
> There never was a man in high position so incapable of not saying anything he thought.[173]

Another layman recalled Archbishop McDonald to have been 'fearless' and a 'bonny fechter',[174] attributes which he needed in full when, in the middle of the 1930s, the eruption of anti-catholic violence in Edinburgh showed that the church's traditional opponents could still be as menacing as new dangers.

The resurgence of the 'No Popery' cry encouraged catholics to close ranks and many were reluctant to venture too far beyond the confines of their own community. Paradoxically, the church may have drawn some reassurance from the re-emergence of an old opponent since the threat it posed to the security of catholics encouraged many to defer to its priests as authority figures. The relegation of the Irish question also boosted clerical influence which was seen in the growth of the Catholic Union during the 1920s; as did the 1918 Education Act. This was a social breakthrough which helped emancipate growing numbers of catholics from permanent immersion in the unskilled working-class. For the first time, it gave the catholic community a multi-class character. It was an advance jealously defended by the church which, in the inter-war years, managed to obtain near unanimous endorsement from its members for the catholic schools system. With religious critics awaiting their opportunity to overturn the 1918 Act, doubt or even debate about the wisdom of separate education was viewed as disloyalty, if not outright heresy, by embattled catholics. The new education settlement underscored the separateness of the catholic community while giving its clerical and lay leaders more time to focus their energy on other areas of community life. The emergence or revival of a wide range of catholic bodies with charitable, political, social, or devotional aims sharpened the identity of catholics as a distinct grouping, but the restraints placed on 'Catholic Action' by the church, allied to its own hierarchical character, prevented most of these groups fulfilling their promise; as did the absence of a cultural infrastructure encompassing a catholic daily paper, a political party, or a catholic university, all of which the community was too poor to provide.

Taking community relations as a yardstick, this was fortunate. If the retention of catholic schools within the state system had been accompanied by a wide range of voluntary initiatives that deepened the introspection of the community, it could have produced an even more hostile response from those protestant Scots still unwilling to accept catholics as fellow citizens even with the Irish question in cold storage. As it was, Scotland was fortunate that the delicate web of community relations was not rent asunder in the inter-war years. The timing of the 1918 Education Act when the country was preoccupied with the outcome of the First World War, may have prevented an immediate backlash occurring. The fact that much of the fighting in the Irish war of independence and civil war occurred in the south of the island was also fortunate in this respect.

World war, the relegation of the Irish question, and the rise of the Labour and Communist parties subtly altered the character and broadened the horizons of the immigrant community. They also made the majority much more aware of its presence than before. This did not necessarily lead to greater mutual respect. But opportunities for co-operation did arise even in the depression-ridden 1920s. The least insular sections of both communities were able to co-operate in struggling against the hardships and injustices of an economic system whose harsh effects were not respecters of religious difference.

Thanks to the swift removal of Ireland from the political agenda, the transfer of political loyalties from the Home Rule movement to the Labour Party was more painless than it might otherwise have been. Identification with the party that after the general election of 1922 was bidding to be the largest one in Scotland, reduced catholic isolation and made the community more open, and less prone to clerical domination. In chapter five, the triangular relationship between the left, the catholic voters, and a resurgent church will be more fully assessed. It was a complex and surprising one that defies easy generalisation. In most other European countries possessing an active socialist movement and a vigorous church, the two forces were locked in bitter conflict. As will be seen, Scotland's religious tensions and widespread catholic support for a programme of reform, helped offset friction on the lines of class versus creed. The Spanish civil war would show that Scotland was not immune from such tensions. But domestic pre-occupations sometimes amounting to a grim battle for survival, absorbed the attention of a community in transition that was far from sure about its ultimate destination.

Notes

1 Cooney, *Scotland and the Papacy*, p. 17.
2 Michael Maguire, 'Charles Diamond reappraised', *Irish Post*, 7 May 1983.
3 Ian Wood, 'John Wheatley, the Irish, and the labour movement in Scotland', *Innes Review*, 31, 2, 1980, p. 80.
4 *Scottish Catholic Observer*, 19 April 1985.
5 *GO*, 29 April 1916.
6 *GO*, 16 May 1916.
7 *GO*, 6 February 1915.
8 McShane and Smith, *No Mean Fighter*, p. 100.
9 *Forward*, 4 September 1918.
10 Nan Milton, *John Maclean*, Pluto Press, London 1973, p. 129.
11 Keith Harding, *The Irish Issue in the British Labour Movement, 1900-1922*, Ph.D. thesis, University of Sussex, 1984, p. 219.
12 Wood, *Innes Review*, p. 80.
13 John Paton, *Proletarian Pilgrimage*, p. 210.
14 Harding, p. 248.

15 Harding, p. 243.
16 *GO*, 27 September 1919.
17 *GO*, 7 December 1918.
18 McShane and Smith, p. 117; Milton, p. 239.
19 James Hunter, 'The Gaelic connection...', p. 6.
20 Walter Kendal, *The Revolutionary Movement in Britain, 1900-21, the Origins of British Communism*, Weidenfeld & Nicolson 1969, p. 290.
21 Handley, *The Irish in Modern Scotland*, p. 298.
22 Michael Collins Papers, University College Dublin Archives, P7/1/11, quoted by Harding, p. 241.
23 Scottish Record Office (SRO), HH/31/ 34, Procurator Fiscal's Report, Glasgow, with reference to Scottish Office file No. 25478/Q/ 92: 'Hostile Propaganda— "Proposed Irish Massacre"', 3 September 1920.
24 SRO, HH/55/68, William Duncan, chief constable of Paisley, to Secretary of State for Scotland, 10

July 1922.

25 Harding, Ph.D., p. 241, quoting Cabinet paper dated 20 May 1920 in the Public Record Office under PRO, CAB/24/ 106.

26 *Scottish Catholic Observer*, 24 October 1969.

27 Handley, p. 299.

28 Handley, p. 299.

29 SRO, HH/55/62, Part 30033/8, Chief Constable of Lanarkshire to the Scottish Office, 9 December 1920.

30 SRO, HH/31/34, 'Police Reports of Political Meetings 1918-   ', Part 25478A/ 79, Report by Procurator Fiscal, Glasgow, 3 September 1920.

31 Report of the General Secretary, third Annual Conference of the Irish Self-determination League, 11 April 1922, copy in the Art O'Brien papers, National Library of Ireland, Dublin.

32 *GH*, 5 May 1921.

33 Canning, *Irish-born Secular Priests*, pp. 272-6.

34 See SRO, HH/55/71.

35 John Burrowes, *Benny Lynch, the Life and Times of a Fighting Legend*, Mainstream, Edinburgh, 1983, p. 63.

36 Tom Gallagher, 'Charles Diamond, 1885-1934, Labour politician and newspaper director', *Dictionary of Labour Biography*, VIII, Macmillan, London, forthcoming; see also Owen Dudley Edwards, 'The Catholic press in Scotland since the restoration of the hierarchy', in McRoberts (ed.), *Modern Scottish Catholicism*, pp. 175-6.

37 Gallagher, 'Charles Diamond'.

38 Interview with William Murphy (Catholic journalist): Glasgow, 13 May 1982.

39 Christopher Hollis, *The Mind of Chesterton*, Hollis & Carter, London, 1972, p. 172.

40 *Catholic Herald*, 2 April 1921.

41 Niall Brennan, *Dr Mannix*, Angus & Robertson, London, 1965, p. 200.

42 Brennan, p. 203.

43 Eoin Kiernan, *Daniel Mannix and Ireland*, Gill & Macmillan, Dublin, 1984, p. 164; see also William Walker, 'Dundee's disenchantment with Churchill: a comment on the

fall of the Liberal Party', *Scottish Historical Review*, 49, 1, 1970.

44 Kevin O'Connor, *The Irish in Britain*, Torc, Dublin, 1970, pp. 141-2.

45 See Michael O'Riordan, *The Connolly Column*, New Books, Dublin, 1979, p. 28; and William Knox, 'William Gallagher' (*sic*), in W. Knox (ed.), *Scottish Labour Leaders 1918-39*, Mainstream, Edinburgh, 1984, p. 117.

46 SRO, HH/55/72, John Carmichael, Chief Constable of Dundee, to Scotland Yard, 5 May 1922.

47 Ernest O'Malley Papers, P17a/ 182, University College, Dublin: they contain vital information about the operations of the Republican movement in Glasgow during the civil war.

48 McPeake's role in the death of Michael Collins has been treated with suspicion because shortly afterwards he deserted to the Republicans, taking with him the armoured car in which he had chauffered the Republican leader. See Marjory Forester, *Michael Collins, the Lost Leader*, Sidgwick & Jackson, London, 1971, p. 338.

49 In the civil war IRA units were habitually termed 'murder squads' by the Free State side.

50 O'Malley papers, P17a/182, pp. 6-7.

51 SRO, HH/55/71, '1923-24 Irish disturbances'.

52 *GH*, 2 October 1923; see also SRO, HH/55/71.

53 *GO*, 14 January 1922.

54 *Catholic Herald*, 23 September 1922.

55 Report of 1922 ISDL conference in Art O'Brien papers; see also *Catholic Herald*, 14 June 1923, 9 May 1925.

56 Maguire, *Irish Post*, 7 May 1983.

57 Obituary of Denis Brogan, *GO*, 27 January 1934.

58 Brian A. Reynolds, *The Formation and Development of Fianna Fail*, Trinity College Dublin, 1976, pp. 422-3.

59 Tom Gallagher, 'How the cumann kept going in Glasgow', *Irish Press*, 7 March 1983.

60 *Forward*, 29 October 1921.

61 *Motherwell Times*, 14 December 1923, for Ferguson's biographical details; *Hansard*, 15 April 1924.

62 *GO*, 4 January 1919.

63 Bill Murray, *The Old Firm*, pp. 84-5.

64 Christopher Harvie, *No Gods and Precious Few Heroes, Scotland 1914-80*, Edward Arnold, London, 1981, p. 100.

65 The ethnic dimension after 1918 is examined in R. Baxter, *The Liverpool Labour Party, 1918-63*, Ph.D., 2 vols, Queen's College, Oxford, 1969.

66 See A. Shallice, 'Liverpool labourism and Irish nationalism in the 1920s and 1930s', *North West Labour History Society Bulletin*, 8, 1982-83.

67 Iain McLean, *The Legend of Red Clydeside*, John Donald, Edinburgh, 1983, p. 182.

68 See Knox, *Scottish Labour Leaders*, pp. 22-6.

69 Obituary of Thomas O'Hare, *GO*, 22 February 1952.

70 *GH*, 7 November 1923; *GH*, 3 November 1926; *GH*, 6 November 1929. Obituary of James McGuire, *GO*, 17 April 1937.

71 *GH*, 27 October 1921.

72 McLean, *Legend of Red Clydeside*, p. 185.

73 John McKee, 'Catholics and education', *Scottish Catholic Observer*, 10 March 1978. For the 1918 Act see also James Treble, 'The development of Roman Catholic education in Scotland, 1878-1978', in McRoberts (ed.), *Modern Scottish Catholicism*, pp. 111-39.

74 Cooney, *Scotland and the Papacy*, p. 87.

75 *Scottish Catholic Observer*, 24 January 1969; Cooney, *Scotland and the Papacy*, p. 87.

76 For the Catholic Social Guild see Ruth Butterworth, *The Structure of some Catholic Lay Organisations in Australia and Great Britain: a Comparative Study*, Ph.D., Oxford University, 1959, pp. 234-41; and Mary Vivian Brand, *The Social Catholic Movement in England, 1920-1955*, Ph.D., St Louis University, 1963, pp. 95-113.

77 *GO*, 3 May 1919.

78 *GO*, 11 January 1919.

79 For T. P. O'Connor and the Irish in Britain after 1918 see L. W. Brady, *T. P. O'Connor and the Liverpool Irish*, Royal Historical Society, London, 1983, pp. 250-3; also F. S. L. Lyons, *John Dillon*, Routledge, London, 1968, pp. 473-5.

80 *GO*, 6 November 1920.

81 *GO*, 18 January 1919.

82 *GO*, 12 April 1919.

83 'Socialism on the Clyde', *Times*, 28 December 1922.

84 McLean, *Legend of Red Clydeside*, pp. 185-6.

85 *GO*, 11 November 1922.

86 Henry Pelling, *The British Communist Party: a Historical Profile*, Black, London, 1958, p. 16.

87 Interview with Harry McShane, Glasgow, 27 April 1982.

88 Interview with Harry McShane.

89 *Irish Weekly* (Glasgow edition), 31 March 1951.

90 For the communist presence in Scottish industrial communities with a significant catholic presence, see Stewart McIntyre, *Little Moscows, Communism and Working Class Militancy in Inter-war Britain*, Croom Helm, London, 1980, p. 161.

91 See Susan McGhee, *Monsignor Taylor of Carfin*, John Burns, Glasgow, 1972.

92 The Carfin phenomenon elicited mixed views from Scottish commentators. For a sceptical account tinged with sarcasm see George Malcolm Thomson, *The Rediscovery of Scotland*, Routledge, London, 1928, pp. 53-61. The writer and critic Edwin Muir was more favourably impressed in his *Scottish Journey*, Mainstream, Edinburgh, 1979 (first published 1935), pp. 176-7.

93 Susan McGhee, 'Carfin and the Roman Catholic Relief Act of 1926', *Innes Review*, 16, 1, 1965, pp. 56-78.

94 The Edinburgh riots of 1935 are the subject of chapter three of my *Edinburgh Divided: John Cormack, No Popery, and Protestant Action in the 1930s*, forthcoming.

95 Cooney, *Scotland and the Papacy*,

p. 89.

96 Patrick Buckland, *A History of Northern Ireland*, Gill & Macmillan, Dublin, 1980, p. 67.

97 *Glasgow Observer*, 26 September 1969; for a history of the Knights in Ireland and elsewhere see Evelyn Bolster, *The Knights of St Columbanus*, Gill & Macmillan, Dublin, 1979.

98 John Lynch, 'Catholic lay societies, 1878–1956', in *Scottish Catholic Herald and Glasgow Observer, Scottish Survey, 1878–1956*, p. xxi.

99 Obituary of Canon Joseph Daniel (1897–1981), *CDS*, 1982.

100 Information from retired teacher who has taught in both state sectors.

101 *Universe*, 2 June 1939.

102 *GO*, 22 January 1938.

103 Interview with J. McLay, Glasgow, December 1983.

104 *GO*, 24 October 1925, 30 February 1926.

105 Rennie McOwen, 'Press reaches milestone on a "pilgrim journey" ', *Scotsman*, 18 April 1985. To its credit, the *Scottish Catholic Observer*, successor to the *Glasgow Observer*, also carried these items in its centenary issue, which appeared on 19 April 1985.

106 See David McRoberts, 'John S. Burns & Sons, 1926–76', *CDS*, 1976, Burns, Glasgow, 1976.

107 Information from James Darragh.

108 Information from several catholic sources.

109 Interview with William Murphy.

110 Cooney, *Scotland and the Papacy*, p. 90.

111 'Obituary of Archbishop Donald Mackintosh, 1877–1943', *CDS*, 1944, Burns, Glasgow, 1944.

112 Information from a private source.

113 Interview with Dr Patrick Connolly.

114 Obituary of A. J. Cronin, *Times*, 10 January 1981.

115 McCaffrey, 'Roman Catholicism in Scotland', p. 298.

116 McCaffrey, 'Roman Catholicism in Scotland', pp. 297–8.

117 James Darragh, 'James Edmund Handley, 1900–1971', *Innes Review*, 22, 1, 1971. Also relevant is the obituary by the same author carried in *The Tablet*, 13 February

1971.

118 Interview with William Murphy.

119 Ian O. Bayne, 'A university institution with its own proud record', *Scottish Catholic Observer*, 9 May 1980.

120 Ian Cameron, *GH*, 10 May 1985.

121 See Compton Mackenzie, *Catholicism and Scotland*, pp. 186–7.

122 See Alice Ivy Hay, *Valiant for Truth, Malcolm Hay of Seaton*, Neville Spearman, London, 1971, p. 95.

123 The story of the Glasgow University Distributist Club is related by Ian O. Bayne (see note 119).

124 R. P. Walsh, 'Distributism', *New Catholic Encyclopedia*, IV, McGraw-Hill, New York, 1967, p. 912.

125 Walsh, 'Distributism'.

126 *Land for the People*, July 1930 (a full run of the journal is in the British Library).

127 *Land for the People*, July 1930.

128 *Land for the People*, July 1930.

129 *Land for the People*, April 1931.

130 Obituary of Monsignor John McQuillan (1889–1971), *CDS*, 1971; see also the obituary of the Irish priest who wound up the scheme, Canon Edward Molumby (1902–82), *CDS*, 1983.

131 He was invited to submit an article on 'the Scoto-Irish' which appeared in the *Scots Observer* on 12 December 1927. The *Scots Observer* praised John McQuillan's Land Scheme plans on 1 June 1929.

132 *Land for the People*, October 1933.

133 *Land for the People*, March 1935.

134 *GO*, 29 September 1923.

135 *GO*, 26 June 1937.

136 *GO*, 12 March 1938.

137 Maguire, 'Charles Diamond reappriased', *Irish Post*, 7 May 1983.

138 *GO*, 23 December 1938.

139 See A. I. Hay, *Malcolm Hay of Seaton*.

140 *GO*, 18 September 1937.

141 John J. Campbell to P. J. Mallen, 30 October 1935, in the Catholic Union file (uncatalogued), Glasgow Archdiocesan Archives. (Hereafter referred to as GAA.)

142 *GO*, 20 September 1963.

143 *GO*, 20 September 1963. Details of the Catholic Union's social work

and of its bid to get the Anti-God Congress banned can be found in the Catholic Union files of the GAA.

144 John J. Campbell to Daniel Mageean, Bishop of Down and Connor, Catholic Union file, GAA.

145 John J. Campbell to Bishop Mageean, 11 December 1935, and to Archbishop McDonald of St Andrews and Edinburgh, 13 February 1936, Catholic Union files, GAA.

146 John J. Campbell to William O'Keefe, Plymouth, 8 July 1936, Catholic Union files, GAA.

147 John J. Campbell warmly thanked Maxton for his assistance, in a letter of 28 February 1936, Catholic Union files, GAA.

148 John J. Campbell to John McGovern, Catholic Union files, GAA.

149 The correspondence relating to specific court cases can be found in the Catholic Union files, GAA.

150 John McQuillan, 'The leakage', St Peter's College Magazine, 14, 54, 1940.

151 Land for the People, July 1930.

152 Interview with William Murphy.

153 Obituary of Father Herbert Rogers (1903–73), CDS, 1973.

154 C. M. Grieve (Hugh McDiarmid), Contemporary Scottish Studies, Leonard Parsons, London, 1926, p. 10.

155 Robert Greacen, 'Taking the Derry boat: Patrick MacGill, novelist, an appreciation', Eire-Ireland, 16, 1, 1981, p. 96; see also Patrick Reilly, 'Catholics and Scottish literature, 1878-1978', in McRoberts, Modern Scottish Catholicism, pp. 185-8.

156 Dave Barnes, 'The navvy's tale', New Socialist, July–August 1984.

157 GH, 19 October 1937.

158 James Freeman, 'Mystery case of Irish potato pickers reopened', GH, 30 November 1982.

159 See Michael McInerney, Peadar O'Donnell, Irish social rebel, Gill & Macmillan, Dublin, 1973.

160 For a history of itinerant Irish labourers see James E. Handley, The Irish Navvy, Cork University Press, 1970.

161 For church hostility towards McGill's work see Ray Burke, 'In Big Brother's shadow', Irish Post, 9 May 1984. See also Ray Burke, 'Patrick MacGill revived', Irish Post, 19 November 1983. Here it was revealed that Caliban Books, in association with Brandon Press, Kerry, were preparing to reissue all twenty-three of MacGill's books. By 1984 Children of the Dead End, The Rat Pit, Moleskin Joe, Lanty Hanlon and Glenmornan had already appeared.

162 Information about Dr P. J. Flood was provided by Dr John Durkan and Mr James Darragh.

163 Obituary of Dr P. J. Flood, CDS, 1966.

164 Private view of a roman catholic layman.

165 John Lynch, 'Catholic lay societies 1878-1956', Scottish Survey, Scottish Catholic Herald and Glasgow Observer, 1878-1956.

166 Information about Fr d'Andria was kindly provided by James Darragh. His obituary in the St Aloysius College Magazine, No. 91, June 1978, was also useful.

167 Lynch, 'Catholic lay societies'.

168 Adrian Hastings, 'Some reflexion of English Catholicism of the late 1930s', in A. Hastings (ed.), Bishops and Writers, Aspects of the Evolution of Modern English Catholicism, Anthony Clark, Wheathampstead, 1977, p. 114.

169 Interview with Fr Anthony Ross, O.P., December 1981. For McDonald's work as archbishop, see also his obituary in CDS, 1951, and W. P. Crampton, 'The archdiocese of St Andrews and Edinburgh', Scottish Survey, Scottish Catholic Herald and Glasgow Observer, 1878-1956.

170 For Monsignor Quill, see his obituary in CDS, 1985. For Fr Walter Glancy, besides there is also an interesting article commemorating his forty years in the priesthood that appeared in the Scottish Catholic Observer on 7 July 1978.

171 Centenary Brochure of John Barry & Sons, Mackenzie & Storrie, Leith 1951.

172 Interview with William Murphy.

173 Frank Sheed, *The Church and I*,
    Sheed & Ward, London, 1974, p.
    181.
174 Interview with William Murphy.

Chapter 4 'The Scottish lion and the Irish bull will not lie down together'

In 1917 the *Glasgow Observer* cheerfully recommended that a retired Perthshire bailie who had unsuccessfully opposed the nomination of the roman catholic Colonel Stirling as the Unionist candidate for West Perthshire 'should be photographed immediately for a museum of antiquity . . . His isolation and failure are evidence of progress.'[1] However, its confidence was completely misplaced as shown by Stirling's defeat in 1918 in what normally was a safe Tory seat.

In fact, hostility to the catholic or Irish presence (and the two terms were interchangeable in describing a population that was now mainly Scottish-born) mounted as Scotland entered the post-war era in a depressed and troubled state. The low morale of Scottish public opinion and of the various institutions and pressure groups which gave it a lead, was due to a variety of factors coinciding: the disproportionately high casualty rate of the Scots in the First World War who had flocked to the colours in greater numbers than people anywhere else in the United Kingdom;[2] the crisis of Scottish heavy industry upon which rested the local economy, that was triggered off by the post-war fall in demand for ships, engineering products and coal, but was made worse in Scotland by the failure of conservatively-minded industrialists to diversify into other areas; and the conversion of much of the working-class to parliamentary and even extra-parliamentary forms of socialism which, in their different ways, were seen to pose a threat to the security and cohesion of Scottish and British society.

As Scotland moved from being almost a co-partner in the British Empire to being an internally divided and increasingly peripheral part of the United Kingdom which had recently shed the troublesome sister isle of Ireland, the mood of sections of the middle-class grew disgruntled and bitter. This spelt trouble for a marginal and unassimilated minority like the Irish in Scotland whose presence 'is regarded with little favour even by enlightened Scottish opinion', the words of a jaundiced nationalist spokesman as late as 1950.[3] They were an undoubted exaggeration then, but much less so in the 1920s. Throughout the inter-war period, even neutral commentators described a community that had been predominantly Scottish-born by the 1890s as 'the Irish' in Scotland, a telling indication that they were regarded almost as strangers in their midst. As Scottish opinion grew more restless and uneasy about the condition of the country and its future prospects, they began to be viewed not just as strangers but as unwelcome intruders.

Vocal elements not without influence in the political parties, the protestant churches and, to a lesser extent in the professions and the business world, viewed them as interlopers who had transformed some of the most densely populated areas of industrial Scotland into alien enclaves and who, by withholding loyalty to their adopted country and scorning its educational and popular institutions, had contributed in no small measure to its malaise.

In the confident atmosphere before the war, when the Scottish economy was in a buoyant state and national prospects seemed un-dimmed, the Irish community was generally ignored by institutions and individuals who later spoke out about its presence, even though it afforded far more examples of being a submerged alien enclave. Scots then looked outwards to the empire and to London where they were influential in politics, journalism and many of the other professions. As they grew more introspective in the aftermath of a disastrous war which had taken its toll of Scottish menfolk and had blighted the prospects of a distinct economic unit that needed to trade to survive, their horizons shrank and many became far more sharply aware of the Irish presence. Statements and developments emanating from the catholic Irish community which, in the past, would have been overlooked by a confident bourgeoisie, elicited a forthright response in a new and unhappier age.

The new highly-charged atmosphere helps explain the violent reaction to a speech made at the end of 1921 by John Phillimore, the catholic convert and professor of Greek at Glasgow University when he delivered a prize-giving address at St Aloysius Academy. He told the audience, made up of catholic pupils, some of whom were bound for higher education, that the universities were open to capture and that education could be used as a means of converting Scotland to roman catholicism. The universities were undefended citadels which would shortly face the missionary energy of the greatest missionary race on earth.[4]

Protestant opinion viewed the speech as an 'insidious plan to infiltrate the universities and turn them into Catholic institutions'.[5] With elections for the Glasgow Education Authority due in April 1922 the protestant church mobilised its members as it had never done

before. The turnout leaped from 27% to almost 60% of the electorate
and catholics lost nearly half their seats on the authority. *The Glasgow
Herald* was to the fore in sounding the alarm and it was berated by the
Observer for 'dropping the quiet grandmotherly dignity which usually
attended its attitude on public matters' and doing 'its utmost to lash
up fear'.[6] The paper claimed that so effective had been its appeal to
protestant creed and heritage that even 'the bulk of Labour voters did
not transfer to Catholic candidates but to Protestant "Anti-Socialist"
ones'.[7] But by the next round of education elections in 1925, the
hubub had died down and all twelve catholic candidates were returned
in Glasgow on a more reduced overall turnout. 53,929 first preference
votes were cast for catholics in 1925 compared with 53,290 in 1922,
which shows how disciplined was the vote mobilised by the Catholic
Union whose ward activists were always able to obtain a higher turnout
than their protestant counterparts whose churches did not have the
same intimate ties with their working-class adherents.[8]

Sometimes freelance militant protestants were returned with these
working-class votes. The last example was Rev James Brisby, an Ulsterman with a religious congregation in Glasgow who was elected to the
School Board several times before 1914.[9] That there were no counterparts on the Education Authority in the 1920s did not mean No Popery
tub-thumpers had lost their audience, but was instead a clear indication
that growing numbers of mainstream clergymen were beginning to
borrow from their highly charged rhetoric. Strongly worded attacks on
the catholic Irish presence in Scotland became a feature of the General
Assembly, the annual gathering of the Church of Scotland, starting in
1923. In that year, the Assembly's influential Church and Nation committee formally approved a report entitled *The Menace of The Irish
Race to Our Scottish Nationality*. It had carried out an investigation
into the Irish presence after strong representations on the matter from
the Presbytery of Glasgow, so it was no isolated outburst but resulted
from a groundswell of concern from presumably ordinary Kirk
members. Published in pamphlet form to ensure wider circulation, the
report speculated about whether Scotland might not be on the verge
of committing 'race suicide' and demanded that means be devised to
'preserve Scotland and the Scottish race' and 'to secure to future
generations the traditions, ideals, and faith of a great people unspoiled
and inviolate'.[10]

The report carried the signatures of the Rev William Munro and
of a High Court judge. It produced a fierce response from the *Glasgow
Observer* which showed how little common ground existed then
between the two main branches of Christianity in Scotland:

> What is an Irishman? What is an immigrant? (For instance, is Bonar Law
> one?) . . . When does an Irishman become a Scotsman. (Is it when recruits

are wanted to prevent a Hun invasion?) . . .

There is a complaint that the ancient glory of Scotland must depart if Roman Catholics or Irish are allowed to increase and multiply. When was Scotland glorious? Was it not in its Catholic days? Did it not owe its proud position among the nations of the world above all to immigrants like Columba and St Margaret . . .

It is time Parliament curtailed the power of such people. The simplest way would be to abolish the stipends of the parish ministers. The rest would follow naturally.[11]

With falling church rolls causing much worry, economic prosperity apparently a thing of the past and emigration removing many of the most energetic Scots, the Kirk seemed inward-looking and dispirited if a perusal of the topics featuring prominently in the resolutions of church synods and debated at the annual General Assembly in the 1920s and 1930s is any guide. By contrast, the catholic population of Scotland was increasing, new parishes were being built, influential people were going over to Rome, and the catholic church was not so reticent as before in displaying its strength in public processions and rituals. In their different ways, these matters only helped to sting a small but growing number of ministers whose church was not as confident of *its* identity and was thus an accurate barometer of Scottish opinion.

Now that most of Ireland had withdrawn from the United Kingdom, a good few Kirk ministers felt that any restraint about mentioning an alien presence in their midst could be lifted. It is no coincidence that 'The Menace of the Irish Race . . .' report emerged when the new Irish Free State had still to reach its first birthday. The closure of Scottish ports to Irish entrants and the repatriation of those Irish already in the country were occasionally advanced as solutions. Although the latter one was a step advocated only by a few, it was rare for those who were vocal on the question of the Irish presence to distinguish between first generation Irish and those whose parents or more distant ancestors hailed from Ireland. All too frequently commentators wishing to prove the urgency of their case, mixed together the Scoto-Irish with the Irish-born to arrive at a figure of anything up to three quarters of a million 'foreign Irish' in the country. A graphic example was provided in 1928 in a speech by Lord Scone, a future Tory MP, as reported by a local newspaper:

There were many thousands of decent, hard-working Irish people Roman Catholics all, but he objected to their presence because it was not right that close on three quarters of a million aliens should batten on Scotland when 100,000 Scotsmen were out of work. If the Irish in Scotland were reduced to even one quarter of a million, the unemployment problem in this country would be so small as to be almost negligible.[12]

In the same year as this speech, the geographer Sir E. J. Russell lent fuel to the agitation of worried Scotsmen by writing in an influential textbook that 'a large foreign population, chiefly Irish, is taking possession, ousting Scotsmen and doing by peaceful penetration what no previous invaders were ever able to do by force'.[13] Although outwardly, the descendants of the original settlers may have adopted the speech and ways of lowland Scotland, those made uneasy by their presence evidently felt that they were unassimalable. Few of their critics gained solace from the fact that, by and large, they were no longer preoccupied with the Irish question and were participating in mainstream British politics. To many Scots, they still retained a distinct and separate identity and the one factor that apparently ensured that this state of affairs would continue into future generations was Section 18 of the 1918 Education (Scotland) Act which preserved and up-graded catholic schools by bringing them within the state system. It was this issue, more than any other, which was a rallying-point for Scots unable to come to terms with the fact that theirs was a multi-cultural society possessing an active minority whose religion Scots had historically come to fear and distrust. The issue was put in a nut-shell by Rev. F. E. Watson, perhaps the main church opponent of the 1918 Act, writing seventeen years later:

> The indignant opposition to the provision of Section 18 of the Education (Scotland) Act, 1918, is that public money is being expanded in educating an increasing section of the population, in the main Free Staters or their offspring, in a faith and a loyalty hostile to the tradition and religion accepted by the vast majority of the Scottish nation . . .
> Why should we feed, clothe, and educate these people who everywhere plot and plan for the downfall of Great Britain.[14]

Frederick Watson may have expressed himself in such forthright terms because he was still imbued with the zeal of the convert, having been a Wesleyan minister for sixteen years before being admitted to the Church of Scotland in 1930. He was also himself a relative new-comer to Scotland, having spent his first forty-five years in the north-east of England.[15] His strong views on the question of 'Rome on the Rates' may explain why, only a short time elapsed before he was taken on in 1931 by the congregation of Bellshill West in Lanarkshire as its parish minister. This was a depressed mining area where catholics and protestants lived in uneasy proximity and where the Orange Order had many adherents in his congregation. Reverend Watson's frequent bids to raise catholic education at the General Assembly and in the press would have gone down well with many of his strong-minded parishioners, but this stormy petrel was only expressing what a large number of ministers and their congregations elsewhere shared, if in a somewhat modified form. Remembering that back in 1872, the Church of Scotland had not been reimbursed when it transferred its schools to the local authorities, many protestants felt it a travesty of justice that a suspect minority faith had been able to receive much more generous terms half-a-century later. Priests had free access to catholic schools which ministers did not have in state ones. There was an angry reaction to the fact that many teachers in roman catholic schools were members of religious orders who would not keep their salary but rather pass it on to the church. Thus it was alleged that the state was directly subsidising its general operations. The same broad argument might have been directed towards the Episcopalian church whose voluntary schools were also transferred to the public upkeep under the 1918 act.[16] This was often forgotten but no outcry was directed at the Episcopalian church which suggests that it was not any principal at stake but the fact that the chief beneficiary of the act was the catholic church which drew such a fierce protestant reaction.

In practice, the implementation of the 1918 act led to surprisingly little friction between local authorities and the catholic church. James Treble has written that 'by the mid-1920s each side was belatedly trying to reduce the sources of potential disharmony to a minimum and to cooperate more closely to promote the educational interests of the catholic children entrusted to their care'.[17] But there was one exception to this rule and that involved a disagreement between the Stirlingshire Education Authority and the catholic church which reached the Court of Session in 1928 and the House of Lords in 1930. The case involved a school built by its catholic proprietors in Bonnybridge in 1925 which the Education Authority declined to place under its jurisdiction. The point at issue was whether education authorities were compelled by law to accept the transfer of schools completed by catholic proprietors after the 1918 act.[18] The House of Lords found in favour of the catholic side which helped prevent similar conflicts arising but the Bonnybridge case was a sore point in protestant circles for years to come.[19] Those opponents of state-financed catholic schools were deprived of a powerful forum in 1929 when the government abolished directly elected education authorities and replaced them with ones whose members were nominated by local councils and the various church groups involved. If they had remained as forums for contentious debate into the 1930s, when militant religious parties were picking up council seats in Glasgow and Edinburgh, it might even have further aggravated an already troubled situation.

Denunciation of Popery was a feature of General Assembly debate well into the 1930s and in one particular year, an Edinburgh daily paper was moved to remark that 'from yesterday's speeches in the General Assembly, one could gather the impression that the most formidable enemy is the Church of Rome'.[20] Some churchmen were alarmed at the success of a Converts Aid Society which in Edinburgh, under W. R. Beattie, a former Episcopalian minister, was able to announce a number of middle-class conversions to roman catholicism in the 1930s.[21] Some churchmen may have half-believed the talented journalist, George Malcolm Thomson when he wrote in his book *The Re-Discovery of Scotland*:

> Well the truth is that Calvinism is going. As a creed it is as dead as the door-nail already; as a system of Church government, it has still as vigorious a life as is possible to any institution whose soul is departed.[22]

But it would be wrong to give the impression that all, or perhaps even most, Church of Scotland ministers felt that they were in deadly combat with a resurgent catholic faith for the hearts and minds of the Scottish people. The protagonists were a small but vocal minority of ministers who had a larger element of the faithful behind them. Most ministers were probably careful to keep out of the firing line and preferred not to get involved while a smaller number, little more than a handful, spoke out when they felt feeling was running dangerously high, against hotheads inside or outside their own church.

For instance, in 1930 the Rev. John Kennedy of St Paul's North Church, Glasgow, repudiated a co-religionist for voicing concern that 12·3% of Scotland's population was comprised of catholics:

> he makes no comment on the fact that 36% (i.e. three times the number of Catholics) belong to no church at all. He unabashedly admits that this pagan million 'are predominantly Presbyterian in their training and outlook'. It may further be added that they are the products of secular education to which we have betrayed our children as catholic Churchmen refuse to do . . .
>
> The Irish nation sets an example to the world in patriotism, church-going, and education based on religion . . . Scotland is no longer a nation at all though it is outstanding for those 'getting on' qualities of which Mr Cockburn is so proud and likes to rival the Jews in running England.[23]

In 1930 other Church of Scotland ministers were prepared to come forward and criticise a play, 'The Trial of Fr Diamond' with mixed marriages as its theme, written and put on by Alexander Ratcliffe, a full-time anti-catholic preacher, which often gave rise to disturbances when it was performed. The Rev. H. S. McClelland, of Trinity Church, Glasgow declared that 'he is absolutely on the wrong lines for he is simply endeavouring to stir up religious biogtry. There are just as good Catholics as Protestants.' The Rev. Hector McPherson, a director of the Protestant Institute commented that 'we must attain our objectives by teaching and example, not sensational methods. It is unscrupulous to carry out attacks by means of a play.'[24]

In 1935, after Ratcliffe and an Edinburgh counterpart had made successful forays into local politics, the Rev. J. M. Dickie was moved to ask in a debate at the General Assembly on the 1918 Education Act: 'was it possible when nationalism was rampant and sheer paganism existed not only beyond the frontiers of the Rhine but in their own midst, that they should engage in a campaign against a Church which, however they deplored its errors, did stand for spiritual things and on the side of Christ'.[25] Within weeks of this sobering intervention, Edinburgh, the site of the General Assembly, was convulsed by angry religious rioting which greeted a three-day roman catholic Eucharistic Congress, even though it was an indoor occasion mainly held on catholic premises. Exultant hardline protestants felt that Scotland's capital had been reclaimed for John Knox and catholics seeking to flaunt their religion taught a well-deserved lesson, but the scale of mob violence alarmed many in the Church of Scotland: even a convinced opponent of the 1918 Act like the Rev. D. M. McGregor felt obliged to write to the *Scotsman* to warn that 'if Protestantism can only be vindicated in such crude ways, its day is nearly done'.[26]

A few bold spirits in the Church of Scotland went beyond conciliatory words and took practical steps to build bridges in their community often at no small risk to themselves. In the Gorbals district of Glasgow, J. Cameron Peddie, an Aberdonian, and minister of Hutcheston parish church for twenty-seven years up to the 1950s, won the respect of many of the young men who formed the gangs that helped to give the Gorbals its unenviable reputation. He found that, contrary to popular belief, religion was not the main cause of the gang warfare of the 1920s and 1930s and that rival gangs could be composed of both protestants and catholics. He won the respect of many of the young in Glasgow's South-side, irrespective of religion, by treating them seriously and giving them premises where they could meet instead of on the streets. He felt that poverty and unemployment were the main causes of Glasgow's gangsterism and he was not the only observer to find that the Gorbals was 'not as black as it was painted'. His congregation 'were quiet decent folk' while the people he met 'in the closes and the streets were friendly, kindly, appreciative'.[27]

Another minister who broke down barriers of mistrust was Henry C. Whitley during years spent in Port Glasgow in the late 1930s. During his first week there, he sought out the local parish priest, Simon Keane (1888–1951), a redoubtable individual, and the friendship which resulted soon had positive repercussions in a town which had known its full-share of sectarian friction:

At the conclusion of this first visit he steered me out to the main street, whether by intent or pure accident I shall never know. The workers from the yard and nearby sail making factory poured thinly out on their way home or to the pubs . . . Priest and parish minister stood together for them all to see. I, at least, was in right up to the neck. The next morning an anonymous letter informed me that I had been seen with the Roman priest and this was a warning to me. Protestants and Catholics don't mix. If I did not take heed, things would be made uncomfortable for me in Port Glasgow . . .

The next Saturday was to throw me right in at the deep end. About seven in the evening my telephone rang—it was the Police inspector. 'Man there is a riot in the Glen; Protestants and Catholics knocking the lights out of one another. Would you come down and see if you can separate your Protestant sheep from the Catholic goats and see if you can get Father Keane. I hear you're both friendly . . .'

I phoned Simon. Fortunately he was in and I told him what happened. 'Right oh, me boy. I'll meet you at the foot of Balfour Street and we'll scatter the Philistines.'

Five minutes later we were striding side by side towards a mob of two or three hundred men—there was a no-man's land of the Glen burn between them. I was scared. Father Simon had a strong walking-stick in his hands and he showed not a trace of fear.

'Come on', he said. 'We'll deal with my flock first.'

Right in among them he went, flailing right and left with his stick and cursing them in the broadest Irish imaginable. In next to no time they began to scatter. Some faces he recognised and his powerful voice called out: 'Go on, Paddy, get home, you scoundrel. I've brought the bloody minister to scare you if this stick doesn't.' One side of the road was cleared. Then we moved to the other. Beside me he whispered: 'Perhaps you should try a word of prayer!' But there was no need—like sheep they scattered. Half a dozen worried policemen and the Inspector joined us . . . They were sorry to draw us in but the suggestion when things really looked dangerous had come from Old Paddy the porter that Father Keane and Mr Whitley might together do the trick. Though it had come to be a regular occurrence whenever there had been a big football game or an 'Orange Walk' . . . , there was never to be another riot in the Glen . . .[28]

In local politics, indivisual churchmen could occasionally help mend religious differences and prevent them from being politically disruptive. Rev. Whitley himself served on the local council in Port Glasgow to good effect while in Glasgow, the Episcopal Canon John McBain was a much respected Labour councillor for Mile-End in the 1920s and 1930s. But perhaps it was the United Free Church minister, James Barr (1861–1949) who made the greatest contribution of any churchman to community harmony by his political interventions. An evangelical minister with no sectarian taint, he was based in Govan after 1905 and he won the respect of a protestant congregation in a district of Glasgow with strong Ulster ties that also included many catholics who admired his work on the Glasgow School Board.[29] His influence may have helped secure the election of Patrick Dollan, a socialist from a catholic background as councillor for Govan in 1913, someone later destined to make his mark on Glasgow's civic life. In 1924 Barr defeated a hardline Orangeman to be elected Labour MP for Motherwell and in 1935 he came out of retirement to stand as MP for Coatbridge and Airdrie, another of Glasgow's satellites where religious rivalry had blighted local politics, which he represented until 1945.

These individual efforts deserve not to be overlooked because they show that even in the most perilous years of community relations in lowland Scotland, there were outspoken figures giving a lead in the direction of sanity and mutual toleration for respective creeds. Perhaps their efforts might have amounted to more and others might have found the courage to join them if the leadership of the Church of Scotland and the catholic church had offered more encouragement. In fact, very little was forthcoming and perhaps more of the blame for this lies with the catholic church. Unlike the Presbyterian churches, its hierarchy was under no constraints from its ordinary membership and it could have given a lead, however symbolic, without facing internal censure. One such possibility involved talks between catholic students at Glasgow university and members of the Student Christian Movement presided over by their respective chaplains. In the late 1930s, a proposal for discussions actually came from the SCM which William Brown, the catholic chaplain at Glasgow was willing to accept. However, on the eve of the first meeting they were unexpectedly overruled by Archbishop Mackintosh, one catholic student still being able to recall how Fr Brown broke down and wept on receiving the prelate's veto.[30] By deliberately isolating itself in this way from civilised contacts, the catholic church invited suspicion and reinforced the ignorance of what ordinary catholics were like. Such introspection, in the atmosphere of the 1930s, was a luxury that could easily have cost the church dear.

The eruption of discord on religious and racial grounds was, from time to time, reflected in the statements and actions of the Tory Party which between 1911 and 1964 was known in Scotland as the Unionist Party. Scottish Tories were probably on much closer terms with the Unionists of Northern Ireland and more understanding of their anxieties than any in England outside Liverpool, so the shared nomenclature, though perhaps coincidental, was appropriate.

In the aftermath of the Anglo-Irish war, a number of MPs and parliamentary candidates pointedly referred to the unwelcome presence of the Irish in their midst. The intention behind such statements was often to use ethnic solidarity in a bid to get workers to resist the appeal of class loyalties being made by the Labour Party and thus remain within the non-Socialist camp. By the collapse of Lloyd George's coalition in 1922, the Tories were able to lay claim to the bulk of the anti-Socialist vote in the main Scottish towns and cities. It was a straight fight between them and Labour now that the Liberal Party's power had been broken except in some rural fastnesses. But, in these straight contests, unorthodox tactics were sometimes used. The worst example arose at the 1925 general election in the seat of Glasgow Shettleston. John Wheatley, the sitting Labour MP and minister of housing and health in the outgoing Labour administration returned to campaign in his constituency with the reputation of having been the most effective member of the outgoing government. But his Tory challenger, Major Reid Miller, a one-armed war veteran, waged a vitriolic campaign against him that dwelt on his Irish birth and religious attachments and he was returned with only a seventy-four vote majority.[31] After the election Reid Miller waged a vendetta against Wheatley which was too much for the Tories who dropped him as the Shettleston candidate. In 1927 Wheatley sued him for libel, but an Edinburgh jury cleared him when the case reached the high court, a verdict which plunged him into depression.

Until the 1930s officers of the Orange Order sat on the Scottish council of the Tory Party.[32] It is doubtful if they enjoyed any definite influence over policy, but they were useful because of the Order's willingness to campaign for the party in working-class areas of Lanarkshire, Glasgow, and Ayrshire where the topicality of the religious question denied the Labour Party a clear-cut advantage. The local Orange hall was often utilised as an election headquarters for the Tories, the practice being maintained in Ayrshire, according to David Lambie MP up to the 1960s.[33] By using the premises of a body that was non-catholic by its statute and decidedly anti-catholic in its behaviour and outlook, the Scottish Unionists were effectively snubbing the catholic minority which made up nearly one-quarter of the population in the west of Scotland. Even Liverpool had roman catholics sitting in parliament as Tories by the 1930s but this development did not arise in urban Scotland till the 1970s.[34]

In order to cultivate the protestant grassroots, members of the Tory aristocracy sometimes consented to being given titular appointments in the Orange Order. This meant reviewing Orange parades and turning up to sit on the platform at annual general meetings, chores which many of them found onerous given the number of apologies for non-attendance which long-suffering Orange gatherings were accustomed to receiving from Tory grandees.[35] Sir John Gilmour, Secretary of State for Scotland from 1924 to 1929 was an honorary deputy grand master, while Colonal A. D. McInnes Shaw, a Renfrewshire MP, later became Scottish Grand Master (although the effective power was held by his deputy, Frank Dobson Dorrian, a coal contractor from

Bellshill).[36] In 1926, McInnes Shaw, along with Sir A. Sprot, MP for Lanark, tried unsuccessfully to remove Scotland from the jurisdiction of the Roman Catholic Relief Act which lifted the ban on open-air catholic processions (and was the work of a roman catholic English Tory MP).[37]

Before leaving office Sir John Gilmour announced his 'intention of seeking an amendment of the law in virtue of which an Irishman landing on these hospitable shores was immediately entitled to the benefit of the Poor Law without the least risk of being returned to his parish and country of origin'.[38] This gesture did no harm among working-class Tories and, in 1931, the year of Labour's electoral crash, a few new MPs even more in tune with their religious and ethnic feelings were returned. One such was William Templeton, an advocate of the compulsory inspection of convents[39] who was Tory MP for the divided but solidly working-class seat of Coatbridge and Airdrie from 1931 to 1935. This was also the parliament in which the most forceful cries for a regulation of Irish immigration to Scotland were heard. That legislation did not result was due to Scottish members being unable to convince English fellow Tories of the urgency of the problem. Reliable evidence gathered by the *Glasgow Herald* (see p. 167) and found in government statistics showed that Irish immigration to Scotland in the 1920s and 1930s was miniscule compared with previous decades. However, popular perceptions were at variance with cold statistics and even liberal Tories like Robert Boothby and John Buchan, who had no religious axe to grind, felt obliged to table questions or make representations about the 'Hibernianisation of Scotland'. In a parliamentary debate, on 24 November 1932, Buchan linked the Scottish malaise with the Irish presence, albeit in a low-key manner:

> something must be done, and done soon if Scotland is not to lose its historic individuality. All is not well with our country. Our population is declining; we are losing some of the best of our race stock by migration and their place is being taken by those who, whatever their merits, are not Scottish. I understand that every fifth child born in Scotland is an Irish Roman Catholic.[40]

A former Chancellor of the Exchequer, Sir Robert Horne (Glasgow Hillhead) was more forthright. He argued that the Irish presence made Scottish home rule, then much in demand, an impossibility:

> There are in the industrial districts of the west of Scotland something like 25% of the population who are Irish and that is far and away the most populous part of the kingdom.
> They could easily form the determining element in the balance between the Scottish parties, and you might find that what you had believed to be

Scottish home rule turned out to be a form of very insidious Irish domination of our politics.[41]

He was followed by Lord Scone (Perth), who bluntly stated that:

culturally the Irish population . . . has not been assimilated into the Scottish population. It is not my purpose to discuss now whether the Irish culture is good or bad, but merely to state the definite fact that there is in the west of Scotland a completely separate race of alien origin practically homogeneous whose presence there is bitterly resented by tens of thousands of the Scottish working-class.[42]

These dogmatic statements followed hard on the heels of electoral successes by the Scottish Protestant League whose honorary president Lord Scone had once been. In 1934, keen to prevent the Labour Party consolidating its newly won majority on Glasgow corporation, the Moderates actually struck up an electoral pact with the anti-catholic SPL. It was given a free run in seven working-class seats while the Moderates were unopposed in more affluent districts where the SPL had taken seats from them last time. No terms were published but, in his election address, the SPL leader declared that 'the Moderate Party have entirely changed their view on . . . my appeal for a revision of the 1918 Education (Scotland) Act as they recently in the Council unanimously supported my motion for action'.[43]

Sir Charles Cleland, a leading local Tory and former chairman of the Glasgow Unionist Association (1914–25) and of the Glasgow Education Authority (1919–28) aligned himself with the SPL on the catholic schools issue shortly before the 1934 municipal election.[44] He was a comfortably off stationer who continued to live in the largely working-class district of Maryhill in Glasgow which, in 1933, still returned a full list of Moderate councillors. He had family links with Northern Ireland through a daughter who had become the wife of Sir Richard Dawson Bates, the hardline minister of home affairs in Northern Ireland from 1921 to 1943. There were other leading Glasgow Tories who, by their track-record, would not have shrunk from endorsing what was an unusual and risky pact with a volatile religious party. One who deserves not to fall from view was Sir John Cargill, chairman of Burmah Oil and a powerful figure behind the scenes in the party up to 1939. This powerful industrial baron was dubbed 'the patron saint of Tory capitalism in the west of Scotland', by Patrick Dollan because of his sponsorship of the Economic League which subsidised anti-socialist propaganda in working-class districts and was behind union-busting activities.[45] Cargill also found the time to be a patron of Glasgow Rangers football club and he was proud of being a descendant of the Rev. Donald Cargill, 'a Covenanter who was executed for his faith on the scaffold at the Cross of Edinburgh in 1681'.[46]

The biographies of Tory power-brokers like Cleland and Cargill show that the alliance with the SPL in 1934 was not a complete aberration. However, it failed in its object to oust the Labour Party from George Square.[47] Pat Dollan consolidated Labour's position but, thereafter, the challenge of the SPL melted away which must have come as a relief to many Tories aware that since they and the SPL were competing for the selfsame protestant working-class votes, they were likely only to cancel each other out and bring solace to their opponents.

Few extra votes had come the Tories way in 1934 by stressing religious difference and the consensus among Tory managers would seem to have been that while there were circumstances in which they would not shrink from adopting the tactic, it only had limited applicability in specific localities. A reading of Gordon Brown's Ph.D. on the electoral strategies of the main Scottish parties in the 1920s provides scant evidence that there was a deliberate attempts by the Tories at senior level to stress religious and ethnic ties in their appeal to working-class voters.[48] If this message was directed almost exclusively to *protestant* workers, it is because the high degree of political organisation among unskilled catholics from the 1880s onwards made them impervious to any Tory appeal. Those who might have wished to employ the religious card in the way it was used in Northern Ireland by the Unionists, would have been restrained by the entry of many Liberals into the Tory Party following the effective collapse of Scottish Liberalism, at least in urban districts. The use of crude religious propaganda would not have endeared them to their new political home. It was not in the Liberal tradition (indeed Liberals had been victims of it for supporting Irish home rule in 1886) and it might have endangered the smooth-running of the non-socialist alliance which made the Tories in conjunction with their National Liberal allies, the biggest Scottish political formation in terms of votes throughout the 1930s and indeed into the 1950s.

Many Tories were more concerned with calming the doubts of newly won ex-Liberals than with confirming the prejudices of the working-class voters who remained loyal for religious reasons. Although there were a few Glasgow seats where this vote had to be cultivated to keep Labour out, much of its Orange support was concentrated in working-class strongholds stretching from Renfrewshire through Lanarkshire across to West Lothian, where Labour only stood a chance of being toppled in an specially disastrous year like 1931. By 1935, even F. D. Dorrian the effective leader of Scottish Orangeism, was facing defeat in his Bellshill council seat[49] and the Grand Master McInnes Shaw was swept aside by James Maxton of the ILP in Bridgeton.

An occasional Tory MP pitched his appeal both towards protestant Orangemen and catholics and could get away with such a tight-rope performance if local circumstances permitted. One such was Colonel Sir Thomas Moore, Tory MP for Ayr from 1925 to 1964. An Ulsterman, service with the British expeditionary force that landed in Russia after the 1917 revolution brought him a wider interest in international affairs and triggered off a lifelong obsession with the danger of communism. In October 1933, he declared that 'peace and justice are the keynotes of his [Hitler's] policy' and he was the 'only major proponent of Nazi Germany among MPs in this early period'.[50] His detestation of communism and sympathy for European fascism made him see roman catholicism as a bulwark against the forces of communist subversion. Thus, in 1932, he found himself opening a roman catholic bazaar in Ayr town hall just hours before he proceeded to a field at nearby Maybole where he was to address a gathering of 4,000 Orangemen. At the catholic function he had declared that 'he was very happy to be associated with his friends in the Roman Catholic faith . . . They were all common stock and they all had the same heavenly father.'[51] Moore did not enlighten the Orangemen about where his previous engagement had taken him but, even though some of his remarks were later published in the local press, the deference which working-class Orangemen displayed towards this upper-class army officer, ensured that he was a welcome guest at their parades on future occasions.

In 1935 the responsibility for religious disturbances which broke out almost simultaneously in Edinburgh and Belfast, was obliquely placed at the door of the Tory Party by Compton Mackenzie, the writer and catholic convert when he wrote:

> we know only too well that the savage, nay the sub-human bigotry of Orangemen is beyond calculation, and we know with equal certainty that such ferocity would never have been tolerated but for the base interest one political party has in fostering it with the hope of political advantage. It is difficult to free the mind of the suspicion that the Protestant agitations both in Belfast and Edinburgh have been systematically fed by the secret elements of the same political party. Yet to divert into dark foul channels the growing discontent of the Scottish people with their position in the world today, which is expressed on one side by a restless socialism rising to communism, on the other by a restless nationalism rising to the idea of complete separation from England, is a very dangerous method of drainage.[52]

If Mackenzie had been more explicit, he would have been courting a possible libel action. But his drift is clear and it is the Tory Party which, however obliquely, is being indicated. However, the evidence is faint and the allegation is greatly weakened by the fact that in the west of Scotland (where the party apparently had much to gain from a working-class divided on religious grounds), there were no major religious disorders in 1935. Walter Elliot, the Tory member for Kelvingrove, later in the year gave his cautious backing for an official enquiry into the Belfast disturbances which the Catholic Union was seeking to bring about.[53] The manipulation of religious feeling was repugnant to him and, as minister of agriculture in 1932 he had also emerged as someone in favour of reaching an accommodation with the republican government of Eamon de Valera newly installed in Dublin.[54] Walter Elliot was a member of the Irish situation committee of the cabinet in 1933 and his preference for restraint may have helped prevent the trade war with the Irish Free State escalating into other areas. Interestingly, another Glasgow Tory MP acted as an emissary between the Dublin and London governments during 1932. This was Captain J. H. Moss who was evidently acceptable to the Irish side.[55]

So, in other words, it would be wrong to assert that Scottish Tory MPs invariably adopted an Orange position on Ireland or related religious matters. Those MPs who did make controversial statements, such as Lord Scone or Sir Robert Horne often represented middle-class or rural seats where they would not have been acquainted with the sensitivity of the Irish issue. Other Tories, representing seats in and around Glasgow usually had cause to be more circumspect and may have been reluctant to be too vociferous in case the peace of their constituencies was disturbed. Sometimes, Orangemen would protest that they were being taken too much for granted and that their elected representatives were dragging their feet over issues dear to their hearts. In 1923, an Orange and Protestant Party had actually been formed when the Scottish Unionist leadership was seen to back the Anglo-Irish peace settlement. However, it had the half-hearted support of Orangemen and quickly disappeared once it was apparent that the 1921 treaty was far from being a sell-out of the Ulster Unionist cause. Thereafter, the Orange Order enjoyed an increasingly subordinate position in Tory ranks and, by the end of the 1930s, no longer had representatives on the party's Scottish council. By now, Tory managers were becoming aware that the Orange Order was better at getting people to march in resplendent uniforms on certain well-known days of the year than it was in persuading them to troop obediently into the polling booths to vote in a predetermined way. The protestant vote was still appealed to, but it was not encouraged to dictate policy. Fewer Tory grandees were prepared to adorn the platform at Orange occasions in the 1930s as the Order's officials were gently pushed to the margins of the party.

It might have been a rather different story if an authoritarian Tory politician had, in the manner of Sir Oswald Mosley, attempted to mobilise a following among the Orange grassroots by appealing to the atavistic feelings of both protestant workers and middle-class elements. In inter-war Scotland, this was a fairly remote scenario since the party preferred to calm public opinion and wean it away from nationalist or left-wing strategies for a Scottish political revival. However, if the political threat from the left had been stronger or if the nationalist movement had been able to capture the imagination of a sufficiently large portion of the Scottish electorate, then it would not have been totally out of character for the Tories to use religion to derail the opposing juggernaut. The Orange card had helped to dethrone the Scottish Liberals in 1886 and there is a lot of circumstantial evidence to show that religious disgruntlement was just as strong in the 1920s and 1930s among parts of the working-class and the church-going lower middle-class. Indeed the possibility of making a political breakthrough by stirring up religious feeling was to be realised in Glasgow in the early 1930s by a fringe party led by a quixotic preacher who nevertheless posed a headache to the established parties by advancing a populist manifesto which possessed a distinct appeal for sections of the protestant electorate.

This was Alexander Ratcliffe whose election to Glasgow corporation in 1931 at the head of an unknown party, after having lived in the city for less than a year amply demonstrated how susceptible part of the electorate was to a religious appeal couched in political terms.

Ratcliffe was born in 1888 in the east coast town of Bo'ness, known for its dissenting Presbyterian traditions. His father was a clergyman attached to the Scottish Coast Mission which preached to sea-farers, first in Bo'ness and later in Leith, Edinburgh's port, where Ratcliffe grew up.[56] Leith had been one of the epicentres of the Reformation and gospel halls and street-corner missions were much in evidence. Besides Ratcliffe, it produced Jacob Primmer and George Malcolm Thomson who, at different times, played upon protestant–catholic tensions in Scotland and it would return a 'No Popery' councillor from the 1930s up to the 1960s, so it is a fair guess that the environment of his youth had a formative role in shaping Ratcliffe's later life.

The Scottish Protestant League (SPL) was founded in Edinburgh by Ratcliffe in 1920. He had earlier been a railway clerk, but he found that he was able to derive an independent living from his religious work. He was a powerful speaker who had the full repertoire of devices and tricks that were used by protestant controversialists to hold the attention of an audience. As late as 1930, he was able to address a packed meeting on convent inspection in the Caird Hall, Dundee, Scotland's largest public hall.[57] He usually charged a small entrance fee wherever he spoke and his ability to draw a capacity audience of nearly 5,000 people in Dundee, a city usually free of sectarian tension, demonstrated just how financially viable his movement was. The age of the mass media had still not pressed far into Scotland and somebody who could tell religious horror stories about churches, convents, and the Vatican and present former nuns and renegade priests to confirm his assault on the wicked church of Rome was an obvious draw even for fickle protestants who did not share his obsessions. Many of the alleged priests and nuns paraded by Ratcliffe and other preachers down the years were charlatans but, in the late 1920s, he was able to win over a serving priest in Glasgow to the cause which was unusual. This was Fr Robert Devitt who was attached to St Michael's parish, Parkhead, until 1927, but was not with Ratcliffe for long.[58] Ratcliffe's various exploits, accounts of speaking tours and denunciations of various figures who failed to meet his exacting standards of being a true protestant, were relayed to a wider audience in a newspaper, the *Protestant Advocate* which appeared intermittently between 1920 and 1931. He had a lively polemical style and the *Protestant Advocate* was both topical and well layed out as was its successor, known as the *Vanguard* or the *Protestant Vanguard* which appeared after Ratcliffe had transferred to Glasgow.

Beforehand he had made several interventions in politics. Widespread hostility to catholic schools being state-aided helped get him elected to the Edinburgh Education Authority in 1925. At the 1929 general election, he stood as a Protestant and Progressive candidate in the seat of Stirling and Falkirk where the Bonnybridge school controversy had occurred. The sitting Labour MP, Hugh Murnin was a roman catholic and Ratcliffe gained 21·3% of the vote. Then and later, he steered clear of both the Unionist Party and the Orange Order, which he never lost an opportunity to criticise in his papers for their reluctance to provide a more trenchant defence of protestant values. Being a rank individualist, temperamentally unable to place himself in a subordinate role, he was unwilling to co-operate with the Orange Order whose officials distrusted him for his egotism and volatility and he thus forfeited an important reservoir of support.

Sensing that Glasgow was a better headquarters for his activities, he moved there at the start of the 1930s. Soon he had his own church building situated near the City Chambers, offices in the commercial district in Bath Street, and a comfortable house in the rich suburb of Bearsden. In his first run for local office, he was returned to the council in 1931 for the Dennistoun ward where he got more votes than all of his opponents combined. This had hitherto been a safe seat for the Moderates (the name then adopted by the Tories in Scottish local politics) in an area of Glasgow inhabited by artisans and lower middle-class elements. In working-class Dalmarnock, Charles Forrester was also returned for the SPL at the expense of a Labour Party still reeling from its crushing general election defeat in October. Dalmarnock was located in the Bridgeton constituency whose MP was the well-known advanced socialist James Maxton. His personal popularity had ensured his survival but the left had problems in this poverty-stricken east end of Glasgow seat. Much of the small-scale sectarian violence that affected Glasgow in the 1930s originated here. The location of the stadium of Glasgow Celtic near to a district where the Orange Order had many adherents caused sectarian tension and, despite Maxton, meant that the left was actually on the defensive in Bridgeton. It was also the headquarters of a protestant gang called the Billy Boys whose leader, William Fullerton, occasionally placed this tough bunch of streetfighters at the service of anti-socialists. It prevented the Communist Party from organsing the unemployed in the district and Charles Forrester used it to protect his meetings.[59]

Forrester was a boilermaker and former Communist who had spent some time in the Soviet Union.[60] By his conversion to 'No Popery' he demonstrated the appeal of traditional values for the working-class even in the midst of a depression. However, he was an inadequate figure, drunk on the night of his election,[61] who was unable to turn Bridgeton into a permanent stronghold for religious extremism. Nor could Ratcliffe, who lacked the common touch and appealed more to the lower middle-classes. Nevertheless, with two out of three candidates being elected in 1931, the SPL did well among contrasting groups and at the expense of both parties.

On what kind of platform did the SPL go before the voters? Ratcliffe claimed that 'it was not a matter of politics that made it necessary for the League to seek representation on the Council, but one of Protestant principle'.[62] Nevertheless, by studying the voting behaviour of the SPL in the council, as well as its election literature, an attempt can be made to locate it on the political spectrum. Rather surprisingly perhaps, a strong case can be made for placing it to the left of the Moderates on socio-economic issues, which are usually the ones that dominate local politics. The city's leading newspaper, *The Glasgow Herald* had no doubts about the matter: the SPL 'was presenting what is essentially a socialist case wrapped up in the garments of religions'.[63]

Catholic schooling was the chief preoccupation of the SPL. However, alone it was not likely to produce an effective political response from the voters. Ratcliffe shrewdly combined his religious propaganda with more material concerns that a wider circle of voters were likely to feel strongly about. Thus the SPL made great play about opposing cuts in social services and increases in rents, while advocating reduced corporation rates. These were rather contradictory and populist postures designed to win support from protestant voters in contrasting districts of the city. The SPL also sought to befriend council employees whose salaries were frozen or else cut by the ruling Moderates in 1931. The *Vanguard* carried the names of councillors who went on expenses-paid trips and it argued that savings could be made by cutting back on waste. Ratcliffe gave an example by never availing himself or special privileges for councillors such as free lunches and he slammed council corruption for which there was anecdotal evidence later confirmed in depth by the investigations of Glasgow's chief constable Sir Percy Sillitoe.[64]

In his bid to woo diverse interests, Ratcliffe had a letter published in the socialist weekly *Forward* shortly before being elected. In it, he assured readers that they had nothing to fear from his election to the council: 'The Protestant councillors will support every measure brought forth in the best interests of the working people. And they will oppose any moves by the Moderates to "down" the working man.'[65]

The SPL gained further ground in 1932 when it won another seat and 11·71% of the total municipal vote in Glasgow. It took working-class Kinning Park from the Moderates but in Dalmarnock, two rival SPL candidates cancelled each other out. This was the first real sign of the fission that would do untold harm to the ultra-protestant cause. But further scope for SPL success still remained with the left divided by the competing Labour, ILP, and Communist parties and, more especially, with the ruling Moderates unpopular due to their austerity measures. Its best year was 1933 when four more protestant councillors were elected in Glasgow, the SPL acquiring 67,000 votes, 23% of the total. The gains were made in the wards of Camphill, Cathcart, Govanhill, and Dennistoun, lower middle-class districts where hitherto the Moderates had been dominant. In some years Moderate councillors had been returned unopposed in those seats and Ratcliffe may have been able to exploit the complacency and neglect which often accompanied electoral one-party rule. The SPL also took votes from the left whose total vote fell collectively by 9% but its chief victim was the Moderates who were replaced in office by a minority Labour administration.

1933 marked the beginning of Labour's long hegemony in Glasgow politics but it was largely thanks to the spoiling role of the SPL that it achieved its breakthrough when it did. Perhaps because of these circumstances Ratcliffe was not regarded as completely beyond the pale by the left and he was even able to contribute articles to the Labour weekly, *Forward*.[66] In a long peice which the editor, Emrys Hughes, had asked him to write in March 1934 in order to clarify the relations between the SPL and Labour, Ratcliffe made some interesting disclosures.

It was revealed that the five-strong SPL group on the council was free to vote as it chose on purely political questions but a whip applied to any with a religious dimension.[67] With this ruling in force, two SPL candidates usually voted with the Moderates, while the rest joined with Ratcliffe in backing him on issues like the need for free school textbooks. Ratcliffe tried to give the impression that he was the most progressive member of the group by citing the time when he had been the only one to back a motion which provided for help to be given to unemployed people suffering ill-health.[68]

Ratcliffe's access to *Forward*, the premier paper of the Scottish left from 1906 to the 1950s can only be described as bizarre when it is realised that he lent his name to a home-grown fascist party in 1933 that withheld membership from roman catholics.[69] The Scottish Fascist Democratic Party was formed by William Weir Gilmour, an ex-coal miner who had graduated to being a surveyor; in the 1920s he had been active in the ILP, was a member of Glasgow Trades Council and a lecturer for the Scottish Labour Colleges. He was drawn primarily to Mussolini's economic policies through his belief in syndicalism and he viewed Italian corporatism as a form of industrial government.[70] In November 1933, Willie Gallacher, the well-known Communist, declared in Glasgow at a meeting where the German playright Ernst Toller was also on the platform, that in Scotland the fascists were not anti-Jewish but anti-Irish.[71] Ratcliffe hosted a large meeting for the Scottish fascists in his Glasgow church and Gilmour maintained his anti-catholicism into the late 1980s as a sprightly octogenarian.[72] Being a free thinker, he bore more resemblance to a continental anti-clerical than to an Orange controversialist, and his assaults on the Roman church focused on its secrecy, love of ritual and superstition, and its desire to wield political influence.

In the first issue of *Commonwealth*, the Scottish fascist monthly, which ran for a few issues in mid-1933, the SFDP unfurled a five-point programme which advocated the expulsion from Scotland of all religious orders, the repeal of the offending clause of the 1918 Education Act and the prohibition of the Irish immigration to Scotland. Gilmour insists that the SFDP rejected Mussolini's anti-democratic spirit and he stresses that he was on good terms with senior British politicians opposed to fascism in the 1930s (letter from Weir Gilmour, 11 December 1986).

Ratcliffe's own anti-catholic stance was not always clearcut or consistent. In a survey of the religious and occupational backgrounds of the 116 members of Glasgow city council, published in a March 1933 issue of *Vanguard*, Ratcliffe was not unduly concerned that six were roman catholics.[73] He vented more fury at the eleven Orangemen who sat as Moderates for not defending protestant interests. He claimed that five of them were on the education committee of the council and asked why they had not petitioned the government to repeal the 1918

Act. Later, when the number of catholic councillors had increased to nine, he remarked that 'this is not many'.[74] More mileage, he felt could be obtained from attacking the Moderates, many of whom were directors, stockbrokers, or retired gentlemen who were set apart from their electors.

Perhaps realising that the catholic community was well-entrenched in Glasgow and that protestant–catholic relations were only tense in a few localities or at certain times of the year, Ratcliffe's anti-catholic stance varied and depended on who he was talking to and where. In his newspaper and, no doubt, in his pulpit, his anti-catholic diatribes were fiercer than in the council chamber or on the hustings; in response to the ILP councillor, Joseph Payne, who claimed that 'the whole foundation of the SPL programme was to "Kick the Pope", take that away and there is nothing left . . .', Ratcliffe agreed:

'Yes we *do* kick the Pope! That *is* our job! It *is* our programme!'[75]

His newspaper usually carried adverts for SPL publications which included such titles as 'The Life of A Carmelite Nun', 'Why Priests Don't Wed', and 'The Horrible Lives of the Popes of Rome'. But his anti-catholic message could be less crude and more sophisticated. In *Forward*, he took issue with a correspondent who had stated that his object 'in life is to exclude catholics from social and political activity . . .'.

> But I must admit that one of my objects in life is to exclude the Catholic Church and her priests from dominating 'Roman Catholics' who desire to take a citizen's part in social and political activity. Moreover, while I am not opposed to Catholics taking a fair share in the administration of the country's affairs, I certainly object to the Catholics being petted and pampered even within the Socialist movement.[76]

Ratcliffe had close ties with militant protestants in Northern Ireland where the local Unionist Party could have been a possible source of support for the SPL if the SPL had assumed a more permanent shape in Scotland. Ratcliffe held a number of speaking tours in Ulster in the early 1930s and Major J. H. McCormick, a Unionist MP in the Belfast parliament chaired one of his meetings, later travelling to Scotland to speak on behalf of the SPL. But relations between Ratcliffe and his Ulster allies were badly strained after an incident in the newly opened parliament at Stormont on 2 May 1933 when a picture depicting King William of Orange being blessed by an ecclesiastical figure resting on a cloud was attacked by a SPL contingent.[77] Outraged protestant hardliners had assumed the ecclesiastical figure to be the Pope and the painting was daubed in paint by Mrs Mary Ratcliffe and then slashed by Councillor Forrester, both of whom were briefly imprisoned by the Belfast authorities before being fined.[78]

In one issue of *Vanguard* Ratcliffe posed the rhetorical question,

'If Home Rule works in Ulster, why cannot it work in Scotland?'[79] Later he delivered a sermon in his church bearing the title 'Would Scottish Home Rule Mean Rome Rule?' Ratcliffe's verdict was that a parliament in Edinburgh would not be detrimental to protestant interests in Scotland and he declared himself willing to support Home Rule in principle, if not the nationalist parties then promoting it. Here he was going out on a limb since most militant protestants in Scotland were staunch Unionists, but Ratcliffe was so much at odds with the protestant establishment that he appeared to enjoy promoting ideas like Scottish Home Rule which were totally at variance with protestant conservative orthodoxy.

Eventually Ratcliffe seems to have fallen out with most of his allies. His involvement with the Scottish Fascists ceased when they deleted anti-catholic articles from their charter later in 1933 and then rapidly disappeared into oblivion. Disputes with an organiser of the SPL over cash reached the courts.[80] More seriously, he found it difficult to retain control over the other SPL councillors and, by 1934, four of the six elected had broken with him. Apparently the SPL leader preferred a vertical chain of command and was reluctant to delegate authority to others even as the SPL was enjoying electoral success. No local branches were formed and Ratcliffe gave senior posts to women, perhaps because he thought them less likely to challenge his authority. In March 1933 he had to appeal through his newspaper for readers interested in being SPL candidates to come forward. Candidates 'do not need to be brilliant speakers but sincere, reliable, and incorruptible'.[81]

In 1934, with councillors defecting, Ratcliffe's movement was fast running out of steam. He could not inspire loyalty because of his quirky personality. One by one he fell out with his collaborators until he was left only with members of his immediate family or those few willing to suspend their critical faculties and offer total obedience to somebody who regarded himself as the sole repository of protestant truth. Thus voters were not impressed with his hastily-arranged electoral pact with the Moderates who wanted to unite the anti-Socialist vote and drive Labour out of power. Neither did all Moderates support the pact whereby Ratcliffe was given a free run in Dennistoun in return for the SPL not standing in traditional Moderate seats. Ex-councillor Matthew Armstrong, an elder of the Kirk came out of retirement to stand as an Independent Moderate against Ratcliffe whom he regarded as 'a menace who needed to be driven from public life'.[82] As a prosperous businessman he was able to finance a strong campaign and contact was even made with the Catholic Union.[83]

Viewing the SPL–Moderate alliance as a threat to catholic educational interests, Archbishop Mackintosh summoned all senior priests to the Catholic Institute in Glasgow on 22 October 1934 to underline the gravity of the position.[84] The Catholic Union mobilised its vote as perhaps it had never done before and Labour stood down in Dennistoun so as not to split the anti-Ratcliffe vote. Armstrong defeated Ratcliffe by 4,745 votes to 4,404 in a cliffhanging contest. The SPL gained 7% of the vote in 1934 and thereafter Ratcliffe drifted to the political sidelines. Standing for Camphill ward in 1937 he got 2,500 votes but was still convincingly defeated. Never again would he enjoy the political limelight. Through the medium of his paper he criticised the first signs of *entente* between the protestant establishment and upwardly mobile catholics as when Lord Provost Dollan and Sir Alexander Swan, the Provincial Grade Master of the Scottish Freemasons were piped into Glasgow's St Andrew's Hall where a masonic banquet was in progress. A horrified Ratcliffe wrote:

> A papist receiving the honours of the Masonic order, and this when the Masonic order is officially cursed and condemned by the Church . . . No wonder the Pope died a few days afterwards.[85]

Shortly after Ratcliffe returned from a visit to Germany in August 1939, his newspaper was able to appear fortnightly instead of monthly. No evidence survives that he received any help from the Nazi authorities but he was prepared to speak up for Germany, refuting claims that people there were starving or that they hated Hitler.[86] By 1940 the Jews had replaced roman catholics as his main bugbear and he contemptuously referred to the Gorbals district of Glasgow as 'Jewland'. An advert in the first issue of 1940, promised articles on 'Our Jewish Usurers', 'the Jews and Crime', and 'Why Germany Put Out the Jews'.[87] Soon after, another edition had a piece entitled 'Britain's Pro-Jew Menace'.[88]

In February 1940 Ratcliffe clashed with Councillor H. D. Longbottom, leader of the Protestant Party in Liverpool who questioned his belief that Hitler was working for the end of 'Popery' in Germany.[89] Later, in June 1940, with Nazi Germany at the zenith of its power, he plaintively remarked in *Vanguard* that 'we are very kind to the Roman Catholics in Scotland, of course the reason being seemingly that we have no Hitler in our midst to eject Popery'.[90]

From the tenor of his statements in 1939–40, one could be forgiven for thinking that Ratcliffe, a protestant iconoclast to the last, wanted to see the triumph of Hitler. During the rest of the war, he campaigned against it in association with the anarchist pacifist Guy Aldred and died in relative obscurity in January 1947.[91]

However unpopular the catholic minority in Glasgow was, its size and degree of organisation made it difficult for Ratcliffe to intimidate his chosen target. Across in Edinburgh, where catholics comprised less than 10% of the population it was, for a while in the mid-1930s, a very different story. Here protestant extremists enjoyed greater political success than in Glasgow and their campaign was laced with anti-catholic violence. Catholic functions were attacked, priests were assaulted in the streets and threatened in chapel houses, and many ordinary catholics were victimised at work. The eruption of strife on such a scale was difficult to explain because the Orange presence was weak in Edinburgh, street violence fuelled by religiously misunderstanding was previously virtually unknown, and the Ulster question had not divided the city as had happened in Glasgow.

The rise of Protestant Action owed more to the angry eloquence of its leader, John Cormack than to the prevailing political situation or previous sectarian unrest. For a brief period he showed that, even in the absence of deep and readily understood divisions, a city or a community can almost be torn apart by the sudden emergence of a charismatic individual who can move people to deeds which they would never normally contemplate.

Born in 1894, the son of Highland parents, he was brought up in a devout Baptist household and, at the age of fifteen, he joined the Argyll and Sutherland Highlanders as a boy soldier. Serving in the trenches in the First World War he later saw action in Ireland during the 1919–21 War of Independence. Collusion between catholic priests and Sinn Fein separatists made him strongly anti-catholic.[92] Such feelings were not assuaged when he worked in the Edinburgh Post Office (GPO) from 1922 to 1934 after leaving the forces. In his new job he was suspected of tampering with mail destined for the Archbishop of Edinburgh and, eventually he was accused of stealing letters and postal orders: No formal charges were ever lodged against Cormack but he was suspended from the GPO in 1932. Already he was speaking on Sundays at the Mound, the venue for open-air speakers in Edinburgh. Initially, this was a gesture of solidarity with his father, a lay preacher who was being maltreated by young catholics in the crowd when he spoke.[93]

Cormack gathered around him a growing band of supporters who fought for control of the streets with young catholics who lived in the crowded tenements of Edinburgh Old Town. These clashes sharpened his anti-catholicism, he found that he could attract a following on account of his physical boldness and speaking abilities, and his thoughts soon turned to politics; in 1933 he formed the Protestant Action Society and one year later he decided to stand for the ward of North Leith in the Edinburgh municipal elections. He was elected, defeating the sitting Moderate, even though Leith, Edinburgh's port was not his home area, nor did it harbour a 'No Popery' tradition at least on the scale of that found in similar small towns in the west of Scotland. In 1886 it had elected William Gladstone when he was championing Irish

Home Rule.[94] From 1918 to 1927, the radical Liberal William Wedgwood Benn was the town's MP. By now, Leith was beginning to be affected by the depression. The export of coal and ancillary trades upon which the viability of the docks depended, ground to a halt with the downturn of the international economy. Severe hardship ensued but the Labour Party, which had received its worst Scottish results in the black year of 1931 in and around Edinburgh, was unable to make much headway. A National Liberal, Ernest Brown, remained the port's MP until 1945. He was a Baptist lay preacher from the south of England. His success perhaps illustrates how, in hard times, the citizens of the port of Leith clung to traditional values and found security in backing a politician with a distinctly religious appeal.

Cormack owed his first and many subsequent victories in Leith to an unusually high poll. In 1934 the average Edinburgh turnout had been 40% but in North Leith it was 58·4% the highest in the whole city. Rowdiness characterised the contest in 1934 and in 1935 when he fielded more candidates, much to the dismay of the local press.[95]

Protestant Action's manifesto was bound to attract controversy. Cormack was on record as advocating the disenfranchisement of roman catholics in Britain and their expulsion from Scotland. Less absurdly, he promised to remove local catholics from all public employment, ban them from having the use of corporation halls, or going ahead with public processions if his party ever won a controlling majority in Edinburgh.[96] The promise of a redistribution of jobs in the depression-ridden 1930s may well account for some part of his electoral support which was always greater than publicly expressed support for his religious views. Cormack was so effective in spreading the impression roman catholics enjoyed preference in corporation employment that they were even believed by sceptics, as a letter from Mr David Harper published in the *Scotsman* on 22 December 1984 shows:

> In the environment of the means test and traumatic unemployment, there was understandable support for the scathing case he made against Irish RC infiltration into the workforce of Edinburgh Corporation Cleansing Department and also into the tramway system which he, I think, nicknamed 'Paddy Reilly's railway'.

No evidence has been found to show that Cormack ever backed up his accusations with detailed figures of the religious background of corporation employees which presumably, as a councillor on various corporation committees, he might have had access to. His claims may have had such a telling impact for the following simple reason: being overwhelmingly working-class, roman catholics working for the corporation were likely to have been found in the most menial open-air occupations where they would come into contact with the general public.

In 1935 Cormack took advantage of his mandate to embarrass and intimidate the catholic authorities in Edinburgh. He gave a warning of the lengths he was prepared to go to shortly before the city council was due to give a civic reception to the Catholic Young Men's Society:

> On the 27th day of April, the peaceful, cultured, enlightened city of Edinburgh, that has never known in my lifetime at least what a real smash-up means, is going to know it that day, if this civic reception comes off.[97]

Councillors Cormack and Marr (the latter newly returned for Central Leith at a by-election) duly turned up outside the City Chambers with over ten thousand people, many of whom barracked the arriving council guests. Fearing trouble a detachment of Gordon Highlanders stationed in Edinburgh Castle was placed in readiness.[98] When the Archbishop of Edinburgh arrived, his car was almost surrounded by a hostile mob before the police brought him to safety.[99] Later, on 10 June 1935, Cormack interrupted the ceremony in which Joseph Lyons, the Australian Prime Minister and a Roman Catholic, was being given the freedom of Edinburgh along with John Buchan.[100] Still more unruly scenes occurred later when a Catholic Eucharistic Congress was held in Edinburgh. Since the first one in Lille during 1882, Eucharistic Congresses had been held to propagate 'the uniquely catholic doctrine of the real presence of Christ in the Eucharist'.[101] This doctrine of transubstantiation was anathema to Cormack and on the evening of 24 June, there was much disorder in Waverley Market where a woman's eucharistic meeting was being held and four priests were set upon by a hostile mob.[102] However, the worst scenes of all occurred at the climax of the Congress on 25 June at an open-air procession of the Blessed Sacrament. This avoided the city-centre and was held in the grounds of St Andrew's Priory, Canaan Lane, in the Morningside district. The next day, the *Scotsman* related how 'as the hour of the gathering approached, tramcar after tramcar brought protestant extremists and others to the scene . . . By 7 p.m., there must have been at least 10,000 people in Morningside Road. Gangs of youths and women shouted "No Popery" ' . . . It went on to report that special coaches containing women and young people were stoned, fighting broke out in the crowd, the police were attacked and baton charges were made.[103]

The atmosphere was ugly and the intimidation of catholics continued on and off for the rest of the summer. Catholic activists stood on all-night vigils guarding their churches and a Catholic Vigilance Association was formed when it was feared that this might have to be a long-term precaution.[104] Worshippers were jeered and taunted as they entered St Mary's Cathedral and retired accountant, John McLaughlin, can still recall how, at midnight mass on a Christmas Eve in the mid-

1930s a few of Cormack's supporters entered St Mary Star of the Sea Church in Leith 'when it was packed to the doors' and 'went to communion simply for the sake of coming out and waving the host saying this is what they believe and it is not true'.[105]

Other Edinburgh catholics still recall how attempts were made to pressurise catholics in their workplace. Archbishop McDonald spoke out at the time about the intimidation of catholics in factory employment.[106] Some catholics in the retail trade were layed off on account of their religion;[107] in other concerns, such as the printing trade, they kept their jobs but none were taken on in future. Some large shopkeepers had already operated a protestant only staffing policy over many years so that Cormack's views were not particularly new, it was rather the extreme methods he used to enforce them that were striking. Even catholics working for the Co-operative Society in Edinburgh were not immune from pressure and they were harassed or intimidated by fellow workers or managerial staff, according to the testimony of at least one catholic who worked for St Cuthberts Co-operative Society.[108] From his own memories of the 1930s, Hugh Brown, Labour MP for Glasgow Provan recalls that there was a distinct lack of sympathy for roman catholics in the co-operative society.[109] No catholic ever became a director of the largest Scottish society, the SCWS at least before 1945 and, earlier in the century, a separate catholic Co-operative society nearly got off the ground in Lanarkshire because of perceived anti-catholic bias.[110]

The Co-operative movement had strong masonic affiliations and freemasons were also strongly entrenched in many local Scottish police forces up to and beyond the 1930s. The police is the other well-known institution which Hugh Brown MP identified as not being particularly sympathetic to catholics at this time. It was not just in the Edinburgh force that catholic officers were conspicuous by their absence. Between the masonic order and the roman catholic church there was little love lost and it would not have been surprising if this was reflected in relations between the police and ordinary catholics; they were, by and large, low wage earners who dwelt in the overcrowded tenements of the Old Town in Cowgate, the Grassmarket, and the Canongate. These were areas where the police frequently had to investigate crimes, albeit of a petty kind linked with drunkenness and petty thieving and, although most of the Old Town's inhabitants somehow managed to remain law-abiding in the fight for economic survival and the maintenance of self-respect, it did not incline the police to view them always in a sympathetic light.

The police stood aside from much of the small-scale sectarian violence that occurred in Edinburgh in the 1930s. Cormack even singled them out for praise at the time of the most serious public disturbances in 1935.[111] He may have won the sympathy of sections of the Edinburgh force for the punishment he had taken from young catholics in earlier days as well as for having made short shrift of elements that the police and Protestant Action were quick to perceive as 'hooligans'. Today Cormack's followers still recall a showdown that occurred with a group of young catholics called the Blackie Boys (named after Blackfriars Street where most of them lived); they engaged in skirmishes with PA's militants until caught unawares by a successful incursion into the Cowgate, their home area, when gang members were taken from their homes at an early hour and beaten up in the street below without the intervention of the police.[112] Afterwards, Cormack capped this success in April 1937 by unveiling a tablet in memory of the Covenanters in the heavily catholic Grassmarket before a crowd of 10,000 people and in the face of little opposition.[113]

Many authoritarian leaders seek to demonstrate their power by penetrating the territory of the opposition and Cormack was no exception. In his bid to rededicate Edinburgh to the memory of John Knox and reclaim it from David Hume and the other men of the enlightenment who set their stamp on it in the eighteenth century, he was aided by a paramilitary movement called Kormack's Kaledonian Klan. It had its headquarters in the Lawnmarket near the district of its catholic opponents. It derived its inspiration from the American Ku Klux Klan and it possessed a number of cars as well as small arms which, in the event, were never used.[114] The emergence of such a body in usually tranquil Edinburgh showed how extreme in some quarters was the antipathy to the small and vulnerable catholic minority in Scotland's capital.

Cormack even shocked some of his allies by the lengths he was prepared to go. As he saw it, roman catholics were beyond redemption even if they displayed a willingness to abandon Romish doctrines and embrace the Reformed tradition. For many years he stubbornly adhered to the view that 'once a catholic always a catholic'. To be born and raised a catholic was a stain that could never be erased. However, others heavily involved in anti-catholic agitation showed more flexibility. Their approach can be summed up in the phrase 'we condemn the sin, not the individual, we condemn romanism as a system but we have nothing but love for the individual'. Few in practice quite adhered to these lofty sentiments but Ratcliffe, Longbottom and others could not quite bring themselves to endorse Protestant Action's objective written into its manifesto: 'As Romanists deal with Protestants in countries where they have full power, so will we deal with Romanists in this country.'[115]

Cormack's call for the expulsion of Scottish catholics, along with the religious orders, may have looked far-fetched even in the 1930s but, for the proposed dispersal of catholics in Scotland, there had been a recent precedent, albeit on a small scale. In 1917, as a result of an Anglo-Russian convention signed with the shortlived Kerensky government, the mainly catholic Lithuanian community in Scotland was broken up.[116] Male Lithuanians who had emigrated to Scotland to work in the Lanarkshire coalfield, were rounded up and shipped to Russia to serve in the Russian army, few if any ever being able to return to join their families in Scotland. In 1940 when Mussolini took Italy into the war on Hitler's side, the authorities rounded up most adult male Italians and placed them in internment camps. If the tension between de Valera's government in Ireland and the British government had flared into something approaching a state of war between the two islands, it is not inconceiveable to think that at least the Irish-born among the catholic community in Scotland might have been deported or even placed in custody.

Among his opponents Cormack was often viewed as a fascist whose threats and strong-arm methods were not to be treated lightly, at least when he was at the height of his influence. But Protestant Action was essentially a religious party and its disregard for nationalism, the primary element in most European fascist movements, makes a *direct* comparison with Hitler and Mussolini inappropriate. It looked back to the Reformation for inspiration whereas mid-European fascism was more modern and revolutionary, drawing its symbols and ideas from an extreme interpretation of the nineteenth century awakening of European nationalism. However, similarities in style and tactics should not be overlooked, all of which suggests that just as catholic fascism was possible in south-western Europe, a protestant variety was not inconceiveable in the north and Protestant Action may have provided at least an outline of it.

Cormack dominated his own movement as completely as Hitler and Mussolini exercised power in their own respective parties. Protestant Action's very existence as a popular movement hinged on the presence of its leader who derived his authority from his magnetism and from the power of the oratory rather than from any office he might hold within the organisation or on the council. Like Hitler, Cormack had the dangerous gift of influencing people to do what he wanted by the power of his speaking voice. James Russell recalls that 'he built up his audience to a crescendo. If he had said, right out to you go and do it, they would have followed his instructions.'[117] Cormack was not unaware of his power. Facing charges after disturbances at a 1936 catholic meeting addressed by Monsignor Ronald Knox, he admitted to the court to having said on that occasion, 'I have only to say one word and this street would flow with blood. . .'[118]

Protestant Action's campaign against a small and vulnerable

minority upon whom the responsibility for the ills of Edinburgh was placed invited comparison with the tactics adopted by the British Union of Fascists against the Jews in the east end of London at exactly the same point in time. They were held up as scapegoats for national and local ills, individual Jews were beaten up, and provocative rallies or meetings were held near to areas of dense Jewish settlement. But there was no catholic petit-bourgeoisie with recently acquired wealth and uncertain social status upon whom Cormack could focus the envy and frustration of less enterprising citizens. The nearest equivalent is the small compact Italian community which emerged in Scotland after 1860. By the 1930s between one-fifth and one-quarter of the Italians in Britain lived in Scotland's cities and towns. But they were unsuitable scapegoats since they had carved out a niche for themselves by specialising in service roles where there was little or no competition from native Scots.[119]

Slogans like 'Toleration Overdone is an Evil' or 'Better a Competent Dictatorship than an Incompetent Democracy',[120] were used by Cormack in public and private and show his authoritarian political outlook. However, in 1936 he disavowed any connection with fascism in a press interview: 'All our energies will be directed against the fascists. When I get control, I will put a ban on fascists in the streets.'[121] In practice Sir Oswald Mosley got as tough a reception from Cormack as from the left when he attempted to hold meetings in Edinburgh. It was not the punitive and illiberal elements of fascism which fuelled Cormack's hostility but Mosley's past and present support for an independent and united Ireland. In England, where feeling over Ireland was lukewarm on right and left, he suffered little damage but, in Scotland, it made him anathema to most potential supporters.

At the 1935 local elections Protestant Action consolidated its position when those standing on a protestant ticket gained nearly one-quarter of the votes polled in Edinburgh. The party was apparently unharmed by its association with violence and Cormack kept the temperature high into 1936 by holding outdoor and indoor meetings on every day of the week, three on Sunday, and occasional rallies in the Usher Hall which held over 3,000 people and which he regularly filled. His arrest, following disturbances at a Catholic Truth Society meeting in February 1936 addressed by Monsignor Ronald Knox, brought more publicity especially when he elected to conduct his own defence at the subsequent trial. Women queued all night to be guaranteed seats in the public gallery and hundreds of his supporters escorted him to court. When he was briefly imprisoned for non-payment of his fine, his hero status was confirmed.[122]

Women would be among Cormack's staunchest supporters for years to come and the party had a far higher proportion of female candidates then was customary for any party in the 1930s. This is not so surprising if it is recalled that there were few other openings for women in protestant life with membership of the Freemasons and any kind of influence in the Orange Order denied to them. One commentator reckons that an important element of his success was the ability he possessed to pour 'excitement into lives that were a vacuum of inactivity . . . and frustration'.[123] At its peak, Protestant Action boasted a membership of 8,000 people in Edinburgh and, given the high turnover, it is not unreasonable to conclude that many must have joined or turned up at demonstrations for the excitment and the novelty, with the religious appeal being incidental. However, Cormack was also able to attract capable helpers drawn by the cause as much as by the charisma of its exponent. Cormack was thus a more practical and accommodating type of leader than Ratcliffe, much better at inspiring loyalty. In 1936 he fielded an organisation that was able to capture 30·84% of the total municipal vote in the city. Six candidates were returned, making a total of nine, and Labour was driven into third place. Seats were taken from both the Moderates and Labour and Cormack realised his aim of driving all catholics from the council; between the two world wars, no other party on the margins of British politics ever did remotely as well in local politics as Protestant Action.

At its height Protestant Action was able to claim both working-class and middle-class backing. Demonstrations and open-air party meetings tended to attract lower income groups while the more affluent and respectable supporters were seen at indoor religious meetings or else, if they were businessmen, preferred to discreetly offer financial support for the movement's election fund or annual bazaar.[124] Many newsagents stocked Cormack's fortnightly newspaper while he claimed to have received telegrams of congratulations from businessmen in all parts of the city after his 1936 electoral triumph.

But thereafter Protestant Action grew too unwieldy as Cormack found it difficult to maintain control over his council group. They were a disparate collection of people who included a fifty-three-year-old Jewess, Esther Henry who was not the only one to have mounted the protestant bandwagon for opportunistic reasons.[125] Opposition to the church of Rome was not enough to keep them united when most of council business concerned non-religious matters. To enable Cormack to remain in control the movement was organised along increasingly authoritarian lines until finally, in 1937, he dismissed the party's executive committee and assumed dictatorial powers. Various councillors defected and in the 1937 local elections, Cormack's judgement appeared to have deserted him when he stood in two seats. Labour took North Leith from him and he failed to be elected in Gorgie because voters were indignant that he would not be giving them his individual attention if he represented two wards. Like Ratcliffe, Cormack suffered from *folie de grandeur* after his electoral break-through and proved unable to consolidate his success. However, he was a more stable personality who had built up a more considerable movement and enough of it remained for him to be returned for South Leith in 1938, a ward he represented without interruption until his retirement in 1962.

As protest movements the SPL and Protestant Action did well because they echoed the prejudices of certain groups of voters at a time when the major parties were exhausted or else divided. Third parties once more did well in Scotland in the late 1960s and early 1970s, but then the Scottish Nationalists and the Liberals had a set of policies and an organisation and were not just built around a handful of personalities or a bundle of negative attitudes. A party based largely on prejudice can only continue to attract voters in a polarised political atmosphere and politically Scotland was among the calmer European countries in the 1930s. The negativism was on full display in the attitude of Ratcliffe and Cormack to each other. The former came across to Edinburgh to campaign against Cormack in the 1937 elections; instead of pooling their energies and forming a nationwide movement, they went their separate ways in the 1930s. Ratcliffe could not bear to be faced with a rival who refused to defer to him and who went on to enjoy much greater political success. Their enmity demonstrated just how difficult it is for protestantism, a faith prone to faction and schism, to participate in electoral politics in the highly successful way its rival has done in catholic Europe.

But in Scotland, if the roman catholic minority had responded to the protestant challenge in the 1930s by setting up its own sectional party, the political battle-lines might have been drawn more firmly and real hostilities might have commenced. The response of Scottish catholic leaders to the threat from Cormack and Ratcliffe was usually a measured one as an ex-member of the SPL recalls: 'the Roman church "took the stick", often ignored the challenge and like the Arabian proverb, the dogs bark but the caravan moves on'.[126] Occasion-ally statements were made by catholics for internal consumption which fuelled protestant anger if reported to a wider audience. A typical example occurred in Edinburgh in 1938 when John A. Barry, address-ing a rally of the Catholic Truth Society, declared that 'the next thirty years will decide whether God or mammon will rule in this country. I am telling you that many young people who are here today will live to see Scotland atheist or Roman Catholic.'[127]

The indifference of major vested interests in protestant Scotland was another powerful obstacle that the protestant parties were unable to overcome. Unlike Ratcliffe, Cormack tried to operate within the

Orange Order so as to win it round to his idea of promoting a full-scale protestant party. Today he is a folk hero in east of Scotland Orange circles, whose portrait adorns several Orange banners. But he had a singular lack of success and after quitting the Order in exasperation in 1939, he was not allowed back in till the late 1950s when, as an elderly veteran of the protestant cause, he was no longer in a position to rock the boat.

The Orange Order has always had a tendency to distrust populists like Cormack who emerge from outside its ranks. It has usually been led by cautious men who defer to nobody in their anti-catholic views but who have come up through a very formal bureaucratic structure and who are content to manifest their hostility to the Church of Rome in backstage lobbying and ritual marches rather than in dramatic political ways. The Church of Scotland likewise was stony ground for anti-catholic zealots. Ratcliffe soon alienated Frederick Watson, the minister most sympathetic to his views[128] while Cormack only received the public support of one parish minister. However, he was quite a well-known figure: Dr James Black, of St George's West Church, Edinburgh, the Moderator of the 1938 General Assembly and a future chaplain to King George VI who 'spoke on our platform many a time' according to a former vice-president of Protestant Action.[129]

Media hostility too in both Glasgow and Edinburgh made it difficult for the religious parties to break out of their electoral ghetto and may well have hastened their demise. Back in 1929 in response to both public interest and mounting agitation on the question, *The Glasgow Herald* undertook a detailed investigation of the facts concerning the immigration of the Irish into Scotland. After publishing its findings in five lengthy articles, the conclusion of the journalist investigating the question was as follows:

> I am satisfied that the current Irish immigration is not large, that compared with the stream of the past it is the veriest trickle, and that it is practically negligible in bearing upon the development of the Irish community in Scotland. That development proceeded almost entirely from the multiplication of the Scoto-Irish—natives of this country but of Irish extraction.[130]

These findings did not deter controversialists who were not going to be dissuaded by inconvenient facts, but they may have had a salutary effect on middle-ground opinion, made uneasy by recent demographic changes but prepared to take its lead from the premier reading outlet of the middle-class in the west of Scotland. So *The Glasgow Herald* may have done a singular service for community relations at the end of the 1920s. But its words did not always have a calming effect on public opinion. A fiercely worded editorial in 1922 had claimed that 'it is no reflection upon the Irish people, but a statement of cold sociological fact that Ireland has been responsible for more of our social troubles in Glasgow than the war and Bolshevik propaganda combined'.[131]

Such outbursts had largely disappeared from the regional press by the 1930s as the Scottish press corps began to realise just how volatile public opinion was on religious matters involving protestants and catholics. On 22 June 1935 *The Glasgow Weekly Herald* published in full, a vitriolic letter from Cormack 'without' in the editors own words 'any attempt at sub-editing or punctuation'. Compton Mackenzie claimed that the bad grammar and clumsy syntax which Cormack exhibited, warned off respectable protestants, but the letter appeared on the verge of the Eucharistic Congress when he drew his biggest crowds and before his greatest electoral victories. Without exception, the press in Edinburgh appealed for calm in the troubled year of 1935, urged catholics not to over-react and spelled out the bleak consequences for Edinburgh unless all of its citizens recovered their senses and exercised restraint. The editorial in the *Edinburgh Evening Dispatch* on 29 April 1935, after the first major public disturbance, warned of 'The Gangster Spirit' loose in Edinburgh on the same day that its rival, the *Evening News* opined that 'we do not want to see Edinburgh ruled from the so-called public forum on the Mound'. These papers were read by many PA supporters, but their editorial message was consistently anti-Cormack both before and after elections. However, they did take adverts for protestant meetings while the *Daily Record* in Glasgow had refused to take adverts for the SPL in 1934 before the crucial municipal elections of that year. One of its columnists even wrote that 'it may be necessary to plead for the running of Glasgow's affairs by a dispassionate commission if sectarianism prevails'.[132] The paper's editor, David Anderson, also tried to get the city's religious leaders to sign a joint declaration calling on voters to reject the intervention of sectarian feeling into party politics. But Archbishop Mackintosh refused to put his name to the appeal because, in an accompanying article, one of his priests was to be criticised for giving a political lead to his parishioners, so the project was abandoned.[133]

The occasional journalist was to be found who reflected popular unease about the Scoto-Irish and who used his pen to magnify the ill-effects of their presence. In the late 1920s the Leith-born George Malcolm Thomson (1899–) did this in a number of remarkable books where, with much eloquence, he sought to convince his complacent fellow countrymen how their very national identity was in peril. The Irish in Scotland are not the only symbols of decline examined in his books but some of his most angry prose is reserved for them. The Scots, 'a nation waiting for a boat', are 'a dying people . . . being replaced in their own country by a people alien in race, temperament, and religion'.[134] Thomson regarded the 'miracle-working' Grotto of Carfin as 'a landmark of the religious and racial revolution . . . changing the spiritual face of Scotland'. Its location was no accident, 'situated in . . . the very heart of industrial Scotland and within easy reach of the main industrial towns'.[135] He recalled how 'the sight of three Irish Catholic priests walking in Princes Street came upon me with the shock of a portent. I waited for some demonstration of wrath from heaven. I looked around appealing to some solid outward symbol of Knox's presence in his own land to fall down and crush the papistical intruders.'[136]

In his *Rediscovery of Scotland*, Thomson had a fictional conversation with a knowledgeable working-class Scot to illustrate the scale in which the Scots were being displaced by the Irish in the factories and docks of their own country:

> you can take it from me, this is the biggest thing happening to Scotland . . . maybe . . . since the Battle of Bannockburn. You may think I am putting it rather high but you remember: I am not going on any rows of figures published by Protestant societies. All I have to say is based on what I have seen with my two eyes, first as a boy helping the steward on a boat plying between Ardrossan and Dublin, then as an apprentice in a Clyde shipyard, after that when I was living in my own native village in the Ayrshire coal district, and finally, as a kind of tramp wandering over Scotland in search of meals.[137]

'I wonder', asked this Scottish Everyman at one point, 'if some day there won't be a Scottish problem in Scotland. On the whole, I don't think so; we're too law abiding, we'll just quickly fade out of the picture.'[138] However, in his other book, *Caledonia or the Future of the Scots*, (a fantastic allegorical tale in which the Scotland of 2027 is sketched out to show how it has been denationalised mainly by the catholic Irish presence), a very different scenario unfolds. Thomson takes as his starting-point the premise that 'the Scottish lion and the Irish bull will not lie down together',[139] due to an essential incompatibility located in the very blood:

> In the old days the hatred between the Presbyterian Scots of Ulster and the Irish was always much more bitter than that between the English and the Irish. The Englishman liked the Irish, ignored them, was amused by them, and at times lost his temper with them. The Ulster Scots could not stand them.
> Who can tell why such repugnances exist? . . . I suggest, without claiming scientific status for it, that it is possibly related to another Scoto-Irish phenomenon, which has often been noted, the sociological failure of mixed marriages between the two races. They resulted in a crossbred type which united the bad qualities of both stocks and bred, in addition, a strange

nullity, an abnormal lack of character and vigour. On the other hand, Anglo-Scottish and Anglo-Irish marriages have been found to produce a more virile and energetic generation. But to leave causes for effects.[140]

The effects were revealed with a vengeance in 1981 when 'the Irish population in Scotland had passed the million mark and . . . the slowly deepening irritation between the races flashed into open war'.[141] In Thomson's colourful essay in futurology regular sieges of the Irish quarter were described, churches Catholic and Presbyterian were burned, troops and armoured cars were twice brought from England to establish martial law in Lanarkshire.[142]

By 2027 the outcome of the race conflict had been settled. When an intelligent young New Zealander, Mr Macauley drops out of the London-Reykjavik-Tokyo express somewhere over Edinburgh he was therefore:

> not altogether astonished when on the first day of his stay in Edinburgh, he encountered a vast and reverent crowd which watched an ecclesiastical procession, with many crucifixes and thuribles. It was the Archbiship of Edinburgh and his clergy, passing on their way to the magnificent new cathedral of St Patrick which reached its glittering white spire two hundred feet over Princes Street.[143]

This fantastic tale shows how apprehensive a number of Scottish intellectuals were about the future. Nor was it all Scottish nationalists who decried the Irish presence. The radical Scottish educationalist, A. S. Neill, worried about its consequences in the 1930s:

> In Scotland we have an intelligent and forceful proletariat, but it is a subservient proletariat. Why? It may be because of the strong Irish element in such places as Clydeside and Dundee, an element that is directed by the priesthood, the priesthood that serves its Lord and Master . . . property.[144]

Another radical who was sceptical about the benefits of the Irish presence was George Orwell, the English novelist: 'Irish Catholics in Britain,' he wrote, 'act as a silent drag on Labour Party policy, but one not sufficiently under the thumb of their priests to be fascists in sympathy.'[145]

Much later, George Malcolm Thomson regretted his anti-Irish outbursts. Work as Lord Beaverbrook's chief assistant took him outside the Scottish milieu and he declared in 1982 that he had not sufficiently thought through his exact views when active in Scottish nationalist politics during the 1920s and 1930s.[146] A close collaborator in those days was Andrew Dewar Gibb, a former Unionist party candidate who joined the National party and later became Regius Professor of Scots Law at Glasgow University. In his *Scotland in Eclipse* published in

1930 he did not need to resort to allegory to drive home his case against the Irish in Scotland:

> In the heart of a dwindling though virile and intelligent race there is growing up another people, immeasurably inferior in every way, but cohesive and solid, refusing obstinately, at the behest of obscurantist magic-men, to mingle with the people whose land they are usurping; unaware of, or if aware, disloyal to all the finest ideals and ambitions of the Scottish race: distinguished by a veritable will to squalour which is mainly responsible for Scottish slumdom; squatting and breeding in such numbers as to threaten in another hundred years to gain actual predominance in the country . . .[147]

Anti-immigrant legislation was not enough. 'No amount of anti-immigration legislation can prevent Irish labourers from having families of twelve nor Irish priests from telling them that to attend a birth-control clinic is a deadly sin.'[148] Unlike Thomson, Dewar Gibb did not mellow and, as late as 1950, in another work *Scotland Resurgent*, the title indicating that nemesis had not yet struck, he advocated the out-lawing of the Ne Temere decree:

> this pronouncement . . . that marriages in a Protestant church or in a registry office are void in the sight of God. The promulgation of this most offensive doctrine which would bastardise most of the people in Scotland, has been declared criminally punishable in New Zealand and New South Wales. Scotland should be able, if she so decides, to secure a similar measure.[149]

Dewar Gibb's professional interest in law inevitably brought him to the subject of the Irish and crime. In *Scotland In Eclipse* he did not put much restraint on his words:

> They are responsible for most of the crime committed in Scotland, which otherwise would be the most law-abiding country in the world. Wheresoever knives and razors are used, wheresoever sneak thefts and mean pilfering are easy and safe, wheresoever dirty acts of sexual baseness are committed, there you will find the Irish in Scotland with all but a monopoly of the business.[150]

In 1922 the *Glasgow Observer*, always exceedingly sensitive about slights directed at its readership, conceded part of Dewar Gibb's case but refuted some of the more damning allegations:

> They may seem to figure very largely in the records of minor crime.
> But they are concerned but little in serious crime.
> Scotland produces her own 'Scotch Jimmies', her own fraudulent Bank Directors, and much the greater proportion of her own murderers and homicides.
> The Irish are mercurial in temperament, and in industrial centres are quite likely to participate largely in street brawls. But the silent, stealthy, sullen Scotch law-breaker, while much less demonstrative in his outbreaks is the

much more serious sinner against order, law, and social amenity.[151]

This was one issue that refused to lie down. In 1938 Dewar Gibb's charges about the Irish and crime were resuscitated by a pamphlet entitled 'Scotland's Dilemma: Province or Nation?' written by a fellow nationalist under the pseudonym of 'John Torrance'. However, its charges were this time refuted by a fellow nationalist, Dr Archie Lamont, writing in *Forward*:

> If 'John Torrance' had been reading either his *Forward* or *The Scots Independent* instead of papers and books published from London, he would know that that figure [on the numbers of Irish in Scotland] . . . is five times exaggerated . . .
>
> In his apparent anxiety to rouse animosity, 'John Torrance' goes on to refer to police-court reports and prison statistics as showing that the Irish make very bad immigrants . . .
>
> 'John Torrance' forgets that there is sometimes a connection between poverty and the incidence of crime . . .
>
> He forgets that the Irish at home have possibly the lowest criminality percentage in Europe.[152]

John McCormick was the leading figure in Scottish nationalist circles in the 1930s and early 1940s. Usually he has been depicted as a moderating influence in the SNP who, in the 1930s, helped to keep it free of extremist influences which might have led it down anti-democratic paths. This is the image he presents in his autobiography, *The Flag In The Wind*, and it is sufficiently well-established for friendly and otherwise reliable commentators to talk about McCormick having 'wanted no part in an appeal to anti-Irish populism'.[153] This is largely but not entirely true. Some correspondence found in Dewar Gibb's papers shows that he backed Dewar Gibb and Thomson in their anti-catholic Irish activities on at least one occasion. A letter from Thomson to Dewar Gibb, written on 3 March 1934, is fairly explicit about this:

> My Dear Dewar,
>
> I am in a businesslike mood so will write a curt official note.
>
> 1. *The Irish*
>
> Your news is excellent. I saw Gibson the other day. He told me of a resolution of the Stepps branch of the NPS demanding action on Clause 18 of the Education Act . . . This will arise at June conference soon. Important fact (secret): it was drafted by McCormick.
>
> So you will see the wind blows in queer directions. I suggest we keep out of this anti-Catholic business, letting it grow as it will, but that we press on with our Irish business.
>
> Cautiously though, otherwise we will merely alienate Gunn . . .[154]

McCormick *was* in favour of assimilating the Scoto-Irish and he placed the blame for their 'un-Scottish social habits and standards' not on their priests or on their own racial inadequacy, but on the failure of Scots to develop a healthy national life to which the newcomers could relate. Once this was done he was confident that 'Scotland . . . will find no difficulty in absorbing the strangers in her midst and turning them into good Scottish citizens'.[155]

Taken as a whole anti-Irish sentiments were probably only a minority taste within the Nationalist movement despite the charge of George Buchanan, MP for Glasgow Gorbals that it was this attitude which in large measure explained why they were gathering support in the early 1930s.[156] Perhaps there were enough Nationalists who were mindful of the warning by the writer Colin Walkinshaw (a pseudonym used by the journalist J. M. Reid) that 'religious strife might offer to some enemies of Scottish nationhood the chance of creating a sort of Ulster problem'. Walkinshaw felt that 'the immediate threat of the Irish to Scottish nationality and independent revival was smaller than that of the English, for the Irish were nowhere in control'.[157] This view was endorsed by G. S. Pryde, a sympathetic observer of Scottish nationalism; writing in the *Sociological Review* in 1935, he declared that:

> Nationalist silence on the subject of the Irish Catholic problem is probably due partly to the desire to avoid antagonising a large, vocal, and organized section of the people, partly to sympathetic admiration of the Irish in point-ing the way by *their* achievement of political autonomy.[158]

In by-elections which the Nationalist party fought in the 1930s, few candidates seem to have made much of an appeal to bigotry or unreason, although this would have won them increased votes in not a few localities. In 1932, the *Glasgow Observer* was even able to support the National Party of Scotland candidate who fought a by-election in Dumbarton.[159] Then, a large percentage of catholic students at Glasgow University seem to have been nationally-minded according to several sources.[160] They played a key role in getting Compton Mackenzie elected as rector of Glasgow University in 1931, the first political success of the Scottish national movement. One of its doughtiest campaigners, Oliver Brown, recalled that during his time at Glasgow University:

> the corporate life of the students was dominated by forceful personalities bearing such names as Boyle and O'Hear, who represented much better than the McLachlans and the McTavishes the 'praefervidum ingenium Scotorum'.[161]

But very few of the better-educated Scoto-Irish ultimately graduated to the SNP (the party was reorganised as the Scottish National Party in 1934). Compton Mackenzie had his own views as to why they were reluctant to fully espouse the Nationalist cause:

when at last there were signs of national re-awakening, the Scoto-Irish students of Glasgow university were in the van of that movement to restore to Scotland her integrity, so prominently indeed that the whole National Party of Scotland was believed by many to be no better than a sinister agent of popery. Anxious to deodorise itself of the combined reek of incense and gunpowder, the National Party allowed a motion demanding the repeal of the 1918 Education Act to be moved by the Secretary of the Party at the annual conference. It is true that the motion was talked out but it was made evident to Nationalists who were also Catholics that the restoration to Scotland of her status as a sovereign nation might mean simultaneously the restoration of that spirit of religious violence, infection by which had first led the way to the destruction of Scotland's nationahood.[162]

But the SNP did not become a total preserve of the Presbyterian lower middle-class. A number of distinguished catholic intellectuals of Scottish lineage were committed nationalists and managed to overlook some of the prejudices directed at both their religion and the Irish ancestry of those who mainly practised it in Scotland. Moray McLaren, Compton Mackenzie, Fionn MacColla, the Hon. Ruaraidh Erskine of Marr and George Scott-Moncrieff were nationally-minded intellectuals who helped defuse the xenophobia of Dewar Gibb, Thomson and others. Apparently they did not see any contradiction in being catholics and supporters of a nationalist movement seeking independence for an overwhelmingly protestant country. Indeed Erskine of Marr and some of the others argued that in the past Scotland's catholic faith had been a bulwark of its independence and that it was no coincidence that her freedom had been quickly squandered when the catholic faith was renounced by nobles and reformers who cared little for Scotland's essential nationhood.[163]

Dewar Gibb and others like him preferred to single out the Reformation, the enlightenment, and Scotland's participation in the industrial revolution and the accumulation of the British Empire as examples of the genius of the nation; indeed his book, Scottish Empire argues that the 'Pax Britannica' was largely a Scottish undertaking. However, these landmarks occurred when Scotland was part of Great Britain or was in the process of shedding its statehood. An appeal to the Gaelic Celtic past would have yielded up a richer and more distinctively Scottish identity. However, this image of Scotland's past had only limited appeal to her mainly industrial population. The dilemma for Presbyterian nationalists was that if they embraced the Celtic cultural heritage, they would be depicted by their opponents as embracing catholicism.[164]

Some nationalists did unwittingly fuel Unionist propaganda that Scottish Nationalism was a catholic plot to subvert the Reformation settlement. A good example is Ruaraidh Erskine of Marr, the second son of the fifth Lord Erskine who was a Celtophile and a monarchist as well as being a roman catholic. In his *Guth na Bliadhna* (Voice of the Year), a periodical for Gaelic speakers and enthusiasts which ran from 1904 to 1920, he remarked that 'Nearly every great evil, religious, political, social and commercial which Alba labours under owes its existence or its continuation to Protestantism'.[165] William Gillies, the first editor of the *Scots Independent* in the 1920s (later the organ of the SNP) echoed this view: 'When Scotland was Catholic, Scotland was free. The Catholic Scots kept her so even when the Pontiff of her Church sided with England.'[166] Gillies does not seem to have been a convert to Catholicism like many of the other intellectuals and propagandists referred to, so the equation of nationhood with catholicism was not necessarily confined to those who might be described as catholic triumphalists.

Roland Muirhead (1868-1964) and Hugh McDiarmid (1892-1978) were separatists who welcomed the Irish presence in Scotland and who hoped that it would have a leavening effect on the Scottish national character, introducing some of those elements and traits which had made nationalism such a vital force in Ireland. Dr Archie Lamont (1907-85) the scientist and SNP propagandist kept in touch with Irish events during the 1930s and he reported on the progress of the young Irish state in *Forward* as well as the nationalist press. Lamont was resident in Ireland during the mid-1930s and he was critical of the censorship laws directed at literature while being enthusiastic about economic progress being made by the new state before World War Two.[167] 'What We Can Learn From Small Nations' was the title of a chapter in *Small Nations*, a book by Lamont published in 1944. In it he wrote that:

> There is a disapproval with which many in Scotland, even those sympathetic to the internationalist point of view, regard the Irish. It is a problem to discover whether this has an origin deep down in religion and national character, or is something imported which obscures the reality.[168]

In 1934 there was an opportunity to clear up misunderstanding when an SNP delegation headed by the Duke of Montrose (1878-1954) and Sir Alexander McEwen (1875-1941), visited Dublin and was received by President de Valera.[169] The delegation also visited Northern Ireland and the Isle of Man and the purpose of their visit was to gather evidence on how devolution worked in practice in those parts of the 'British Isles' which had won autonomy or outright independence from London. William Power (1873-1953), a Glasgow journalist and leading figure in the SNP during the 1930s and early 1940s was another visitor to Ireland during this time. He was favourably disposed towards the Irish generally while not underestimating the great changes that would have to be made if the Irish Free State was to be transformed from a backward agricultural nation to a modern and economically prosperous one. In his memoirs published in 1937, he had kind words for the Irish leader, Eamon de Valera 'whom we used to think mad, but who . . . has proved one of the most farseeing administrators in Europe'.[170]

It was Oliver Brown, perhaps the most energetic of all SNP propagandists during this century, who displayed the most positive attitude towards the Irish in Scotland and their Scoto-Irish heirs:

> During the terrible years of English domination, Ireland exported large numbers of wage-slaves to be employed in this island as hewers of wood and drawers of water for their alien masters. The peasants, uprooted from their native soil and herded into overcrowded slums quickly degenerated and the police court records began to bear a monotonous list of Murphy's and O'Reilly's convicted of being drunk and disorderly.
>
> There is, however, another side which has not been considered, the positive contribution made by these Irish immigrants and their offspring to Scottish life. Can we begin a distinguished list with any greater name than that of James Connolly, once employed in the Cleansing Department of Edinburgh Corporation? (If that was his right position, how many Lord Provosts of Edinburgh have been fit to be scavengers?) John Wheatley comes next as the only minister who so far has left a legislative achievement to his credit. John McGovern is one of the few forceful personalities in a Parliament which but for him would more closely resemble the Nazi Reichstag. William Gallacher maintains a high standard of personal morality in a Party not distinguished by its regard for moral scruples.
>
> Paul Vincent Carroll has achieved eminence in drama. Scholarship is represented by Professor D. Brogan who has succeeded Lord Bryce as the chief non-American authority on the American Constitution, by Dr Patrick MacGlynn, the Terentian scholar of Glasgow University and Drs Handley and Farmer who have enriched the history of Scotland by their researches in hitherto neglected fields. Sir John Lavery and Patrick Downey made a great contribution to Scottish painting. Among 'best-sellers' Dr Cronin is the most popular of the novelists that Scotland has produced in this century . . .
>
> This is a most remarkable record and we thoroughbred Scots are not sufficiently grateful because we do not deserve it. Yet even as I write these words I recognise the falsity of this distinction; for these people are no longer to be reckoned as Irish except in origin—they are now an integral part of our national life—however much they may be rightly attached by sentiment to the country of their origin.
>
> For it is now absurd to describe a McGinty or a Reilly as necessarily Irish as to proclaim that an Inglis must be English, a Fleming must be Belgian or that a Wallace must be Welsh.
>
> For in spite of sectarianism, the barriers between the long established inhabitants and the grandchildren of emigrants, are being broken down and even sectarianism itself has been steadily declining in the past twenty years with the corresponding decline in the influence of institutional religion.[171]

Oliver Brown and others of a similar persuasion were more representative of nationalist party feeling than the likes of Dewar Gibb by the end of the Second World War. This explains why Scottish nationalism could be commended in the 1974 edition of the annual Scottish catholic yearbook in quite fulsome terms:

Scotland's national movements have been free of a paranoia that haunts similar movements in other countries. Scottish Nationalism was, and is, a responsible, democratic and intelligent force . . . [172]

This was a small vindication for the Nationalists of the 1930s and 1940s who preferred to treat the Scoto-Irish as an integral part of the Scottish community. But even if the Nationalists had, without exception, been sympathetic to the Scoto-Irish or had sung the praises of Irish independence, it probably would not have made much difference to their electoral fortunes in the west of Scotland. In the 1930s and beyond the Scoto-Irish were more concerned with material advancement or simple survival than with sorting out their relationship with the Scottish nation and the Labour Party was the obvious vehicle for them.

Notes

1 *Glasgow Observer*, 10 February 1917.
2 Harvie, *No Gods and Precious Few Heroes*, pp. 10-11.
3 Andrew Dewar Gibb, *Scotland Resurgent*, Observer Press, Stirling, 1950, p. 180.
4 The speech is paraphrased in Murray, *The Old Firm*, p. 127; *GH* reported it on 21 December 1921.
5 Brogan, 'Catholics in changing social conditions'.
6 *GO*, 1 April 1922.
7 *GO*, 1 April 1922.
8 *GO*, 28 March 1925.
9 Steve Bruce, 'Popular Protestantism and politics in Scotland and Ulster', in J. K. Hadden and A. D. Shapre (eds.), *Prophetic Religion and Politics*, 1985.
10 *The Menace of the Irish Race to our Scottish Nationality*, William Bishop, Edinburgh, 1923.
11 *GO*, 19 May 1923.
12 First carried by the *Perthshire Constitutional and Journal* and reprinted in the *Protestant Advocate*, March 1928.
13 Sir E. J. Russell, *Great Britain:*
Essays in Regional Geography, quoted in Andrew Dewar Gibb, *Scotland in Eclipse*, Toulmin, London, 1930, pp. 54-5.
14 *GH*, 8 May 1935.
15 Frederick Ernest Watson (1884-1954), *Fasti Ecclesiae Scoticane*, 9, 1929-54, Oliver & Boyd, Edinburgh, 1961, p. 123.
16 McCaffrey, 'Roman Catholicism in Scotland', p. 299.
17 J. H. Treble, 'The working of the 1918 Education Act in Glasgow archdiocese', *Innes Review*, 31, 1, 1980, p. 28.
18 Treble, 'The working', p. 28.
19 'Bonnybridge Roman Catholic School v. Stirlingshire Education Authority', *1930 Sessions Cases, Cases decided in the Court of Sessions and also in the Court of Justiciary of the House of Lords*, T. & T. Clarke, Edinburgh, 1930, pp. 27-30.
20 *Edinburgh Evening News*, 2 June 1932.
21 Pat Bolan, *Scottish Catholic Observer*, 3 May 1985.
22 George Malcolm Thomson, *The Re-*

discovery of Scotland, Kegan Paul, London, 1928, p. 35.

23 *GO*, 6 November 1930.

24 *GO*, 22 February 1930.

25 *Scotsman*, 31 May 1935.

26 Quoted in Mackenzie, *Catholicism and Scotland*, p. 169.

27 Rev. J. Cameron Peddie, 'The man who really broke the Glasgow gangs', *Evening Citizen*, 19 January 1955.

28 Henry C. Whitley, *Laughter in Heaven*, Hutchinson, London, 1962, pp. 47-8.

29 See Albert Bogle, 'James Barr, B.D., M.P.', *Records of the Scottish Church History Society*, 21, 1983, pp. 189-207.

30 Recollection of James Durkan.

31 Ian S. Wood, 'John Wheatley . . .', p. 81.

32 Harvie, *No Gods and Precious Few Heroes*, p. 100.

33 Interview with David Lambie, MP, London, 26 April 1984.

34 James Reynolds, Liverpool Exchange, 1929-32; John Shute for the same seat from 1933 to 1945.

35 See *Protestant Action*, 7 January 1939.

36 Interview with J. G. MacLean, member of the Protestant Action Society.

37 McGhee, 'Carfin and the Relief Act', p. 71.

38 Dewar Gibb, *Scotland in Eclipse*, p. 59.

39 *GO*, 5 July 1930.

40 *Hansard*, 261, 24 November 1932, p. 262.

41 *Hansard*, 261, 24 November 1932, p. 245.

42 *Hansard*, 261, 24 November 1932, p. 330.

43 Ratcliffe's election address is quoted in a memorial of the Archbishop of Glasgow, 1935, in the Catholic Union files, box 11, Glasgow Archdiocesan Archives.

44 John J. Campbell to Archbishop Mackintosh, 6 November 1934, Catholic Union, Box 3, GAA.

45 *Forward*, 29 June 1935; see also Murray, *The Old Firm*, chapter 5, 'Hooligans in high places'.

46 The Bailie, 'Profile of Sir John Cargill', *Glasgow Weekly Herald*, 9 July 1932.

47 See Tom Gallagher, 'How Glasgow turned pink', *Scotsman*, 5 November 1983.

48 Gordon Brown, *The Labour Party and Political Change in Scotland: the Role of Five Elections*, University of Edinburgh, Ph.D., 1982.

49 *Vanguard*, 25 December 1935.

50 Richard Griffiths, *Fellow-Travellers of the Right, British Enthusiasts for Nazi Germany, 1933-39*, Constable, London, 1980, p. 157.

51 *Vanguard*, 4 January 1933.

52 Mackenzie, *Catholicism and Scotland*, p. 177.

53 Catholic Union, Box 9, Correspondence to 1935 Parliamentary Elections, GAA.

54 Deirdrie McMahon, *Republicans and Imperialists, Anglo-Irish Relations in the 1930s*, Yale University Press, New Haven and London, 1984, p. 176.

55 McMahon, *Republicans and Imperialists*, p. 101.

56 More biographical data about Ratcliffe can be obtained from reading a semi-autobiographical series in his newspaper entitled 'Twenty-five Years of the Hustings', published in successive issues of *Vanguard* starting in April 1937. See also chapter 4 of Steve Bruce's *No Pope of Rome*.

57 *Protestant Advocate*, 7, 10, November 1930.

58 Robert Devitt was attached to St Michael's, according to the 1927 CDS; in the following year his name was included among the list of clergy but he was not attached to any parish.

59 See Murray, *The Old Firm*, p. 157, and McShane, *No Mean Fighter*, pp. 205-6.

60 McShane, *No Mean Fighter*, p. 205.

61 Bruce, *No Pope of Rome*, p. 60.

62 *Forward*, 3 March 1934.

63 *GH*, 6 November 1933.

64 For Sillitoe's exposure of political corruption in Glasgow, see his own autobiography, Cloak without Dagger, London, 1955, and A. W. Cockerill, *Sir Percy Sillitoe*, London, 1975.

65 *Forward*, 21 October 1931.

66 Ratcliffe published articles in *Forward* on 13 June 1931 and on 3

March 1934.

67 *Forward*, 3 March 1934.

68 *Forward*, 3 March 1934.

69 See *Vanguard*, 1 July 1933.

70 Interview with William Weir Gilmour, Edinburgh, 19 December 1986 (carried out jointly with Ian Wood).

71 *Forward*, 4 November 1933.

72 *Vanguard*, 1 July 1933.

73 *Vanguard*, 11 March 1933.

74 *Vanguard*, July 1937.

75 *Vanguard*, 29 September 1934.

76 *Forward*, 13 June 1931.

77 The SPL's version of the incident was published in *Vanguard* on 20 May 1933. This issue also reprinted an article entitled 'Attack on Pope's picture', taken from *The Northern Whig*, a Belfast daily paper which reported the incident on 3 May 1933.

78 Graham Walker, 'Painting framed by Controversy', *Irish News* (Belfast) 5 May 1983.

79 *Vanguard*, 3 January 1934.

80 *Forward*, 3 November 1933.

81 *Vanguard*, 11 March 1933.

82 Letter from William Speirs, ex-member of the SPL, 14 March 1984.

83 Letter from H. Grace to John J. Campbell, 23 October 1934, Box 9, Catholic Union files, GAA.

84 Catholic Union files, box 3, Letter of Canon William Daly to all Glasgow parish priests, GAA.

85 *Vanguard*, March 1939.

86 *Vanguard*, 14 October 1939.

87 *Vanguard*, 6 January 1940.

88 *Vanguard*, 20 January 1940.

89 *Vanguard*, 3 February 1940.

90 *Vanguard*, June 1940.

91 *Glasgow Herald* carried a short obituary on 14 January 1947.

92 See John Cormack, 'My hectic life', *Protestant Telegraph* (Belfast), 11 January 1969.

93 The personal details about John Cormack's early life were provided by his sister, Mrs Dora Wight, in an interview on 18 July 1983. Additional information about how he came to form Protestant Action was given by McDonald Morris in a series of interviews carried out in December 1984. A series of articles by Cormack himself entitled 'My hectic life' which appeared in Ian Paisley's *Protestant Telegraph* during January–February 1969 also yield some interesting information.

94 Alistair B. Cooke, 'Gladstone's election for the Leith district of Edinburgh in July 1886', *Scottish Historical Review*, 49, 170, pp. 172–94.

95 *Edinburgh and Leith Observer*, 25 October 1935.

96 John Cormack, 'If I were dictator of Edinburgh', *Daily Record*, 6 October 1937.

97 *Daily Record*, 18 April 1935.

98 *Protestant Times*, 4 May 1935.

99 *GO*, 4 May 1935, *Bulletin*, 29 April 1935.

100 *GO*, 15 June 1935.

101 Colm Kiernan, *Daniel Mannix and Ireland*, Gill & Macmillan, Dublin, 1984, p. 210.

102 *Scotsman*, 25 June 1935; *Scottish Daily Express*, 25 June 1935.

103 *Scotsman*, 26 June 1935, *Daily Record*, 26 June 1935, *Scottish Daily Express*, 26 June 1935.

104 *GO*, 10 August 1935.

105 Interview with John McLaughlin, Edinburgh, 21 August 1984.

106 Archbishop McDonald's statement about the Edinburgh riots was issued in July 1935 and is reproduced in full in Compton Mackenzie's *Catholicism and Scotland*, pp. 178–9.

107 Mrs Molly Regan, interviewed in Edinburgh on 18 June 1985, was able to cite a number of examples from her own personal experience.

108 Mrs Molly Regan.

109 Interview with Hugh Brown MP, London, 26 April 1984.

110 I am grateful to Professor John Butt for this information.

111 *Protestant Times*, 18 May 1935.

112 McDonald Morris.

113 *Edinburgh Evening News*, 26 April 1937.

114 McDonald Morris.

115 *Protestant Action Society, List of Aims*, n.d. (1935).

116 See Murdoch Rodgers, 'The Anglo-Russian military convention and the Lithuanian immigrant community in Lanarkshire, Scotland (1917–20)', *Immigrants and Minorities*, 1, 1, 1982.

117 Interview with James Russell, former vice-president of Protestant Action, Glasgow, 10 June 1985.

118 *Protestant Times*, 25 April 1936.

119 See Joseph Farrell, 'The Italians who came, saw, and conquered', *Scotsman*, 12 December 1983.

120 'Toleration overdone' was displayed in Cormack's newspaper in a prominent position; 'Better a competent dictatorship . . .' was a favourite saying of Cormack's, according to James Russell.

121 *Edinburgh Evening Despatch*, 5 November 1936.

122 *Edinburgh Evening News*, 8, 14 April 1936.

123 Colm Brogan, 'Catholics in changing social conditions'.

124 J. G. MacLean.

125 Interview with Lionel Daiches, Edinburgh, 22 August 1984; conversation with David Daiches, Edinburgh, March 1984.

126 Letter from William Spiers, 14 March 1984.

127 *GO*, 3 February 1938.

128 *Vanguard*, 3 January 1934.

129 James Russell.

130 *GH*, 25 March 1929. The findings of the series are summarised in Handley, *The Irish in Modern Scotland*, pp. 309–11.

131 *GH*, 23 August 1922.

132 Rosslyn Mitchell, ex-Labour MP and solicitor, writing in the *Daily Record*, 6 November 1934.

133 1935 Memorial for the Counsel of Archbishop Mackintosh, Catholic Union, box 11, GAA.

134 George Malcolm Thomson, *The Rediscovery of Scotland*, p. 86; *Caledonia, or the Future of the Scots*, Kegal Paul, London, 1927, p. 10.

135 Thomson, *The Rediscovery*, pp. 53, 54.

136 Thomson, *The Rediscovery*, p. 34.

137 Thomson, *The Rediscovery*, p. 43.

138 Thomson, *The Rediscovery*, p. 43.

139 Thomson, *Caledonia*, p. 14.

140 Thomson, *Caledonia*, pp. 75–6.

141 Thomson, *Caledonia*, p. 76.

142 Thomson, *Caledonia*, p. 76.

143 Thomson, *Caledonia*, p. 70.

144 A. S. Neill, *Is Scotland Educated?*, Routledge, London, 1936, p. 85.

145 Shane McElhatton, 'Orwell: no friend of Irish Ireland', *Irish Times*, 17 January 1984.

146 Interview with George Malcolm Thomson, London, 26 March 1982.

147 Dewar Gibb, *Scotland in Eclipse*, pp. 56–7.

148 Dewar Gibb, *Scotland in Eclipse*, p. 57.

149 Dewar Gibb, *Scotland Resurgent*, p. 183.

150 Dewar Gibb, *Scotland in Eclipse*, p. 55.

151 *GO*, 26 August 1922.

152 *GO*, 8 January 1938, quoting from *Forward*.

153 Wood, 'John Wheatley', p. 83.

154 Dewar Gibb collection, National Library of Scotland, letter from George Malcolm Thomson dated 8 March 1934. The Scottish novelist Neil Gunn (1891–1974) is referred to in this quote.

155 John McCormick, *The Flag in the Wind*, Gollancz, 1955, p. 53.

156 *Hansard*, 261, 24 November 1932.

157 Colin Walkinshaw, *The Scots Tragedy*, Routledge, London, 1935, p. 175.

158 G. S. Pryde, 'The development of nationalism in Scotland', *Sociological Review*, 27, 3, 1935, p. 276.

159 *Glasgow Observer*, 12 March 1932.

160 Interview with Archie Lamont, Carlops, Midlothian, 15 December 1981. See Sydney MacEwan, *On the High C's*, Burns, Glasgow, 1974 and Mackenzie, *Catholicism and Scotland*, pp. 186–7.

161 Oliver Brown, *The Extended Tongue*, n.d., p. 29. The pamphlet is one of several hundred published in a microfilm edition entitled *Scottish Nationalist Pamphlets, 1844–1973*, EP Microfilm, 1980.

162 Mackenzie, *Catholicism and Scotland*, pp. 186–7.

163 Patrick Reilly, 'Catholicism and Scottish literature', in McRoberts, *Modern Scottish Catholicism*, pp. 190–4, 199–202.

164 Bryan S. Turner, 'State, civil society and national development: the Scottish problem', *Australia and New Zealand Journal of Sociology*, 20, 2, 1974, pp. 169–72.

165 Guth na Bliadhna, 2, 2, p. 300, quoted by Jack Brand, *The National Movement in Scotland*, Routledge,

London, 1978, p. 187.

166 *Liberty*, vol. 2, No. 3, March 1921, quoted in Brand, *The National Movement*, p. 188.

167 E.g. Archie Lamont, 'How a Scot sees Ireland', *Forward*, 23 May 1936.

168 Archie Lamont, *Small Nations*, MacLellan, Glasgow, 1944, p. 79. See 'The Duke and de Valera, what was said in Dublin', *Forward*, 28 July 1934, a satirical impression of the visit.

170 William Power, *Should Auld Acquaintance* . . . , Harrap, London, 1937, p. 139.

171 Brown, *The Extended Tongue*, pp. 28-9.

172 *CDS*, Burns, Glasgow, 1974, p. 353.

Chapter 5 **The Labour-Catholic alliance tested and reaffirmed, 1922–45**

After the mould-breaking general election of 1922 working-class catholics proved more consistently loyal to the parliamentary left than possibly any other element of the Scottish population usually aligning with the left. Having voted in a disciplined manner for the Liberals up to the First World War, the Labour Party became the new repository of catholic support. To a surprising degree the small catholic middle-class, largely drawn from the teaching profession, voted in much the same way as working-class catholics which demonstrated an apparent unity of interests in the community transcending class issues.

One important reason catholic teachers had for backing the Labour Party was its unwavering support for the much contested 1918 Education Act which increased their tenuous professional standing. Pragmatic reasons, and in time sheer habit, also accounted for much working-class catholic support for Labour. Catholic religious leaders drew some reassurance from this fact. They were suspicious of a party whose constitution proclaimed it to be socialist and which yet received the votes of many ordinary catholics. They were determined not to allow any party to unduly influence the views of their flock on social and ethical considerations concerning their role as citizens in a fast-changing society.

It was still taken for granted by perhaps most catholics that the authority of the priest stretched far beyond the simple practice of faith and could be applied to regulate their everyday lives. One of the few areas of catholic life where the priest's influence did not extend to was the work-place where ordinary catholics became receptive to new ideas that stressed their membership of a distinct class rather than any common religious brotherhood. In continental Europe the church and new political forces representing the socialist left or else middle-class radicalism, collided violently in their efforts to win the newly industrialised masses round to their rival philosophies. In Scotland, as in much of the rest of northern Europe, conflict between organised religion and the labour movement was avoided. Anti-clericalism was not a feature of the Labour Party either before or after it achieved its electoral breakthrough and indeed many Scottish Labour leaders derived their ideas and reforming zeal more from religious sources than from socialist tracts; gradually the more perceptive roman catholic clergy became aware that Glasgow's first wave of Labour MPs in the 1920s could be more accurately described as impassioned democrats than as red revolutionaries.

However, the transfer of catholic loyalties to the Labour Party was endured rather than accepted. The church did not have much choice since there were no alternative avenues available more in keeping with catholic ultramontane mores that it could mobilise support for. The largest political party was still the Conservative party which had a long record of being inimical to those religious and patriotic values dear to the heart of ex-Irish working-class catholics. In 1885 Parnell had persuaded many newly enfranchised catholic voters in Britain to vote Tory in a complicated tactic designed to secure Irish Home Rule. But subsequent generations of Irish voters had become too politically aware to easily stomach such an order and only in an emergency would Scottish church leaders have even contemplated emulating Parnell's command. If it had been the Liberal Party rather than the Tories which had survived as the chief alternative to parliamentary socialism, catholic spokesmen at specific moments (especially in the 1930s) might have sought to channel working-class votes towards it. But, for various reasons, the church failed to step into the role of political broker vacated by the Home Rule Party in the early 1920s.

The fact that there was a vacuum in church leadership in the archdioceses of Glasgow and Edinburgh at a time of rapid political change was (it can be argued) of crucial importance. The danger that an all-out assault on socialism might only alienate part of the catholic community and unintentionally help boost the influence of the Communist Party in certain districts may also help to explain the church's relatively low profile at the start of the 1920s. The danger would have been appreciated most of all by local activists in the Catholic Union who, to a greater degree than most parish clergy, were in tune with the political mood in the catholic community.

By the end of the 1920s the Labour Party had come to be recognised as the lesser of several evils by influential currents in the church; it was prepared to put up with frequent lectures from the church and its supporters in the religious press and the various movements of the catholic laity. Many years would elapse before the party dared to challenge clerical spheres of influence concerning not just the catholic community and education but social and medical questions.

A far-sighted clergyman might even have concluded that catholic interests were better served by bolstering the catholic custom of voting Labour than by any alternative political course. In the west of Scotland the Labour Party was more dependent on the catholic vote for its overall majority than was the case anywhere else in Britain. So it was rather more willing to pay wary heed to the views of local church leaders. If the community had voted Liberal (or, however improbably, Tory) it is highly unlikely that church views on public affairs would have been taken into account in the formulation of sensitive public issues (to the degree that occurred when Labour was in office before 1939), so it is hard to view the support given by working-class families to the cause of modest political and social reform as being damaging to the interests of the church. This also came to be the stance of a small but growing number of bishops in the urban dioceses of Scotland and England. Some of their priests were of a different persuasion and did not bother to conceal their reactionary views. They comprised priests from upper-class old catholic backgrounds (rare in Scotland) and Irish ones from well-off families in the rural southern counties that could 'afford' a priest.[1] However respected such priests may have been bowing to their spiritual role, the fact that they came from a different society, indeed a rural one, may have made an industrial population less disposed to heed their political instructions than if they had been native clergy possessed of the same reactionary ideas. The abolition of education board elections, for which a priest had normally headed the catholic list must also have encouraged his parishioners to see him as a less 'political' figure than before. Priests no longer stood for election and the church was thus deprived of its principal opportunity to demonstrate the political influence it exercised over the working-class catholic faithful.

Nevertheless, truculent clergymen continued to denounce individual left-wing candidates who did not show their office sufficient respect or who exemplified a strand of socialist policy which was deemed not to be in harmony with church attitudes. In the 1930s it would not have been unreasonable to conclude from the sheer frequency of such collisions that the catholic church and a left-wing party were not destined to go on sharing the allegiance of catholic voters and that sooner or later a full-scale confrontation was bound to occur, where ordinary catholics would be obliged to choose between the party that advanced their material interests and the guardians of their religious faith. However, on looking inside the catholic church, it would soon become clear that different power-brokers behaved in the same autocratic and high-handed way towards each other as individual priests did towards politicians looking for support in their bailiwicks. So the frequency of clerical attacks on 'upstart' candidates of the left may not have been a sign of a looming showdown in the catholic community for the hearts and minds of guileless catholic workers but was perhaps more illustrative of the types of discourse normally in use between catholic power-holders in moments of stress.

Occasionally, some catholic interests could appear as disunited and rancouress as the labour movement with differences of opinion and personality clashes only being kept in check by the local bishop's ability to impose his authority over quarrelling factions. One illustration of discord in senior catholic ranks was provided in Glasgow after 1922, the year in which the elderly Charles Byrne was eased off the education authority where he had been the chief lay catholic representative for over twenty years. Instead of going quietly and being satisfied with the papal knighthood conferred on him, Byrne, some years later circulated a pamphlet in which he claimed that he had been the victim of a plot hatched by Monsignor James Mullin, a senior clergyman. Words like 'treachery' were freely employed and Byrne charged that Monsignor Mullin had even urged that catholic votes be given to Sir Charles Cleland, the Tory leader on the education authority who 'would be as good as half-a-dozen Catholic representatives' (Mullin's alleged words).[2] The arrival of a new archbishop in 1922 calmed matters somewhat but Donald Mackintosh soon began behaving in a highly autocratic manner which was not the best example for newly-ordained priests in Glasgow fresh from the Scots College in Rome where the initial prestige of the Italian dictator, Mussolini, left its mark on quite a few of them for the rest of their priestly careers. In 1940 when Britain was fighting for its existence against the twin tyrannies of Nazi Germany and Fascist Italy, Mackintosh made a remark in a letter to John Campbell, secretary of the Catholic Union, which captured his own authoritarian outlook:

> I cannot refrain from remarking that 'Democracy', in the sense in which it is commonly interpreted, is just a charter for all who take it on themselves to fuss about other people's business! I hope this remark will not alarm the Lord Provost [Patrick Dollan]. If it does, well, I am ready to defend the basis of my remarks . . . and . . . I am ready to do that . . . also in public!![3]

By now, Archbishop Mackintosh was a chronic invalid who was unable to get around his archdiocese or properly supervise its activities. However, instead of delegating business to his staff, he centralised power in an almost obsessive way so that the growth of the archdiocese was much slower than otherwise it might have been. It was only under his successor that a programme of building churches got underway when they were already needed in his own time when the cost of labour and materials was much cheaper than later they would be. By the late 1930s Mackintosh was even insisting on typing his letters from his own sick-bed rather than allow the Vicar-General to perform this simple chore. In some regards, arguably the most influential figure in the archdiocese after the archbishop was his full-time nurse, Miss Duncan, a protestant who shielded Donald Mackintosh from visitors, acted as his intermediary, and accompanied him to Rome and on his convalescent trips abroad. Miss Duncan used to roundly abuse Archbishop McDonald of Edinburgh (whom Mackintosh viewed as a rival) when members of the laity phoned up for advice or instructions.[4] Another protestant, was the archbishop's chief financial adviser, outwardly a commendable ecumenical gesture, but more illustrative of his remoteness from ordinary catholics.

The more outgoing and democratic style of the Archbishop of Edinburgh could not have been in sharper contrast to his Glasgow counterpart. It has even been claimed by a lay catholic with deep respect for historical truth that when McDonald's scheme for a college to train priests and teachers in St Andrews was effectively sabotaged by local protestant interests, a number of lay catholics aware of the rivalry between the two senior bishops in Scotland had reason to suspect that the tip-off had been given by someone close to Mackintosh.

The infighting which occasionally marred the internal life of the catholic church in Scotland provided a useful backdrop for assessing the turbulent relations between individual religious figures and the forces of the left. In some ways, as will be seen, the left got off lightly compared to how rivals within the church sometimes settled accounts with each other; influential lay figures sometimes displayed the egotism and caprice of domineering princes of the church, perhaps none more so than Charles Diamond, 'the Catholic Harmsworth' who, by the 1920s, controlled a large publicity empire of local catholic papers. As has been seen, he placed his papers' editorial line behind the Labour Party between 1918 and 1922, mainly on account of the situation in Ireland. But inevitably, just as in earlier political involvements (as an Irish Nationalist MP in the 1890s and then as a conditional supporter of the Liberal Party), Diamond fell out with his erstwhile political allies. After 1922, the high-point of the quixotic relationship between this newspaper proprietor and the mass working-class party of the left, his backing for Labour became increasingly qualified. In April 1923, following a visit to Rome where he was granted a private audience with the Pope, he set out the limits of his support for Labour and alluded to the circumstances in which it might be withdrawn. His views were publicised on 11 April 1923 in the official Vatican newspaper, *Osservatore Romano*, under the heading 'In England, Catholics, Political Parties and the Labour Movement'. Some passages are worth quoting:

The present position of Catholics in Great Britain in relation to the political life of the nation is not altogether unhappy . . .

The British Labour Party is not specifically a Socialist Party . . .

Several attempts have been made by certain Catholics to create antagonism between Catholics on the one hand and the Trade Unions and Labour Party on the other by saying that both these latter were socialistic. Up to the present the attempt has failed and though the Holy See has been approached on the matter, no official veto has been imposed on Catholics entering the Trade Unions or the Labour Party.

. . . When the Holy See makes a pronouncement on the point all Catholics will listen and obey . . .

Perhaps it is inevitable that co-operation between Catholics and the Labour Party as it exists in England, is not to be found in other countries . . .

Just as Catholics work hand in hand with non-Catholics for political and social ends without detriment to their principles, so they can co-operate with Socialists without embracing Socialism . . . It is clear then that the Catholics of Great Britain, though small in numbers, have no intention of allowing to pass unnoticed Socialist and Communist errors just as they do not permit Protestant errors to pass with impunity. They recognise that while Protestant-ism as such is a lifeless thing, quite the contrary is true of Socialism and Communism. These are in their first stage of existence; it is only in Russia that they are seen in action.[5]

Diamond did not contest the 1923 general election for Labour and he condemned party candidates who were secularists, such as H. G. Wells, standing for the London University seat and also a critic of catholic education:

we can say that Catholic education has survived others and will survive Wells. But if the Labour Party is to give its approval to such 'extra-official pronouncements', it will not be paving the way for its assumption to power in the very near future.[6]

The new line of qualified support for Labour was spelt out in an editorial carried by all his papers shortly before the November 1923 election:

Where any Labour candidate shows a truculent, atheistical, or anti-Catholic disposition, we should advise no one to support him. In this way, the Catholic vote could be extremely powerful in determining the issue in many con-stituencies.

The Tory Party is the party of privilege and monopoly. It is repulsive to every Catholic of democratic instincts.

Liberalism is played out.

The battles of the future will be between Labourism and Toryism and, unless Labour is revolutionary or anti-Catholic, it will command an over-whelming majority of Catholic support.[7]

Early in 1924 Labour formed a minority administration under Ramsay MacDonald. Until near the end of the government's eight month life, the *Observer* refrained from any sharp comment on its performance. When it did so, the leader-writer criticised Labour in office not for its radicalism but for its timidity:

> With regard to Ireland, we are firmly convinced that there are members of the Labour Party who are quite prepared to betray Ireland and who would be just as ruthless against any attempt to establish an Irish Republic as the Cromwellians themselves . . . It all goes to show that Labour in office and Labour out of office are two very different things. Nearly half of the Labour Party in Parliament have now secured jobs with good salaries attached, and their anxiety seems to be to hold office and to draw their salaries at whatever cost to their past professions and their constituency . . .
>
> The truth is that they are all anxious to impress the country with their moderation, which is excellent in its way and may help to get them back to power but they should not so readily throw over the principles of liberty and justice and fair-play which we expect to see them put into operation.[8]

After the fall of the Labour government the owner of the *Catholic Herald* newspaper group was an unsuccessful Labour candidate in the Clapham district of Wandsworth during the general election fought in the autumn of 1924. His campaign was conducted from a Rolls Royce, the cause of much comment in Fleet Street. Diamond's rejoinder was a characteristic 'Why Not! There was a time when the automobile was the monopoly of the capitalist candidate but that day has gone for good.'[9]

'Vote Labour' was still the watchword of the *Observer* in 1924 but with added qualifications. This time readers were urged not to vote for fellow Labour candidates of Diamond's who displayed an equivocal stance on communism. In his campaign he insisted that 'a majority of Labour Party members are not socialists'.[10] No longer was Diamond prepared to treat socialism as a harmless fad within an undoctrinaire Labour Party. During the spring and summer of 1924 he wrote a weekly column setting out the differences between socialism and labourism which was syndicated in all his newspapers. True socialism, he argued, was incompatible with liberty and religious freedom and communism was really the ultimate goal of serious-minded socialists.[11] Besides his own volatile personality, his more truculent attitude to the chief ideology of the left may have stemmed from several different factors: his failure to make a new political career for himself as a Labour MP; Labour's lukewarm support for Irish self-government as demonstrated by MacDonald's backing for the Northern Ireland state; and perhaps the feeling that the left simply was not to be trusted given the deeds being carried out in the Soviet Union in the name of 'socialism'.

Diamond's anti-socialist offensive ran counter to the position of John Wheatley as a catholic *and* a socialist, one that he had defended in the letter-columns of the *Observer* nearly twenty years before. Busy with cabinet responsibilities in 1924 Wheatley did not respond. Both he and Diamond had much in common, being self-made men of Irish birth who had made careers in British publishing, mixing business and politics in the process. John Wheatley was both a devout catholic and a successful publisher whose business motto allegedly was 'There cannot be no socialism (sic) in business under capitalism: the man who thinks different is not in business long.'[12] Diamond might have endorsed these hard-headed sentiments but Wheatley's belief that socialism and the roman catholic faith could he harnessed together for the good of mankind made him even more dangerous than a left-wing secularist given the appeal of such a model for 'impressionistic' catholics. Thus it was only long after his death in 1930 that the *Glasgow Observer* felt able to pay tribute to both the courage and achievements of Wheatley. In 1924 the Diamond press largely ignored the housing bill which as minister of housing and health he pushed through parliament, it being the one substantial legislative achievement of the first Labour government. After 1922–23 it was less than effusive in urging support for Wheatley in his marginal Shettleston constituency. Instead, on numerous occasions, it sought to refute Wheatley's belief that socialism and the catholic faith could be harnessed together for the good of mankind. With unconcealed glee the *Observer* published two contradictory quotes from Wheatley on the subject in a 1925 editorial. One was an extract from a *Daily Herald* article of 23 March 1925 in which he wrote that 'the Catholic church does not oppose state ownership as advocated by the Labour Party: THE LABOUR PARTY IS A SOCIALIST PARTY: therefore the Catholic church does not oppose socialism'.[13]

The editorial remarked that 'Wheatley was using his customary jesuitical method of reasoning'. It went on:

> Unfortunately for Mr Wheatley, he declared in *Forward* of 3 November 1923 that 'There is no good blinking the fact that the policy announced at Plymouth will seriously strain the Labour Party. IT WOULD NOT DO SO IF IT WERE A SOCIALIST PARTY. BUT IT IS NOT.'
> Just how the ingenious and cunning Mr Wheatley can explain such a contradiction is a matter for himself.[14]

Later in 1925 the *Observer* came back to the attack:

> Wheatley has held office and has been as cunning as he is insinuating in his conduct since he was first returned to the Parliament as a Labour member. The ILP is still within the Party and it is just as objectionable in its ways as

are the Communists. In fact, the ILP is practically a Communist Party.[15]

Earlier the *Observer* had pulled no punches in an editorial which itself was full of insinuation:

> Mr Wheatley MP is apparently determined to be in the very forefront of the extremists in the socialist camp.
> That way lies notoriety if not fame.
> However, his clap-trap about this Government 'desiring war' with Russia would not deceive the inmates of a lunatic asylum . . .
> We remember some time ago when he came out with another scream about the time to come 'when every man in this country who made any money should be called on to explain how he made it'.
> There is one way of making money—the moneylender's way.
> Mr Wheatley is no moneylender.
> But moneylenders put their clients into the County Courts by the tens of thousands, and we know a concern that carries on business over the country under different names, and which uses the County Court against its customers as freely as any moneylender, and we should think more freely than most.
> We are sure Mr Wheatley knows something about it . . .
> . . . he . . . talks with a double tongue on social, political and economic questions. We say that Mr Wheatley in his own affairs displays all those characteristics of capitalism and all those harsh methods . . .[16]

In 1924 Diamond had snorted with disapproval when Wheatley was credited with having said that the capitalist system would end in five years.[17] He obviously had faith in the system, which may help to explain why he was so antipathetic towards the view of one of its most eloquent detractors. An editorial with his characteristic stamp and simply called 'Capitalism' declared in 1926:

> There is not a Trade Union in the country that is not a capitalist and drawing money on invested money . . . What is wrong is not the use of capital, is not 'capitalism', but the abuse of a thing good in itself.[18]

Fewer aspects of Labour Party behaviour troubled Diamond in the west of Scotland than in London and the south generally, but as the 1920s wore on he was increasingly reluctant to overlook internal developments which ran counter to his own views. One was the leftward drift of the ILP, which was bringing it into increasing conflict with its parent body, the Labour Party. The issue was a complex one since the champion of the ILP left in the west of Scotland was James Maxton MP, a staunch defender of catholic education interests, while it was Patrick Dollan, a lapsed catholic who organised the more moderate elements. Diamond was attentive to these nuances but, in 1926, he inveighed against the ILP describing it as 'the cell of all the worst features of the Labour movement . . . whose affinity to

Bolshevism, in many respects, we have more than once referred to'. In the same issue of the *Observer*, readers were warned that 'there are principles embodied in the constitution of the ILP which, if well understood, make it impossible for any Catholic to join that body'.[19] John Wheatley belonged to the ILP, (a point the *Observer* would not have needed to drive home to many of its readers), but so did Joseph Sullivan, a right-wing catholic miners leader whom the paper had just congratulated for being nominated to fight a Lanarkshire by-election as a Labour candidate.[20]

During 1926 Diamond seemed to go out of his way to stoke up incidents that would justify a suspicious attitude towards the Labour Party on the part of his working-class readers. His Scottish press outlets gave publicity to a motion from the Patrick and Shettleston branch of the ILP in Glasgow urging the annual conference to support the abolition of PR in the Education Authority elections. The *Observer* viewed the motion as tantamount to calling for the disenfranchisement of catholic voters in parish and educational elections and warned that its acceptance would be viewed as an 'enemy act'.[21] For some time Diamond had been an outspoken advocate of PR in local and parliamentary elections because he felt it would enhance the influence of catholics within the party they had chosen to support after 1918. Given the uniform way catholics traditionally had voted in areas where their numbers were concentrated, he believed that the character of the Labour Party could have been altered by a solid phalanx of catholic members returned from multi-member constituencies. Under PR Diamond would have been able to urge support for some Labour candidates while withholding it from others without standing accused of being disloyal to the party, a position of influence he would have relished.

Labour candidates who supported artificial birth control would certainly have been blacklisted by Diamond. It was the surfacing of this issue that led him to sharpen his invective against the radical wing of the parliamentary left during the late 1920s, possibly more than any other. Aware of how capable religious interests were of driving a wedge between the party and its catholic following if it grew too out-of-step on questions like birth-control, Glasgow-based activists on different wings of the party urged caution. *Forward* refused to take adverts from those advocating birth-control[22] but in women's organisations affiliated to the Labour Party strong support existed for a Labour government authorising public health authorities to give contraceptive advice. As health minister in 1924 John Wheatley carefully avoided giving such an undertaking although hardpressed by an influential deputation that included H. G. Wells and Dora Russell. His case for inaction was the deep division of opinion within the working-class over birth-control and the need for the express authority of Parliament, rather than an individual minister's sanction, before the demand for birth-control could be accepted.[23] Ian Wood, Wheatley's biographer, reckons that his handling of the whole issue 'was perhaps the only instance in his career of church teaching being the deciding factor in a political decision he made, or in this case, avoided making'.[24]

At the ILP's annual conference in April 1926 Jean Roberts, a Glasgow delegate (and a future Lord Provost of the city) unsuccessfully tried to shelve a motion in favour of birth-control by arguing that 'as socialists they were not going to be side-tracked by having birth-control brought in as a red herring. The fight is between socialism and capitalism.'[25] The same thing happened at the Labour Party's annual conference later in the same year: a motion of the national executive committee argued that the party should not take an official attitude on the question but it was defeated, albeit narrowly. The *Observer* then announced that 'the Labour Party as such is committed to the obscene and scandalous policy of birth-control' although in its previous issue it had declared this not yet to be the case which showed how erratic the pronouncements of Diamond's paper sometimes could be.[26] But whatever way it was to be interpreted, the outcome of the Labour Party conference produced a new situation which catholics could not ignore:

> This raises in a very specific manner the whole question of the relations between Catholics and the Trade Unions and Labour Party. We are able to speak on the matter with some authority and with some right to a hearing for ours are the only Catholic journals in the country that have any claims upon the Labour movement and that have made sacrifices for its welfare and fought its battles to the best of our ability . . .
>
> *The Tablet*, of which His Eminence, Cardinal Bourne is the chief Trustee . . . has never concealed its politics which have been Tory and reactionary. This fact, however, has never prevented it from claiming and being accepted as an official Catholic organ which we, in our journals, have never pretended to be . . .
>
> We place our journals and their policy under the direction of the Holy See, and whatever instructions or commands emanates from Rome on these great issues, to them we give our obedience and adhesion in advance.[27]

Next year, at the 1927 municipal election in Glasgow, both the *Observer* and *Forward* agreed that the birth-control controversy had cost the party support.[28] Four of the five seats lost had been held by catholics and the *Observer*'s editorial proclaimed that 'the mere mention of birth control is enough to set the Catholic electorate on its hind legs'.[29]

In 1928 the *Observer* urged voters to back a Moderate in a council by-election in Hutchestown. The paper accused the Labour Party of 'bigotry' for not nominating a catholic in perhaps the most catholic ward in the city.[30] This action by the local party showed that the age of the 'catholic mafia' was still some way off. The Moderates opportunistically chose a catholic who failed to be elected, thus highlighting the limits of Diamond's influence even in a favourably disposed locality where, ultimately, the voters preferred to allow their judgement to be swayed by political rather than ethnic-religious considerations. Of course the mood of the electorate could change. Labour was then experiencing a recovery in support confirmed not long afterwards by the 1929 general election after which it formed a government.

In 1933, James McLaughlin, a catholic standing against the Labour Party as an Independent won a seat in the Gorbals ward with the *Observer*'s backing. There were special circumstances since the sitting councillor, James Strain, a Co-operative Party[31] member had just been expelled from the council after being found guilty of corruption charges.

Any catholic standing as a Moderate in Glasgow municipal elections was usually a shopkeeper, publican, or businessman, who was not eligible for a Labour nomination for being too 'capitalistic'. In some years the Moderates adopted such candidates in inner city wards where a large part of the electorate shared his religion but it was a tactic that never once paid off before or after 1945. One of the few catholics (perhaps the only one) nominated in a winnable Tory council seat during the 1930s was that young solicitor, Francis Campbell, brother of the secretary of the Catholic Union who stood for the normally Tory ward of Glasgow Exchange in 1934. In a year when sectarian feeling was higher than usual thanks to the intervention of the SPL, Campbell failed to get elected, presumably because his religion disqualified him in the eyes of a number of Tory voters who preferred to abstain.

Charles Diamond was perhaps enough of a realist to see that he could not hope to produce a wholesale switch in the voting habits of his readers. In housing, education, and health the Labour Party stood for the interests of a community mainly located in the very lowest income brackets and in its calmer moments the *Observer* still admitted this fact. No longer prepared by 1929 even to offer conditional backing for the Labour Party, his newspaper group altered the way in which it delivered political advice at election time. It urged readers to ignore party labels and vote for a candidate on his or her merits. In 1929, for the very first time, members of each of the non-communist parties standing (thus including the Tories) were given space in Diamond's papers to appeal for support. The *Observer* singled out five issues which it deemed to be the crucial ones for catholic voters. Ireland was not included in a list which stressed the importance of catholic schools, birth control, the dangers of socialism, the danger of protection, and unemployment.[32] 'Until the catholic church speaks out against the British socialists as she does against the Continental brand, Catholics are free to vote for members of any of the three parties,' was its eve-of-poll verdict.[33] Five Labour parliamentary candidates who, as Glasgow councillors, had supported the inclusion of birth-control literature in libraries were deemed to be unworthy of catholic support.[34] One of them, John S. Clarke was condemned because 'as a press writer he has repeatedly rubbed the Catholic fur the wrong way'.[35] The *Observer* stressed that his opponent was 'an extremely enlightened Conservative whose attitude to the Catholic school question is quite satisfactory'.[36] Fearing defeat, the *Observer* alleged that John S. Clarke 'appeared at a Catholic meeting prior to the contest and practically apologised for his infidel writings'.[37]

By contrast, George Buchanan, who represented Glasgow Gorbals, refused to reply to the *Observer*'s pre-election questionnaire and said that he preferred to give his opinion if asked at a public meeting in his constituency. A popular MP, representing the division of the city with the strongest catholic presence, his boldness illustrated the limitations of the *Observer*'s influence and in no seat does its verdict appear to have greatly influenced the outcome in an election where Labour was destined to do well.

But by 1930, with the hapless Labour government attempting to combat the depression with orthodox treasury measures that bore down on its worst-off supporters, its popularity had fallen off sharply. When John Wheatley's death necessitated a by-election in Glasgow Shettleston, the *Observer* offered its most controversial advice yet. It urged catholic voters to support the Tory candidate, William Templeton, who was not at all sympathetic to catholic interests. Indeed, during the final stages of the campaign, it was revealed that he supported the compulsory inspection of convents, a traditional demand of hardline anti-catholics.[38] What prompted the *Observer* to take this extreme step was the record of the Labour candidate, John McGovern. Early in his career he had committed a grave transgression when 'he opposed a Catholic priest who stood . . . for the parish council and supported an opposing candidate, the priest being defeated. The Irish electorate in Shettleston are strong Labour supporters, but with most of them, their faith comes first and they cannot be expected to vote for a candidate who has made it his business to secure the defeat of a priest.'[39] A former altar boy, who became a supporter of the anarchist Guy Aldred and who was not afraid to condemn religious involvement in politics, McGovern seemed to personify the dangers inherent in a catholic becoming involved with full-blooded socialism. He won but with a majority reduced to less than 700 votes.

Perhaps this was the best possible outcome from Diamond's point of view. He could argue that Labour had been taught a salutory lesson with a majority slashed to the barest minimum while not having to accept the responsibility for the election of an anti-catholic Tory. However, the erratic behaviour of the popular catholic press at this time may have weakened its credibility, with readers capable of savouring its often highly-charged and pointed editorials while not always carrying out the advice contained in them.

Diamond's reputation in the 1920s was also beginning to suffer due to his involvement in a series of costly libel actions. They arose because 'he was temperamentally incapable of distinguishing between his opponents ideas and their personalities. He yielded on too many occasions to the temptation merely to insult his opponents rather than rationally refute their arguments—an exercise his intellect was well-equipped to do.'[40] When his company was wound up in the mid-1930s following his death, the liquidator found that 'in his later years "the profits were largely absorbed by the cost of libel actions" '.[41] His earlier genius in money-making deserted him as he entered his seventies and advertisers were increasingly reluctant to be associated with his improper vendettas. Revenue from his main weekly publication *The Catholic Herald*, dropped by nearly half between 1924 and 1932.[42] Circulation of the Scottish editions of his papers remained higher than elsewhere but while his influence in education elections remained clear up till 1929, (the year of their abolition), it is doubtful, once Labour voting became an ingrained habit for most of his readers, if he was able to tip the electoral scales to any meaningful extent. Undoubtedly many local and parliamentary candidates felt it necessary to give the appropriate answers to his frequent pre-election questionnaires, but the clash between the church and the left which might have enabled the true extent of his influence to be assessed, never arose perhaps because the Labour Party was mainly in opposition and thus not charged with carrying out policies possibly repugnant to catholic interests.

Reluctantly Diamond concluded that a catholic party was not the solution for British catholics dissatisfied with those already on offer. Not only did the British electoral system make its success unlikely but there was not enough common ground among catholics to make it a practical proposition. Diamond was reluctant to force a situation which would have shown that catholics did not have an identity of outlook on political issues and that the pull of class loyalties could in certain recurring situations be stronger than the wish to obey the priest. The political content of speeches made by autocratic clergymen hostile to the claims of socialism were usually discreetly ignored by parishioners who instinctively felt differently. The concentration of Scotland's urban catholics in the lower income groups which were faring worst of all in the post-1929 depression and experiencing the full rigours of unemployment, means test, workhouse, and general deprivation meant that the left was their natural home despite the outbursts of clergy who saw reality through a narrow set of ecclesiastical lenses. Even the Diamond press seemed to realise this much in 1931 when it gave its backing to McGovern and Maxton in a general election in which Labour was routed in both the UK and Scotland. Both men were returned and only in South Wales did the left do better than in Glasgow. Each of the other Glasgow Labour survivors, Neil Maclean (Govan), William Leonard (St Rollox) and George Buchanan (Gorbals) had a strong catholic presence in their constituencies. With or without the encourage-ment of the catholic press, the Scottish catholic working-class was already earning the reputation of being perhaps the most loyal element to support Labour.

The choice of parties to support on the left increased in 1932 when a large part of the ILP disaffiliated from the Labour Party to become a completely separate entity. Tension between the parent body and the ILP (which had taken care of much of Labour's educational and propaganda work) had steadily increased after the radical James Maxton became ILP chairman in 1926. A complete break loomed as Maxton stepped up criticism of the 1929–31 Labour govern-ment for its lack of faith in socialism as 'the one practical social system that can meet the world's needs'.[43] He and his allies refused to support government policies that were considered harmful to the working-class and when Ramsay McDonald formed a coalition government with the Tories and National Liberals in 1931, Maxton took it as final proof of the moral and ideological bankruptcy of the Labour Party. Maxton, the orator and agitator for socialism missed the steading influence of John Wheatley and it has been argued that a total split could have been avoided if the strategist in this unique political partnership had not suffered an untimely death in 1930. Oswald Mosley described Wheatley in the 1960s as 'the only man of Lenin quality, the English [sic] left ever produced'.[44] (This was not just the view of an English fascist. Maxim Litvinov, Soviet foreign minister in the 1930s saw Wheatley as 'the only man in England who could make and push through a Socialist revolution'.)

Maxton proved to be mistaken in his belief that the economic crisis had created something approaching a revolutionary situation that would enable the ILP to supplant Labour as the party of the working-class. Among the unemployed the depression bred grim resignation rather than a defiant espousal of socialism. The damage done to Labour by MacDonald's defection was much less than first imagined since few others followed him out of the party. After 1932 the ILP possessed only five MPs, three of whom represented Glasgow seats. Maxton had been unable to carry the bulk of the Scottish ILP with him, but as events failed to keep in step with his utopian hopes, what grass-roots support he had was increasingly confined to Clydeside where the ILP also had an elected presence in local government.

The split in the parliamentary left demoralised many political activists and bewildered less committed voters. It seemed an ideal opportunity for the Catholic Union and the catholic press to step in and urge west of Scotland catholics to back whatever formation that appeared least objectionable to catholic beliefs and interests. Almost everything about Maxton (and his colleagues) suggested that they ought to receive short shrift from the catholic lobby. Maxton was an atheist who had supported the affiliation of the Communist Party to the Labour Party and, moreover, he was an admirer of the Soviet Union. How then, is one to explain the latitude he received from the catholic lobby through his twenty-four years in parliament? The *Observer* and the Catholic Union treated him with forebearance and with a certain affection. In 1935, not long after he had been collaborating with the Communist Party in organising the unemployed, John Campbell in a letter to another prominent catholic wrote that 'I am very glad to see Maxton's result in Bridgeton and particularly the unexpected majority he had'.[45] Much earlier, in 1923, he received a glowing write-up from the *Observer* which few other Labour MPs could have hoped to get:[46]

> Ever since he went to Westminster, Mr Maxton's part in parliamentary proceedings has made him a national figure and placed him definitely in a category of Labour intelligentsia *[sic]*. His personal charm of manner has endeared him to hosts of his constituents. His favours to Catholic interests and his special knowledge of school questions and of the natural need for absolute equality in education legislation will render him a particularly useful friend to Catholic school interests if these should be attacked by bigots hereafter.[47]

Despite his reputation as a committed socialist, the *Observer* seemed absolutely confident that Maxton was a dependable ally prepared to come to the aid of the roman catholic church if its educational interests were threatened. Until the end of the 1930s this issue was the chief priority of the catholic political lobby in the west of Scotland and its salience would seem to be the reason why Maxton could rely on generous support from such an unlikely source. In his seat, Bridgeton, Orange sympathies among the protestant working-class were stronger than possibly anywhere else in Glasgow and the church may have concluded that his ability to defuse sectarianism in local politics more than compensated for his heretical political ideas. Maxton's warmth and eloquence meant that he received a huge personal vote which the Orange Order tried and failed to dent. Glasgow catholics like John Campbell may have conlcuded long before Westminster Tories like Churchill and Baldwin (with whom Maxton was on friendly terms), that despite his unkempt appearance, he was far from being a dangerous revolutionary. One of his biographers has shown that essentially he was a constitutionalist, who wished to see the triumph of socialism but felt that it 'could come about only through the orderly and peaceful transition of society and not through violent upheaval'.[48] *Forward* showed that his fiery language was not even taken seriously by more moderate socialists when it remarked after the 1931 electoral rout that alas Maxton would now have to postpone the revolution till Christmas.[49]

One incident just before his election to parliament illustrated why Maxton may have thought it important not to alienate himself from catholic interests. In 1922 he had stood for the Education Authority elections along with Canon Anthony Mullins, the parish priest in the Sacred Heart parish Bridgeton. When Canon Mullins emerged at the top of the poll, Maxton was the last candidate to be returned. In 1926, as the ILP was moving left under Maxton's guidance, the *Observer* reminded its readers of this incident, the moral apparently being that when a priest and a socialist were in contention, many catholics would automatically vote first for their spiritual pastor.[50]

Maxton always cultivated the catholic community in his Glasgow Bridgeton seat. From it he derived proportionately more votes than from non-catholics which is confirmed by the attitude of the two main juvenile gangs in his constituency: the protestant 'Billy Boys' were staunch supporters of the Unionist cause at election time while the catholic 'Norman Conks' 'are in the main devoted followers of Maxton'.[51] As a supporter of Glasgow Celtic he was a regular visitor to Parkhead stadium which lay within his constituency and he thus identified with the folk loyalties of a section of his voters. In 1934 he even paid an unsuccessful visit to Eamon de Valera, the Irish leader, to petition him to allow the exiled Leon Trotsky to settle in Ireland.[52] If there was any catholic criticism of this offbeat scheme it was muted. At Westminster Maxton had long ago proved his worth whenever the 1918 Act, the Magna Carta of Scottish catholic education came under attack from opponents; for instance, during the passage of the Church of Scotland Property Bill in 1925, he even took issue with fellow Labour MP James Brown (MP for Ayrshire South) over whether the Presbyterian church was prejudiced against the parts of the 1918 Act concerned with the maintenance of catholic schools. Maxton insisted that the established church in Scotland was culpable here and that the bill should not be passed.[53]

Later, in 1930–31, Maxton disillusioned some left-wing colleagues by refusing to come to the aid of Sir Charles Trevelyan, minister of education, when his education bill came under attack from right-wing Labour MP James Scurr, who tabled an amendment demanding more resources for catholic schools. The historian, A. J. P. Taylor contended that the incident revealed 'Labour had acquired its own sectarian lobby'.[54] In her memoirs Jennie Lee, the Labour MP for North Lanarkshire in 1929–31, recalls that although Trevelyan 'was the only friend we left-wing ILPers had among government ministers', Maxton refused to defend his bill.[55] She recalls how he and John McGovern:

> got hold of me, literally got hold of me, to explain 'the facts of life' in the west of Scotland. I could challenge the authority of the Labour Party and still survive, but if I also antagonised the Labour vote, there was not the slightest hope I could hold my seat.[56]

This may be an oversimplification written in hindsight of a complicated situation which, for instance, does not quite explain how John McGovern, the renegade catholic, was able to hold on in Shettleston despite confronting the church on a number of issues. In deciding its response to particular politicians, the catholic lobby was not just motivated by ideological considerations as the Maxton case amply shows. Arguably the introduction of sectarianism into local politics during the early 1930s pushed the fear of ultra-leftism into the background. Certainly a perusal of Catholic Union papers during the years Alexander Ratcliffe was on the council in Glasgow provides much evidence for this view. John Campbell might nothave quarrelled with the view of Glasgow presented to readers of *The Spectator* in 1934 by Tom Johnston, the Labour politician:

> Here in Glasgow is the last place in Britain ever likely to get a Communist revolution; the Isle of Wight perhaps, or Oxford or Cheltenham—but not here. If you doubt it, pay a visit to Glasgow on July 12 when one-third of the population goes out with its icons—usually William Prince of Orange on a white horse—and drums and fifes, while another one-third of the population waves green flags tauntingly and throws (empty) beer bottles at the drums.[57]

However, the advance of religious extremism in Glasgow politics was halted by Ratcliffe's defeat later in 1934, the year in which Charles Diamond, the stormy petrel of catholic journalism, wrote his last embattled editorial. His death on 19 February 1934 aged seventy-five, also marked the removal of a turbulent influence on west of Scotland politics. Evidence from the last years of his life showed that Catholic Union activists in Glasgow did not share, at least to the same degree, his dislike of socialism and its electoral standard-bearers. The influence wielded by Diamond on politics in difficult to assess with any precision but the large sales the paper enjoyed in Scotland and the large number of local editions he printed indicate that it was greater there than in other areas of Britain with large immigrant communities. Certainly

Diamond's press outlets are a very useful barometer for locating the different cross-currents in the catholic community and it explains why they have been an important source of material for this book.

Whatever influence Diamond exercised in his last years on catholic public opinion (and it appeared to be declining from a peak somewhere around the early 1920s), his death undoubtedly marked the end of an era. It coincided with the award of £750 damages to Mrs Sheehy Skeffington whom Diamond had accused of hypocritically speaking on Republican platforms while collecting a British pension for the murder in Dublin of her pacifist husband by a British officer in 1916.[58] When no payment was forthcoming Mrs Sheehy Skeffington applied for the compulsory winding up of Diamond's New Catholic Press Ltd. Eventually it was sold for a mere £12,000 to Ernest Vernor Miles who had only become a roman catholic in 1932.[59] His partner, Sir Thomas Jones (former secretary to the cabinet) was given day-to-day charge of the Scottish press outlets. Although educated at Glasgow University and a member of the ILP in his youth, Jones was unfamiliar with the Glasgow catholic community (he was not a catholic himself) and circulation began to go into decline.

The *Glasgow Observer* generally stayed out of the dispute between the two wings of the once united Labour Party after the 1932 split. Rallying the forces of moderation was a capable political leader with unimpeachable anti-communist credentials whom the paper was none-theless reluctant to endorse too loudly. Patrick Dollan may have been of impeccable Irish catholic lineage but he had ceased practising his religion quite early in life and had gone on to marry a protestant and fellow socialist, Agnes Moir, their only son James being educated at a non-catholic school. However, the *Observer* and Catholic Union did not make too much fuss about Dollan's personal situation no doubt because he had proved to be a welcome ally in politics.

Dollan preferred to remain in local politics even though his organising skills had contributed greatly to the 1922 electoral landslide in Glasgow which sent to Westminster a contingent of forceful left-wingers determined to acquaint parliament with the miserable conditions of the working-class in the west of Scotland. In contrast to Maxton's visionary outlook, he was pragmatic and hardheaded. He was distrustful of simple and sweeping solutions, believing that 'Socialism in our time will be achieved in the town and burgh councils'.[60] He turned down many offers, not just in Scotland of a Labour seat, preferring to stay in touch with the grassroots of the Labour movement and test his administrative skills within the arena of local government. Dollan had never been a marxist and this type of experience placed him increasingly at variance with some of the Clydeside MPs including John Wheatley, a formative influence in his youth. In 1925, at the

Scottish conference of the ILP, Dollan defeated Maxton's resolution favouring admission of the Communist Party to the Labour Party.[61] He was well able to imagine the reaction of the catholic church if such a union had been consummated, but the proposal also affronted his own view of socialism and how it might be achieved. At the start of 1931 he wrote:

> There is no easy road to socialism or we would have traversed it by now. The realisation of socialism can only be accomplished by hard thought and hard work, for which we have to equip ourselves by training and experience. Socialism is impossible without the consent of democracy.[62]

As chairman of the Scottish ILP from 1926 to 1931, Dollan had closer links with the rank-and-file than any of the MPs. He was able to make sure that a majority in Scotland followed his evolutionary course and was not pushed in a more militant direction. He worked hard to stitch up an alliance with fellow moderates from the trade unions and the Co-operative Society so as to keep Glasgow safe for reformist socialism while Maxton and some of his colleagues fulminated in parliament against the evils of the capitalist system and the way it had ground down the people of the west of Scotland. The nub of their outbursts, which initially led them to defy the rules of parliament, concerned housing conditions. Dollan felt that there were occasions such protests went too far, thus making his task as a local government chief hoping to attract jobs and favourable publicity to the Glasgow of the 1930s a difficult one. In his retirement he accused Maxton and the Gorbals MP George Buchanan of having made the districts that elected them 'more notorious than the Bowery in New York or Whitechapel in London', thus jeopardising Glasgow's reputation:

> They alleged that Scotland was the worst housed country in Europe. That its infant mortality was the worst in any civilised country. Wheatley and the others made a general case but... Maxton and Buchanan chanted the poverty theme of Bridgeton and Gorbals in preference to any other ...
> ... It was at this period that Gorbals undeservedly got its notoriety as one of the most abysmal city wards in the English-speaking world.[63]

Dollan was very attached to his native city and, however he may have changed in other respects as his political career evolved, he never drifted away from his roots. At election time he showed his identification with the rhythm of Glasgow life by touring the constituencies and falling into the vernacular of every district, using each local dialect with great flair.[64] Gilbert McAllister, James Maxton's first biographer, summed Dollan up as 'a clever journalist, a dangerous enemy, a valuable friend, a man with his full share of Irish wit . . . as keen in his way as ever Maxton was in securing socialism'.[65]

In 1932 Dollan's political skills and local knowledge were wielded to greatest effect when he managed to keep the bulk of the Scottish ILP loyal to the Labour Party. A Scottish Socialist Party (SSP) was formed (with Dollan as chairman) that was supposed to perform the same crusading tasks in educational work and general propaganda as the ILP had done before disaffiliation. However, it failed to display the same idealism and commitment to socialism and in 1940 the SSP was merged with the Labour Party after losing a court case to the ILP about the ownership of property and assets which had been in dispute since the 1932 split;[66] many of the most fervent idealists had, of course, remained with the ILP while its more moderate rival was increasingly preoccupied with municipal responsibilities.

In 1933 the first Labour administration was formed in Glasgow and Dollan became city treasurer. By now he was viewed even by opponents as a quintessentially Glasgow figure so attempts by militant protestants to stress his Irish catholic ancestry had little effect. However, the Labour administration was in a minority and had to rely on upwards of half a dozen ILP councillors to remain in power. They were mainly concentrated in East End wards taking in the parliamentary seats held by Maxton and McGovern. Meanwhile in 1933 and 1934 ILPers standing for re-election were able to rely on the backing of the Catholic Union, which in some wards seemed more kindly disposed towards the ILP than the Labour Party.

In 1934 senior clergy including the Rector of St Mungo's Academy, the chief catholic school in the city, presided at a Catholic Union meeting which unanimously decided to support the ILP's John Heenan in Shettleston.[67] Across in Govan, Labour's John Storrie, a devout catholic and keen member of the St Vincent de Paul society might have been expected to receive the same backing from the Catholic Union. However, at least one branch was more sympathetic to a radical Labour councillor in the neighbouring seat of Fairfield who was a non-catholic: Tom Kerr 'is a man well disposed towards Catholics and he has always upheld their rights on the Council'.[68] The catholic activist quoted here advocated a policy of non-interference while the hope of John Devine, a local priest was that 'every favourable vote will be recorded for John Storrie'.[69]

Catholic Union election correspondence from this period shows that local committees were allocated a certain degree of autonomy, although John Campbell, the energetic secretary, could be relied upon to intervene if they became too wayward. Fear of giving victory to a hostile Moderate or to a SPL candidate by a split in the Labour vote lay behind much of the Catholic Union's electoral strategy in the early 1930s. Sometimes it seemed to be even more concerned about maximising the natural Labour vote than the rival left-wing parties which were engaged in a bitter battle for supremacy that would eventually see the ILP, the weaker protagonist, disappear from the local council by the 1940s. The Catholic Union was also aware of the practical support given by ILP councillors to their unemployed constituents, many being catholic and several of its councillors (Joseph Payne and John Heenan) were themselves catholics.

The behaviour of the Catholic Union in the crucial period when Dollan was laying the foundations for a Labour domination of Glasgow municipal politics that would stretch over decades, would thus suggest that they were giving the moderate left no special favours. This tends to dent the view that influential 'co-religionists' of Dollan played a crucial role in helping him turn a movement that had flirted with revolutionary politics into a conventional force ready to reach an accommodation with capitalism. Trade union officials and members of the Co-operative societies seem to have been far more instrumental in pushing the Labour Party in Glasgow to the right. A mere six out of 116 Glasgow councillors in 1933 were roman catholics, a figure that only began to appreciably rise in the 1950s. Dollan was the only member of the Labour leadership in the city before the war of a catholic background; he welcomed the support of catholic Labour councillors but there is not sufficient evidence to show that he went out of his way to draw prominent catholics into the party.

But Dollan's views gradually moved in a direction which might have caused some disillusioned activists to wonder if he was not returning to his Irish catholic roots. Back in 1911 he had argued that it was better for the Labour movement's electoral prospects to be put back twenty years than for it to make an alliance with branches of the Home Rule movement involved with the licensing trade.[70] However, twenty-two years later he took issue with Dr Arthur Salter, Labour MP for Bermondsey in the columns of *Forward* over the latter's equation of teetotalism with socialism.[71] Dollan had soon to reply to charges from John McGovern, ILP MP that Glasgow magistrates were in the habit of demanding bribes in return for issuing pub licenses.[72] The Labour Party had scarcely been installed in office and a decade earlier such a charge would have been inconceiveable, highlighting as it did the extent to which the party had moved away from its prohibitionary idealism.

Relatively few magistrates had been chosen from the catholic community when McGovern uttered his charge. But the number steadily increased in the 1930s especially after the appointment of John Stewart, a councillor representing Hutchestown, as the first Labour Lord Provost of Glasgow in 1935. In 1937 the *Glasgow Observer* proudly announced that six catholics had been appointed justices of the peace (JPs) on the recommendation of Glasgow's Lord Provost to the Lord Chancellor. They included John Campbell, secretary of the Catholic Union, Dr John Colvin, a doctor and the son of the well-known lay catholic Dr Thomas Colvin, (appointed a JP in 1901), Patrick Lynch, chairman of the Gorbals division of the Labour Party and a member of the Catholic Social Guild, and Herbert Green, the owner of a chain of cinemas.[73]

These names usefully illustrate the types of catholics a Labour Lord Provost thought would make suitable appointees to the bench. Dollan himself became Lord Provost in 1938 and his gift for public relations won round many of those in important walks of life apprehensive that an ex-agitator with an Irish name had become Glasgow's first citizen. In the words of the *Glasgow Herald*, 'he revealed himself as unexpectedly the right man in the right place' and the customary knighthood awaited him when his term of office expired in 1941.[74] Having turned down an OBE in 1938 he was one of the first prominent socialists to accept a knighthood which, to his left-wing critics, was the logical culmination of a career latterly spent helping to make 'Red Clydeside' safe for capitalism.

Patrick Dollan's son has admitted that he was 'one of those prepared to accept the best of capitalism if it will advance socialism'. On two occasions, when his civic plans were blocked, he successfully appealed to parliament which may have helped to reconcile him to the existing political order.[75] In 1936, he was insisting that 'the British Labour . . . movement must reaffirm its belief in democracy amidst the doubts and confusion created by Dictatorship and civil war . . .'[76] In May 1937 he declared that 'we socialists are bound to admit that our movement has made more progress under the monarchy than the pioneers thought possible . . . there is no evidence that the monarchy in this country has, at any time, tried to interfere with working-class aspirations'.[77] This statement brought an outcry from Labour activists and veiled criticism from even fellow revisionists like Tom Johnston. He followed Dollan's article in *Forward* with one in the same paper entitled 'The Cost of the Monarchy' in which the size of the Civil List was the subject of withering criticism. Dollan back-tracked in the same issue when he conceded that if constitutional monarchy impeded the road to progress, it would have to be taken on.[78] But his revisionist views were once more on display in 1938 when he declared, after having talked with young Glasgow businessmen, that some 'are preaching socialism without realising they are. The important point for Socialists is that young capitalists have revised their old ideas and are adapting themselves to new situations and circumstances. Socialists will require to do likewise.'[79]

Dollan's attitude to war also underwent a radical alteration. Having declared in 1934 to the annual conference of the SSP that 'the membership of the SSP would under no circumstance take part in war', he changed his views sharply in later years.[80] By 1938 he was arguing that it was the duty of Socialists to preserve democracy by any means necessary, including armed force and he was organising the war effort in Glasgow soon after the outbreak of hostilities. This rightward trajectory harmed his reputation as a radical in the Scottish labour movement and by 1943, critics were dubbing him 'the most popular Tory Provost Glasgow has ever had'.[81] Eventually it was followed by a reconciliation with the church in the early 1940s when his wife also became a catholic convert.

A significant pointer to this reconciliation had been given by Dollan shortly after being installed as Lord Provost. It was the tradition for the new incumbent to march with his bailies and councillors to Glasgow Cathedral, the main Presbyterian church in the city in a custom called the 'Kirkin' o' the Council'. Dollan honoured this convention but decided to broaden its scope. A notice duly appeared in the corridors of the City Chambers inviting bailies and councillors to accompany him to St Andrew's roman catholic cathedral. Dollan in thus challenging precedent was honouring a promise to a late friend, Dr Willie Kivlichan, a police surgeon and footballer who had played for both Celtic and Rangers. There was a heavy police presence in case of trouble but it passed by uneventfully even though the milling crowds carrying Dollan's party along Clyde St was so large that at one point people were in danger of being swept into the river Clyde.[82] This gesture by the first catholic to become Glasgow's Lord Provost was perhaps a symbolic illustration that the city's catholics were no longer a submerged minority whose role in city affairs could be comfortably overlooked.

But Dollan was perhaps the medium rather than the conscious architect of changes which altered the *leftist* character of politics in Glasgow. His period in the limelight coincided with the dawning of the age of the Labour machine, one that was more concerned with managing and planning than with advancing ideas. The changes flowing from Labour's assumption of power in British cities were a nationwide phenomenon, but they were particularly striking in Glasgow given the earlier radical character of labour politics there. Dollan brought an unruly left-wing region in line with the requirements of London-based metropolitan socialism. But he was no machine boss on the Irish American Tammany Hall model. His powers of exposition and argument and the fact that the Labour Party in Glasgow was increasingly of one mind about many important ideological issues after 1933 meant that he did not have to be. Even ILP councillors were eventually brought into the fold, some becoming Labour members of parliament.

Dollan lived in a tenement flat, suffered occasional criticism for his sleight-of-hand methods from colleagues, and retired from politics soon after the age of sixty, which is hardly the career pattern one would expect of a Scottish 'Boss Tweed'. Charges of corruption were never levelled at him personally but, after 1933, a number of Labour, ILP, and Tory councillors were jailed for fraud and larceny. In 1941, the year in which Dollan's term as Lord Provost ended, no less than six members of Glasgow Corporation had been convicted by the courts, mainly for corruption charges.[83] Tom Johnston, the new Secretary of State for Scotland, and a puritanical socialist who still adhered to rigid views on drink which Dollan had gradually discarded, linked graft with the misuse of licensing acts.[84] He and Dollan clashed in the press about the best means to solve the problem. Dollan criticised Johnston for having 'given the impression . . . that Glasgow has a monopoly of graft offences':

> These occur in every part of the country. Wherever profit is to be made out of municipal transactions, there is always a tendency for graft unless regulations are strict and enforced without fear or favour.[85]

Percy Sillitoe, Glasgow's chief constable, claims that in 1941 Tom Johnston warned him that 'if I get any more of that sort of thing and other people were convicted he would have to consider very seriously putting in a Commissioner to act in place of the Corporation'.[86]

Shortly before the outbreak of world war the Labour Party on Clydeside had faced an even more awkward challenge, one which brought it into direct confrontation with the catholic church and placed in question its ability to rely on the votes of its most loyal support group. This crisis of loyalty was triggered off by the eruption of civil war in Spain in July 1936. Almost from the outset the *Glasgow Observer* pledged its support for the rebels under General Franco who had risen against the Republican government in Madrid, thereby plunging Spain into three ferocious years of war. News of wisespread persecution of priests, monks, and nuns in Republican-controlled areas where anarchist influence was strong, roused catholic feelings abroad and Glasgow was no exception. The *Observer* became a channel for the propaganda of the Spanish right so that tendentious page one headlines like 'I saw Guernica Bombed and I Accuse Basque Government' were not uncommon.[87] Even the Glasgow Distributists revealed themselves to be pro-Franco,[88] as did James Shields, the author of *Gael over Glasgow*, a recent novel about the catholic community which had not been unsympathetic to the left.[89] Huge open-air masses of reparation for the crimes committed against the church in Spain were held at the Carfin shrine in Lanarkshire. The Scottish hierarchy was always represented and sometimes as many as 70,000 people are reckoned to have taken part.[90]

Simultaneously in Spain, young working-class catholics from Clydeside and Dundee were fighting for the anti-fascist side as members of the International Brigade. They helped swell the Scottish contingent which was the largest of any British group to go out to Spain and their willingness to lay down their lives for this cause graphically illustrated that the catholic community spoke with more than one voice on this emotive question. Writing in the 1950s Anthony Hepburn was to point out that 'there are still a number who "fell out" with the Church over Spain'.[91]

Spain was the mirror for ideological, religious, and social tensions that had resonance in the rest of Europe and indeed much further afield, which may explain why it had such a strong impact in Glasgow, a city with a delicate balance of competing religious and political interests. Perhaps it was the realisation that the emotions generated by the Spanish war threatened to do serious damage to the cohesion of the church, especially in a number of working-class districts, which prompted a few bishops to restrain their more militant lay activists.

In the archdiocese of Westminster, where the Catholic Evidence Guild was divided over whether 'we should do Franco propaganda from our platform', Frank Sheed recalls that Cardinal Hinsley's opinion was sought and he opted for non-intervention.[92] In Glasgow during the first months of the war, Archbishop Mackintosh felt compelled to publicly rebuke the *Glasgow Observer* for making a pre-election attack on the Labour Party without his authority. *Forward* viewed the paper's line as 'an unscrupulous attack on the Labour Party . . . in which an appeal was made to working men and women to vote against Labour candidates in the municipal elections'. The *Observer* article had stated: 'the situation has now changed for the Labour advocates have now joined the war against Christ'.[93] *Forward* of 10 November 1936 then went on to make a bold claim about dissension in catholic ranks:

> The frantic appeals by Roman Catholic capitalists to their poorer brethren to vote against Labour have not the official backing of the Church authorities in the west of Scotland. The Catholic Union and similar organisations have declined to identify themselves with any capitalist campaign against Labour.[94]

The *Glasgow Observer* of 14 November 1936 showed that *Forward* had been on the right lines when it published an apology regarding the anti-Labour advice it had recently given to voters; it was in fact a second apology since Archbishop Mackintosh felt that the first one had been too vague and not sufficiently contrite:

> We again wish to repeat that we were expressing nothing but our own opinion, but we also acknowledge that we failed by an elementary oversight to recognise that in publishing anything in the domain of Faith and Morals . . . we, as Catholics, are bound by the general law of the Church, which enjoins

previous submissions of such proposed publications to be sent to the local Bishop . . . We further find that in so acting we departed from the practice of the former administration of the *Glasgow Observer*. We have apologised to the Archbishop of Glasgow . . . and His Grace had graciously accepted 'the apology as closing the matter'.[95]

It is very likely that Archbishop Mackintosh insisted on this abject public retraction less because of the content of the offending editorial more because his *imprimatur* had not been sought by the newspaper. The incident amply displayed his autocratic style but it can be assumed that he felt far less displeasure with Labour policy over Spain than did impetuous catholic journalists depending ultimately on his patronage for the sale of their product. One lay catholic has summed up Archbishop Mackintosh's view of politics as follows: 'given the two fundamental rights of freedom of worship and freedom of education, he felt it was no function of the Church to express a preference among political parties'.[96]

The Archbishop may have been reassured by the Labour Party's policy favouring British non-intervention which it adhered to in the earlier stages of the war. Arthur Woodburn, secretary of the Labour Party in Scotland since 1932 saw Spain as a Trojan horse for the Communist Party to use and he reflected the official Labour movement's cautious and guarded response to the intense local activities that had mushroomed around the Spanish war.[97] In Glasgow alone, by 1937, there were fifteen Spanish Aid committees raising funds for the Republicans and organising medical aid and foodships.[98] In April 1937 their activities led to a split inside the ruling Labour group in Glasgow Corporation. A dispute arose about whether permits ought to be granted to corporation transport workers to raise funds for the Republican cause in depots where they worked. Two Labour bailies defied the whip, voted against, and were expelled from the Labour group of councillors and from the city party.[99] Both were roman catholics: James McLaughlin who had been received into the Labour Party after being elected for the Gorbals ward in 1934 as an independent; and Alexander McGregor, a publicity-conscious solicitor who was honorary secretary of the Catholic Truth Society and chairman of the Catholic Evidence Guild in Glasgow and 'an indefatigible worker for Catholic issues'.[100]

McGregor became a leading figure in the Friends of Nationalist Spain, the Scottish offshoot of a London-based mainly lay catholic body formed in March 1938. During that month an even bigger split loomed inside the Glasgow Labour group when the town council debated an application by the Friends to hold a public meeting in St Andrew's Hall. In an acrimonious debate three Labour councillors joined McGregor and the Progressives in speaking out in favour of granting the application. The depth of feeling in the debating chamber was shown in a speech by one of their opponents Bailie Tom Kerr (Fairfield, Labour):

> You [the Progressives] may take over to your side certain members of the Labour Party, and you will be welcome to them. Take them with you. We have nothing to lose by being defeated, and a great deal to gain so far as purity of, and loyalty to, the party are concerned . . .
> Many of us are taking what might be regarded as political risks. We have thrown everything into the pool. We have considered the pro's and con's of the question and what it might mean in the matter of votes from a certain section of the community in Glasgow.[101]

Later in the debate, when Bailie Crawford, another Labour member from Fairfield, rose to speak, Patrick Dollan interjected with a remark about not making an injudicious speech. As late as July 1938 Dollan was appealing for unity in the Labour group which illustrates the degree of tension there may have been beneath the surface over Spain.[102] Since Labour used to be banned from holding meetings in public halls, Dollan did not think that the party should employ this tactic against others, however much it disagreed with their views. This view he advanced in a June 1938 article in *Forward* in an article entitled 'Free Speech and Free Thought is the Way to meet Franco-ism'.[103] It was an argument elaborated by Councillor Rosslyn Mitchell (Knightsbridge, Labour) at the climax of the debate:

> The heat generated by this discussion shows how dangerous it is for a public authority to depart from the fundamental principle upon which the democracy of this country has been obtained . . .
> I am opposing anybody in authority putting up a bar against free speech . . . Mr Kerr put four different arguments. He asked that we should put political thoughts out of account and then he started a great tirade against General Franco and his supporters. Then he went on to suggest a sectarian issue. I say this—the Roman Catholics have just as much right to speak their opinion from St Andrew's Hall as anybody else.
> A great deal of trouble has been caused by the fact that we have departed from a principle and are saying we are going to let a hall—which does not belong to a majority of this council, but to the Citizens—to those who hold our views and refuse it to those who have not our views. That is the very negation of democracy. It is the foundation on which the edifice of tyranny will be erected, and when there is tyranny in the air, no matter from what quarter it comes, I oppose it.[104]

Mitchell and five other Labour councillors (including the Lord Provost John Stewart) voted in favour of allowing the 'Friends' to hold their pro-Franco rally in St Andrew's Hall. Another fourteen Labour and ILP councillors abstained which enabled the motion to be carried by fifty votes to thirty-eight. The caution of some ILP councillors may have stemmed from the fate of Councillor John Heenan, who went down to defeat in Shettleston and Tollcross in 1936 in a straight fight with the Progressives; in 1937 Joseph Payne lost Cowcaddens and was pushed into third place behind the Progressives and Labour which won the seat. Both men were catholic ILPers (Heenan had been the *Glasgow Observer*'s labour correspondent in the early 1920s) and both forfeited the support of the Catholic Union for having supported the Republican cause in Spain.

John McGovern MP accused the *Observer* of waging a campaign against its erstwhile contributor because he had broken ranks over Spain.[105] But in 1937 Heenan resigned from the ILP, citing as his reason the party newspaper's deprecation of the need for those Spanish catholics fighting Franco to go to mass.[106] Fenner Brockway wrote from London to say that 'the Glasgow ILP . . . will not be the same without you' but Heenan declined to reconsider.[107] He was followed in 1939 by the ILP member for Glasgow Gorbals, George Buchanan. Beforehand he had *declined* to adopt the party line of support for the Republican government according to fellow MP, John McGovern.[108] Although he had received a record 75% of the vote at the last general election, he felt in danger, especially after the Labour Party had adopted a popular local candidate who was reputed to have clerical backing.[109] Not reassured by his thumping majority, Buchanan took the Labour whip in 1939. A parliamentary colleague once remembered him saying of his electorate: 'there is very little between their cheers and their jeers'.[110]

Probably the most combative left-wing politician over Spain anywhere in Britain was John McGovern. At the 1935 general election the Catholic Union had not opposed him in his Shettleston seat; it was left up to local branches to decide their own policy. But relations took an ugly turn in December 1936 when, in the words of the *Evening Times*, a Glasgow daily paper, McGovern issued 'a slashing attack on the Roman Catholic church for its alleged interference with the political opinions of its members'. The *Evening Times* had obtained a copy of a letter McGovern had sent to the secretary of the Catholic Union in which he blamed the church for making Glasgow 'the cockpit of sectarian warfare'. According to the paper, 'he alleged that at every election the clergy obscures the living issues and induces Catholics to vote not as a class but as a creed'. The letter pulled no punches in elaborating the point:

> The issues raised here have been birth control, secular education, 1918 Education Act, Home Rule, Belfast inquiry, Matrimonial bill, lunacy clauses, mental defectives etc but never a case of war, means test, unemployment

benefit, housing, pensions, Poor-law scales, etc.

When the Catholic Union recently urged an ILP Parliamentary Group to move amendments to the 1935 Housing Act and allow more persons to the room than the National Government had made provision for, the argument used being 'that it would discourage birth control', I thought it was the worst approach ever made to me, and the limit in black reaction and gross impertinence.[111]

The *Glasgow Observer* replied in kind by somewhat mischievously linking McGovern with 'gang warfare' in a story which turned out to have little bearing on the dramatic headline.[112] In May 1937 McGovern issued a writ against the *Catholic Herald*, the English counterpart of the *Observer* because of 'brazen lies against myself'. In an election leaflet at the end of 1937 he claimed that 'the owner paid me the sum of £100 and all expenses, and made a complete apology in the *Catholic Herald*.[113]

McGovern was a turbulent figure who, in a parliamentary career spanning almost thirty years, was rarely known to mince his words on a subject about which he felt strongly. The question of Spain undoubtedly saw him at his most vitriolic. In January 1937, before an audience of 2,500 in a cinema in the Parkhead district of Glasgow (with hundreds more outside unable to get in), he vented his indignation about the record of the catholic church in Spain in perhaps the most anti-clerical speech ever given by a Glasgow Labour MP. The church in Spain was assailed, among other things, for paying low wages to the workers on the trams and buses which it owned. Uproar ensued when McGovern associated himself with those workers who had denounced the Spanish clergy as 'the enemies of the people'. One member of the audience could be heard above the tumult. 'Talk away John, it'll be your last Christmas; we'll send you where we sent John Heenan,' to which McGovern replied, 'Do your worst; if I had a thousand seats I would lose them on this issue; my self-respect is more important to me than any seat in this city.'[114] Even stormier scenes then ensued when McGovern claimed that money to buy bombs was being collected in British churches and at the point when he named one local priest as being 'an apostle of Christian terrorism'.[115]

In June 1937 the high-point of the Spanish controversy in Glasgow was perhaps reached when a debate was held in a packed St Andrew's Hall in which McGovern was pitted against the catholic lecturer, Douglas Jerrold who had actively helped Franco in the initial stages of the uprising.[116] McGovern was, in characteristic vein, declaring at one point that 'religion exists today not because of the support of the clergy but in spite of the support of the clergy'.[117] He had an English counterpart in Josiah Wedgwood, MP for Newcastle-under-Lyme. In the first Labour government he had been Chancellor of the

Duchy of Lancaster but, by the late 1930s, he was sitting as an independent Labour member. Wedgwood went further than McGovern in a 1937 letter to Anthony Eden, the Foreign Secretary in which he talked about English 'Catholics as ever loyal to Rome, but all are the enemies of this country's state and faith'.[118]

Percipient members of the Catholic Union and the church hierarchy were able to see that, in the main, socialists driven into an anti-clerical position over Spain (or whose longstanding distrust of church interference in politics was reinforced by events there), were hardly representative of their party, even less of the voters who had returned them to Westminster. In Glasgow, John Campbell, secretary of the Catholic Union, worked hard to prevent a complete break between the catholic lobby and the left arising from the provocative behaviour of a few politicians like John McGovern. At its 1937 AGM he successfully repudiated the demand from some sections of the Catholic Union that it stand its own people in local elections to oppose 'anti-God' candidates. Campbell and others also showed their essential moderation in the case of Councillor McInnes of Townhead who some wished to punish in 1937 because he had been 'primarily responsible for the expulsion of two Catholics, McLaughlin and McGregor from the Labour Party . . .' When one of the speakers in the ensuing debate pointed out that, as one of the whips of the Labour group, McInnes was simply acting under instructions in moving the expulsions, the matter was allowed to drop.[119]

But it can be safely assumed that the Catholic Union did not campaign as assiduously for preferred Labour candidates as it had done in years past when a sectarian threat had also been in evidence. At the 1938 municipal elections, the lack of involvement may have been reflected in the turnout which at 45% was the lowest in nine years. Labour received 44·25% of the vote with the Tories a close second with 43·50% but the 9% of the vote still obtained by the ILP meant that the two left-wing parties had a comfortable majority in the corporation.

As Patrick Dollan skilfully edged the local party away from radical or exposed positions which could have plunged the non-communist left in Glasgow into further turmoil, the chance of a confrontation receded even before the Spanish civil war ended in victory for the Franco side. By 1939, both he and John Campbell were talking very similar language about the danger of communist infiltration into the Labour Party. In April 1939 the Lord Provost was able to report that twenty-one out of twenty-two Scottish Labour MPs completely repudiated Sir Stafford Cripps's Popular Front scheme. Significantly this information was relayed by Dollan in the first issue of the *Scottish Catholic*, 'a news digest and fiction magazine' which did not survive the outbreak of war.[120] Further developments were to convince lay catholics made apprehensive by the Spanish war that the Labour Party in Glasgow was after all in safe hands: the winding up in 1940 of the pacifist-inclined and nationalist-minded SSP, founded by Dollan as a successor to the ILP in 1933 but from which he dropped out in 1936 as his definition of socialism increasingly diverged from the party's; also the transfer of power in 1940 from the city Labour Party to the Labour Council group which was deemed to be more immune from communist influence and more in tune with the party's slide towards orthodoxy and respectability.

By 1940 the Labour Party in the west of Scotland was 'safer' for catholic voters than at any time in the past and the Catholic Union allowed its vigilance to drop. The files of the Glasgow Archdiocesan Archives taper out after this year, the war having disrupted its infrastructure and programme of activities. John Campbell had ceased to be secretary by 1945 and in post-war general elections the Catholic Union had a distinctly low profile. Even the survival of John McGovern in politics caused it little unease. Before the end of the Spanish conflict he had begun to make his peace with the church. As a result of two visits to Spain, on one of which he narrowly escaped death at the hands of Spanish communists, his enthusiasm for the Republican cause diminished. Like George Orwell he had been dismayed by the way the Republican government had allowed local communists under instructions from Moscow to crush the libertarian left in the Barcelona fighting of May 1937.

The suppression of the POUM which in a number of ways was the Spanish equivalent of the ILP deeply angered McGovern and confirmed the hostility to communism which had been engendered by disputes with local communists about agitation on behalf of the unemployed, a cause he had been linked with earlier in the 1930s. An article with the title 'What I saw in Spain: the Communist Menace Today: Why the Popular Front must be Opposed' appeared in *Forward* under McGovern's name in June 1938.[121] In later years he became one of the most inveterate anti-communists in the Parliamentary Labour Party which he joined after Maxton's death in 1946. Naturally catholic press attacks on him eased off and by 1951 a regular correspondent in the *Observer* was arguing that John McGovern was the obvious successor to Ernest Bevin as foreign secretary.[122]

Undoubtedly, the Spanish civil war engendered more heat and controversy in Glasgow than perhaps any other British city, but the political after-effects were remarkably few. If a general election had intervened between 1936 and 1939 or if the Labour Party and the Catholic Union had been under the direction of less pragmatic figures than Dollan and John Campbell), the outcome might have been different. Perhaps a rift similar in kind though not in degree to that which erupted in Australia in the 1950s and which led to the formation of two Labour Parties might even have loomed. Archbishop Mannix of Melbourne encouraged a breakaway formation because of perceived communist infiltration of the Australian Labour Party. A large proportion of working-class catholics who had hitherto supported the ALP transferred their loyalties to the Democratic Labour Party which won seats in the federal parliament thanks to Australia having a form of proportional representation and for almost twenty years the ALP was deprived of office.

The split in the Australian left had these major consequences even though it was largely confined to one state, Victoria. On more than one occasion Glasgow had shown that it could be out of step with political trends elsewhere in Labour-voting areas of the country. It was a distinct political entity with a mood and style all of its own. The survival of an ILP parliamentary party largely drawn from Glasgow is a prime example of its individuality. But this was at the cost of dividing the radical left and letting moderates into the ascendancy by the end of the 1930s.

Perhaps the fact that the Labour Party had already split in a way that was beneficial to catholic interests encouraged those behind the catholic lobby to hold their fire in the late 1930s. Workers with a clear religious orientation, entering the party, did so with the approval of the Catholic Union; it may have been felt that benefits to be obtained from an emergent Labour Party more in tune with catholic values were not worth jeopardising over a short-term foreign emergency, no matter how emotive the subject or how uncomfortable some of the implications were for embattled Glasgow catholics. Undoubtedly some catholics were unhappy that not one of their co-religionists represented a Glasgow parliamentary seat by the late 1930s.[123] As a result, the *Observer* was moved to comment in 1937 that 'there is no member of parliament for the city who could be trusted to voice Catholic aspirations and Catholic ideals in the House of Commons as well as protect Catholic interests'.[124]

The Catholic Union was more realistic in its appraisal: it concentrated its energies on Glasgow Corporation where Labour was in power with catholics to be found in its ranks, rather than on distant Westminster where the party was usually out of office and catholic members were far less likely to be able to alter its character.

All this was cold comfort for forces on the right hoping to see the left in Glasgow weakened by religious dissension. Mostly they were to be found outside the catholic community. The Earl of Glasgow, Ayrshire landowner and backer of various far-right causes between the wars, was a patron of the Friends of Nationalist Spain, but catholics would have drawn little comfort from the fact that he had earlier founded a Union of Scottish Loyalists, a name that would have conjured

up unfavourable images for many of them.[125] The much better-known
Sir Oswald Mosley found that urban Scottish catholics had no special
brief for his British Union of Fascists (BUF) even though many were
appalled that their church was under attack in Republican Spain; Weir
Gilmour claims that his SFDP unintentionally deprived the BUF of a
base in Scotland after 1933. The anti-catholicism of his shortlived
fascist party permanently soured the fascist image in the minds of those
Scottish catholics who were potential adherents to the BUF.[126] Even
when Mosley appointed Victor Duffy, an English catholic, to be the
BUF's Scottish organiser, it made no difference and served only to
produce dissension in existing Scottish BUF ranks. Thus Scotland can
be contrasted with the north of England where relatively large numbers
of catholics *were* receptive to the BUF.

Glasgow's catholic community threw up only one well-known
public figure who placed himself unashamedly on the right of politics.
This was Colm Brogan (1902–77), a school-teacher at St Mungo's
Academy and also at St Gerard's secondary school in the 1930s who
possessed an acute and incisive mind whose judgements were expressed
in caustic and witty terms in part-time journalism. Notwithstanding
the fact that his father, Denis Brogan had been a prominent campaigner
in Glasgow against British rule in Ireland, he gravitated to the right
early in life. Michael de la Bedoyere, editor of the *Catholic Herald*
summed up his political outlook in the following way:

> In . . . school he learnt to detach himself from the illusions of contemporary
> liberalism and socialism and thus came to associate himself with their political
> opposite, Toryism.
>
> But his Toryism was highly individual and it served him more as a con-
> spicuous pedestal from which to denounce the left than as a platform on
> which to build a different political structure. Fundamentally, the constructive
> side of his thought was Catholic and democratic in the serious sense of the
> word.[127]

Brogan was a complete individualist who revelled in controversy
but, in Glasgow, he was a somewhat isolated figure whose talents did
not find as much of an outlet as in London, to where he moved in 1946.
There he became 'one of the few journalists and pamphleteers of the
Welfare era to assail the ideas and institutions of the left with the same
zest and skill that Socialist intellectuals devoted to the personalities and
positions of the Right'.[128] As well as being a leader-writer with the
Daily Telegraph, he also wrote for the *Glasgow Observer* and he was the
author in 1954 of the eloquent book *The Glasgow Story*. Brogan never
lost touch with his native roots and he retained enough of Clydeside's
egalitarian spirit to make him an unorthodox Tory. *The Times* recalled,
on his death in 1977 that 'he had no reverence for the Conservative

establishment. It was disconcerting for conventional Tories to discover an ally contemptuous of the Crown.'[129] If the Scottish Tories had not seemed so caste-like and unwelcoming to members of a community which was extremely conservative in its social mores and in its religious outlook, others might have joined this lone-wolf extrovert in moving towards the political right.

In the west of Scotland there were deeply religious catholics, concerned by the spread of communism at home and abroad—the principal danger of the age in their eyes—who responded in an original way to the perceived threat in their midst. Their concern led them to form the Catholic Workers Guild in July 1941, the month in which the Soviet Union became Britain's ally following the surprise attack mounted by Hitler on Stalin's Russia.

This movement perhaps deserves to be regarded as the most sophisticated and distinctive of the catholic organisations which absorbed the energies of lay people before 1945. It was the brainchild of members of the laity who formed it with a practical aim in mind and who kept control of its activities thereafter. The backing of the archdiocese was sought, but its founders retained their freedom of action and thus, the CWG was one of the few catholic groups where the laity actually arrived at the decisions as well as carrying them out.

Much of its independence from assertive clergy stemmed from the environment in which the CWG largely operated; many of its activities centred around the self-enclosed world of the industrial shop-floor where it combatted the ideas and proselytism of marxists. In outlook the CWG was not old-fashioned or merely reactive since it acknowledged the existence of injustice in the workplace, encouraged the growth of trade unionism, and promoted educational classes whose aim was to turn out catholic trade unionists alive to reform and prepared to use their Christian ideals to shape a more just and better society.

The founders of the CWG were Anthony Hepburn (1904-66) and James Darragh (1919-). Hepburn's father had been the owner of a small bakery, in the running of which he had been guided by catholic social principles as enunciated in the more recent papal encyclicals. As a young man Anthony Hepburn was one of a number of catholics to be attracted by Scottish nationalism. He trained as a librarian and spent many years in the Mitchell Library, Glasgow whose director he eventually became. It may have been his library experience which alerted him to communist propaganda and the range of outlets the party was prepared to use in order to further its ends. In 1940, the *Glasgow Observer* reported his concern about how bodies like the Left Book Club were systematically used to recruit potential members of the Communist Party: 'their way to success is through reading. "Read and Learn" is also Mr Hepburn's motto for Catholics':

His aim is to establish Catholic libraries in the big city parishes where there is a strong Communist membership. The library would be run by a small group which would take a keen interest in individual members, so far as their reading is concerned, and in time they would have a complete answer to every Communist challenge.

'This may be a long and tedious way,' said Mr Hepburn, 'but in the end it would be well worth while.'[130]

In the same article Mr Hepburn 'expressed the opinion that the Catholic press had neglected badly the important job of informing its readers against associations which have the faintest connection with Communism. The power of the Communist Party . . . is not just in its numerical strength, but in those comparatively harmless organisations which are under its influence . . .'[131] This was justifiable criticism perhaps also meant for some of the lay associations supposed to be guarding against communist encroachments inside the catholic community. A number had become too narrowly devotional or overly interested in 'study for study's sake' rather than as a preparation for action. Even the Catholic Union sometimes gave the impression of being fully absorbed in husbanding the catholic vote in the most advantageous direction for catholic interests to be aware of what the communists were getting up to between elections. Given the internal conflicts which had absorbed it in the 1930s, the Labour Party was abandoning many of the social, educational, and propagandistic activities which it had previously found time for; it was increasingly becoming a voting machine in conjunction with the trade unions, so this gave the Communist Party added scope to seek out new recruits by diversifying its activities.

In 1940 Hepburn put his accumulated knowledge of Communist popular front tactics into print when he issued a booklet called *Communism In Scotland*. Very few copies survive and even the Mitchell Library does not have one. It was put to me that the pamphlet was sufficiently accurate and hard-hitting for its targets to go out of their way to buy it up and remove it from libraries which had obtained a copy. In thirty-two pages Hepburn set out to detail Communist tactics and influence in bodies as varied as the Co-operative movement, the Home Guard, Scottish nationalism, Housewives committees, the armed forces, and the industrial shopfloor. The pamphlet sought to demonstrate how these various outlets were used to spearhead opposition to the war, spread Marxist 'education', raise funds for the party, and obstruct industrial production, a strategy geared towards boosting the interests and long-term objectives of the Soviet Union which in 1940 still enjoyed cordial ties with Nazi Germany. Hepburn was not reassured by the small turnout at the 1940 congress of the Scottish wing of the Communist Party (CPGB): 119 delegates representing 3,000 members: 'the power of the Communist Party . . . is not in its numerical strength, but in the comparatively harmless organizations which are under its influence'.[132] Furthermore, the hardcore membership of the party was, he claimed, composed of men who are 'trained, fanatical disciples, with one consuming purpose in life—the achievement of Communism in Scotland by an armed civil war. It contains many men who went specifically to Spain for military experience likely to be useful in the future.'[133]

Hepburn was aware that many veterans of the war in Spain were Scottish catholics, not all of whom were CPGB members but who were bound to have come under strong party influence. His partner James Darragh later noted that of the 407 men listed as killed fighting with the British International Brigade for the Republican side in Spain, no less than ninety-one were from Scotland, many with names such as Burke, Casey, Connolly, Duffy etc.[134]

The CWG was opposed to banning the Communist Party. Hepburn felt that such a step would be 'a grave mistake' that would only force many of its members underground and make their activities hard to detect and counter.[135] With party politics in abeyance and a general election held over till the end of the war, it was felt there was little point in utilising the political arena to frustrate communist intentions. The consensus among those who formed the CWG was that to be effective it needed to concentrate its energies in the areas where the Communist Party was applying most pressure and making the greatest headway which, in the early years of the Second World War, was the trade union and industrial world.

The membership of the CWG was recruited in the place of work which made it unlike all other catholic organisations, including the vocational guilds, which were organised on a parish basis. Besides ordinary industrial workers, it gained adherents from some catholics reluctant to go into uniform who gravitated to the nearest shipyard or munitions factory where they found work in a reserved occupation, exempt from military service. Others, including James Darragh, were in war work because they had been exempted from military service on health grounds. The membership of the CWG was 'a motley collection of workers skilled and unskilled, male and female, undergraduates and graduates, veterans of older Catholic organizations and complete newcomers'.[136] In August 1941, one month after being formally launched, it was claimed that thirty unions were represented in its ranks.[137] The *Glasgow Observer* regularly gave Anthony Hepburn space to report on its activities. His last report appeared in October 1942, the month he joined the Royal Air Force. His colleague, James Darragh, prevented from joining the forces by a tubercular condition, stepped into his shoes so that a wide number of Glasgow catholics continued to be aware of the CWG's efforts to frustrate communist plans on the industrial front; despite its laudable efforts, friction with other catholic bodies sometimes proved unavoidable as James Darragh relates:

> The old Catholic organizations were . . . in the hands of men who were too old or too unfit to go to war; I was young; the opportunities for misunderstanding were ever present. I . . . managed to have a virtual monopoly of Catholic newspaper coverage; Catholic societies expected newspaper reporters to cover their meetings, but the staff for doing so did not exist during the war and the societies had no sense of how to do the job for themselves; every Monday morning I delivered to the three Catholic newspaper offices in Glasgow, press copy properly typed, double spaced, wide margins, written in newspaper style for immediate use. The Catholic newspapers, perenially short of copy, were grateful and used my material. Fine from the CWG viewpoint, but the other Catholic societies did not like it although they did nothing to help themselves; the Catholic Social Guild in particular thought we were stealing their thunder.[138]

Eventually a joint committee of the two groups helped smooth over initial differences. The CWG was not concerned with publicity for its own sake, but used it to alert as many catholics as possible about the means Communists used to ensnare the unwitting, above all in the workplace. The message it consistently reiterated was that the party exploited shopfloor grievances and injustices for its own ends, which were dictated from abroad. That did not mean bad conditions or unfair practices simply had to be endured because the motives of those prepared to challenge them were fundamentally suspect. The CWG argued that workers should take action themselves to right injustice in the workplace and thus remove the conditions which enabled the communists to gain a hearing. In January 1942 Hepburn rebuked catholics for failing to support a young co-religionists heavily involved in trade union affairs. He related that:

> Very few Catholics in the union gave him support, while others, because he was not afraid to talk about conditions, and was keen on one hundred per cent unionism, dubbed him a 'Communist'.
>
> This charge to a man who not only believes in the faith and practices it, but believes in the values of trade-unionism, makes militant Catholics very bitter indeed. We have a big job before us to educate our own people.[139]

After 1941, with the war economy working flat out to supply armaments and supplies for the different theatres of war, grievances about safety standards, rates of pay for overtime, and general conditions of work continued to surface despite the atmosphere of solidarity engendered by the patriotic wave sweeping over the country. In the first two years of the war the CPGB had been anxious to exploit whatever grievances it could, but this tactic was abruptly dropped when the Soviet Union joined the Allies in 1941 and began to receive military aid from Britain.

Momentarily stunned by the complete turn-around in events caused by the German invasion of Russia, the Communist Party quickly recovered its poise, dropped its opposition to a war between 'two rival imperialist camps' and urged maximum support for the global anti-fascist struggle. For the sake of the war effort and the Anglo-Soviet alliance, communist industrial activists now tended to overlook grievances that they would hitherto have been keen to exploit. The emergence of the country they had long idealised in their propaganda as a partisan with Britain in a desperate military struggle against Nazism, boosted the credibility of the CPGB among many British workers, but it also enabled the CWG to make headway in drawing attention to the ulterior motives that lay behind the somersault in communist tactics. If no other way of solving a shopfloor dispute presented itself, the CWG did not back off from condoning industrial action and it urged that workers should speak their minds as individuals, pointing out that peaceful agitation for economic justice was not at variance with Christian social ethics. It reiterated that Communist silence about grievances which, shortly beforehand, it had been keen to exploit or invent, only served to show how much the party was the creature of a foreign power which had launched unprovoked attacks on weaker states like Poland and Finland and had annexed the Baltic republics of Estonia, Latvia, and Lithuania before being repaid in the same coin by Hitler.

It is hard to know what impact the CWG's campaign had in the war years. Membership was small and fluctuating and its message was mainly directed to fellow catholics. However, the fact that the CPGB made less wartime inroads in the trade union movement on Clydeside than in some other parts of Britain might, in part be attributed to its vigilance. The catholic community had, in the past provided a small but significant stream of party recruits and with highly-motivated religious activists for the first time challenging the party on its own chosen terrain, the effect cannot have been altogether negligible. Certainly if the wave of militancy which swept Clydeside in the First World War is used as a benchmark, the party had good reason to be disappointed with its performance locally during the Second World War. At the 1945 general election, it was unable to benefit from the sympathy many workers had for Russia at a time when Labour Party organisation and membership in the Glasgow district was in rather a sorry state.[140]

Being an unorthodox catholic body which operated beyond the reach of the institutional church meant that some old-fashioned priests were liable to misunderstand the motives behind the CWG and question its worth. There was still no lack of such priests in Glasgow during the 1940s and, when a body adopted the same industrial practices as the Communists in order to organise catholic workers and be in a position to undermine the credibility of their political foe in the eyes of the workforce, it may, for some, have been going too far.

The CWG had an important ally and protector in the Jesuit, Fr William d'Andria who had been encouraging catholics in different occupations to form their own guilds since the early 1930s. James Darragh feels that it was Fr d'Andria who was instrumental in securing episcopal approval for the CWG in Glasgow.[141] He carried sufficient weight to smooth over any concern felt in church circles about the social radicalism of the CWG swamping its religious message. Darragh in particular was deeply influenced by the Catholic Workers Movement of New York whose mainstays, Dorothy Day and Pete Maurin gave witness to their faith by campaigning for the victims of injustice in ways that could have seemed dangerously radical to more conventional catholics. Darragh was also influenced by the Belgian priest, Canon, later Cardinal Cardjin whose Young Catholic Workers Movement pioneered a 'See, Judge, Act' approach to further its activities which both he and Hepburn felt was a model that ought to be emulated in Scotland. However, episcopal approval was not forthcoming and this remained the case even when a new and more sympathetic archbishop, Donald Campbell was installed in 1945; the memory of young Free French servicemen urinating and copulating under the windows of Bishop's House in Oban were perhaps too vivid for Campbell (previously Bishop of Argyll and the Isles) to expect that the Gallic source of the 'See, Judge and Act' approach would be of much benefit to Scotland, or so it has been suggested to me.

With Archbishop McDonald still in charge across in Edinburgh, the atmosphere was more conducive for such new departures. In 1941 the archbishop gave heart to the CWG by stressing 'the vital necessity for Catholic workers and professional men to join their trade unions and professional associations and to direct the efforts of those organisations into Christian channels'.[142] He also gave his blessing to a three-day conference on social reconstruction after the war organised by the Edinburgh university Catholic Student's Union in the spring of 1942.[143] Each year he continued to send two young priests to Oxford or Cambridge to take degrees in social science subjects and thus be in a position to train lay people to play a vigorous role in trade unions and politics. The idea never quite worked since most priests who had taken degrees found themselves too busy with parish work to devote sufficient time for motivating the 'lay apostolate' in these directions.[144] However, two priests, Walter Glancy and Patrick Quille simply made time and at the end of 1942 they were giving a series of public lectures in Edinburgh which showed a more reasoned approach to socialism on the part of the church by seeking to greatly qualify its condemnation of socialism:

> Socialism is a word which is loosely used to cover, very different shades of meaning. Taking 'Socialism' in its broadest sense, as emphasising the common good, the unity of men, the rights of society, over the individual, and the consequent obligation on the individual to promote the common good, it is almost as old as history. We find it proclaimed as far back as 1300 BC. We see it in St Thomas More's *Utopia*, and in a host of writing since. There has even been a school of thought called 'Catholic Socialism'.
>
> But the 'Socialism' which is put forward under the name of 'Communism' is the scientific socialism of Marxism. Marx despised all previous Socialists as utopian dreamers and idealists and preached a new scientific socialism. It is of this form of socialism that the Pope is speaking when he says that 'No one can be a sincere Catholic and a true socialist'.[145]

To hear these sentiments coming from Scottish priests would have greatly encouraged the pioneers of the Catholic Socialist Society such as John Wheatley. In its concern with the workplace and economic issues, and by its desire to show doubting churchmen and catholics under the sway of communism that Christianity had a place in the factory or shopfloor, the CWG shared some of the missionary qualities of Wheatley's CSS. But in their campaign against communism, CWG activists could not entirely overlook more traditional challenges to the faith. In October 1942, just prior to joining the RAF Anthony Hepburn made reference to these:

> For those who live close to reality, there can be seen plenty of signs of opposition to Catholicism. It will be a task of Catholic industrial workers, full of the same zeal to make sure that post-war Scotland is not built on Stormont lines.[146]

Although the demands of wartime production meant that signs like 'No Catholics' or 'No Irish need Apply' were becoming things of the past outside factory gates, Hepburn would have been aware that the old sectarian ways had not been totally banished by the war. Larger numbers of catholics were able to gain employment in industrial concerns which had been secure protestant strongholds because of a national crisis that was likely to be temporary in duration not as a result of any permanent change in the way labour was employed. Even in the midst of an egalitarian revolution produced by the 'people's war' in which Britain was engaged, old practices continued to be re-affirmed. Early in the war Lord Provost Dollan was able to draw important engineering firms to the new industrial estate at Hillington in Glasgow,[147] but the vitality of religious identity in the workplace was shown by the phenomenal speed with which freemasonry established itself, along with recruitment practices where catholics came off second best.

On showing the Duke of Kent around early wartime Glasgow Sir Patrick Dollan managed to put a brave face on it when the royal visitor remarked that 'he must have a difficult time because of the large number of Irish in Govan and elsewhere':

> I told him that I had represented Govan for thirty years during which I had never had trouble with any of the citizens and that he was on his way to inspect the Govan Civil Defence Force. At the end of the inspection, he had a tremendous reception from the Govan boys and when we went out into the street I said, 'You have just now been cheered by the Irish and the Scots of Govan. Could you tell me which was Irish and which was Scots'?[148]

The Irishness of the immigrants may have been receding into the background in the 1940s, but religious differences that were reflected in education, local politics, and the structure of the labour market meant that 'catholic' and 'protestant' remained discordant phrases in Clydeside for some considerable time yet. Shared wartime experiences may have brought people closer together, but two antagonistic traditions on Clydeside still frustrated the emergence of a single community sure of its identity and sense of belonging.

Notes

1 Willy Slavin, 'Roman in the Gloamin', *Cencrastus*, No. 11, 1983, p. 23.
2 Charles Byrne, *Hindrances to Catholic Organization, Education and Progress*, Glasgow, 1928.
3 Catholic Union files, box 8, Archbishop Mackintosh to John Campbell, 20 November 1940, GAA.
4 John Durkan.
5 Charles Diamond, 'In England, Catholics, political parties and the labour movement', *Osservatore Romano*, 11 April 1923, reprinted in the *Glasgow Observer*, 26 May 1923.
6 *GO*, 24 November 1923.
7 *GO*, 17 November 1923.
8 *GO*, 19 July 1924.
9 *GO*, 25 October 1924.
10 *GO*, 25 October 1924.
11 Diamond's articles were published as a book, *How Socialism Cannot Come and Remain*, in 1925.
12 John Paton, *Left Turn*, p. 148, quoted in William Ferguson, *Scotland 1689 to the present*, Oliver & Boyd, Edinburgh, 1968, p. 367.
13 *GO*, 9 May 1925. The capitals appeared in the original.
14 *GO*, 9 May 1925.
15 *GO*, 10 October 1925.
16 *GO*, 3 January 1925.
17 *GO*, 11 October 1924.
18 *GO*, 5 June 1926.
19 *GO*, 20 March 1926.
20 *GO*, 13 March 1926.
21 *GO*, 27 March 1926.
22 Knox, *Scottish Labour Leaders*, p. 33.
23 Ian Wood, 'John Wheatley', in Knox, *Scottish Labour Leaders*, p. 280.
24 Wood, p. 280.
25 *GO*, 10 April 1926.
26 *GO*, 23 October 1926.
27 *GO*, 23 October 1926.
28 *Forward*, 5 November 1927.
29 *GO*, 5 November 1927.
30 *GO*, 7 July 1928.
31 The Co-operative Party was not a separate party in its own right but

one of the socialist organisations affiliated to the Labour Party; James Strain was not a roman catholic.

32 *GO*, 18 May 1929.

33 *GO*, 25 May 1929.

34 *GO*, 25 May 1929.

35 *GO*, 18 May 1929.

36 *GO*, 25 May 1929.

37 *GO*, 8 June 1929.

38 *GO*, 5 July 1930.

39 *GO*, 21 June 1930.

40 Maguire, 'Charles Diamond reappraised', *Irish Post*, 7 May 1983.

41 Maguire, *Irish Post*, 7 May 1983.

42 Maguire, *Irish Post*, 7 May 1983.

43 Bill Knox, 'Maxton: rebel waiting for an answer', *Scotsman*, 22 June 1985.

44 Robert Skidelsky, *Sir Oswald Mosley*, Macmillan, London, 1981, p. 169.

45 John Campbell to John Cruden, 16 November 1935, Catholic Union files, GAA.

46 See note 45.

47 *GO*, 1 December 1923.

48 Knox, 'Maxton', *Scotsman*, 22 June 1985.

49 *Forward*, 31 October 1931.

50 *GO*, 11 April 1925.

51 Gilbert McAllister, *James Maxton: Portrait of a Rebel*, John Murray, London, 1935, p. 95.

52 *Daily Record*, 3 May 1934.

53 *GO*, 11 April 1925.

54 A. J. P. Taylor, *English History, 1914-45*, Oxford University Press, various editions, p. 353.

55 Jennie Lee, *My Life with Nye*, Jonathan Cape, London, 1981, p. 81.

56 Lee, *My Life with Nye*, p. 81.

57 Tom Johnston, *Spectator*, 11 February 1934.

58 Obituary of Charles Diamond, *GO*, 24 February 1934 and 10 March 1934; see also Maguire, *Irish Post*, 7 May 1983.

59 Jim Coffey, *Scottish Catholic Observer*, 19 April 1985, p. 10.

60 'P. J. Dollan—a future Lord Provost of Glasgow', *Bailie*, 2 March 1935.

61 R. E. Dowse, *Left in the Centre*, Hutchinson, London, 1966, p. 40.

62 *Forward*, 28 February 1931.

63 Unpublished memoirs of P. J. Dollan, vol. 1, pp. 19, 60.

64 Interview with James H. Dollan (son of Patrick Dollan), Glasgow, 7 April 1982.

65 McAllister, *Maxton*, pp. 85-6.

66 Christopher Harvie, *Scotsman*, 23 July 1983.

67 Catholic Union, box 9, James McGrory to John Campbell, GAA.

68 Catholic Union, box 9, Alexander McCann to John Campbell, 17 October 1933, GAA.

69 Catholic Union, box 9, Rev. John Devine to John Campbell, 24 October 1933, GAA.

70 Wood, 'John Wheatley', *Innes Review*, 1980, p. 78.

71 *Forward*, 10 June 1933.

72 *Forward*, 16 December 1933.

73 *GO*, 20 March 1937.

74 Obituary to Sir Patrick Dollan, *Glasgow Herald*, 31 January 1963.

75 T. Gallagher, 'Red Clydeside's double anniversary', *Bulletin of Scottish Labour History*, No. 20, 1985, p. 8.

76 *Forward*, 19 September 1936.

77 *Forward*, 8 May 1937.

78 *Forward*, 29 May 1937.

79 *Forward*, 31 December 1938.

80 *Forward*, 31 March 1934.

81 Helen Corr and Bill Knox, 'Patrick Dollan', in Knox, *Scottish Labour Leaders*, p. 97; W. O. Brown, *Edinburgh Clarion*, No. 44, June 1943.

82 Information from William Murphy, catholic journalist.

83 *GH* editorial, 12 December 1941.

84 'Graft in Glasgow', *GH* editorial, 11 February 1942.

85 Letter from Dollan, *GH*, 19 February 1942.

86 Sir Percy Sillitoe, *Cloak without Dagger*, Pan, 1955, p. 138.

87 *GO*, 20 November 1937.

88 Interview with retired sheriff John Bayne.

89 For the novel see R. D. Elliot, *The Glasgow Novel*, unpublished Ph.D., University of Glasgow, 1979.

90 Ian Wood, 'Scotland and the Spanish civil war', *Cencrastus*, autumn 1984, p. 14.

91 Anthony Hepburn, 'Political and industrial relationships', *Glasgow Observer and Scottish Catholic Herald, Scottish Survey, 1878-1955*.

92 Frank Sheed, *The Church and I*, p. 200.

93 *Forward*, 10 October 1936, quoting the *Glasgow Observer*, 3 October 1936.

94 *Forward*, 10 October 1936.

95 *GO*, 14 November 1936.

96 James Darragh.

97 Wood, *Cencrastus*.

98 Wood, *Cencrastus*.

99 Wood, *Cencrastus*, p. 15; *GO*, 27 February, 3 April 1937.

100 *GO*, 13 July 1935.

101 Tom Kerr's speech of 21 March 1938 as copied by John Campbell, box 4, Catholic Union, GAA.

102 *Forward*, 18 June 1938.

103 *Forward*, 18 June 1938.

104 Rosslyn Mitchell's speech of 21 March 1938 as copied by John Campbell, box 4, Catholic Union, GAA.

105 *Forward*, 21 January 1937.

106 John Heenan to James Carmichael, Catholic Union, box 9, GAA; it is not known how the Catholic Union acquired this correspondence.

107 Fenner Brockway to John Heenan, 24 September 1937 (see note 106).

108 John McGovern, *Neither Fear nor Favour*, Blandford Press, London, 1960, p. 171.

109 *GO*, 20 March 1937, was looking to Dr John Colvin as a likely parliamentary candidate in the Gorbals.

110 Jean Mann, *Woman in Parliament*, Odhams, London, 1962, p. 123.

111 *Evening Times*, 30 December 1936.

112 *Evening Times*, 30 December 1936.

113 'Shettleston and Tollcross Ward, Personal Appeal from John McGovern MP', leaflet for 1937 Glasgow municipal elections in Catholic Union files, GAA.

114 *Forward*, 21 January 1937.

115 *Forward*, 21 January 1937.

116 Charles Petrie, 'Douglas Jerrold', *Dictionary of National Biography, 1961-70*, Oxford University Press, 1981, p. 586.

117 *Forward*, 12 June 1937.

118 *GO*, 18 September 1937.

119 John Campbell to A. Barker, 28 October 1937, Catholic Union files, box 8, GAA.

120 *Scottish Catholic*, No. 1, April 1939; it lasted till September 1939.

121 Wood, *Cencrastus*.

122 *GO*, 9 March 1951.

123 McGovern did not count, owing to the fact that he was then estranged from the church.

124 *GO*, 20 March 1937.

125 *Forward*, 18 June 1932. The Scottish Loyalists were formed following a call for stewards to defend free speech when National Government candidates were speaking in the 1931 election campaign. The Earl of Glasgow claimed that 1,600 people responded to his appeal in Glasgow and Edinburgh.

126 Letter from William Weir Gilmour, 12 December 1986.

127 Michael de la Bedoyere, 'Colm Brogan', in Matthew Hoehn (ed.), *Catholic Authors: Contemporary Biographical Sketches*, St Mary's Abbey, USA, 1952, p. 58.

128 Obituary of Colm Brogan, *Times*, 29 January 1977.

129 *Times*, 29 January 1977.

130 *GO*, 17 May 1940.

131 *GO*, 17 May 1940.

132 *GO*, 17 May 1940.

133 Anthony Hepburn, *Communism in Scotland*, Burns, Glasgow, 1940, p. 1.

134 James Darragh, 'The Catholic population of Scotland, 1878-1977', in McRoberts (ed.), *Modern Scottish Catholicism*, p. 246, n. 36.

135 *GO*, 17 May 1940.

136 Letter from James Darragh, 1 December 1982.

137 *GO*, 15 August 1941.

138 Letter from James Darragh to Paul Fitzpatrick, 25 October 1982 (copy sent by James Darragh to the author, 21 January 1983.

139 *GO*, 2 January 1942.

140 The downturn in the Labour Party's activities is shown by Christopher Harvie's 'Labour in Scotland during the Second World War', *Historical Journal*, 26, 4, 1983, pp. 921-44.

141 Interview with James Darragh, 3 August 1982; James Darragh, 'Obituary of Fr William d'Andria SJ (1895-1977)', *St Aloysius College Magazine*, No. 91, June 1978, pp. 68-9.

142 *GO*, 5 December 1941.

143 *GO*, 8 May 1942.

144 Letter from Charles Smith, Edinburgh catholic, 28 June 1985.
145 *GO*, 27 November 1942.
146 *GO*, 23 October 1942.
147 Interview with Mr J. McLay, Glasgow, 20 December 1982.
148 Patrick Dollan, unpublished memoirs, vol. 2, pp. 134-5.

Chapter 6 **Embarking on a fresh journey, destination uncertain: Scottish catholics, 1945–70**

In 1945, as troops were demobilised and conditions only slowly began to return to normal at home, Scottish catholics might have been forgiven for displaying guarded optimism about the future. Those of military age who had enlisted in the armed services generally found that domestic rivalries were put aside: they were not systematically discriminated against on a religious or ethnic basis, promotion was often open to those who displayed aptitude or courage, and more than a few were decorated on the battlefield. The steady but undemonstrative way in which catholics on all fronts played their full part in the war disarmed some of their critics who had previously viewed them from afar as an unassimilable sub-group immersed in ghetto life and unlikely to acquit themselves well in the patriotic struggle against Hitler because of past anti-British associations. The shared comradeship that is a legacy of wartime proved a great leveller which psychologically equipped many catholics to play a more active role in shaping their own environment.

The prospect of returning to their own communities and taking up where they had left off in 1939–40 did not appeal to many, especially those who could remember only long periods of unemployment perhaps punctuated by casual bouts of menial low-paid work: the horizons of those in a religious minority which comprised a large proportion of the underprivileged in industrial Scotland, had been stretched, their expectations raised. They had been influenced by the wartime propaganda which promised a better life for all in peacetime and not a few hoped that it would mean an ending of some of the restrictions which had prevented catholics competing in the labour market, especially in skilled trades. The wartime emergency and attendant labour shortages had created some openings in occupations which for generations had been the reserve of the protestant labour aristocracy, but the ending of the war showed that the extent of change in recruitment practices, especially in private industrial concerns, had only been limited: Catholics were less prepared than before to meekly accept subordinate status. If the clock had been turned back to the wintry 1930s, most would have ungrudgingly accepted their lot, but some could have been expected to display the anger and alienation which, in the Britain of the 1980s, had emanated from underprivileged Afro-Caribbeans whose aspirations for a modest degree of economic advancement have not been realised.

This bitter scenario was not played out because the expectations of working-class catholics were raised just at a time when the state was proving more responsive to the needs of underprivileged sectors of the population as a whole. A comprehensive set of educational and social reforms were approved by parliament even before the termination of the war, which pointed the way ahead. Having borne the brunt of the war effort, ordinary citizens were in no mood to accept the frugal peace that had been offered by the victors in 1918. The desire for a fairer distribution of wealth and resources was confirmed when the Labour Party was swept into office with its first ever overall majority. For the first time, the party which the catholic minority had broadly identified with since the settlement of the Irish question, was now in a position to act decisively to remedy some of the outstanding grievances which the community shared with others in the lower-income bracket.

Thanks to the wartime coalition of the three main parties, a more harmonious political climate existed which meant there was less chance of divisive issues like religion being used to frustrate Labour's plans. These plans included the introduction of a free health care service for all citizens and the provision of state assistance for the unemployed or those unable to earn a regular income—bereft of the hated means test. The welfare state was the cornerstone of Labour's reforming programme and, along with the expansion of state education, it greatly contributed to reducing tensions and rivalries within the working-class as indeed did the gradual onset of full employment. The arrival of easier times thus reduced the impact of cultural and religious differences in working-class communities as was shown in 1946 when militant protestants tried in vain to mount a popular campaign against the government's decision to demobilise thousands of Polish soldiers in Scotland and allow them to settle with their wives and families.

The arrival of the refugee Poles added a new dimension to the Scottish catholic community while the return of the Italians from prison camps to restart their retail businesses, restored to it the entrepreneurial element which otherwise it would have lacked.

Rev David McRoberts, the most authoritative Scottish catholic historian of the post-war years, has described a church that was emerging into 'a rather strange new world of problems and ideas where the nineteenth century tradition was no longer adequate'.[1] For two years,

Glasgow, the largest archdiocese, with three-quarters of Scotland's catholics, had been rudderless following the death of Archbishop Mackintosh in 1943. No obvious successor was discernable at least from within the archdiocese. Able and talented priests such as P. J. Flood had not been given responsibilities in areas where their pastoral qualities could have had a galvanising effect (at least not for long enough). A great many of the senior clergy were tacitly out of the running because they were Irish by birth and training.

Into the vacuum stepped Donald Campbell, Bishop of Argyll and the Isles until his transfer to Glasgow in 1945. At first glance, there was little to suggest that he might be able to offer the effective leadership which had often been lacking since the time of Eyre, the first archbishop. He had mainly been accustomed to rural parishes and belonged to one of the tight-knit Highland families that had provided a long line of bishops. Campbell was the third cousin of his predecessor in Argyll, the second cousin of his successor, and the nephew of the co-adjutor archbishop of Glasgow from 1919 to 1921.[2] One seasoned observer described him as 'friendly and unpretentious but lacking in depth'.[3] Nevertheless, he had an open mind and was happily free from the complexes that other senior figures in the church had about lay initiatives. The latter view was the reflection of James Darragh, then an activist in the Catholic Workers Guild during the 1940s.[4] Campbell took a keen interest in the CWG's efforts to combat communist influence in bodies such as the union of housewives in Glasgow and he placed the diocesan offices, then in Renfrew Street, at its disposal for meetings.

In 1948 the formation of the Archdiocesan Council of Social Action was authorised with Fr John Carter as its director and Darragh as its secretary. Its purpose was to encourage the application of catholic principles in all spheres of social activity, to provide training for Christian leadership in the field of social action, and to get catholic organisations fully involved in improving social conditions.[5] But it never got close to fulfilling any of these objectives. Anthony Hepburn, the founder of the CWG, opted for a more reflective approach and in 1949 Darragh joined the civil service in London, preferring an independent career to becoming a protege of the archbishop who had expressed a wish to send him to Cambridge for postgraduate studies which inevitably would have incurred obligations.

Before long, the commitment to social action was run down thanks to changes of personnel within the church itself. In 1948 James Ward, a new Vicar General was appointed who was both a traditionalist and a capable administrator. Campbell got the credit for the wave of reorganisation in the archdiocese largely carried out by Ward. He gave effect to Campbell's wish to see the 'big barrack-style presbyteries with six curates broken up in favour of smaller units'. Forty-one new parishes were established in Campbell's time, each with a new church, and thirteen new churches were built in existing parishes. But there was little room in Ward's scheme of things for social action in which the laity would inevitably have to play a big role. Fr Carter was eased out of the Archdiocesan Council almost before he could make his mark. It has been said that Ward was only interested in two vocational organisations, the St Vincent de Paul's Society and the Legion of Mary, organisations which would not make a social revolution but whose purpose was to pick up the debris of society or else encourage religious devotion. By the mid-1950s Ward was virtually running the Glasgow archdiocese with Campbell, increasingly isolated from the senior clergy and the laity, on his way to becoming a largely ceremonial bishop.

Anti-communist activities without a social focus continued to be approved as long as an active threat was seen to exist from that quarter. One priest, Fr Vincent Cowley (1913–76), formed a Roman Catholic Shop Stewards' Movement to oppose the CPGB in union elections, various campaigns 'being carried out under his strict direction by a few laymen whom he chose and trusted'.[6] Being chaplain of a convent Cowley's duties were light, so he had the time to devote to these activities. Money was also forthcoming from employers organisations[7] and, in 1950 Cowley deployed his machine in West Fife against Willie Gallacher, the Communist MP. His Labour challenger, Willie Hamilton recalled that the Labour Party had hitherto been 'feeble and frightened' in West Fife and that even the redoubtable Patrick Dollan had shied away when approached in 1945 to oppose Gallacher.[8] On that occasion he was comfortably returned but in 1950 those lay catholics from industrial Scotland and beyond whose overriding priority was the defeat of communism, descended on the Fife mining seat. Speakers at anti-communist rallies included two former leading Communists who had become catholic converts in 1948, the Englishman Douglas Hyde and the less well-known Hamish Fraser, a veteran of Spain and the International Brigade who was the only British volunteer to serve on the Brigade's staff as an officer of SIM, the Spanish secret police then under Soviet control.[9]

Fraser was the author of a pamphlet justifying the Nazi–Soviet Pact—*The Intelligent Socialist's Guide to World War II*—which sold out in less than a week and led to his appointment as the Scottish CP's propaganda secretary. Having been a party group leader in John Brown's engine and boiler works at Clydebank in wartime he became disenchanted with Marxism and joined the roman catholic church before becoming a teacher in primary schools in Ayrshire. In 1950 Fraser contributed to the crushing defeat of Willie Gallacher. 'I was defeated before polling began, the Catholics concentrated against me,' was the

MP's verdict.[10] Until his death in 1986 Fraser would be a tireless foe of liberal catholics at home and abroad who wished to move the church in a less absolutist direction and he edited the periodical *Approaches* which appeared irregularly but had a worldwide circulation of over 3,000.[11]

As the Cold War atmosphere intensified, catholics who wished to display social concern in the workplace or in the community, not just to frustrate communism but as a desired end in itself, were increasingly overtaken by campaigners like Cowley with a more singleminded and limited objective. The CWG, with its emphasis on reflection on study, was regarded as increasingly 'harmless and ineffective'. The Edinburgh-based Fr Walter Glancy (1914–80), the Scottish priest probably most committed to spreading catholic social teaching throughout society, even suffered the accusation of being tainted with communism.[12] A sign of the times was the establishment in Glasgow during 1950 of the right-wing 'Blue Army of Our Lady of Fatima' whose inaugural meeting was addressed by John J. Campbell. In a tough speech he said:

> Most of the Communist leaders in Great Britain were renegade Catholics. They had got to face up to that. They had got the guts to do the fighting— Communists knew that so they tried to get lapsed Catholics to take up a fighting attitude.
>
> 'Let us start and pray for the return of the Communist leaders here in Glasgow . . . becuase nothing hurts the Communists so much as when they know that their members have returned to the Sacraments.'[13]

Banner headlines in the catholic press greeted the resignation of Harry McShane from the party in 1953, but it was 'in protest against the iron discipline and bureaucracy of the party'.[14] McShane remained a pillar of the Scottish radical left into his nineties and he had no desire to exchange communist orthodoxy for the religious variety. Nor had the young combative Lawrence Daly who after quitting the CPGB in 1956, the year of the invasion of Hungary, formed the Fife Socialist League which attracted a number of young catholic workers.[15] The activities of militants like Daly and Mick McGahey of Lanarkshire— who remained in the party after 1956—showed that the catholic community was yielding talented recruits for the party even in the hard-fought 1940s and 1950s. But the improvement in social conditions experienced by most, if not all, of the working-class meant that their message now lacked the impact it once had in the inter-war period.

Only a relatively small number of priests and laymen were actively involved in checking a communist foe that was now more influential abroad than at home. In the post-war decades, the church was fully stretched trying to cope with the enormous population shifts brought about by the need to rehouse families outside the densely overcrowded inner city of Glasgow.

The 1951 census had shown a population of 119,000 in Clydeside living three to a room, the average in England being one person per room except for a very few areas.[16] Glasgow corporation had 80-90,000 families on its housing waiting list in the early 1950s; because housing had been an emotive issue in the city since the rent strikes of the First World War, the corporation was under pressure to act quickly. It responded by building large housing estates around the perimeters of the city, allowing for density a great deal higher than had previously been thought appropriate in such developments. They were put up with such haste that there was minimal provision of facilities and amenities.[17] Ten per cent of Glasgow's population was decanted on to these estates, others moved into high rise flats in the 1960s (the decade when multi-storey housing was seen as the exciting answer to remaining housing needs), while new towns were built at East Kilbride in Lanarkshire and Cumbernauld north of Glasgow to which upwardly mobile working-class catholics were able to gravitate. Between 1961 and 1975, when the human exodus from the city was at its height, Glasgow's population fell from 1,055,000 to 825,000;[18] between 1951 and 1977 the population of the eight inner city catholic parishes slumped from 69,000 to 13,000.[19]

Although the resources at the disposal of the church and the energies of numerous priests were stretched often to breaking-point by the levelling of well established communities and by the geographical upheavals of the post-war decades, it was not caught unprepared. Largely in response to the internal requirements of the church, the vast archdiocese of Glasgow had been divided up into three separate units in 1948. The county of Renfrew, to the west of Glasgow became the diocese of Paisley, the county of Lanark became the diocese of Mother-well, and the city of Glasgow together with the county of Dumbarton became the new archdiocese of Glasgow. This group of dioceses was erected into a new ecclesiastical province of Glasgow in which the two dioceses of Motherwell and Paisley became suffragan sees of the Glasgow archdiocese which had now attained the same metropolitan rank as the archdiocese of St Andrews and Edinburgh. Glasgow in 1948 was left with an estimated catholic population of almost 300,000 people whose spiritual care was in the hands of 298 priests in fifty-eight parishes.[20] The split was an admission that the old archdiocese had outgrown the administrative capabilities of the church, the population having risen from 309,700 in 1900 to 522,900 in 1951 (that represented an increase of six per cent in the catholic population of the west of Scotland which stood at 24% of the region's total in 1951).[21]

Although the tendency for some farflung working-class communities especially in Lanarkshire to be overlooked by Glasgow has been rectified, the reorganisation continued to have its critics. Eyebrows had been raised about including new Glasgow housing estates like Easterhouse and Garthamlock in the Motherwell diocese in order to ensure a sensible spread of population. The viability of the Motherwell diocese itself had been questioned because it has no recognised urban regional centre and comprises an area facing a difficult economic future as coal and steel, the mainstays of the local economy, have been relentlessly scaled down, beginning in the 1950s.

But generally, people grew accustomed to the new ecclesiastical arrangements which were far easier to come to terms with than the wholesale change in the fabric of Glasgow life wrought by the planners in the post-war years. Large dreary housing schemes situated miles from traditional centres of activity and lacking amenities such as cinemas, libraries, social clubs or public houses, were the unimaginative outcome of what had been one of the most ambitious slum clearance schemes in Europe. They were a kind of parody of Glasgow's traditional tenement life, quite incapable of generating the same kind of community spirit.[22] One of the few voices raised against these 'concrete jungles' had been Cornelius O'Leary, parish priest of St John's in the Gorbals.[23] This was appropriate since the area that had been the hub of Glasgow catholic life up to the 1950s was to suffer more completely at the hands of the planners than possibly any other working-class community in Glasgow. It had few friends and plenty of detractors thanks to the dubious reputation it had been given by the novel *No Mean City* of 1935 by Alexander MacArthur and K. Long. The Gorbals became a byword for squalor and violence throughout the English-speaking world, a stigma that was reinforced by Robert McLeish's play *The Gorbals Story*, made into a feature film in the 1950s.

The area certainly had its share of social problems thanks to overcrowding and the 1930s slump, gangs existed, but they were a threat to one another rather than the general public. The Gorbals was Scotland's most cosmopolitan district, (having absorbed a succession of immigrant groups—Irish, Highlanders, Jews, Lithuanians—) through which people could walk in safety in the 1930s.[24] Nobody was better qualified to speak about the Gorbals than Dr Patrick Connolly who—along with his brother Eugene—practised medicine there for thirty years. In 1982, when it was announced that the Gorbals was losing its parliamentary seat, he was moved to write about it:

> it is a wonderful place to practice medicine. The people were hard-working, everyone knew everyone else, no one was ever left alone when they were in trouble. The folk downstairs would send a pitcher of soup to the old biddy upstairs, the old would babysit for the young couple . . .
>
> The place had a reputation that was undeserved. My wife is from the south of England and her folk used to think that I was out every night tending to

the victims of razor gangs in the street. Pure mythology! I never in all my life encountered one bit of trouble, only mutual respect and courtesy among a community that actually cared.[25]

The tenements levelled in the 1950s and early 1960s were replaced by multi-storey flats populated by newcomers to the area. By now the Gorbals community had been split up and sent to different housing estates. Dr Connolly regards this as a tragic error: 'instead of scattering them, they should have been resettled as one group; a new community could then have been created on the outskirts of the city'.[26] Speaking in a much darker vein, the journalist John Burrowes—seeing how 'its heart and soul' were 'ripped out'—wonders if it was not all 'master-minded by someone who had a vengeance on the once colourful community'.[27]

Glasgow was not alone in witnessing these cataclysmic changes. In Edinburgh a Tory council ensured that most of the working-class was banished to rather desolate housing schemes on the outskirts of the city so as to sweep social problems from view and cash in on tourist receipts by enhancing the city's picture-postcard image. The population of the five oldest city parishes declined from 22,000 to 9,000 as catholics from the old town began to trek to windswept estates. But, in the east, the pace of change for catholics was altogether less drastic than in the west.

Gordon Gray was appointed Archbishop of St Andrews and Edinburgh on the death of Andrew Joseph McDonald in 1950. Although then, at forty years of age, the youngest bishop in the world, he was a traditional figure less keen on innovation than his predecessor. One outspoken priest remembers a favourite motto of his having been 'you must not disturb our good ordinary Christian people';[28] 'he saw pro-cessions as the most suitable example of Catholic public activity' (the acerbic view of one senior layman). The Association of Catholic Trade Unionists, an Edinburgh counterpart of the CWG, faded from the scene although it is not clear whether this occurred before or after Gordon Gray's arrival. Different accounts have been given but perhaps the one that carries the most weight was provided by Fr Walter Glancy who had been given permission to set it up in the 1940s. At the forthieth anniversary of his ordination in 1978, Lord Wheatley asked him what had happened:

He explained that the Association of Catholic Trade Unionists was set up for better understanding of the papal encyclicals and greater emphasis on Catholic social teaching. It made great progress with 120 actual people, an office. But suddenly it was stopped because it was said that it did not have a sufficiently spiritual foundation.[29]

A senior catholic in public life has described Glancy as 'one of the best minds in the Catholic Church. He was quite open to new ideas as long as they had merit in them.' However, no honour or promotion came his way after the 1950s. Another innovator whose work was frustrated was Brother Clare, headmaster of St Mungo's Academy in Glasgow. He had been asked to draw up a new version of Catechism based on the modern Baltimore one but it was rejected by Archbishop Gray in favour of an old-fashioned text which has been described as 'the penny catechism writ large within hard backers'.[30]

Having his roots in Banff, Gray wished to uphold the Scottish identity of the church. He had been shaken by the eruption of Protestant Action in the 1930s and did not want to encourage the church's enemies to brand it as an alien force in Scottish life. For a while, in the 1950s, he even banned the sale of *The Irish Weekly* at the back of churches in his archdiocese. Edited by Edinburgh catholic Michael Fallon, it provided news for Irish immigrants in Scotland and enjoyed a circulation of 16,000 in the late 1940s.[31] The ban was not always enforced by priests in outlying West Lothian parishes with mining communities of Irish descent and it gradually fell into disuse. But one well-known Glasgow catholic, a resident of Edinburgh for over fifty years has been able to detect a difference of attitude among catholics towards their Irish ancestry in these two principal centres:

> Those in Edinburgh tend to conceal their Irish connections more often than in Glasgow. Under the influence of traditional Scottish Catholics from the north, they can be disparaging of the Irish in a way that is not often heard in Glasgow.[32]

This underlying feeling was referred to with unusual frankness in a catholic press article marking the retirement of Gordon Gray in 1985:

> It is his very Scottishness that marks him out from most of the Catholics he served as Bishop over the last 34 years. Yet that consciousness of his roots serves not to promote superiority but rather a quiet empathy for those who by family background and upbringing feel themselves drawn from the different Irish tradition.
>
> He opened a seminary at Drygrange to allow the future priests to be trained within their own diocese and their own traditions. He championed the training of teachers at Craiglockart in Edinburgh in the sound belief that teachers needed to be seen by parents and pupils alike as products of their own region and not imports from Ireland or Glasgow.[33]

The east–west tension between the upholders of the native catholic tradition and those representing the immigrant stream was not exacerbated by Gray who placed a strong emphasis on tact and diplomacy in most of his relationships. His predecessor had dreamt of a national seminary at St Andrews with the west, inevitably, being the only reliable source of finance. The idea was promoted in Glasgow by Archbishop Campbell (before his elevation he had been a suffragan bishop of St Andrews and Edinburgh), but it was opposed by his chapter (senior clergy). Campbell prudently decided not to force the issue since he would merely have alienated his leading priests for the forseeable future.

This incident graphically illustrates the limits of a bishop's power. The tensions producing it stemmed in part from the fact that the Scottish catholic church had no recognised head or Primate. St Andrews and Edinburgh is the senior diocese but the incumbent does not have the formal authority over his fellow bishops that the Archbishop of Westminster has in England. Inevitably, a situation of overlapping powers, and no clearly defined responsibility, has hampered long-term decision-making, encouraged a degree of inertia, given bishops with strong personalities an advantage, and led to a degree of duplication of resources best seen in the creation of separate seminaries in the east and the west when the numbers of vocations warranted one establishment.

Those directing church affairs rarely if ever voiced their disagreements in public. Especially in the immediate post-war years a serene and confident image was presented with the strength of west of Scotland catholicism being celebrated by vast rallies, such as the one in St Andrew's Hall in 1948 to mark the centenary of St Vincent de Paul Society in Glasgow, or the immense throng in Celtic Park in 1949 when Archbishop Campbell celebrated Mass in the presence of Archbishop Godfrey, the papal representative in Britain, on the centenary of the formation of the CYMS. A priest, speaking at a Catholic Truth Society meeting in 1951, could even be reported as saying that 'if Catholics had the zeal of the Communists or the Salvation Army, they could win Scotland in ten years'.[34] However, blind faith was not enough in an increasingly complicated age. In areas like trade union work, where catholics could have made an impact by deed and example, pioneering priests like Walter Glancy got little help from their colleagues (even those sent to university) because they were preoccupied with parish duties.[35] Docility was a virtue stressed from seminary days onwards, simple faith was important; it was dangerous to ask too many questions.[36]

Firmly orthodox priests could even be suspicious of the work of the Newman Association, an organisation of catholic graduates formed in 1945 which stimulated a wide range of study through lectures and conferences. Even though it had been formed by a small group of graduates, mainly scientists engaged in industry, who had grown alarmed at the extent of communist influence on the shopfloor and the success of bodies like the Left Book Club in defining the political agenda in the post-war years, it was not immune from suspicion.[37] In Glasgow, when it began to make use of the facilities for study offered by university extra-mural departments, this was not universally welcomed. 'Aquinas', growled Canon Joseph Daniel when he heard that the teaching of Aquinas was to be the subject of a course one winter, 'Give them Aquinas and you'll turn them into Marxists'.[38]

Monsignor David McRoberts, who taught church history and scripture at the Glasgow diocesan seminary from 1948 to 1963, often had occasion to rail against the short-sighted and anti-intellectual character of the bishops, and the clergy, from whom they were chosen. Described in his official obituary as 'one of the most influential Catholic clerics in Scotland since Bishop John Geddes', poor health and independence of character ruled out a career on the bench of bishops and enabled him to concentrate on scholarly work on the pre- and post-Reformation church from which much of his fame is derived.[39] From 1951 until his death in 1978 he edited *The Innes Review*, the journal of the Scottish Catholic Historical Association which was launched at a Newman Association conference in 1949. In 1959 an archival centre for the Church was opened at Columba House in Edinburgh, for which McRoberts acted as keeper after 1973. His predecessor and successor as keeper, the Reverends William Anderson and Mark Dilworth OSB were both distinguished scholars, but 'he was always dismayed . . . that there were so few clergy willing to work in literary or historical fields':

> I imagine our seminaries are largely responsible. The staff at Blairs, Cardross and Drygrange never seem to contribute even to *The Glasgow Observer*.[40]

In 1960, on the 400th anniversary of the Reformation in Scotland, when *The Innes Review* produced a special issue on how and why it occurred, the journal was accused of spreading 'protestant scandal' after a contributor mentioned that the sixteenth century Cardinal Beaton had fostered illegitimate children. The matter went before a meeting of bishops but was dropped when Bishop Scanlan of Mother-well quietly declared that the claim indeed had validity and that Beaton had tried to legitimise his offspring.

David McRoberts conveyed his impression of the life and character of the Church and the men who ran it in his time to a diary, now in the Scottish Record Office, which will be made available on the deaths of all the bishops alive in 1978, the year of its last entry. Perhaps the only other churchman of his own time to merit comparison with him as a scholar was the Marist Brother Clare, (James Edmund Handley). As a catholic teacher he was exceptional in his range of interests and commitments. Later, as a research fellow at Glasgow University, John

Durkan, a retired history teacher, was to produce new appraisals of sixteenth century Scotland and its place in Europe which won him plaudits from other historians, but the catholic teaching profession as a whole rarely distinguished itself in other fields. Perhaps because of the constraints placed on them in earlier times when they deferred to religious superiors on pain of dismissal, few teachers have made a name for themselves in political, cultural, or social fields and they cannot be described as an especially dynamic or innovative group even in the life of the catholic community. Of course, many of the most gifted and conscientious teachers were fully absorbed in the expansion of catholic education which occurred with the raising of the school-leaving age after 1944 and the attendant need for more senior secondary schools for a community whose schooling had usually ended at the primary level. But the anonymity of teachers down the generations of Scottish catholic life still remains striking.

The catholic teaching body expanded prodigously in the post-war years but this was not reflected in the activities of the Don Bosco Society, the guild of catholic teachers, which began to fall from view in the 1950s along with other bodies such as the CYMS, the Union of Catholic Mothers, and the Catholic Union whose activities were once headline news in the catholic press. The need to monitor the activities of dangerous radicals in the Labour Party had receded as 'Red Clydeside' entered the history books and militant protestants found themselves no longer in a position to threaten catholic education, leaving the Catholic Union with a much diminished role. In 1961 when falling circulation required the various regional catholic papers to come together in one weekly known as the *Scottish Catholic Observer*, this was also a sign of the times.

The peak years for seminary students and ordinations were 1959 and 1960 (both at 184 students). A fairly steady decline set in thereafter which 'thus pre-dates the second Vatican Council and is not a consequence of it', according to James Darragh.[41] The community which used to yield up a plentiful supply of vocations was slipping into history. Scottish catholics were 'no longer so concentrated geographically, or so unified in outlook and social experience as . . . in the inter-war period'.[42] The levelling of old communities, the drift to the suburbs, housing estates and new towns, the growth of a professional class, the rise of the consumer society, the arrival of the mass media with its jarring values, and the alteration of the status of women could not fail to affect catholics, often profoundly. For increasing numbers the local church and the clergy no longer gave meaning to their lives in the way these pillars of the faith had done for their parents and grand-parents. An estimated 120,000 catholics lost contact with the Church in Scotland between 1951 and 1976 compared with some

52,000 between 1931 and 1951.[43]

Archbishop Campbell's death in 1963, while on a pilgrimage to Lourdes, signalled the end of an era. The chapter (that is the senior clergy) recommended the capable Vicar General James Ward as his successor. But Bishop Scanlan of Motherwell was appointed instead. His friendship with the Scots-born Cardinal William Heard (1884–1973), a senior Vatican bureaucrat, counted in his favour. Although old and infirm, Heard 'knew what levers to pull', and one source reckons that 'between 1960 and 1972 he made the bishops in Scotland'.[44] Many priests felt that at sixty-four Scanlan was too old to undertake the responsibility of running Glasgow and they were not too happy with stories of his autocratic style when in Motherwell. But his essential conservatism in a time of flux was reassuring. Its appropriateness is open to doubt on the eve of the pathbreaking Vatican Council, but he marked a welcome break with his predecessors by playing a full role in the civic and social life of Glasgow and taking his place at public occasions as a religious leader of the city.

Scanlan was a law graduate from Glasgow University and only the second native of the city to be appointed its archbishop. He had moved in different worlds both as a military chaplain and a church administrator in the Westminster diocese. A more outgoing figure adept at public relations was inheriting Glasgow as the social advances of the previous two decades were combining to produce a less insular and more achivement-orientated community. The expansion of secondary and tertiary level education and the growth of local employment as a result in the upsurge in the world economy and greater investment in the public sector, were creating opportunities for upward mobility which had proved elusive for even the brightest members of past generations of immigrant catholics.

By the 1940s the time had long gone when the only professions open to roman catholics who wished to break out of the working-class were bookmaking or pub ownership.[45] The burgeoning responsibilities of the state in the post-war world meant that catholics could now aim to enter the local or national civil service secure in the knowledge that their religious or school background would not be the handicaps they could prove to be still for those seeking white-collar positions in large areas of the private sector.

The lower-income groups were among the principal beneficiaries of post-war expansion and catholics benefited disproportionately because they were massively over-represented in these categories. The raising of the school leaving age to fifteen in 1947 placed an extra 60,000 Scottish pupils on school roles and a disproportionate number were catholics.[46] Whereas in 1921 catholic secondary pupils in Scotland had only been 3·3% of the catholic school population, by 1972 the proportion had risen to 31·2%;[47] even more significantly catholics made up no less than 39% of secondary school pupils in Glasgow by 1972.[48]

Increasingly catholic secondary education was being seen as a preparation for higher education and careers, not just for a tiny minority. Gone were the days when the only hope of university education for a working-class catholic lay in obtaining a Carnegie bursary or relying on an affluent member of the family (in the unlikely event one was available).[49] After 1945 a grant was automatically available from the Scottish Education Department for university applicants who fulfilled the conditions of entry while grants were also available for ex-servicemen as well as for trainee teachers.

The number of catholic students at Glasgow University trebled from 700 in 1956 to an estimated 2,000 in 1972.[50] In a given year many more were to be found at Scotland's other seven universities as well as at technical colleges and, by the 1980s, it was estimated that the catholic student community in Glasgow was the largest such in Britain.[51]

In 1958 James Gordon, a brilliant student debater and winner of the coveted 'Observer' Mace Trophy became the first roman catholic to be elected president of Glasgow University Men's Student Union, others stepping into his shoes in later years. Gordon was a product of St Aloysius College, the selective fee-paying catholic school, which catered for the offspring of Glasgow catholics mainly active in the professions. A strikingly high proportion of west Scotland catholics destined to make their mark in law, medicine, or public administration after 1945 were old Aloysians. Run by the Jesuits, St Aloysius gave the impression to some of being a tense academic environment in which everyone was pushed and where little priority was given to recreation, art, or technical subjects. In the 1950s and 1960s a great rivalry grew up between it and Hutcheson grammar school, the senior non-catholic Glasgow independent school, for receipt of the university bursaries awarded each year to outstanding pupils by the Scottish Education Department. Each summer the prize-winners along with their schools are announced in *The Glasgow Herald* in order of merit, and in the early 1950s much rejoicing ensued in catholic middle-class ranks when Frank Cairns became the first Aloysian to come top in this competition.[52]

But although prominent in student politics and in the convivial aspects of undergraduate life, the growing catholic student body has remained anonymous in other respects and has shown little intellectual curiosity. Anthony Ross, OP, formerly Catholic chaplain at Edinburgh University, has looked for an explanation in their schools which 'have been even more strongly exam-orientated than others and less critical of the authoritarian character of the Scottish educational system'.[53] Even T. A. Fitzpatrick, a former vice-principal of Notre Dame College of Education, the catholic teacher training centre in Glasgow, pointedly wondered whether preparation for the heady atmosphere of intellectual freedom was seen by catholic teachers as the major responsibility it undoubtedly was and he goes on to speculate:

> Were their products less well prepared to face the liberty of university or adult life. Did a spirituality which emphasised self-denial and withdrawal from the world result, whatever its merits, in attitudes of non-involvement and compartive lack of commitment.[54]

Catholic students fitted easily into, and indeed reinforced, the conservative ethos of Glasgow University although it was derived from its middle-class Presbyterian past, and they grafted on their own mores. Down to the late 1970s it laid claim to the last sexually segregated student union in Britain, the student unrest of the previous decade having passed it (and most other Scottish universities) by. Archbishop Scanlan's 1967 warning against 'perfidious . . . humanism in Glasgow University' was somewhat alarmist, apolitical hedonism being far more prevalent.[55]

If they did not emigrate from Scotland altogether, a very high proportion of graduates still headed for a career in teaching by the 1960s. Family and peer group influence combined to make this seem the natural thing to do. 'Why study more mathematics when you know enough already to preapre people for their Highers', Anthony Ross OP recalls a principal teacher of the subject saying to an exceptionally brilliant graduate who had been offered a postgraduate scholarship.[56] In the late 1940s, when James Darragh was one of the first local catholics to study economics at Glasgow University, the reaction from friends and relatives was 'You can't teach with that'.[57] By contrast with his own community Darragh noticed how the Jews of Glasgow were far less hidebound and more willing to grasp new opportunities. He remembered a Russian Jew who used to be a door-to-door salesman in his parish whose son became a professor of medicine at Glasgow University, a trajectory that was rare in catholic Glasgow until quite recently.

Admittedly an acute shortage of catholic teachers did exist in the post-war years as a result of the sharp increase in the school population and the ability of qualified women to go into professions like nursing where previously it had been difficult for a catholic to advance very far. Catholics proved unable to produce from their own ranks enough teachers to serve the needs of their schools, despite an emergency scheme for the recruitment and training of large groups of new entrants into the profession after 1945. It is instructive that a very high proportion of music and arts teachers in catholic schools were non-catholics, another illustration that catholics were lagging behind in the cultural and artistic field even in the less arduous conditions of the 1945-70 era.[58]

The Scottish catholic experience has yet to produce a novelist of any distinction though, over the past decade, Marcella Evaristi, a talented playwright of Italian extraction, has emerged. Perhaps it is also worth adding a note that the appreciation of classical music in the west of Scotland has grown immensely, thanks in large part to the Cecilian Society, founded at Glasgow University by James Boyle, a future Sheriff and member of a large catholic family that had been encouraged to stage amateur dramatic shows in their large house in the suburb of Pollokshields for the benefit of visitors.

Despite the necessary recruitment of non-catholic teachers, the catholic system sought to preserve its identity in a number of symbolic ways as, for example, by the gearing of its holiday pattern to the church liturgical year, by acceptance of the church's discipline in the matter of Mass attendance and observance of fasting and abstinence, and of course by religious instruction in the essentials of the catholic faith:[59] under the terms of the 1918 Education Act, the church was able to insist that evidence of competence to teach religious education was a necessary prerequisite for a full-time teaching appointment as a catholic teacher in a catholic school. A formidable case could be made for the condition applying to primary teachers who were expected to play a major role in the preparation of children for the Sacraments but, in the 1960s, it seemed increasingly out of place in the secondary sector where teachers are employed as specialist subject teachers. Many felt that they simply did not know enough about the church and the faith to teach religious education in sufficient depth in view of the changes in theological perception and liturgical practice that were occurring in the aftermath of the Second Vatican Council—or else because they may have felt spiritually unprepared themselves.

Through its representatives on the local authority's education committee, the Church also had the power to vet applications for promoted posts in catholic schools. When a vacancy for a senior appointment exists, the representative, usually a priest, will be informed and shown a short-list of applicants. He can block a candidate by refusing to give him or her a certificate of approval of character and belief. This action may occur after consulting with the candidate's parish priest to find out if he is a regular Mass attender and whether his private or family life makes him suitable to be in a post of responsibility in a catholic school.[60]

Ecclesiastical vetting procedures are a grey area. There is no evidence that they are used indiscriminately, but being reliant on sometimes unverifiable information and 'gossip' about a candidate, they may be open to abuse. They may also cause those catholic teachers who identify with a professional rather than a religious role to be less outspoken than they otherwise would be. The lack of group consciousness long evident throughout the profession was perhaps enhanced by the institutional split between the denominational (catholic) and non-denominational sector of state education.

A shift occurred in 1961 with the outbreak of a teachers' strike in Glasgow. It started in St Augustine's, a catholic school, due to the action of Arthur Houston, who formed a breakaway union from the Educational Institute of Scotland over the EIS leadership's lack of militancy on the perennial pay issue. The strike spread to non-denominational schools in Glasgow before being settled with Houston eventually rejoining the EIS as a full-time salaried official; it represented a watershed for all teachers, who were not highly politicised compared to other public sector employees and helped to narrow the psychological gulf preventing effective collaboration between teachers in the two state sectors.

However, Houston remained something of an exception among catholic teachers until the 1980s; the majority tended to channel their radicalism into the Labour Party while it was middle-class teachers from the non-denominational sector who often made the EIS the focus of their political activities. As late as 1985 only eighteen out of 160 places on the EIS national council were held by dedicated roman catholics; they formed a separate national committee within the union to specifically oversee catholic educational interests.

It may be that union-minded catholics declined to put their names forward for election through being reluctant to identify with a committee dominated by senior teachers who see their chief priority as guarding the 1918 settlement. A separate body, the West Catholic Association of the EIS, has this as its overt aim and the EIS reserves four places on its national council for it; periodic elections are held for these places, they are open to catholic teachers based in catholic schools, not to non-catholic teachers in these schools or catholic teachers in the non-denominational sector.

To round off discussion of the complicated system of teacher representation in Scotland, mention should be made of the rival but much smaller teachers body, the Scottish Secondary Teachers Association. The SSTA is a more conservative body than the EIS and it may be no coincidence that for many years its General Secretary was James Docherty, a catholic, while John Vallelly an ex-catholic headmaster, was a former SSTA national President.[61]

Few catholics displayed entrepreneurial flair despite their improved circumstances. James Gordon, who in the 1970s, after an earlier incarnation as a TV political journalist and unsuccessful Labour parliamentary candidate, became the founder and managing director of Radio Clyde, one of Britain's most successful local radio stations, has made the revealing comment that 'in my younger days the idea of going out and starting your own business in the 1950s would have taken most people aback . . . the professions were regarded as the natural post-university outlet for catholics'.[62] Any with business flair were quite likely to be in the ranks of those who moved away from Scotland. An estimated 900,000 people left Scotland between 1945 and 1975, effectively wiping out the nation's natural population increase. James Darragh reckons that catholics 'were at least proportionately represented in this great movement and . . . because of their circumstances in Scotland, may have been proportionately over-represented'.[63]

Among the best-known emigrants from a Scottish catholic background who made their mark after 1945 were James Loughran, the conductor and Old Aloysian, the hotel and retailing magnate, Charles Forte, and Sean Connery, the film actor who started out as a coal-heaver in Edinburgh. Jack Coia, the award-winning architect, was unusual in that he was able to establish an international reputation in his profession while remaining in Glasgow.[64] Distinguished civil servants from a Glasgow catholic background included James Darragh, who rose to a senior level in the Board of Trade before being appointed in 1972 to oversee the rescue of shipbuilding on the Clyde, an ironic responsibility given the past lack of success of catholics in securing employment in many of the Clyde yards. James Mellon, President of Glasgow University Catholic Society in 1948 entered the diplomatic service and has become Her Majesty's senior representative in Ghana and then Denmark. James McGuiness, a leading member of Walter Glancy's ACTU, became a senior civil servant in the Scottish Office charged with responsibility for drawing up the legislation for the Scottish Assembly proposed under an Act of Parliament in 1978. They were among the most accomplished members of the catholic community who were entering the civil service in the post-war years. That more did not make names for themselves in this and other spheres is an indication that a good many catholics were not taking full advantage of the opportunities that lay before them in the post-war world.

One upwardly mobile catholic Tom Carberry went on to become professor of business studies at Strathclyde University, having entered the ministry of labour in the 1950s. By the end of that decade it was found that west of Scotland catholics were heavily represented at clerical officer level in this ministry. Questions were discreetly asked and it was discovered that with religious discrimination still being quietly practised in areas like banking and accountancy (or else perceived to exist there by catholics, which is a different matter), they were naturally gravitating to areas where it was felt that they were not likely to be penalised. Tom Carberry sums up the process in the following way:

> If they were already under-represented in one area, it was logical that they would be over-represented in another one. Beforehand they had been over-represented in the ranks of the unemployed. Now they were going to be over-represented in the public sector.[65]

The administration of local government also drew suitably qualified catholics in the post-1945 years. Perhaps the best-known example is Sir Lawrence Boyle, the Edinburgh-born catholic. He trained for the priesthood until ill-health compelled him to focus on a less demanding vocation. As a local government officer he resolved to apply himself to be better than the next person in his work which overlapped into part-time study for various university qualifications. Although he was aware that scope for discrimination existed, he was thus in a difficult position to penalise and, after being County Treasurer in Midlothian, he came to Glasgow in 1962 as Deputy City Chamberlain. His boss, Mr Esselman, who oversaw the city's administration, hailed from Aberdeen which lacked comparable religious differences and he was not influenced by sectarian considerations when appointing senior staff in Glasgow Corporation (the same could not have been said about his predecessor). In 1969, while a non-socialist administration held office in Glasgow, Boyle succeeded him as City Chamberlain; only one councillor opposed his nomination on religious grounds, while there was strong support from the ruling Progressives who, because of his administrative record were reluctant to lose Boyle to another authority.

In increasing numbers the legal profession drew recruits from catholics of an immigrant background, who had hitherto largely made their mark in the criminal statistics. As many as three catholic judges were to be found in Scotland before the Second World War. But Skerrington, Moncrieff, and Carmont were from a landed or upper-class background. John Wheatley, the nephew of the Labour minister of the same name, was the first member of the west of Scotland immigrant community to make his mark in this elite profession. In 1972 he was appointed Lord Justice Clerk, the senior Scottish judicial appointment. To become an advocate, the Scottish equivalent of a barrister, more than adequate private means were vital and the Wheatley's were one of the few catholic families in the west able to offer the necessary support. No other catholic in the west became a barrister until after 1945, but now it is reckoned that there are a reasonable number. The reputation Wheatley made at the bar meant he was soon receiving commissions from many different sections of the Edinburgh community. In 1947 he was appointed Solicitor-General for Scotland after having been elected Labour MP for Edinburgh East. He faced little or no hostility on account of his religion during the campaign. To become Edinburgh's first catholic MP a decade after the eruption of serious religious discord, showed how, in the meantime, the atmosphere had changed there.

In the west of Scotland during the 1950s increasing numbers of catholics were coming forward in the solicitors' branch of the legal profession. Although not as prestigious as the bar, the financial rewards are easier to come by than those at the bar while the social status of a solicitor was at least as high as that of a family doctor. Joseph Beltrami and Laurence Dowdall two of Scotland's best-known criminal lawyers in the post-war years, were pioneers of the new wave of catholic lawyers. For all its elitist characteristics the Scottish legal profession passed the religious test regarding those catholics seeking to breach its citadels with flying colours. It did not close ranks to keep catholics out but accepted those with the necessary qualities and persistence into its elitist ranks.

John Bayne, a dedicated catholic lay activist, as well as a former Labour parliamentary candidate, was a sheriff at Glasgow from 1959 to 1979. During this time it became possible to reach the judicial bench through a apprenticeship as a solicitor rather than as an advocate and several other catholics have been appointed sheriffs; James Murphy, Sheriff of Strathclyde since 1976 was formerly a partner and founder member of the well-known inter-denominational legal firm of Ross Harper & Murphy, created in 1961. It was a politically ecumenical firm as shown in 1970 when the future sheriff campaigned for Winnie Ewing, Hamilton's Nationalist MP, despite the fact that the Tory candidate was his own partner, Ross Harper.[66]

The St Thomas More Society exists for catholic lawyers but only a minority have shown any keen interest in it. In the 1970s a meeting in Glasgow addressed by Lord Wheatley and attended by the archbishop was held in order to resuscitate it. Perhaps the fact that a very high proportion of Glasgow catholic lawyers trained for the priesthood made it seem worth while. But despite great enthusiasm on the night, nothing came of it. The open secular environment in which lawyers move makes it difficult to organise on a confessional basis even for sporadic events—in the opinion of a senior member of the profession.[67] Another source reckons that catholic lawyers were too busy becoming prominently involved in the Glasgow Bar Association, an association of Glasgow solicitors of all denominations or none, enabling members to make appropriate contacts and advance their careers.

Not surprisingly, among members of the educated middle-class who had emerged from the old industrial proletariat, there was a growing temptation to 'show that catholics are just the same as other people, to conform to the current social, political or cultural fashion, to try not to be noticed as Catholics'.[68] Elsewhere the same observer writes that 'there were those who maintained two distinct compartments in life, one in which they did religious things without much energy, and with an eye on mother, a second in which they were busily preparing to "get on" in the world'.[69] A growing division within the community based on social distinction could be observed by the 1960s. Despite the efforts of the Newman Association, a strong tradition of catholic intellectualism which could be taken as the hallmark of an educated catholic community whose faith and culture were being integrated, was still conspicuously absent.[70] In the post-war years, new parishes sprang up in middle-class areas where none had previously existed, denoting the growth of an owner-occupier sector within the catholic community, but the Church could not quite manage to play the integrative role it had performed in the inner-city parishes of the immigrant community.

The trek out of the immigrant catholic enclave to a socially and religiously mixed neighbourhood was a decisive event for those who undertook it. Professor Tom Carberry recalls moving from a room and kitchen in Cumberland Street, the Gorbals, to a three apartment corporation house in Govanhill when aged nine in the 1930s. Although the anti-catholic SPL had enjoyed some success there earlier in the decade, he does not remember the family encountering positive hostility:

> One sensed various things though . . . Firstly . . . that we were the first Catholics living up that close and that our arrival was viewed with some apprehension by the neighbours; mind you they were very discreet in giving voice to that apprehension . . .
> The first day that we were there after the removal my mother was told in a very nice and polite way what was expected of her. I think that would have been told to any incoming neighbour but, looking back on it, I think it was done with a certain emphasis to make sure we did not step out of line . . . Occasionally there was a little flurry . . . around things like silver jubilees and coronations. The expectation was that everyone should put out flags. We didn't put out Union Jacks . . . and there was maybe the odd comment made. However, that being said, I think we were pretty readily assimilated.[71]

People interact more intensively in working-class neighbourhoods than in middle-class ones so more scope for friction exists between members of families who express the kind of partisan attitudes that have given a sharp edge to the community divide in Glasgow. Occasionally neighbourly disputes with a religious dimension reached the courts and were reported in the press, but it is perhaps surprising that more instances of friction did not emerge as families from well-defined working-class communities found themselves thrown together on new housing estates. Gang warfare was a feature of life on some of the new Glasgow housing estates, especially in the late 1960s, but the evidence suggests that these gangs were formed on a territorial rather than a religious basis;[72] no evidence has emerged that, in allocating tenancies for new corporation housing, factors payed especial heed to the possibility of religious friction emerging and took steps to offset it. But this is an area in which more thoroughgoing research remains to be done. Officials in corporation housing departments wielded immense power and, if they reflected the disparaging view of working-class catholics held by other power-holders, it may help to explain why, starting in the 1930s, they were sent in large numbers to a poorly constructed estate like Blackhill. It was allocated for those among the working-class who could not be designated 'clean and respectable' and it rapidly developed 'a reputation for illness and violence that surpassed that of the old slums themselves'.[73]

In middle-class areas which catholic professionals began to enter after the 1940s, there was no expectation of trouble. But scope for misunderstanding existed and at least one community, Eastwood, in the southern suburbs of Glasgow but located in Renfrewshire, split on quasi-religious grounds over the proposal to build a catholic secondary school in the area.

By 1966 there was a demand for such a school and a suitable site was available. However, the locally dominant Conservative Party dragged its feet over allowing planning permission. It reflected the views of many residents, who were soon aware that the proposed school would also cater for children from nearby Glasgow council estates. Between the wars over three-quarters of newly built housing in Glasgow was in the public sector[74] and many Eastwood residents were hyper-sensitive to the prospect of daily encroachments from the products of council houses who could not be expected to share their respect for property or middle-class standards. But catholic parents had no wish to continue sending their children to over-crowded schools in Glasgow and, according to one observer, were keen to see their desire for full equality and full social acceptance met by sending their children to a middle-class school in the area where they lived.[75] This dispute rumbled on into the 1970s with entrenched positions being taken up in a split suburban community. In the mid-1970s Thomas Winning, the new Archbishop of Glasgow, is reported to have told the Tory Party leader, Margaret Thatcher, in no uncertain terms while she was visiting Glasgow, of the importance the catholic hierarchy attached to the building of the school.[76] In the hierarchy's eyes it would ease the worrying temptation for middle-class catholics to send their children to a more convenient non-catholic school.[77] (Already a growing minority of pupils at Hutchison Grammar, the top Glasgow fee-paying school, were from comfortably off catholic homes.) Whether or not this apocryphal story is strictly accurate, previously expressed support for Eastwood Tories from Conservatives outside the area quickly dried up and the school was eventually built.

This episode may have shown achievement-oriented catholics that they could not always shake off their ethnic past or express their religious and educational preferences without paying some cost. It is likely that very few Orangemen were to be found in Eastwood or similar districts that began to admit catholics. But the Masonic Order remained a potent social force in middle-class Glasgow as a glance at the still copious Masonic notes in the daily press in the 1950s and 1960s would soon make clear.

It was middle-class businessmen with masonic loyalties who (as directors and senior shareholders) ensured that Rangers football club still retained an all-protestant image by declining to sign catholic players in the forty years after the Second World War. An unguarded statement in 1967 by Matt Taylor, the club's vice-chairman, showed how outdated religious ties blended in with strong financial considerations to account for this anachronistic policy: 'it is part of our tradition. We were founded in 1873 as a Presbyterian Boys' Club. To change now would lose us considerable support.'[78]

Only in the late 1960s, when recurrent crowd trouble from a section of Rangers' following began to mar the image of Scottish soccer, did the local press begin to campaign in earnest against its religious exclusivity. Alex Cameron of *The Daily Record* demanded 'a vigorous clean-out of inbred bigotry which coincidence no longer begins to explain or excuse'.[79] Earlier, in the mid-1960s, various Glasgow elites had begun to be outspoken perhaps aware that a correlation existed between football disorder and Glasgow's accelerating industrial decline. Magistrates were instructed to hand down stiff penalties to soccer hooligans; Sheriff Daiches QC spoke in 1965 of 'this disgraceful behaviour which is making this city a byword in Europe'. The chairman of the Scottish TUC wrote to the city's magistrates arguing that Old Firm violence was having a damaging effect on Scotland's image among industrialists while the Lord Provost made a plea to both clubs to sever their sectarian identities.[80] But the inertia of Scottish society allowed the waves of criticism to lap harmlessly around Rangers; earlier, Celtic had been under greater pressure from the administrators of Scottish football. At the beginning of the 1950s, it was almost expelled from the Scottish Football Association for refusing to cease the practice of flying the Irish tricolour at its ground. George Graham, secretary of the SFA, and a freemason and an Orangeman, was the team's chief antagonist.[81] But Rangers came to Celtic's defence at this moment which, at first glance, may seem surprising, but is not really so: Rangers and Celtic are like Siamese twins dependent on each other for their economic well-being. One would not enjoy the same economic success and prestige without the closing of ranks induced by the other's presence.

An impressive gesture of respect was accorded to Celtic by its old rival when Rangers chairman, John Lawrence was at Glasgow airport in 1967 to be among those welcoming back the Celtic team from their European Cup triumph in Lisbon; the Church of Scotland later passed a motion of congratulations at its General Assembly.

Celtic has never refused to play Rangers on account of either its signing policy or the openly sectarian element who have made the running among its supporters. But a number of middle-class catholics still have something of a chip on their shoulder about the latitude supposedly given to Rangers either by referees, senior football officials, certain journalists or else the police, perhaps because the survival of Rangers as one of Glasgow's leading institutions places a questionmark over their own status in the city. Catholic professionals perhaps only a generation removed from the working-class have waxed indignantly about having never seen a Rangers player ordered off at an Old Firm game before a Celtic player or about the partiality of referees who have ensured that 'they never lost in any FA cup final since 1929 whereas Celtic has'.[82] In 1986, the Celtic manager David Hay even declared that, if it was up to him, Celtic would join the English league, words prompted by refereeing decisions at the Skol cup final which Celtic adherents found it hard to stomach.

Even though such reactions may denote something of an inferiority complex among catholics caught uneasily between the working-class and the middle-class, some basis for a lingering sense of grievance remained. After 1945 ambitious and self-confident catholics could still be systematically rebuffed in certain white-collar occupations such as banking for no good reason. A lingering suspicion still existed that catholics and social problems went hand in hand which acted to the disadvantage of the job applicant.

In the 1950s Richard Buchanan a Glasgow catholic councillor with a surname that gave no clue to his religious identity, recalls what he found on being appointed to the board of the Royal Infirmary in Glasgow. Interviewing applicants for a senior nursing post, he was struck by the fact that the retiring matron ruled out the most promising candidate with the words, 'Oh but she's a Catholic'. However, her abilities impressed the other members of the interview panel and she got the job, but Buchanan still remains appalled at the open and obvious way that her religion was treated as a disqualification by an older member of the nursing profession who, by the candour of her remarks, did not feel she was expressing views that were in any way unusual.[83]

In Coatbridge, which with five catholic secondary schools, is the Scottish town with the largest proportion of catholics among its inhabitants, no catholic could get a job in any of its banks until late in the post-war era. For many years James Breen, the headmaster of a selective entry school with a good academic reputation grew increasingly exasperated until, in the early 1960s, he decided to personally confront Coatbridge bank managers about the situation. Several of those that he saw informed him that they recruited new staff on the recommendation of existing employees and that there was no conscious policy to exclude catholics. But when Breen said to one manager, 'I know for a fact that you contacted Airdrie High School about suitable recruits', all he could say was 'Oh I forgot to approach your school'. Another manager, reacting positively to Breen and perhaps not realising the significance of what he was saying, said that 'I will phone head office in Edinburgh to see if the ban [on catholics] is still in place'.[84] The headmaster had discovered an unspoken embargo and the chances are that it was duplicated in other Scottish towns; in time catholics began to be taken on as bank employees in Coatbridge but it was a slow process.

Lower down the professional scale catholics tended not to pursue jobs as engineers, firemen, technicians, printers and quantity surveyors because of the received wisdom that they were simply hitting their heads against a brick wall. In Coatbridge Mr Breen remembers taking a school party to a local authority public works only to be spat on by workers in an upper storey of the building. Professor Tom Carberry is just one of several respondents who mentioned that in the post-war decades, a whole range of establishments (some, well-known names), would still not take on catholics. But when a labour shortage occurred in many skilled occupations during the expansionary years of the 1950s and 1960s, the situation became more fluid. With increasing numbers of well-trained and qualified catholics coming on to the labour market, some employers began to waver if the alternative was a poorer-qualified protestant. This is the impression Carberry derived from the 1950s and he illustrated it in the following way:

> Who gets the 100 IQ jobs as Clerk of the Water Board? Is it the 115 IQ papist or the 105 IQ drummer from the Lord Carson Memorial Band? When the choice lies between the 115 IQ and the 115IQ a lot of the discriminatory firms had no doubt about whom to appoint. When the choice lay between a 115 IQ catholic and a 105 IQ protestant, doubts crept in. When it lay between an applicant with a 135 IQ and another with 105, they knew what side their bread was buttered on . . . It was in that situation that many employers decided to stop discriminating.[85]

Old recruitment patterns based on protestant solidarity or disdain for a community that had hitherto been regarded as synonmous with the submerged working-class, began to alter due to other reasons. Local family-based concerns were increasingly taken over by national or multinational firms whose personnel section had a more meritocratic set of criteria for recruitment. If local managers remained in charge, scope existed to continue with the old hiring practices, but 'if a *debâcle* occurred, you had to justify your approach to someone coming up by train or plane from London':

> You were always liable to get a situation where a character was sent up who was Eton-educated and belonged to the Brigade of Guards, but it transpired eventually that either he was a Catholic or his wife was; it all helped to make you that bit more careful about what you said regarding religion.
>
> The other possibility was that you were taken over by an American company and the man who flew in to oversee the changeover was an Italian-American or an Irish-American . . . Equally it could have been somebody from the Bible Belt but you never knew who was going to arrive from the American parent company. In that situation, employers who had been discriminating found it prudent to cease being discriminatory or else be less discriminatory than before.[86]

Alex Ferry, a leading trade unionist, was able to comment authoritatively about the changes he glimpsed on the shopfloor in the west of Scotland during the same period. Born a catholic in Glasgow in 1931, the son of an Irish father and a Scottish mother, on being widowed she remarried a protestant who became a convert (though he did not practice the faith) and the children were brought up as catholics. He entered the job market in the 1940s when he recalls the question of one's denomination still played a significant part in deciding what type of job a Glaswegian acquired:

> It was still much more difficult for a Roman Catholic to be employed in the craft trade than it was for others . . . I discovered that myself when I was trying to find an apprenticeship. The employer . . . would ask you what school you had gone to (that was the immediate give-away) and if you tried to cover it up, you were then asked about the Boy Scouts and the Boys Brigades; this was supposed to see what kind of individual you were but really it was a hidden questionnaire about your background and religion.
>
> Notwithstanding that, I managed to get an apprenticeship in one of the less desirable engineering companies in Clydebank . . . When I moved into the Singer Sewing Machine Company in 1954 . . . the effects of discrimination were even more glaring. The tool room where I was, employed around 300 people . . . You could have counted the Catholics on the digits of your two hands and, in the shop in which I worked, I was the only Catholic.[87]

Alex Ferry relates that the situation changed between 1954 and

1966 not through any affirmative action on the part of trade unions or employers but owing to the shortage of skilled men which made it difficult to adhere to the old recruitment policy. The better conditions of the 1950s reduced rivalry within the working-class but mutual suspicion could be rekindled in surprising ways. Alex Ferry recalls that in 1956 when the unions in the engineering industry negotiated an extra days holiday and recommended to members that it be taken on Christmas Day, 'all hell broke loose' at Singers. December 25 was still not a recognised holiday in all walks of Scottish life and it was felt that catholics would be the chief beneficiaries since for them it was a more significant occasion on which they were required to attend Mass. Alex Ferry recalls that the matter had to be put to a ballot and that it was carried only by a small majority despite the fact that more than half the workforce were women who might have been expected to be keen to be with their families on that day.[88]

Alex Ferry was already a union officer at Singers by 1956 and he recalls attempts by the Singer management to take advantage of religious differences to split up the workforce. A lever was to hand in the free-masons who had many adherents among the rank-and-file who were keen to seek promotion up the ranks of this male-bonding organisation:

> You could actually see people changing . . . With those you had been on friendly terms with, a wall was erected once they joined . . . When they went to a meeting or a function of the Masonic Order and the managers were there, somehow this gave them the impression that they were important. And that was reflected in their attitude when industrial disputes arose.[89]

Standing for his first elective office in 1964, Ferry found that his religion was so unpalatable for some engineers that they preferred to vote in the first ballot for his Communist rival despite their lack of sympathy for the Communist cause. This was particularly the case in the Dennistoun area of Glasgow which had been the power-base of Alexander Ratcliffe in the 1930s. In the second ballot, the Dennistoun branch swung into line after remonstrations from other protestant engineers supporting Ferry who then went out of his way to win the trust of branch officials in that district. He reckons that he managed to 'prove to them his determination to serve the entire membership irrespective of what anybody's religion was'.

Religion also produced some disconterting alliances in the Electrical Trades Union (ETU) according to the journalist, George Scott. In the early 1960s he talked to one Clydeside ETU member who had voted for Frank Haxell, the Communist, as general-secretary in preference to John Byrne 'because Byrne was a Catholic and I couldn't vote for a Catholic'.[90] Another Tory reckons that the traditionally large vote on Clydeside for Haxell (who was removed after charges of ballot-rigging were upheld in the courts) 'was not a Communist vote but an anti-Catholic vote'.[91]

It is perhaps appropriate that the first Scots catholic to rise high in the union world did so in the USA. This was Lanarkshire-born Philip Murray (1886–1953) who left Scotland in 1902 and for twelve years was head of the powerful Congress of Industrial Organisations.[92] Alex Ferry eventually became President of the Confederation of Shipbuilding and Engineering Unions. He is impressed with the way that religious segregation has largely retreated from the industrial world on Clydeside. He is hopeful that it will not be revived by the post-1973 recession, but is still able to point to some employers who 'want to know what religion you are':

> Of course when you query that and say that it leaves room for discrimination, you are told that it is just in case somebody is taken ill and we know that we've got to send for a minister or a priest. But when you look at the proportion of Catholics employed by companies who operate in this way, you often find it is amazingly low and that they are usually in the worst types of jobs.[93]

Catholics have tended to do well with the expansion of the service economy which has filled part of the gap left by the declining manufacturing sector. Some successful catholics who maintain something of a catholic enclave mentality, belong to the Knights of St Columba, a secretive body formed on masonic lines which only grants membership to practising catholics. In 1965 it was a catholic source that publicly aired the claim that 'Knights use their influence to get another Knight a position in teaching, in local government, or commerce'.[94] The Catenian Association existed for slightly more elevated catholics in business and the professions. One source describes it as 'operating in a quasi-masonic manner (though without such elaborate ritual) to put upwardly mobile catholics in touch with one another . . . Their activities involved organizing dances at which young middle-class catholics could meet other young middle-class catholics and these dances were still flourishing up to the early 1960s.'[95]

Anecdotal evidence points to a large number of working-class Scots still having a subliminal or active fear that public officials, whether they be policemen or social security officials, are liable to discriminate against them on religious grounds. This became obvious to one social security officer with militant protestant affiliations, when he was placed in charge of one urban district for five years:

> If I went to a house and saw a nail on the wall, then I guessed that nail had contained a holy picture which had been removed when the householders discovered that I was coming to do an inspectoral visit—just in case they didn't get a grant which they were entitled to.
> It was a completely irrational fear.[96]

The upheavals of war, the relocation of so much of the urban population in new communities, and the onset of moderate prosperity, certainly dealt a blow to old religious prejudices and rivalries, but their banishment to the darker corners of Scottish life was a slow process as the above illustrations have shown. The differing receptions catholics received as they moved into new housing estates, middle-class suburbs, the factory shop floor, or the university showed how community relations remained in a state of flux well after 1945.

Old political moulds also remained obstinately in place on Clydeside after 1945. In the general election of that year there was only a 2½% swing to the Labour Party in Glasgow compared with Edinburgh's 14·5% and the UK average of 12%.[97] Glasgow had the lowest turn-out of any one of Britain's fifteen largest cities which, at 65%, was 7% down on the 1935 figure. Out campaigning in a working-class and Orange part of the Ayrshire town of Irvine, David Lambie, the future Labour MP, found animosities still in place in 1945 when a man came out of his house carrying a crowbar with which he threatened to smash the canvasser's car unless he moved off.[98] Notable outbreaks of violence occurred at Old Firm matches in 1946, 1949, 1952, 1953, 1955, 1957 and 1958, which only served to underline that war and reconstruction had not relegated an inter-tribal conflict that still absorbed so much of the commitment and energy of Glasgow's soccer mad young.[99] Growing up then in the 1950s, the writer James Campbell recalls that 'Scottish patriotism was superceded by loyalist patriotism which conflicts with it'.[100]

Donald MacDonald, a Church of Scotland minister, recalls that his Highland background had not prepared him for the rigours of Glasgow, which he came to in the 1950s. He arrived from North Uist, an island largely inhabited by Presbyterians; neighbouring Benbecula was comprised almost equally of protestants and catholics while South Uist was 90% catholic, yet he recalls 'there was really no friction . . . no strong awareness of difference between us'. In Glasgow he 'came down to earth with a thud in his first summer' on taking a part-time job in a Bridgeton photographic factory 'where suddenly you discovered that there were some people who did not sit with one another at teabreak, people who did very different things over the weekend . . . it was really then that I discovered how badly divided the community actually was'.[101]

Living in the Partick district he 'discovered that there were protestant and catholic pubs . . . that some people . . . would cross the road rather than walk in front of the catholic chapel; I remember the intense catholicism there was on the other side of the coin—people passing the chapel who would take their hat off . . . These were the formative impressions.'

The local media had learned from experience not to probe too deeply into the tangled mix of loyalties that still divided Glaswegians. C. M. Oakley, the Portsmouth-born historian of Glasgow, made the revealing comment shortly after the war that 'there is no subject on which writers and speakers about Glasgow are less willing to dwell than that of the Irish in Scotland'.[102] No lead was forthcoming from the BBC, which failed to beam a spotlight on Scotland's religious and social problems. From 1933 to 1957 BBC Scotland 'became a by-word for puritanical parochialism' under its Controller, the Rev. Melville Dinwiddie.[103] That a Presbyterian minister could hold down such an influential post in the public domain and mould it to his own narrow tastes shows how invisible were the roman catholics (14·7% of Scotland's population in 1951, 25·6% of Glasgow's).[104] Given that they were either ignored or disparaged in many cases, roman catholics often reacted defensively on the rare occasion that they sought to define their role beyond their own parish. This passage from Colm Brogan's *The Glasgow Story* (1954) is a good illustration:

> The Catholic population of Glasgow is bedded down. It is there, it is large, it is growing, and it cannot be got rid of by any methods short of those favoured by Herr Himmler.[105]

At least the fact that a catholic was writing a history of his native city (regarded still as one of the best) was a sign of identification with it if not with wider Scottish society. Those few Scots who sought to inhabit the no man's land between the two communities did not always find life easy. In the Gorbals, some of the local catholic clergy were suspicious of the Rev Geoff Shaw, a Presbyterian minister who chose to do youth work from a crumbling tenement in Cleland Street at the end of the 1950s, and who was soon to be a legend in his own lifetime.[106] His daring new departure bore fruit and inspired emulators in Glasgow's bleak new housing estates. *The Evening Citizen*, one of Glasgow's afternoon daily papers, was less successful at mould-breaking. It almost crashed financially one summer in the late 1950s after carrying an article very critical of the Orange Order. A readership boycott ensued which caused such panic that Donald MacDonald, then a journalist on the paper, recalls tht nothing critical was written about the Order in the Glasgow press for many years to come.[107] Across in Edinburgh Compton Mackenzie was able to notice a welcome improvement in the atmosphere:

> Few statements have given me as much satisfaction to make in any article or book I have written as to be able to say that since I came to Edinburgh in 1953 I have not received one anonymous letter from an indignant Protestant, not even one pip from an Orangeman. Without any doubt, the Edinburgh of today is much more tolerant than it used to be.[108]

But the same Edinburgh still returned the protestant firebrand John Cormack to the council and would continue to do so until his retirement in 1962. He survived increasingly thanks to the backing of the ruling Moderates who gave him a free run in his Leith ward because of his ability to keep Labour out and bring over apathetic voters who might normally have stayed at home. Although he still spoke regularly at the Mound, his election literature and council record shows that he was now more concerned with the 'menace of socialism' than with that of Rome, at least in his political role. He acquired a quieter and more responsible image which enabled him to make the rare transition from street agitator to local political institution. He became known as the last resort for people in trouble and was Edinburgh's first full-time councillor. He had a reputation for incorruptability and frugality which won him the respect even of opponents. Flashes of the old Cormack sometimes reappeared as when he challenged the roman catholic head of the council health committee, who was opposing his motion that a small annual grant be given to the first family planning clinic set up in Edinburgh, to tell the council 'what he did as a married man . . . and only having two of a family'.[109]

By the 1950s Cormack's long years of service on the council placed him in line for appointment to the magistrate's bench as a bailie. However, his colleagues hesitated to take this step right up until 1955, the year before he became the longest-serving member, or 'Father' of the council. This caution was understandable: in Scotland, unlike England, the local magistrate sat alone which made his power to fine defendents and send them to prison rather more open to abuse. In the past Cormack had linked roman catholicism with crime and, if he had taken this view literally while discharging his judicial role, it could have brought further unwelcome publicity to the city of Edinburgh. After earlier failing to agree among themselves, the ruling Progressives elevated Cormack to the local bench in 1955. One councillor, Robert McLaughlin, was allegedly told by him that he would not discriminate against catholics and, although he sometimes hit the headlines for delivering an idiosyncratic verdict, he seems to have honoured that pledge.[110]

Councillor McLaughlin was one of four roman catholics elected as Progressives in Edinburgh during the 1950s. Their nomination, election, and appointment to senior convenorships and committee chairmanships would seem to show that at different levels the Progressives were unhampered by blinkered prejudice and unamenable to pressure from Cormack about whom to choose as a public representative. Three of the four (McLaughlin was from a poor background in Leith) were middle-class catholics who stressed their Scottish identity (one, George Hedderwick, was Archbishop Gray's brother-in-law), so they were easily absorbed into the Edinburgh establishment. A number of tactical compromises managed to smooth over previously yawning religious differences in Edinburgh without the need being felt to remove their source which was a typical Scottish compromise in the post-war years that catholics in public life tended to accept. Across in Glasgow catholics who conformed were granted proper recognition by the local elites, then mainly protestant in composition, but there were rather fewer of them. One example is Sir Patrick Dollan who was the first winner of the St Mungo Prize for citizenship in 1939 and who, after his death, was singled out for praise in 1969 by John Lawrence, the Glasgow builder and chairman of Rangers football club:

> I knew the Dollans for many years and always held them in high esteem. Sir Patrick was an admirable administrator, efficient, conscientious, full of drive and enthusiasm, tempered by common sense.[111]

Such latitude was not forthcoming from the Orange Order which saw Dollan as the first of a wave of catholic Irish politicians who were seizing control of Glasgow's public affairs for their own sectional interests. In 1955, its paper, *The Vigilant* set out its uncompromising views not just on the catholic faith but on its adherents which made no concession to the times in which they were written:

> I am now absolutely convinced that the Roman Catholics will resort to every lie, every trick and every crime in the annals of society to defeat the Protestant freedom which we enjoy. They hate us . . . Do not descend to the immoral level of Rome. Preserve your principals. Love God and your neighbours. Let your motto be 'Ye shall know the truth and that truth shall make you free'.[112]

These were the words of Alan G. Hasson, a young and energetic Church of Scotland minister who had formed the paper because 'a medium for the expression of matters vital to our Cause has been a long-felt want'.[113] In fact the Order was rudderless, having entered a period of stagnation in which it hardly did much else beyond maintaining the ritual of the annual processions and commemorations and giving occasional political service to the Tory Party. A vacuum at the top of the Order existed when Hasson burst onto the protestant scene in the early 1950s. He rapidly made his name as minister attached to the parish of Bonhill, Dunbartonshire where his fiery sermons attracted full congregations. He was all for confrontation with roman catholics as his fellow minister James Currie recalls—'once when a big lorry knocked over his gatepost at the Manse, he kicked up blazes and represented it as a catholic plot against him'.[114] Having moderated his views in later years while losing none of his religious fervour, Hasson characterised his assault on Rome in the following terms:

I became a moral fanatic, convinced that I stood almost alone doing battle with the powers of evil, exemplified by the Catholic Church.

The Lord God had blessed me with great gifts of mind and spirit, and to my everlasting regret I buried my talents in the malodorous midden of the Orange Order, a dung heap of hatred, blindness and bigotry. Here was a political organisation paying lip-service to the Cause of Christ, parading an open Bible whose magnificent truths could not penetrate the closed minds of sectarian bitterness. The whole organisation was an affront to the Spirit of Christ—and I became their leader.[115]

After a whirlwind rise Hasson was elected Grand Master in 1958 while still only in his early thirties. He broke through because he was such an impressive contrast to the worthy but colourless figures who had been at the helm in previous decades. To make his presence felt at the annual Orange walk in Glasgow he got himself a large chestnut horse on which he rode, dressed in a red hunting coat, white breeches, a top hat and clerical collar.[116] He sought to revive the Order as a political force while still anchoring it to firm Reformation principles: a campaign was waged against drink at rallies and against failure to attend church regularly. He sought to make church attendance a condition of membership and condemned the slackening of standards that he observed all around him:

An Orangeman . . . ought to be an observer at the ordinances of public worship, keeping only the Sabbath day and living so that his whole walk and conversation shall correspond with and sustain his . . . religion.

Is the Order living up to these ideals today? The answer is No! . . . some would do the cause of Protestantism more good by leaving us than by remaining. Yet I believe that the chief fault lies with our leaders. Private, District and Grand Lodge leaders are not ruling the lodges according to the Constitution but rather . . . with re-election in mind.

. . . Let us not have Brothers Finance, Popularity, Timidity or Scaredness, selling our privileges for gain . . .

. . . to the staunch regulars who do uphold the constitution . . . we must unite in our lodges to force our Masters to act, and we must use every weapon at our disposal, even ridicule.[117]

Hasson almost seemed intent on rousing ordinary members against the cautious and bureaucratic office holders in much the same way as Mao Tse-tung was to do in China during the late 1960s. However, the politically quiet and materialistic late 1950s were not the best time to launch a cultural revolution inside the Order so as to make it a more assertive force set fair to re-evangelise a nominally protestant Scotland. Internal opposition grew against his high-handed and capricious rule and, in 1959 he suspended lodge members *ad hoc* in one of the largest districts, Armadale in West Lothian. The flamboyant and visionary Alan Hasson was really something of an odd-man-out at the head of an organisation whose caution and routine were features of stability as well as stagnation. The growing paranoia inside Scottish Orangeism was reflected in an anonymous article that appeared in *The Vigilant* in 1958:

> I fear not Rome. I fear not Communism. I do fear my own brothers and sisters who are gossips and slanderers.
>
> In my private lodge, No. 242, Bellshill, I have found a group of very imperfect brethren. I cannot extol their virtues . . .
>
> To sum up with potent thoughts and deductions. Fear God, honour the Queen, and love the Brotherhood. Don't talk of any lodge business outside the brotherhood . . . In all cases support the brethren, remembering that we are a nation on our own, despised and rejected.[118]

In 1960 Hasson suffered a nervous breakdown and was replaced as Grand Master. He then spent some years in Canada before returning in 1971 to Britain where he was arrested and charged with having embezzled Orange Order funds to the tune of £10,300 during his time as Grand Master.[119] There followed two tangled trials at the second of which, the appeal, the case against Hasson was found not proven.[120] The presiding judge, Lord Wheatley was a roman catholic as was the defence lawyer Joseph Beltrami; today Hasson, who has changed his name to Alan G. Cameron, speaks up for co-existence between protestants and catholics while still adhering to the belief that a spiritual reawakening is necessary to cure the social and political ills afflicting Scotland. Of his time as Grand Master he now writes: 'I became possessed by the demons that accompany power and prestige, and I became a demagogue. I was under the spell of my own slogans and prejudices.'[121] He is to the Orange Order what Trotsky was to the Soviet Union under Stalin, a destructive influence driven by vaulting ambition and erractic judgement.

The Hasson affair was not a terminal blow to the standing of the Orange Order. It had enough inner resources to be able to bounce back, but this traumatic episode had revealed the pitfalls of placing too much faith in charismatic leadership. Under greyer but more level-headed stewards, it conducted its affairs in a more low-key manner after 1960. They had to face new challenges to Orange cohesion which did not emanate from the Vatican. As the redevelopment of Glasgow gathered pace in the 1960s, bulldozers levelled areas like Kinning Park, and parts of Partick, Whiteinch and Govan where Orangeism had been especially strong thanks to their shipbuilding associations. The demolition of areas in the east end like Dalmarnock, Bridgeton, and Parkhead, associated with weaving or heavy engineering, came later but would be just as devastating. The decline of shipbuilding on the Clyde and the winding down of the Ayrshire and Lanarkshire coalfields in the 1950s posed another questionmark about the viability of the Order in the absence of traditional industries around which the lodges had grown up. Emigration from the Orange heartlands of Ulster was also a casualty of the economic downturn. Some of the most dedicated Scottish officials had strong Ulster family connections and the damming up of this source of renewal stood to alter the character of the movement in subtle ways. It may have made it more pragmatic and less unyielding in a political and religous sense and more open to influence from the wider Scottish society even as the Ulster conflict flared up in earnest in the 1970s and 1980s. Somehow it was able to retain a mass membership despite the above challenges and the growth in religiously mixed marriages and the further spread of secularism within the working class.

Here it should not be overlooked that the Orange Lodge fills a void in the lives of men and women in dozens of anonymous towns and villages across Scotland with bleak economic prospects. There is keen competition to ascend the lodge hierarchy and pursue the degrees which denote a brother's seniority. The spread of licensed Orange social clubs shows how the Order has come to terms with the pub-orientated life of post-industrial Scotland in a way that its much larger Ulster counterpart still refuses to do.

Lodges have spread to new housing estates, to new towns like Cumbernauld and towards the east of Scotland in line with the shift in jobs and population. Orange officials now see no point in denying that membership has been lost in the course of these upheavals.[122] Many lodges in depressed areas waive the payment of dues for unemployed members so as to prevent numbers falling. However divisive some of its features appear, Orangeism remains an expression of communitarian values at a time when working-class lifestyles are becoming increasingly privatised and centred around the home with its consumer goods and television.

Increasingly the Labour Party has become the political beneficiary of a movement which is an authentic if flawed expression of working-class culture in Scotland. As links with the freemasons and other elite groups lessened, members began to vote increasingly along class lines. The Scottish Tories who dropped 'Unionist' from their title in 1965 deferred less and less to Orange prejudices. This was shown graphically in Bute and North Ayrshire where Sir Fitzroy Maclean, a British army officer, was nominated for the safe Tory seat in 1959. Many party workers were Orangemen and Labour convassers used to jest with them that they were unconscious agents of Rome since Maclean had married one of the Lovats, a Highland catholic family and his children were being brought up in their mother's faith.[123]

John Adam, the Scottish Grand Master in the 1960s, was arrested in 1962 outside an ecumenical gathering, but the increase in catholic-protestant dialogue does not seem to have greatly troubled the bulk of the membership.[124] One activist reckons that the anti-ecumenical movement ran out of steam in the 1960s because most of those who identified with Orangeism were largely unchurched. It is interesting that Dr Ian Paisley's Ulster-based Free Presbyterian Church failed to spread to Scotland in spite of frequent trips to drum up support during and after his rise to prominence in the 1960s.

In Ulster there is no shortage of clergymen willing to act as Orange chaplains: 'some use the lodge to gain church members and to increase their standing in their town or village'.[125] But after the Hasson episode, only a handful of Church of Scotland ministers were prepared to associate with the Order. Hasson himself, writing in 1956 gave the following explanation:

> Ministers . . . see some members of the Order whose behaviour is reprehensible and conclude that this is our general standard.
>   Many . . . think that we are uneducated, ill-informed, prejudiced, and they look upon the Order as a collection of cranks, a bunch of bigots, or a troupe of trouble-makers.[126]

Gone were the days when an applicant for membership had to have signed by a minister a document that specified that he or she attended church and took Holy Communion so many times per year.[127] A minister like James Currie who identified with traditional protestant values without condoning sectarianism, is an exception. In Glasgow's working-class Pollok estate where he was minister from 1955 to 1972, he boosted the size of his congregation at a time of declining membership elsewhere in similar parishes: 'I have gone out on a limb for the Orange Order,' he declared, a movement which 'upholds sound principles and gives Protestants a voice.'[128] When his successor refused to lay on an annual church service for Orange parades, attendance at church plummeted, but those at the helm in the Church of Scotland seem prepared to shoulder this cost in certain localities for the sake of mending fences with the catholic church.

The 2nd Vatican Council, inaugurated by the liberal Pope John XXIII in 1962, set in train changes which made the catholic church far less dogmatic and introspective in its style and teachings and opened the way for meaningful dialogue with many of the protestant churches. It thus signalled the end of the Cold War between protestants and catholics in all but a few parts of the world and 'ecumenism' became the new catchword for those on both sides of a previously gaping chasm wishing to build bridges and establish realistic inter-church contacts. Malcolm Muggeridge's definition of the ecumenical movement as three men coming out of a pub on a Saturday night who are so unsteady that they have to support each other if they are to get home, perhaps has more validity for England than for Scotland, but even there, the realisation was dawning in the 1960s that the churches were working on a weakening base and that, in order to preserve what were essential values, they would have to come closer together and acknowledge that they had more in common than divided them.[129]

A landmark in ecumenical relations was the visit paid to the Pope in 1962 by the Moderator of the General Assembly, the Very Rev A. C. Craig, the first holder of the office to make that journey.[130] In 1969 Fr J. H. Dalrymple took up the invitation for a catholic priest to attend the General Assembly. In 1971, a member of the hierarchy, Bishop James Monaghan was present and in 1975 Archbishop Thomas Winning addressed the Assembly in 'a speech that was very warmly received'.[131] The first official talks between the two churches since the Reformation had taken place in 1971 when the catholic hierarchy accepted an invitation from the Assembly to establish a dialogue on the meaning of marriage.[132] Many informal talks had already taken place, the inspiration for which came from the Right Rev Columba Mulcahy, the Abbot of the Cistercian monastery at Nunraw. Although belonging to one of the enclosed contemplative orders, this small dynamic Irishman followed the call of the Vatican Council for the religious orders to adopt their way of life to modern conditions and their work to the contemporary needs of the Church; generally the religious orders in Scotland, as elsewhere, have shown more readiness to adapt to the changing times than have parish-based clergy.

In the Church of Scotland the driving force behind ecumenism was the Iona Community led by the redoubtable Very Rev Dr George MacLeod, later Lord MacLeod of Fuinary. He was not one of those in the ecumenical movement who believed in talk for the sake of talk and who fell over backwards not to offend the other religious party. He raised issues such as the catholic church's hostility to mixed marriages in the hope that a meaningful dialogue could ensue with beneficial results. In 1966 a warning note was sounded by him on this question in *The Scotsman* which showed how slow progress had been in places:

> It is surely improper for public monies, monies subscribed by members of other branches of the Christian Church in Scotland to be used in part to facilitate the teaching of young children that a Roman Catholic married, in say St Giles Cathedral, to another member of Christ's Church is living in sin.[133]

The attitude of many catholic priests to a mixed marriage was conveyed in the official obituary of Canon William Mallon (1904-73), a Glasgow priest:

Firmly and trenchantly he preached the old faith. Mixed marriages were not encouraged. 'Trust Our Lady and she will get you a good Catholic husband'—this was the advice he gave many a girl considering a mixed marriage, and he was often proved right.[134]

Canon Mallon operated in the era when catholics had to seek clerical permission to attend protestant weddings or funerals or to eat meat at weddings held on a Friday. If a catholic was asked to be the best man at a protestant wedding, again permission was required and it was not always forthcoming. These ground-rules applied in many catholic parishes up to the 1960s. Parents who accepted the prevailing orthodoxy were often devastated if one of their children contracted a marriage with somebody not belonging to the church. John McCormack Campbell, a Presbyterian minister in Glasgow (and a convert from Catholicism) was appalled when one such catholic girl was kidnapped by her father and two brothers on the steps of his church and 'he blazed the story over all the papers'.[135] But the church gradually modified its line on mixed marriages after 1970. A written undertaking from both priests that they would do everything in their power to ensure that their children would be brought up in the catholic faith was replaced by a verbal promise to that effect from the catholic partner.

Catholic rigidity or the unguarded observations by catholics that a reunited church would be predominantly catholic in doctrine and ethos roused suspicion in some quarters that ecumenism was a 'take-over bid' or a 'cover' for trying to win converts to catholicism despite high-level denials. One prominent convert to Rome in the 1960s was Ronald Walls, a Presbyterian minister who had been active in the early ecumenical movement and who became a catholic priest.

The Right Rev Andrew Herron, a Church of Scotland administrator and former Moderator, remains wary about where the ecumenical movement might be leading and is critical of George MacLeod's stance on the issue.[136] Both men were on opposite sides of the debate over whether bishops should be appointed and placed in charge of kirk presbyteries (districts) which gripped the church in the mid-1950s. The recommendation was thrown out and for Herron it showed that 'there might not be enough life to launch a revival in Scotland but there is still enough to start a fight religiously speaking'.[137] He thinks that diversity in the Christian tradition is enriching and is not prepared to discount the possibility of a split occurring in the Kirk—with himself among the seceders—if the ecumenical movement progresses so far as to cover the essential differences between the reformed and roman tradition in the Christian Church. He feels that that term ecumenism is used too loosely when it has at least two separate senses: the creation of better relationships among denominations and the creation of unity among denominations. He is an ecumenist in the first sense but an anti-ecumenist in the second sense.[138]

The official obituaries of Scottish priests who died in the 1970s and 1980s show far more examples of priests who had misgivings over the major religious changes taking place in the 1960s than of any who had positively welcomed change and sought to implement it in their parish work.[139] If instructed by a higher authority, some priests reluctantly went along with ecumenical initiatives while inwardly desiring to tell non-roman catholics the errors of their ways; 'they believed themselves to be in possession of everything that was good and true', recalls Fr John Fitzsimmons, an ecumenically-minded priest. Donald MacDonald, in his Partick parish, found that the scope of dialogue depended on the individual response to churchmen on the ground rather than the policy of their superiors, or the wishes of parishioners:

> One of the Presbyterian misconceptions is that everything is decided from Rome . . . but I discovered that if the priest up the road just wants to shut the door of the Presbytery and says none of these new ideas are coming in, they don't come in.[140]

When a charming but conservative Irishman was replaced in Partick by Fr Gaetano Rossi, 'you could practically feel the atmosphere changing overnight . . . anything he was asked to participate in he agreed to'. This accord bore practical fruit when the clergymen realised that the council had plans to demolish the whole of Partick. A local association was formed to save the district: 'it was the sort of thing that could not have been done by the minister or priest alone, but with the two of us, it was almost an unstoppable force in the area'.[141] What remains of tenement life in Partick today was saved by their timely co-operation.

Orangemen were not entirely untouched by the ecumenical spirit as Fr Cornelius Burke showed in the Ayrshire parish of Kilwinning. He was 'a man with a remarkable personality from whom religious differences meant less than nothing'.[142] He had the local Orange flute band raise funds for his church and was welcome inthe local Orange club until his death in 1972 at the age of fifty-one. Archbishop Scanlan of Glasgow was similarly able to break down barriers:

> He and his attire were to become very familiar in George Square and other public places in the city. It was a side of life of which the clergy knew very little. Where he got the key I do not know, but in a short time he had opened all doors to the civic and social life of the city.

The climax of his open diplomacy came on 5 January 1971 in the aftermath of the Ibrox disaster in which sixty-six Rangers supporters were crushed to death at the end of an Old Firm match. The archbishop arranged a Requiem Mass to which he invited the leaders of the city along with the Rangers and Celtic football clubs. His obituary records that 'when the manager of Rangers FC appeared on television to announce that Rangers as a club would attend Requiem Mass in St Andrew's Cathedral, it was the greatest piece of religious news ever heard in Glasgow in my time'.[143]

Gestures which received far less publicity also had a vital bearing on community relations: in Partick, Donald MacDonald records the atmosphere in 1967 when he invited a nun to preach at one of his services, an event unprecedented in Scotland:

> Quite a number in my congregation were suspicious . . . the usual question was raised: 'Are you likely to get asked back yourself?' There was a massive turnout . . . and we got picketed by Pastor Jack Glass . . . His supporters infiltrated the congregation and . . . the moment Sister Catherine got up to start speaking, pandemonium broke out.
>
> It was fascinating to see some of the congregation who I knew had Orange leanings and were hardline Protestants, grabbing hold of Jack Glass's supporters and physically flinging them out of the door . . . He put people's backs up. It was . . . old-fashioned working-class courtesy—this was no way to treat a guest, no way to treat a woman in chruch.[144]

A rebuke to bigotry which had even more resonance in wider society was the appointment of Jock Stein, a non-catholic, as manager of Celtic in 1965. Stein's family associations (centred around the Lanarkshire coalfield) were vehemently protestant, but he fitted in easily with the team seen as the tribal champions of catholic Glasgow.[145] In 1967 Celtic won the European Cup in Lisbon, a victory seen as a great Scottish success by many non-adherents since Celtic was the first team from Scotland to win this coveted trophy. This was perhaps a dramatic example of how greater contact with the outside world was breaking down the parochialism and ethnic rivalries in Scottish life from which sectarianism sprang. In a quieter way the boom in foreign holidays after the 1950s, which took many Scots to southern Europe and indeed to Ireland, may have caused many to come back with a more benign view of the catholic features that were hard to ignore in their own country.

One area where adult protestants and catholics came into increasing contact was in the schools. Though the catholic authorities firmly refused to accede to the growing clamour in the 1960s that denominational (catholic) and state schools be integrated, they had long ago accepted the presence of non-catholic teachers in their schools. Without them the schools would have ground to a halt since Scottish catholics could not produce from their own ranks enough teachers for their own children: 'If not exactly a middle-class profession' teaching 'expresses an instinct for middle-class status and the Catholic community is predominantly working-class'.[146] To make matters worse, catholics newly arrived in the middle-class as doctors, lawyers or indeed senior-level teachers were not encouraging their own children to go into education. By 1978 non-catholics accounted for 22·7% of teaching staff in catholic secondary schools, the proportion varying locally from 11·3% in Lanarkshire to 62·1% in Fife.[147] One catholic head-master pinpoints the better discipline often to be found in catholic schools as well as their openly Christian ethos as explanations for why they may attract certain types of non-catholic teachers.[148] But properly qualified non-catholics have far less chance of promotion than catholic teachers with the same qualifications. One reason given is that senior teachers are supposed to take a forward role in regard to sacramental duties. But leaving that fact aside, there have been some catholic head-teachers so wedded to the present system that they have sought to ensure that every department in their school has a catholic at its head whatever the circumstances. Despite such preconceptions, relations between the two groups of teachers in denominational schools appear to be satisfactory.

If denominational and state schools were sited close to one another, relations between the two headmasters often had a vital bearing on community relations in the locality. Hugh Brown MP recalls that when two new schools were built in the Cranhill district of Glasgow in the 1950s, the rapport between two 'excellent' headmasters had a very beneficial effect in the area.[149]

Outside the metropolis in areas where old divisions had a longer life span it was less easy to curb friction in the educational sphere which had a obvious religious basis, even if the will was there. This was broadly the experience of Tom Kirkwood, who came from the relatively trouble-free town of Dundee to Bannockburn in Stirlingshire, where he was headmaster of the catholic primary school from 1962 to 1971. Observing that community relations had room for improvement, he sought to build bridges, and one of his first acts was to stop his pupils coming to school wearing Celtic scarves: 'I told them that this was a provocation to the others and the parents were quite co-operative.' However, he was fighting an uphill battle as the following incidents may make clear:

1. The custom whereby children collected food parcels to take to the older people in the village was extended to all regardless of religious attachment with the co-operation of local protestant ministers. Next year Mr Kirkwood sought to get both the local

primary schools to join forces in this endeavour but, despite the enthusiasm of the other headmaster, he could not get enough support from protestant parents.

2. The outcome of the first football match between Mr Kirkwood's school and the local non-denominational one. 'It was an eye-opener—some of the Protestant fathers were yelling to their sons to "get stuck into them Popish bastards". As a result one of my boys had to be taken to hospital.'

3. The friction that occurred when protestant and catholic children used the same bus home from school. When the headmaster complained to the bus inspector he was told, 'You know, Mr Kirkwood, I have parents of protestant children phoning me to ask for separate buses for their children. They do not wish their children to share the bus with catholics'.

4. The refusal of any of the local ministers to condemn the smashing of a statue of Our Lady in the grounds of the local catholic church. This happened on three consecutive years when Celtic defeated Rangers and, on each occasion, the culprits apprehended by the police turned out to be members of the Orange lodge.

5. The 'persecution' of a catholic family by their Orange neighbour, who reported to the council that their house was filthy, only for the health inspectors to find it spotless; and who played Orange tunes on the gramophone so that neighbours several doors away complained, at a time when the catholic couple's ten-year-old boy was dying of leukaemia.

This harrassment only stopped when a protestant miner, on hearing of it, threatened to beat the Orangeman up unless he left the family alone. Tom Kirkwood was himself glad to move elsewhere when he reached sixty and could take early retirement, having received little solid backing from local leaders for his bid to bring pupils and parents separated by religion closer together.[150]

These strains were reflected in political behaviour until at least the end of the 1960s. There is clear evidence of a strong correlation between religious denomination and party choice in urban Scotland. In relatively harmonious Dundee, a survey into voting behaviour carried out in 1968 found that 39% of workers from a Church of Scotland background voted Conservative compared to only 6% of workers from a catholic background.[151] Taking the community as a whole, those in the sample who were actually affiliated to the Church of Scotland, identified even more strongly with the Tories: 61% Tory, 39% Labour according to the 1968 survey.[152] Among the catholic sample in Dundee there was a tendency for regular attenders to have a greater propensity towards Labour voting than those nominally attached to the church, which ran counter to the trend in the Church of Scotland sample.[153]

Until the 1964 general election Scotland had a greater proportion of working-class Conservatives than the north of England which had a not dissimilar class structure.[154] The capture by the Tories of the shipbuilding constituency of Glasgow Govan in 1950 and 1951 (a Labour seat continuously since 1918) had shown that working-class Conservatism still had plenty of life in it. Until the late 1960s the Tories still held on to a swathe of working-class wards like Kinning Park, Whiteinch, Partick, and Govanhill associated with Clydeside traditional industries, the composition of whose workforce had remained solidly protestant. Dennistoun went Labour in 1963 but this was a fluke result brought about by the intervention of a 'Protestant Ratepayers' candidate which showed that the Conservative camp was not immune from religious tensions.

In 1945 Sir John McEwen lost the hitherto safe Tory seat of Berwick and Haddington which he had held since 1931: when he entered parliament he was a Presbyterian but his wife was a catholic and he became a convert to Rome in 1940. Political observers disagreed whether it was this special factor or the general swing to the left which lost him the seat. The same question was asked twenty years later when his son, Robin McEwen was given the opportunity to become the first catholic Tory MP to represent a Scottish constituency since the end of the war. In 1965 a by-election took place in the marginal Tory seat of Roxburgh, Selkirk, and Peebles. McEwen lost to the Liberal, David Steel, the son of a well-known Church of Scotland minister. Somebody close to McEwen's campaign commented: 'the Border country does not appear on the surface to be as prejudiced as many other parts of Scotland but deep in the thoughts of these morose Border people prejudice does lie buried'.[155]

In the hitherto safe Tory seat of Glasgow Pollok, Robert Kernohan a staunch protestant with an Irish-sounding name lost in 1964 'because of a revolt by Protestant voters who thought the Tories had chosen a Roman Catholic'.[156] Kernohan was diffident in his comments about the result but admitted that during the campaign, and especially on polling day, the question was frequently asked by voters: 'Is Kernohan a Catholic?'[157]

Turning to Labour it is a curious fact that more unskilled workers became Labour MPs in England and Wales in the post-war decades than in Scotland. The tight-knit nature of Scottish working-class communities means that they are often very conscious of hierarchy and seniority within their own ranks. But a religious factor was also present since the unskilled working-class was disproportionately catholic, especially in the west of Scotland. It is striking that Labour's most loyal support group in Scotland provided so few of its MPs in the 1945–70 period. Selection meetings may have been reluctant to nominate catholics in certain constituencies for fear of alienating protestant voters. That it was not a groundless fear may have been shown in the case of Mary McAllister, a catholic nurse returned for Labour at a by-election in 1958 for the marginal seat of Glasgow Kelvingrove: in the subsequent general election she lost after a campaign in which electoral graffiti had drawn attention to her religion in a derogatory way.[158]

In the same 1959 election, a showdown occurred in the normally safe Labour seat of Coatbridge and Airdrie when Labour nominated James Dempsey, a roman catholic, to fight against Mrs C. S. Morton a sister of the great Rangers football hero of the inter-war years, Alan Morton, who was standing for the Tories. She lost by only 795 votes, an extraordinary result that went flatly against the trend in the rest of Scotland where Labour made spectacular gains. Clearly large numbers of protestant working-class voters allowed their religious folk loyalties to gain precedence over their normal class allegiances.

Besides the two already mentioned, only six newly elected Labour MPs were drawn from the catholic community between 1945 and 1970, two seats (Glasgow Gorbals and Bothwell in Lanarkshire) providing four of these. Perhaps the relegation of the Irish struggle, which up to the 1920s had pushed many of the Scoto-Irish into politics, should also be counted as an explanation. Thereafter, on only one occasion did it assume any particular importance in British politics before the late 1960s. That was in 1948–49 when, under a Labour government, attention began to be focused on the methods used to shore up permanent Unionist rule in Northern Ireland. MPs from Scotland like Neil Maclean, John McGovern and Willie Gallacher were to the fore in condemning the ill-treatment of the nationalist minority (although they were not prominent in The Friends of Ireland group largely drawn from Labour MPs in England with Irish ancestry).[159] An Anti-Partition League was formed in Britain and Ireland which, by 1949 claimed to have twenty-two Scottish branches.[160] Addressing one of its meetings in Govan town hall, Neil Maclean, the local MP left no doubt about his own position: 'What was the use,' he said, 'of sending British armies into the continent to crush the Hitlerism of Germany if they allowed the Hitlerism of Northern Ireland to continue.'[161] Later, in October 1948, Eamon de Valera, the champion of Irish nationalism, arrived in Glasgow on the second stop of an anti-partition tour of Britain. On the first day he addressed a capacity audience of 3,000 in St Andrew's Hall, Glasgow with another 1,400 waiting outside. The next day he was accorded a civic reception by the Lord Provost of Glasgow and he went on to address students at Glasgow University before being entertained to dinner by the Patrick Pearse branch of his party Fianna Fail. Fellow guests included a Presbyterian minister, Rev John McKechnie, professor of Celtic Studies at Glasgow University and Robert McIntyre, briefly Scottish Nationalist MP for Motherwell in 1945 and later to be president of his party. Five Scottish bishops were there and, in a welcoming address, Archbishop Campbell hailed de Valera as 'one of the greatest Christian statesmen in Europe'.[162]

Despite this impressive line-up the conditions for reviving the Irish question in the west of Scotland had largely vanished in the previous quarter century: emigration from Ireland was down to a trickle and the Scoto-Irish had acquired new political allegiances from which they could not be easily diverted because they were a product of their every-day circumstances and not any dim ancestral memories. This was shown in 1949 when the Labour government helped pass a bill that strengthened the union of Northern Ireland with Britain (without insisting on better Unionist treatment of the catholic minority) follow-ing the declaration of an Irish Republic in Dublin which chose to leave the Commonwealth. Neil Maclean defied a Labour ban on anti-partition activities by addressing a large rally in Govan early in 1949 but most of his Labour colleagues in Scotland supported the bill (harsh criticism mainly came from some English Labour members).[163]

At the 1950 general election, four Anti-Partition candidates stood against sitting Labour members. All but one fought Scottish seats and they included the Scottish Nationalist, Oliver Brown who stood in Greenock under the slogan 'Ireland United, Scotland Free'. The best result was obtained in Glasgow Gorbals by William McGuinness who won 1,959 votes, or 4·7% of the poll. He had been treasurer of the local Labour Party when he went to see George Buchanan, the Gorbals MP only to be advised to drop Ireland if he wanted to get ahead in the party.[164] When a by-election arose in 1948 McGuinness supported for the nomination Alice Cullen, a catholic convert who declared that it was precisely because of Ireland that she had entered politics.[165] However, when she absented herself from the Commons on the day of the crucial Irish vote, McGuinness turned against her, his path out of the Labour Party eventually taking him into the SNP (where he would be among the first Glasgow roman catholics to become prominent in its ranks).

Thereafter the interest of most west of Scotland Labour MPs in Ireland was largely a sentimental one. Even though he had to contend with a strong Orange presence in his Bridgeton constituency, James Carmichael MP attended the commemoration of the 1916 Easter Rising in Dublin year after year.[166] Carmichael had belonged to the ILP until succeeding James Maxton in parliament in 1946. On crossing over, he and ILP colleagues had been astonished to find that the membership of the Labour Party in Glasgow was not much bigger than that of the ILP.[167] Concern over possible Communist infiltration and the desire to keep the control of constituency and ward affairs in the hands of a select and dependable group of people often meant that the local power-brokers were reluctant to encourage new blood, so that it was not unknown for applicants wishing to join the Labour Party never to receive an answer or a party card. Once elected, some councillors seemed to stay in place for ever, Labour's dominance reducing the possibility of defeat. The quality of candidates was restricted by the difficulty working men had in getting the necessary time of work to attend to council business:

> Councillors tended to come from a narrow range of occupations: self-employed shopkeepers, publicans, trade-union officials, insurance agents and railwaymen, who were somewhat rare and fortunate in having provision for leave of absence—without pay—included in their conditions of employment.[168]

As the party's arteries hardened, dull and mediocre councillors were increasingly noticeable as was the low calibre of the new intake of Scottish Labour MPs who had an increasingly marginal role in the Parliamentary Labour Party after 1945. It was a sign of the times that few, if any, MPs from Scotland identified with the radical Bevanite wing of the Labour Party in the 1950s.

When the history of Scottish Labour politics after 1918 began to be chronicled in the 1970s, it was tempting to ascribe the gradual slide towards anonymity and conformity on the Scottish left in large measure to the strong catholic presence, especially at municipal level, and to the fact that the party drew much of its support from a community with strongly conservative social instincts. However, this interpretation needs to be somewhat tempered: other Labour local authorities in England and Wales displayed many of the same bureaucratic and authoritarian tendencies, some to a much greater degree than in Glasgow, without the presence of a Labour-voting catholic community. Besides from the 1930s to the 1960s its grip on the party machine was more in the realm of folklore than of fact, so much so that in 1946 one catholic councillor complained that 'the Catholic population of the city were too slow and seemed to think it necessary almost to apologise for their very existence. They should demand more. What was needed was more Catholic councillors in the Corporation.'[169]

It was only in the 1960s that the number of Glasgow Labour councillors from a catholic background began to match the degree of electoral support which the community traditionally gave the party. By 1968 around one-quarter of Glasgow Labour councillors were catholics. Their visibility coincided with a rash of corruption cases involving Labour councillors, at least one of those convicted being a catholic lawyer. In Glasgow scope for corruption existed for a number of reasons: the housing shortage and the perennial scarcity of public house licences (when much of Glasgow was still 'dry') meant that pressure to show favouritism could often be exerted on councillors by relatives wanting a better house or publicans in search of a licence. This trade had always attracted catholics owing to the strength of temperance views among Presbyterians and catholics were still disproportionately affected by the housing shortage. Since most building contracts went to Direct Labour Organisations, the market for private firms was small and competition among them fierce which could also envelop councillors who were felt to be able to pull strings.

Rumours abounded during the late 1960s about the existence of a separate catholic caucus within the Glasgow party. William Taylor, the respected leader of the Labour group from 1962 to 1969 admitted that catholics were occasionally elected to important convenorships even though they lacked the capacity to hold high office. He had his suspicions about the operation of a separate caucus but, when he asked certain colleagues, they would never acknowledge its existence.[170] It was a sign of the times that William Brogan, a Glasgow schoolteacher (and brother of Colm, the Tory iconoclast) was asked to stand for a Labour ward in Glasgow when he was not even a member of the party.[171]

Patrick Trainer, a long-serving Labour councillor, is sure that his colleagues were simply too divided among themselves to form a 'Catholic Mafia'.[172] MPs Hugh Brown and David Lambie who were familiar with the Glasgow Labour scene in the 1960s likewise failed to come across evidence of a religious caucus at work.[173] Lambie doubted whether Labour councillors habitually acted as spokesmen for their church even on sensitive issues, although his West Fife colleague, Willie Hamilton recalls having to point out to a pushy senior cleric in the area that he could expect no special favours from him following the Communist defeat in the constituency in 1950.[174] There is no evidence before the 1970s that catholics systematically voted for catholics in parliamentary nominations. Hugh Brown MP was impressed by the way religion was not raised in the Glasgow Shettleston nomination of 1959. Crusty old John McGovern, long reconciled to the faith, was succeeded by a Jew, Myer Galpern in a seat with plenty of catholic activists. In Dundee, where catholics provided the bulk of Labour votes, they were not strong enough to displace John Strachey, the Eton and Oxford-educated upper-class former Marxist who represented Dundonians from 1945 to 1963, even though many were alienated by his patrician style. His biographer showed how he was a fish out of water and what kind of member his constituents preferred:

> He and his wife were shocked by the bitterness and low-level of education of the half-starving Dundee working-class . . . Many Dundonians would have preferred a more earthy if less distinguished member. Strachey was not easy for Scottish trade-unionists to get to know or understand . . . He and Celia his wife, always looked forward to the moment when, on their journey south, the signpost proclaimed them to be in England again.[175]

Catholics were largely excluded from the ranks of those Labour officials eligible for office because the effects of upward social mobility were not felt in earnest until the 1960s. During that decade the rise of the new left and various kinds of social rebellion challenged many of the traditional moral values with which catholics identified. In 1965 Lord Wheatley sounded a warning note at the congress dinner of the Educational Institute for Scotland (EIS), the largest Scottish teacher's union, when he said that those who 'snear at and criticise what is called the Establishment, and that meant anybody in authority', were 'getting too much support and publicity from the mass media'.[176] Shortly beforehand, Brother Clare, criticising 'the politically threadbare phrase "We've never had it so good" ', expressed his fears for the future and asked, 'What are the planners up to?' He even quoted with approval the words of von Hayek, then still an obscure Austrian economist, that 'there is no justification for the widespread belief that, so long as power is conferred by democratic procedure, it cannot be arbitrary'.[177]

Despite the instinctive conservatism of many priests and teachers, catholics entering the middle-class remained surprisingly loyal to old political ties although they might now be living in neighbourhoods with no clear ethnic or religious identification. The 1968 Dundee survey showed that a startling 88% of non-manual working catholics still identified with the Labour Party. The feeling of belonging to an under-privileged minority not yet in the mainstream of Scottish life may have clung to a surprising number of those who moved from traditional neighbourhoods. The claim made in 1964 by political journalist, James Gordon that 'most Catholics seem only too anxious to vote Conservative as a status symbol to complete their break with their working-class background' was not really borne out in practice.[178] Even the maverick Colm Brogan who was a paid-up member of the Conservatives in England, admitted that he would drop out of membership if he moved into a number of Scottish constituencies where the party still had 'an Orange aura'.[179] Writing in 1962, he recognised that 'the Scottish Catholic middle-class of remotely Irish descent is either sentimentally "Labour" or quite staggeringly apolitical'. He went on:

> Among these, there must be a large majority whose natural symapthies lie with the Conservative Party . . . They stay away . . . because that party can be represented as anti-Catholic, or at least tolerant of the intolerant.
> This is bad, but not only for the Scottish Conservative Party. It is also

bad for the Scottish Catholic community. A minority group such as our own which is not economically self-sustaining needs to have sympathetic friends among those who handle public funds and have their fingers on the levers of public power . . .

One Protestant Conservative who wrote to me said that he and his like wanted to get rid of the shellbacks who are still thinking in terms of the Home Rule battles before the First World War. He said that he and his like will not be able to do anything unless able young Catholics are willing to come forward and take the places of the people they want to push out.[180]

Just before the 1964 general election the *Scottish Catholic Observer* published a letter from one priest, Francis McHugh counselling Tory support because the party was for 'maintaining sound values'.[181] This was a debatable claim in light of the recent Profumo affair and he was rare in his outspokenness. The clergy generally maintained a low profile in politics at a time of consensus between the major parties, many of the younger ones coming from working-class or lower middle-class homes that identified politically with the Labour Party. Some may even have been aware that the welfare state promoted by Labour since 1945 fitted neatly into traditional catholic doctrine holding government responsible for meeting many social and economic needs.

The 1964 election saw Donald Anderson, a Hamilton-born catholic (educated at St Aloysius College, Glasgow) nominated as the Tory candidate for the previously marginal seat of Glasgow Scotstoun. He was unsuccessful and it was not until 1969 that the first catholic Tory was returned to Glasgow Corporation.[182] This was Cyril Lombardi, winner of a by-election for middle-class Pollokshields. He was a director of companies in the wine and spirit trade and, appropriately, he hailed from the Italian community which had no anti-Tory complexes over Ireland or past discrimination. Lombardi was followed by Henry McGoldrick and Gerald Somers, ex-president of Glasgow University men's union both being elected to the Corporation in the early 1970s. None of these three made a major impact in local politics and, in hindsight, their elevation would seem to indicate a growing toleration by middle-class Presbyterians of catholic candidates rather than a swing to the right by any large section of catholics.

The Scottish National Party (SNP), an emergent force in politics during the 1960s, also had its share of catholic candidates at parliamentary and municipal level. In the early 1950s John Campbell identified himself with the Scottish Covenant movement campaigning for Home Rule along with fellow law catholics, John Bayne and Michael Byrne. On being asked how the catholic minority would fare under a Scottish parliament, he responded: 'if you expect the Protestants in the Six Counties to go in with the Catholic majority in the rest of Ireland, we must similarly be prepared to go in with the majority in

Scotland'.[183] Sir Patrick Dollan argued in the press with Campbell that:

> Great Britain is too small to permit of its being carved into tiny units. A favourite Communist strategy is to preach home rule for every other country except Russia . . . The most consistent supporters of Home Rule in Scotland are Communists and fanatical anarchists . . . The Scottish people as a whole are better off than the people in any other country except America and for this they have much to be grateful for British guidance and cooperation.[184]

H. J. Paton, author of *The Claim of Scotland*, might have been thinking of Dollan when he wrote concerning the Scoto-Irish, 'it is not unknown for them to proclaim that Scotland has all the self-government she requires, when they succeed in joining the Establishment'.[185] Nationalist feeling died down until the 1960s when the SNP began to acquire support among parts of the lower middle-class in small town Scotland, among working-class 'floating' voters, and among residents of new towns like Cumbernauld. In 1967 the SNP finally won a sensational by-election victory in the Labour stronghold of Hamilton. It has been partly attributed to 'the Orange vote in Larkhall and else-where' swinging to the victor, Mrs Winifred Ewing, in a bid to ruin Labour's hope of victory.[186] In trying to break into Labour strong-holds in west central Scotland there is no evidence that the SNP systematically played the Orange card, but irritation with catholic fidelity to Labour sometimes emerged as in the words of the SNP's Iain McCormick:

> Politically many of these Scots fail to appreciate that they are now as Scottish as anyone else, and fail to see that Scotland's future is their future.
>
> It is more the pity that so many working-class Catholics regard it as an article of faith to vote Labour come-what-may. Such a vote is meaningless and only matched in futility by the ritual Conservative vote of working-class Orangemen.
>
> Catholics could make a great contribution to the Scotland of the future were they to cast aside the 'ghetto' approach to Scottish politics now.[187]

As well as being a son of Dr John McCormick, one of the party's founding fathers in the 1930s, McCormick, later an SNP MP, was him-self a catholic convert. However, at least one of the fifteen SNP councillors elected to Glasgow Corporation in 1968 and 1969 was a catholic from a working-class background—namely Tom Brady, an electrician who briefly represented the Calton ward. Most of these gains were not made in the remaining working-class Tory seats but in Labour strongholds like Maryhill, Shettleston, and Cowcaddens where protestant manual workers with Tory or weak Labour affiliations swelled the SNP vote. Local Labour complacency, corruption cases, and the unpopularity of the Wilson government helped engineer this upset. Although the nationalist challenge quickly collapsed in no small part due to the inexperience of its elected representatives, Labour was in a troubled state down to and beyond the 1960s, internal differences over denominational schools contributing to its malaise.

A survey conducted in 1966 had shown that a majority of Glasgow Labour councillors, party workers, and electors favoured school integration:

School integration: preference of Labour councillors, party workers and electors, 1966 (%)

	For	Against
Councillors	77	21
Party workers	83	21
Electors	60	36

Source: McLean, *Legend of Red Clydeside*, p. 229, quoting Ian Budge *et al.*, *Political Stratification and Democracy*, Macmillan, 1972, p. 92.

Even within catholic ranks muffling dissent over this issue 'was not as easily accomplished as it had been in earlier, more perilous days when the self-preserving instinct to close ranks soon quietened any protest'.[188] A 1967 survey found 63% of Glasgow catholics in favour of integrating protestant and catholic schools, a figure that has not been repeated in subsequent surveys.[189] Catholic schools were then going through a crisis which only abated in the early 1970s, caused by the rising curve of student numbers and the lack of sufficient staff. 'Many catholic schools were on the point of collapse', much to the alarm of some middle-class catholics, who discovered that as late as 1972–73 the average pupil-teacher ratio in catholic secondary schools was 20·5%, compared to 17·3% for non-denominational ones. The fact that university honours graduates formed only 19·3% of teaching staff in catholic schools in the most populous region of Scotland, compared with 24·8% for non-denominational ones, raised further disquiet about the quality of education in the catholic sector.[190] But the bulk of upwardly mobile catholics still faithful to the church were not yet prepared to defy their bishops over schools just as they showed few signs of renouncing completely their Labour Party loyalties.

Nevertheless, in 1969, Richard Buchanan, one of Glasgow's two catholic Labour MPs, broke ranks and declared that 'integration up to the intermediate state . . . must come about because of the chronic shortage of teachers'.[191] Much more serious was the decision of the Glasgow City Labour Party in March 1970 to pass the resolution that 'segregation of schools on religious grounds be terminated but that provision for religious instruction be continued in accordance with individual belief'.[192] Although the resolution was not binding on the

Labour council group (then in opposition), senior Labour figures were aghast at the decision. Daniel Docherty, the Labour spokesman on education said:

> A decision like this is political suicide . . . If those people want to lose the next election; this is a sure way of doing it. There will be a riot in the country if this sort of thing is forced through.[193]

With a general election looming, Labour's William Ross, Scottish Secretary of State even took the unusual step of allaying catholic fears about the future of their schools in a party political radio broadcast.[194] But the guardians of catholic schools were not easily pacified. The church was aware that, contrary to rumour, it could rely on few Labour councillors to faithfully reflect its views on education and indeed other public issues with a religious dimension. Devout councillors like John Storrie who used to chide colleagues like Richard Buchanan for 'eating meat on an obscure saint's feast day' in the corporation restaurant had given way, by the late 1960s to more secular catholic representatives usually lacking ties with any of the catholic groups and who 'toed the line' on separate schools less out of conviction than because it was too costly politically to do otherwise.[195]

Fr John Tracy, the Jesuit headmaster of St Aloysius College, the catholic fee-paying school, was not mollified by assurances that the Labour council group had no intention of implementing the decision of the city party. He was already concerned with Labour plans to axe fee-paying schools that were dependent on state backing and, during the 1970 general election, he sent a letter to the parents of his 850 pupils suggesting that they should not vote Labour if they wished to save the school.[196] One of the school governors was John Mains, leader of the Labour group, and he resigned from the board in protest. It is unclear what political effect, if any, such statements had. Labour was voted out of office in 1970 but no seats changed hands in Glasgow. However, in 1967, Rev Geoff Shaw (a senior figure in Scottish local government when it was revamped in the 1970s) had been a casualty of the schools question. He was standing for the marginal Labour ward of Kingston and went on record as saying 'I believe the continued separation of Roman Catholic and Protestant children at separate schools is one of the main contributory factors to the bigotry and intolerance in our midst'.[197] His biographer reckons that from then on the election in this inner Glasgow ward was as good as over. A local catholic priest preached against Shaw and one 'went so far as to say that to vote for Shaw was to break the First Commandment'.[198] In a declining inner city ward with a high proportion of elderly people, some accustomed to acting on advice from the pulpit, Shaw lost.

Eleven years later, the Archbishop of Glasgow read a lesson at his funeral and described him as 'a personal friend and dedicated Christian, dedicated to the causes of social justice and to the well being of the people of the Region'.[199] In the meantime a *modus vivendi* had been restored between the two institutions to which most catholics pledged their spiritual and political allegiances. The Labour Party chose to support denominational schools as long as they were seen to have the backing of catholic parents, although motions hostile to the segregated system continued to be submitted to the party's Scottish conference well into the 1970s.

The cracks in the consensus over education followed hard on the heels of disagreements within Scottish catholic ranks over the extent to which the reforms emanating from Rome should be implemented. For news from Scotland the Vatican relied on the apostolic nuncio in London whose concerns were mainly with the English church. Scotland's remoteness was only partly assuaged in 1969 when Archbishop Gray was elevated to the rank of cardinal. William Heard, the other Scot in the college of cardinals, had been a member of the central preparatory commission for the Ecumenical Council and from 1962 to 1964 he had taken part in all four sessions of the council where he was 'far from being a diehard conservative'.[200] However, the catholic church in Great Britain was ill prepared for change and the result was considerable confusion about belief and practice, a sudden and widespread weakening of Catholic identity, a polarisation of opinion, and a weakening of acceptance of the authority of the Church'.[201]

This at any rate is how an official church agency described the reaction of the English church to 'Vatican II' and it would not altogether misrepresent the Scottish response either. Elderly priests and laity found it difficult to come to terms with the replacement of the Latin Mass with English, the repositioning of altars so that priests no longer celebrated with their backs to the congregation, and the phasing out of so much ritual and ceremony. The introduction of a new ritual, whereby worshippers wish each other the sign of peace by shaking hands was another unwelcome innovation for those priests reared in a more austere tradition. The Vatican Council proved a traumatic experience for old style priests like Canon Joseph Daniel, of whom there were many, 'with their strong attachment to the tradition of a triumphalist Church'.[202] Even Monsignor David McRoberts, who 'as a young man . . . had favoured change', felt little sympathy with many aspects of the post-Vatican II world. His obituarist recalls that:

> although he was no theologian, he had no difficulty in identifying the 'new insights' as simply old heresies writ fresh. The liturgical changes depressed him—maimed rites, as he somewhere describes them, with little of that liturgical orderliness, and nothing whatsoever of the consoling beauty of the

Church's traditional music . . . The speed with which changes had been introduced seemed to show a lack of sensitivity: 'one gets the impression that . . . are clutching at any gimmick just to give the impression that they are doing something. All that seems to result from that sort of thing is that the older generation are alienated while the younger generation are left quite unimpressed.'[203]

Tensions between the generations was perhaps most strenuously reflected within the priesthood itself during the 1960s. Men still took charge of parishes after their prime and many tended to see the parish as their property. Under a priest of the old school a curate could be 'treated as an adolescent' and discouraged from showing initiative.[204] In the 1960s growing numbers began to question their subordinate role to autocratic parish priests. Since Scottish priests did not have a national council which met periodically as in England, they lacked the institutional forum in which to ventilate their concerns and compare notes with others. Many who underwent a 'crisis of identity' and began to 'query the relevance of their recluse seminary training to the realities of life', abandoned the priesthood and went to university as mature students to gain professional qualifications in social work or in education; some fell in love with women whom they later married, others returned to the ministry more qualified for the tasks ahead but the church could ill afford to forfeit the energy and commitment of those who cut adrift in the 1960s.[205]

The laity were not apparently traumatised to the same degree by the pace of change or by frustrated expectations regarding such sensitive issues as the celibacy of priests and the extent to which the hierarchical church should accommodate democratic procedures in its institutional practices. A survey of the *Scottish Catholic Observer*'s readership in 1967 found that 72% preferred the Mass in English compared with 68% of English and Welsh catholics polled in a similar survey, while 32% felt Vatican II had resulted in too much change as opposed to 28% who felt there had been too little.[206]

The issue that undoubtedly produced the greatest degree of anxiety and unrest within the clergy and between the church authorities and the laity in the 1960s and indeed beyond was artificial birth control. Planning a family by the use of artificial contraception was an accepted convention in a protestant and increasingly secular society like Scotland and here catholics found themselves under greater pressure to accept church teaching or else to conform to social norms than in perhaps most other European countries. In 1968 a commission set up by Pope Paul VI to review the church's prohibition on artificial birth control found itself split, but with a clear majority stating that the church's teaching could change without losing theological respectability.[207] In the encyclical *Humanae Vitae* Paul VI chose to accept the minority report. While slowing the progress of the ecumenical movement, *Humanae Vitae* did not result in a widespread drift from the church. Instead people began to 'shop around' and look for priests who appreciated the personal and family difficulties involved in arriving at a decision over birth control and who were prepared to underline the role of individual conscience in making a choice about regulating one's family. Rennie McOwan detected the growth of 'compartmentalised Catholicism' in the late 1960s whereby 'people said in effect that the encyclical was not an infallible document, that the hierarchy had got it wrong, and they carried on making decisions in conscience according to their circumstances'.[208]

Such a dilemma mainly affected middle-class catholics. In dioceses like Motherwell where the church was overwhelmingly working-class and where tight-knit communities had not been subject to as much physical disruption or social changes as in Glasgow, the old folk catholicism blended in more successfully with new innovations in liturgy and practice than was the case elsewhere.

In 1968 two Scottish-based priests actually debated *Humanae Vitae* from differing standpoints in the main Scottish catholic weekly[209] although Gerard Hughes, the catholic chaplain at Glasgow University was the only one in Scotland to publicly express his misgivings about the line taken by the encyclical. The pastoral letter from the Scottish hierarchy endorsing it was among the firmest emanating from any national church in the catholic world which showed how isolated Fr Hughes was.[210] A counterblast from a small but highly articulate section of the laity then ensued (an unusual development in the context of modern catholic Scotland) with the formation of the Scottish Lay Action Movement (SLAM) at the end of 1968. The driving force behind SLAM was the Glasgow solicitor James Armstrong who, in politics, was a firm Tory with a libertarian perspective. Along with other catholics mainly drawn from the liberal professions, he sought to 'encourage intelligent debate on the problems facing Christians' and to foster the conditions that might allow more say for the laity in the running of the church.[211] In a letter to Archbishop Scanlan in 1968 he was asked to 'broaden and intensify dialogue with the laity' on the question of birth control.[212] When SLAM changed its name to the Scottish Catholic Renewal Movement in 1969, it issued a more forthright statement that referred to 'considerable discrepancies which exist from parish to parish and especially diocese to diocese, each a source of confusion and scandal'. It complained that the laity 'who contribute all the financial resources of the Church, have little or no say in how these are deployed' and that 'the true status of women is not reflected in the Church'.[213] For a time the SCRM made Glasgow a lively centre of theological and ecumenical discussion by inviting to the city some of the most progressive of contemporary catholic theologians such as Hans Kung, Karl Rahner, Edward Schillebeeckx, and Gregory Baum whose meeting in 1977 was picketed by a small group of ultra-traditionalists.[214]

A more serious collision had occurred in October 1971 when Archbishop Scanlan informed the clergy that 'the so-called Scottish Catholic Renewal Movement had not received approbation from the Scottish hierarchy. . . and therefore had no authority to use the title "Catholic" '.[215] (Earlier that year, when Glasgow University awarded the archbishop an honorary degree along with Hans Kung, the radical theologian, Scanlan very ostentatiously walked out just prior to the reception for Kung.[216]) Rather surprisingly the SCRM agreed to drop the word 'Catholic' from its title. It subsequently survived until the mid-1970s before running out of steam and disappearing altogether. By now James Armstrong was increasingly alienated from the church as an institution. Moreover the SCRM had been unable to follow up the success of its well-advertised public meetings by organising regular debates within the Scottish catholic community. Unaided by the stimulus of outside speakers its impact at parish level or even in the official lay apostolate, was negligible. A major oversight was the failure to organise on a democratic basis—a committee was never formally elected nor an AGM held.[217] As the 1970s wore on those Scottish catholics who were attempting a total rethink of their religious commitment in the contemporary context were dispersed, demoralised and defeated, some to become progressively alienated from the church itself and others to become immersed in purely secular political activities.

A life spent in a hierarchical church where obedience from the laity was taken for granted meant that Scanlan was unable to handle the emergence of a movement like the SCRM. However, he was less unbending towards ecumenical activities in the higher education sphere. In 1965 an Interdenominational Chaplaincy Centre was set up at Strathclyde University, the second university in Glasgow, which Columba Ryan, of the Dominican Order helped make a success.[218] At Glasgow University, the Rev Professor William Barclay, a well known biblical scholar and a Kirk minister, became the Catholic Society's honorary president in 1970 after having addressed it on scripture.[219] But in 1971 the Glasgow University chaplain Gerard Hughes SJ faced dismissal by the Archbishop who had objected to him giving Holy Communion at interdenominational services to non-catholics. The case received prominent coverage in the local press and a petition carrying 3,000 signatures, gathered by the students was presented to the archbishop appealing for a change of heart. Fr Hughes also had the support of his order, the Jesuits, and negotiations between the Jesuit Provincial and Thomas Winning, newly appointed auxiliary bishop in Glasgow produced a compromise that allowed him to stay on for at least another year; the Jesuit review *The Month* noted that this was the first instance in Britain, certainly in Scotland, of a prelate bowing to public opinion and reversing a decision, but it could just as easily have been said that in few other dioceses would such firm disciplinary procedures have been attempted in the first place.[220]

The Scottish Catholic Observer tried valiantly to reflect the issues that were confronting the church in the moral and secular sphere in the 1960s even at the risk of being controversial. Under Rennie McOwan in the early 1960s 'it had a brief period of brilliant and challenging editorship'[221] with circulation standing as high as 40,000 copies.[222] Now that the daily press reported much catholic news (a sign of the minority's advancing integration), it was felt that, to remain viable, the paper should grasp the opportunity to be the platform for discussions about the issues inside and outside the church affecting the catholic community. However, being dependent on church sales meant the paper was vulnerable to priests who did not relish frank debate. It was not unknown for entire parish sales to be cancelled because the parish clergy were offended by some item. The pressure also came from the very top in the early 1960s:

> Bishop James Ward . . . asked the *Glasgow Observer* . . . to withdraw from its pages the serialisation of Xavier Rynne's book on the debates of the Vatican Council.
> Other diocese did not want it withdrawn: it went into the east edition and came out of the west. The west clergy bought the east edition.[223]

Apparently the bishop was worried about the impact on the 'simple west of Scotland faithful of reported extracts from the disputes that were occurring among the bishops of the world assembled in Rome. In 1974 Vincent Hastie, the paper's editor (the fourth appointment in four years), was drawn to publicly criticise priests who banned the paper because it had given advance publicity to the visit of radical priest Daniel Berrigan to Glasgow as the guest of the SCRM.[224] Another casualty was Colm Brogan, the catholic Tory, growing increasingly crusty in his old age: in 1974 the editor of the *Scottish Catholic Observer* admitted that 'a number of people very high in the echelons of the Roman Catholic Church in Scotland made it patently obvious to me that they had considered his writings vitriolic and they would rather he would not write'.[225]

By muzzling Brogan the catholic authorities made it plain that they preferred to calm opinion and still debate. The *Observer* might have been better able to stave off church directives if a broadly based lay movement had emerged in Scotland which could have acted as a separate pole of influence.

In England pastoral councils (consultative bodies of 'clerics, religious and laity which can be established as a permanent institution or as an *ad hoc* body as required by the bishop')[226] had emerged in a number of dioceses. By 1980 this movement was strong enough for a National Pastoral Conference to be held in England where the representatives of the laity debated the state of the church and made a series of recommendations for reform in its structures and practices, some of which were favourably received by the hierarchy. But no equivalent gathering took place in Scotland even though a Scottish Catholic Lay Apostolate Council existed with the approval of the hierarchy. Sheriff John Bayne, a former chairman of the council pointedly reminded the church in 1974 that at the 1965 session of the Vatican Council it was agreed that the laity 'share in the priestly, prophetic and royal office of Christ, and therefore have their role to play in the mission of the whole People of God in the Church and in the world'.[227] Sheriff Bayne, in his own words, stated that Vatican II had established that 'an individual layman is permitted and sometimes even obliged to express his opinion on things which concern the good of the church'. For Bayne lack of progress in Scotland could be explained on the following grounds:

> Only three of the eight dioceses have a diocesan lay council and accordingly the representatives of the other five dioceses are not selected by the laity, and have no link with the people they are supposed to represent . . .
> Sad to relate, there are priests who see no need for parish councils, and who believe that the basic duties of the layman should be confined to praying, obeying, and paying. 'Lay participation' in some parishes extends only to such necessary tasks as taking up the collection at Sunday Mass. Are they scared that yielding responsibility will mean a challenge to their position or are they unwilling to shoulder the extra responsibility of running (as they see it) a parish council.[228]

Parish councils tended to function best in middle-class parishes in the manner envisaged for them. Here parish clergy were less likely to have a paternalistic attitude towards the laity and were more inclined to regard them as 'professional equals', people with skills that the parish council could make use of.[229] In the diocese of Paisley and Dunkeld, parish councils were conspicuous by their absence in the 1960s and 1970s—indications of the local bishops' lack of enthusiasm for the concept of the lay apostolate.

But in a time of flux when morale was low because of the unprecedented pace of change inside and outside the church in Scotland, it is not surprising that where they could, priests opted for the tried and tested formulae. The extent of the malaise was revealed in a frank assessment published in 1977 as part of the obituary of Archbishop

Scanlan who had retired in 1974 on reaching his seventy-fifth birthday:

> During that decade [1964-74] the Church suffered a dismal decline. There were many causes but the most obvious is emigration from Glasgow. During those ten years Glasgow lost the equivalent of twenty good healthy parishes. Further, there is no doubt the morale of the clergy declined in those ten years. Again many causes could be deduced; aftermath of the Council, longer wait for parishes, the decay of so many city parishes, for nothing saps the morale more than saying Sunday Mass in a church virtually empty, but I think a major factor was diocesan finance. When he came to Glasgow the diocese had large reserves. When he resigned without in any way attributing blame to him, the fact was that all these reserves had gone. I well remember how shattered my contemporaries were when the late Bishop Ward revealed to a Senate meeting that the diocese was in financial difficulties.
>
> They found it hard to accept the reality that now they were in a poor diocese. To what extent the Archbishop grasped these facts, I do not know. Usually the stokers are aware the ship is sinking before the captain.[230]

The social changes and new economic opportunities that opened up after 1945 ameliorated the physical condition of the catholic community while still leaving it predominantly working-class. The raising of long-established working-class communities as part of an ambitious and flawed process of urban development, weakened the hitherto strong group identity of the catholic community and hastened the process of assimilation with the rest of society.

Buffeted by environmental changes, Vatican II, and the growth of materialist and secular values, the church lost ground especially in the newer communities where so many Scottish catholics were located by the end of the 1960s. Many priests lived to see the traditions and values they had long accepted as norms set aside or disrupted and it was often an embittering experience since the pressure for change was emanating from the heart of the institutional church as much as anywhere else.

At least denominational education, the guarantee of catholic faith and morals was not directly threatened in the 1945-70 period, one which in fact saw an unprecedented expansion in the catholic education sector. But teacher shortages and the expectations of middle-class catholic parents which denominational schools could not always meet, placed strains on the system and, by the end of the 1960s, the more percipient observers could see even stiffer challenges ahead caused as much by demographic changes as by the hostility of certain non-catholic sectors.

Whether catholic schools helped to instill a strong religious consciousness or merely provided a catholic identity with vestigial religious overtones is debatable although the situation varied from school to school. Although they were not in themselves a direct cause of conflict, separate schools helped to encourage the survival of the overall religious divide in Scottish society. Without them, the assimilation of catholic and non-catholic children in Scotland would undoubtedly have occurred at a faster rate.

Luckily, the major changes of the post-war years were not complicated by a revival of the Irish question, but evidence from the 1940s and 1950s showed that there was still plenty of indigeneous mistrust and friction to be overcome. Improvements in community relations reflected in inter-marriage figures and a growth of new opportunities for catholics in the labour market did not occur uniformally and there were clear variations in region, occupation, and district.

Much of the impetus for better understanding arose from structural changes in the economy and in the physical environment which sometimes had their origins outside Scotland in the international economy. Instead of giving a lead, elites modified their behaviour to reflect the more open and less internally divided post-war atmosphere, but a concerted effort to foster greater tolerance and mutual respect was not forthcoming: inertia and fear of bold experimentation still paralysed much of Scottish society. It is significant that up to the close of the 1960s, religious sectarianism was still a taboo subject not talked about in the public forum in case the extent of this fissure within Scottish society produced uncomfortable shock-waves that disturbed the peace of institutions, political parties and communities that had not always managed to contain religious differences within their own ranks.

Progress was measured by small gestures and unspectacular shifts in mood and style rather than by a wholesale assault on, and repudiation of institutions and practices that emphasised religious and ethnic difference. The ecumenical movement of the 1960s marked a bolder departure. Without exaggerating its impact, it emerged at a fortuitous moment in Scottish life since with Northern Ireland exploding into conflict after 1968, new challenges to the fragile web of community relations in the west of Scotland were not slow in presenting themselves.

Notes

1 David McRoberts, 'The archdiocese of Glasgow', in *Scottish Survey, Scottish Catholic Herald and Glasgow Observer, 1878-1955.*

2 *Western Catholic Calendar, 1975,* Burns, Glasgow, 1975.

3 John Durkan.

4 Interview with James Darragh, 3 August 1982.

5 *Statutes of the Archdiocesan Council for Social Action,* Glasgow, 1945.*

6 Letter from Charles Smith (Edinburgh roman catholic), 28 June 1985.

7 Charles Smith.

8 Talk with Willie Hamilton MP, 3 April 1984.

9 Both men produced works describing their conversion:

Douglas Hyde, *I Believed*, Heinemann, 1952, and Hamish Fraser, *Fatal Star*, Burns, Glasgow, 1954.

10 *GO*, 3 March 1950.

11 Details of Hamish Fraser's life are obtained from his obituary in *The Times*, 29 October 1986.

12 Obituary of Walter Glancy, *CDS*, 1981.

13 *Irish Weekly*, 31 March 1951.

14 *GO*, 31 July 1953.

15 Letter from Lawrence Daly, 4 June 1986.

16 Thomas J. Fitzpatrick, *Catholic Secondary Education in South-west Scotland before 1972: its Contribution to the Change in Status of the Catholic Community*, Aberdeen University Press, 1986, pp. 104-5.

17 Checkland, *The Upas Tree, Glasgow 1875-1975*, p. 67.

18 Checkland, p. 72.

19 Darragh, 'The Catholic population in Scotland, 1878-1977', in David McRoberts, *Modern Scottish Catholicism*, p. 223.

20 McRoberts, *Scottish Survey*.

21 Darragh, 'Catholic population', p. 230.

22 Checkland, *The Upas Tree*, p. 68.

23 Obituary of Cornelius O'Leary, *CDS*, 1975.

24 John Burrows, *Benny Lynch*, p. 2.

25 Dr Patrick Connolly, *Sunday Standard*, 7 March 1982.

26 Interview with Dr Patrick Connolly, 29 April 1984.

27 Burrowes, *Benny Lynch*, p. 2.

28 Private communication.

29 *SCO*, 7 July 1978.

30 Private communication.

31 Interview with Michael Fallon, Edinburgh journalist.

32 Privately expressed opinion.

33 James Coffey, 'Scotland's cardinal', *SCO*, 10 May 1985.

34 *GO*, 2 November 1951.

35 Charles Smith.

36 Interview with the Rev Anthony Ross OP, 21 December 1981.

37 M. P. Murray, 'In Retrospect, an historical view of the early days of the Newman Association in Glasgow, 1945-46', unpublished Ms; interview with J. McLay, 20 December 1982.

38 Anthony Ross OP, 'The development of the Scottish Catholic community, 1878-1978', in McRoberts, *Modern Scottish Catholicism* , p. 51. Fr Ross later identified Canon Daniel to me as the author of this remark.

39 Obituary of Right Rev. David McRoberts (1912-78), *CDS*, 1980, p. 377.

40 McRoberts, Obituary, *CDS*, 1980, p. 387.

41 Darragh, 'Catholic population', p. 221.

42 Fitzpatrick, *Catholic Secondary Education*, p. 151.

43 Cooney, *Scotland and the Papacy*, p. 95.

44 Private opinion.

45 View of David Lambie MP, interview, 26 April 1984.

46 Fitzpatrick, *Catholic Secondary Education*, p. 115.

47 Fitzpatrick, p. 152.

48 Darragh, 'Catholic population', p. 234.

49 Interview with Professor Tom Carberry, 30 April 1984.

50 McRoberts, *Scottish Survey*; interview with Bishop Joseph Devine, 21 August 1981.

51 Fitzpatrick, p. 152.

52 Information from Ian O. Bayne, a former Aloysian.

53 Anthony Ross OP, 'Resurrection', in Duncan Glen (ed.), *Whither Scotland*, Gollancz, London, 1971, p. 121.

54 Fitzpatrick, *Catholic Secondary Education*, p. 153.

55 Cooney, *Scotland and the Papacy*, p. 84.

56 Ross, 'Development of the Catholic community', p. 50.

57 Interview with James Darragh.

58 Interview with Dr Patrick Reilly of Glasgow University, 14 May 1982.

59 Fitzpatrick, p. 148.

60 Interview with Dr Thomas J. Winning, Archbishop of Glasgow, 4 July 1986.

62 I would like to thank those members of the teaching profession and officials of the EIS who provided information about how the denominational sector is represented in the EIS.

62 Interview with James Gordon, 25 March 1986.

63 Darragh, 'Catholic population', p. 224.
64 Obituary of Jack Coia (1899–1981), *Times*, 18 August 1981.
65 Interview with Tom Carberry.
66 I am grateful to Ian and John Bayne for the information about the Scottish legal profession in the above two paragraphs.
67 Private communication.
68 Fr Anthony Ross OP, 'The church in Scotland', in J. Cummings and P. Burns (eds.), *The Church Now*, Gill & Macmillan, Dublin, 1980, p. 28.
69 Ross, 'Development of the Catholic community', p. 51.
70 Fitzpatrick, p. 151.
71 Tom Carberry.
72 Interview with Hugh Brown MP, 26 April 1984; see James Patrick, *A Glasgow Gang Observed*, Eyre Methuen, London, 1972. This was the pseudonym used by the name of the son of a senior member of the Catholic teaching profession in order to penetrate the gangs.
73 Smout, *A Century of the Scottish People*, pp. 55–6.
74 Checkland, *The Upas Tree*, p. 40.
75 W. J. McKechin, *A School in Eastwood Park: a Case Study in Local Authority Decision-making and Public Participation*, Paisley College of Technology, Working Paper, No. 9, 1979, p. 49.
76 McKechin, p. 23.
77 McKechin, p. 39.
78 Quoted in Murray, *The Old Firm*, p. 222.
79 Murray, p. 223.
80 Quoted in H. F. Moorhouse, 'Professional football and working-class culture: English thought and Scottish evidence', *Sociological Review*, 32, 2, 1984, p. 302.
81 Gerald McNee, *The Story of Celtic, an Official History, 1888-1978*, Stanley Paul, London, 1978, p. 7; Murray, *The Old Firm*, p. 63.
82 Opinion of Patrick Reilly; letter from Neil J. McDermott in *GH*, 30 November 1986.
83 Interview with former MP Richard Buchanan, 16 June 1986.
84 Conversation with retired headmaster James Breen, 4 July 1986.
85 Tom Carberry.
86 Tom Carberry.
87 Tom Carberry.
88 Interview with Alex Ferry, 23 November 1984.
89 Alex Ferry.
90 George Scott, *The RCs*, Hutchinson, London, 1967, p. 98.
91 Scott, *The RCs*, p. 98.
92 Obituary in *GO*, 16 October 1953.
93 Alex Ferry.
94 Gerald Dunne, 'The Knights of St Columba, the case against', *SCO*, 21 May 1985.
95 Ian and Gill Bayne.
96 Private information.
97 R. B. McCallum and Alison Readman, *The British General Election of 1945*, Frank Cass, London, 1964.
98 David Lambie MP.
99 Moorhouse, 'Professional football', p. 301.
100 James Campbell, *Invisible Country*, Weidenfeld & Nicolson, London, 1984, p. 3.
101 Interview with the Rev. Donald MacDonald, 16 April 1984.
102 C. M. Oakley, quoted in Moray McLaren, *The Scots*, Penguin, London, 1951, p. 91.
103 Harvie, *No Gods*, p. 128.
104 Darragh, 'Catholic population', p. 230.
105 Colm Brogan, *The Glasgow Story*, p. 195.
106 Ron Ferguson, *Geoff, the Life of Geoffrey M. Shaw*, Famedram, 1979, pp. 101–2.
107 Donald MacDonald.
108 Compton Mackenzie, *My Life and Times, Octave X, 1953-63*, Chatto & Windus, 1967, p. 47.
109 John Cormack, 'My hectic life', *Protestant Telegraph*, 22 February 1969.
110 Interview with John McLaughlin, 21 August 1984.
111 Dollan Memorial Library Brochure, 1969.
112 *Vigilant*, December 1955.
113 *Vigilant*, No. 1 (n.d.).
114 Interview with the Rev. James Currie, Dunlop, Ayrshire, 26 March 1986.
115 Iain McGregor, *The Holy Terrier*, Edinburgh, typescript, n.d.
116 *Scotsman*, 9 July 1966.
117 *Vigilant*, September 1958.

118 *Vigilant*, November 1958.
119 Details of the case in Joseph Beltrami, *The Defender*, Chambers, 1980, p. 124; also interview with Alan G. Cameron (formerly Alan Hasson), 18 December 1984.
120 Beltrami, *The Defender*, pp. 123-37.
121 Iain McGregor, *The Holy Terrier*, p. 2.
122 Interview with David Bryce, Grand Secretary of the Orange Lodge of Scotland, 21 August 1984.
123 Interview with David Lambie.
124 *Scotsman*, 9 July 1966.
125 David Armstrong and Hilary Saunders, *A Road too Wide*, Marshall Pickering, 1985, pp. 62-3.
126 Alan G. Hasson, 'Why are the ministers of the Church of Scotland not in the Orange Order?' *Vigilant*, January 1956.
127 Daniel Houston, Orange Order officebearer, quoted in Peter Kearney, *Conflict in Religion*, Ms in the Mitchell Library, Glasgow, p. 30.
128 *Conflict in Religion*, Ms, Mitchell Library, p. 30.
129 Interview with the Rev. Donald MacDonald.
130 Obituary of the Very Rev. A. C. Craig, *Times*, 28 August 1985.
131 James Quinn SJ, 'Ecumenism and Scottish Catholics', in McRoberts (ed.), *Modern Scottish Catholicism*, p. 208.
132 Quinn, 'Ecumenism', p. 208.
133 *Scotsman*, 23 April 1966.
134 Obituary of Canon William Mallon, *CDS*, 1974, p. 324.
135 Interview with the Rev. James Currie.
136 Interview with the Rev. Andrew Herron.
137 See note 136.
138 See note 136.
139 These obituaries are carried in the *Catholic Directory for Scotland*.
140 Interview with the Rev. Donald MacDonald.
141 See note 140.
142 Canning, *Irish-born Secular Priests*, pp. 23-4.
143 Obituary of the Most Rev. Donald Scanlan, Archbishop of Glasgow, *CDS*, 1977, pp. 373-4.
144 Donald MacDonald. See chapter 7

for Pastor Jack Glass's role as a militant protestant leader.
145 Hugh McIlvanney, *Observer*, 15 September 1985.
146 William Walker, *Glasgow Herald*, 2 April 1974.
147 Ross, 'The church in Scotland', p. 29.
148 Interview with Peter Mullen, headmaster of Holyrood Roman Catholic Secondary School, 5 August 1986.
149 Interview with Hugh Brown MP.
150 Letter from retired headmaster Tom Kirkwood, Corpach, Fort William, 6 March 1982.
151 J. G. Kellas and P. Fotheringham, 'The political behaviour of the working-class', in A. Allan MacLaren (ed.), *Social Class in Scotland Past and Present*, John Donald, Edinburgh, n.d., p. 159.
152 J. M. Bochel and D. T. Denver, 'Religion and voting: a critical review and a new analysis', *Political Studies*, 18, 2, 1970, p. 208.
153 Bochel and Denver, p. 212.
154 Kellas and Fotheringham, 'The political behaviour', p. 150.
155 Scott, *The RCs*, p. 45.
156 James McMillan, *Anatomy of Scotland*, Leslie Frewin, London, 1969, p. 97.
157 Scott, *The RCs*, p. 49.
158 Information from Ian O. Bayne.
159 Bob Purdie, 'The Friends of Ireland: British labour and Irish nationalism, 1945-49', in T. Gallagher and J. O'Connell (eds.), *Contemporary Irish Studies*, Manchester University Press, 1983.
160 *Irish Nation*, February 1949.
161 *Irish Weekly*, 13 March 1948.
162 *Irish Weekly*, 23 October 1948; Michael Fallon, *SCO*, 17 December 1982.
163 *Irish Weekly*, 22 January 1949.
164 Interview with William McGuinness, 3 May 1983.
165 William McGuinness.
166 Interview with Lord Carmichael (formerly Neil Carmichael MP), 25 August 1981.
167 Interview with William Taylor, former leader of the Labour group on Glasgow Corporation, 1962-69, September 1981.
168 Ferguson, *Geoff*, p. 180.

169 Clr Daye, *Catholic Herald*, 20 September 1946.
170 Interview with William Taylor.
171 Interview with William Brogan, Rutherglen, 22 July 1982.
172 Interview with Patrick Trainer, Labour representative for the Springburn ward on Glasgow Corporation and Strathclyde Regional Council since 1963.
173 Interviews with Hugh Brown MP and David Lambie MP.
174 Interview with Willie Hamilton MP.
175 Hugh Thomas, *John Strachey*, Eyre, Methuen, London, 1973.
176 Lord Wheatley, *SCO*, 8 January 1965.
177 Brother Clare, *SCO*, 4 December 1964.
178 James Gordon, *SCO*, 9 October 1964.
179 Colm Brogan, *SCO*, 9 September 1962.
180 Colm Brogan, *SCO*, 21 December 1962.
181 *SCO*, 4 September 1964.
182 *SCO*, 17 October 1969.
183 *Irish Weekly*, 18 November 1950.
184 *Bulletin*, 1 December 1950.
185 H. J. Paton, *The Claim of Scotland*, Allen & Unwin, London, 1968, p. 179.
186 Anthony J. C. Kerr, *SCO*, 22 December 1967.
187 Iain McCormick, *SCO*, 19 May 1967.
188 McKechin, *School in Eastwood Park*, p. 54.
189 Kellas, *Modern Scotland, the Nation since 1970*, p. 71.
190 Annual General Meeting of the EIS, 4-6 June 1981, Minute No. 639.
191 *SCO*, 4 July 1969.
192 *GH*, 10 March 1970.
193 *GH*, 18 March 1970.
194 *GH*, 18 March 1970.
195 Dick Buchanan MP for the John Storrie tale.
196 *GH*, 16 June 1970.
197 Ferguson, *Geoff*, pp. 161-2.
198 Ferguson, *Geoff*, p. 162.
199 Ferguson, *Geoff*, p. 162.
200 Obituary of Cardinal William Heard, *CDS*, 1974, p. 367.
201 'Catholics in England and Wales, the present state of the church', Catholic Information Service, London, 1982, p. 3.
202 Pat Bolan, obituary of Canon Joseph Daniel, *SCO*, 6 February 1981.
203 Obituary of Right Rev. David McRoberts, *CDS*, 1980, p. 387.
204 Cooney, *Scotland and the Papacy*, p. 82.
205 Cooney, p. 78.
206 *SCO*, 26 July 1967.
207 Rennie McOwan, 'Catholics and contraception in the real world', *GH*, 10 April 1985.
208 McOwan, 'Catholics and contraception'.
209 *SCO*, 16 August 1968.
210 Cooney, p. 100.
211 Cooney, pp. 101-2.
212 Cooney, p. 101.
213 Cooney, p. 101.
214 Interview with James Armstrong, 28 May 1982.
215 Cooney, p. 103.
216 Interview with retired sheriff John Bayne, 8 May 1982.
217 Recollection of Ian O. Bayne.
218 Interview with Tom Carberry.
219 Cooney, p. 111.
220 Cooney, p. 104.
221 Owen Dudley Edwards, 'The Catholic press in Scotland since the restoration of the hierarchy', in McRoberts (ed.), *Modern Scottish Catholicism*, p. 182.
222 Interview with former editor, William Murphy.
223 Rennie McOwan, 'The Observer and Vatican II', *SCO*, 19 April 1985.
224 *Scottish Daily Express*, 10 March 1974.
225 *Scottish Daily Express*, 11 March 1974.
226 John Cunningham, 'Church administration and organisation', in McRoberts (ed.), *Modern Scottish Catholicism*, p. 85.
227 *SCO*, 20 September 1974.
228 *SCO*, 30 December 1977.
229 Private source.
230 Obituary of Archbishop Scanlan, *CDS*, 1977, pp. 376-7.

Chapter 7 **Is one community emerging from two traditions in Ulster's shadow?**

Scotland was taken as much by surprise as the rest of the United Kingdom by the eruption of bitter internal conflict in Northern Ireland starting in October 1968. The deceptive quiet of the previous forty-five years had caused most Britons from the political class to think that the Anglo-Irish conflict had been permanently settled by the device of partitioning the island and allowing the Unionists in six of Ulster's nine counties to have home rule within the UK. A navel-gazing Westminster was shown how wrong it was in 1968 when the downtrodden catholic minority, comprising one-third of the population of Northern Ireland, began to campaign for civil rights and an end to blatant favouritism shown towards the protestant majority in the allocation of jobs, housing and regional development. Although the campaign was for the adoption of British democratic standards in Northern Ireland rather than Irish unity, the Unionists over-reacted; peaceful protests led by middle-class catholics then gave way to furious rioting in the catholic nationalist ghettoes. British troops were deployed in 1969 to prevent law and order collapsing altogether; Britain soon got even more deeply embroiled as extreme nationalists took advantage of the power vacuum to revive the IRA. Its bombing campaign of 1971–72 helped topple the Unionist government and Britain stepped into the Ulster cauldron by closing the Stormont parliament and introducing direct rule from Westminster, but it was unable to end the violence or devise an acceptable political solution.

The west of Scotland was the part of mainland Britain closest to Northern Ireland not just geographically but emotionally and also in terms of the ethnic composition of its inhabitants and their religious ties. Journalists looking for a fresh angle on the conflict wondered whether it was not a matter of time before Glasgow, which had always enjoyed a turbulent image when Belfast was deceptively calm, erupted into fratricidal violence. It was noted that the behaviour of Orange and republican flute bands that travelled over to Northern Ireland rallies from Scotland was often more provocative than that of their local counterparts; and that it was soldiers in Scottish regiments who had been involved in the first clashes with Belfast youths in March 1970, disturbances that marked the end of the catholic community's 'honeymoon' with the British Army. Glaswegians watched uneasily as fresh sectarian graffiti began to appear on bus shelters and on the walls of housing schemes. Insulting or complimentary references to the Queen or the Pope and dates marking earlier stages of the conflict, such as 1690 or 1916, gave way to slogans about 'Bloody Sunday', 'PIRA', and the UDA and UVF, two paramilitary responses to the Provisional IRA from the loyalist or protestant side.

While trying to get on with their own lives Glaswegians cast an anxious glance over their shoulders and worried about the amount of local political fall-out from the Ulster explosion. Looking back in the mid-1980s Church of Scotland ministers Andrew Herron and Donald MacDonald still remained surprised that battle had not been drawn by some of the local factions that took their lead from the partisans of orange and green in Ulster.[1] The ecumenical movement was only getting underway in the west of Scotland and had much suspicion about the motives behind it to break down. Better known than any ecumenically-minded clergyman in the early 1970s was Pastor Jack Glass, a flamboyant preacher and crusader against the Church of Rome who was compared to Ian Paisley, the towering demagogue who, by his violent oratory and militant tactics, had done untold damage to the chances of a moderate solution prevailing in Northern Ireland during the late 1960s. Glasgow also had to contend with the Old Firm conflict, a source of internal discord absent even from Northern Ireland.

But as the Northern Ireland conflict dragged on year after year leaving Scotland relatively untouched, predictions of imminent disaster were less commonly heard. Despite the legacy of immigration from Ireland it became apparent that the west of Scotland was not an extension of divided Ulster but part of a nation with its own history, traditions and institutions which had evolved a more low-key way of solving its problems. In a number of important respects it enjoyed crucial advantages over Northern Ireland which made it difficult for the conflict to spread: housing was integrated and most communities were religiously mixed; the trade union movement was not at the mercy of competing sectarian interests as in Belfast was able to set an agenda that stressed what the working-class had in common; and the police force was ceasing to be drawn largely from one religious source as had long been the case in Ulster. Even the Old Firm matches may have unwittingly played a role in directing the intense rivalry of the west of Scotland youth away from politics and religion. 'Perhaps', in the words of a Glasgow chief constable, 'the ritual of these events has been instrumental in providing an outlet for the differences between the two communities', however uncomfortable it has been for those neutral citizens inconvenienced by the anti-social behaviour of Old Firm supporters.[2]

Northern Ireland erupted as growing intermarriage across the religious divide was making it less feasible to talk about the watertight protestant and catholic communities in the west of Scotland. However, sympathisers were to be found who were prepared to give active support to the combatants on both sides by providing safe houses for men on the run, organising solidarity demonstrations, and offering humanitarian aid. This was particularly true of militant protestants who often turned out to have relatives or close friends in Northern Ireland. Each year the Orange Order helped renew these bonds as lodges paid fraternal visits back and forth across the Irish Sea to commemorate the symbolic events of the protestant calendar. No catholic equivalent to the order existed in Scotland which helps to explain why Glasgow's identification with Irish republicanism has only been expressed in a sporadic or disorganised way. There is plenty of evidence to suggest that the post-1968 troubles helped revive the order at a time when nominal membership was increasing, especially among younger generations of Orange families where sons expected to don the Orange sash, preferred instead to follow, in their spare time, sport or other leisure pursuits. In Partick only a dozen old men could be found to assemble behind the Orange banner in the mid-1960s recalls Donald MacDonald, then a local minister, but once protestant Ulster was seen to be under threat from enemies within or without, Orange events suddenly seemed less hackneyed and once more hundreds were to be found marching behind the banner in this working-class Glasgow district.[3]

While residual sympathies were revived by post-1968 events the great bulk of the Scottish population showed no desire to make the Ulster quarrel its own. It was a subject that was not raised at first out of fear that the genie might be let out of the bottle in Scotland but increasingly from a feeling of boredom and distaste. So the resurgence of the Orange Order and the disturbing zeal of some of the cause's adherents was a deceptive indicator of Northern Irelands importance to Scotland. Those who wished to make it a pressing local issue were thoroughly isolated from the bulk of public opinion. Scots who might have half-tolerated religious or pro-Irish zealots because there did not seem to be any harm in doing so or because they suddenly remembered their own catholic Irish ancestry or Calvinist childhood, emphatically refused to give them houseroom once the toll of death and destruction mounted just sixty miles from the Scottish coast. *Scottish* national

consciouness also grew as Ireland burned and bled in the early 1970s
and was partly reflected by the electoral success enjoyed by the SNP
in 1974.

By then the IRA was taking its campaign of terror to the mainland
but Scotland and Wales were not included as targets because Irish
republicans viewed their inhabitants as fellow Celts who had likewise
to endure English overlordship. Scots of nearly all political hues were
left unimpressed by this dispensation but some may have been secretly
relieved that the delicate web of community relations escaped what
would have been its stiffest test if bombs had been planted in Scottish
cities. Whether the Scots would have acted with the indifference and
cold contempt that the southern English displayed towards IRA bombing in their cities and towns is simply impossible to say. One MP, David
Lambie, whose mid-Ayrshire constituency is near to the Ulster coast,
was aware of solidarity activity going on in his area but he had been
informed that neither side wished to spread the conflict to Scotland
and that, even in the event of civil war breaking out in Northern Ireland,
they would not bring the fight to Scotland.[4] So, as in 1919–21
Scotland's function has chiefly been that of a safe haven and source of
arms rather than as a minor theatre of the conflict itself.

Anyone aware of the degree of solidarity with the Irish republican
cause emanating from Glasgow after 1918 might have been surprised
at the lack of response shown in the 1970s. Of course, the terms of
the conflict had changed: most of Ireland was free and a majority in
the remaining part wished to stay with Britain. More to the point, the
bulldozers had levelled most of the inner city districts which had
nurtured a distinct Irish sub-culture. This sub-culture was not being
reproduced (IRA graffiti aside) because emigration from Ireland to
Clydeside had dried up in the post-war decades; booming southern
Britain was becoming a more attractive destination of families in the
rural west whose younger offspring, without hopes of land inheritance
had previously set off for Scotland. In 1986 the largest Irish community in Scotland was to be found in the lower middle-class parish
of Christ the King in Glasgow's southern suburbs:[5] those first generation Irish remained more interested in self-improvement than in re-
enacting old quarrels. Even the AOH, a catholic body some times
viewed as a pale imitation of the Orange Order has been the soul of
moderation. It is strong in Lanarkshire and still stands for Irish unity
but it condemns violent means of achieving this end: and relations
with its Orange rival are sometimes good enough for flutes and other
instruments to be lent out when required by the other side.[6]

Archbishop Winning is pleased that the vast majority of Glaswegian
catholics have no time for the IRA.[7] In 1973 his church was briefly
embarrassed when the police discovered a cache of weapons in the

chapel house of St Teresa's, Possilpark not long after Fr Bartholomew Burns had gone into hiding before returning to Ireland from where he avoided extradiction much to the annoyance of the Orange Order. Ironically, two years before, workers at the *Scottish Daily Express* headquarters in Glasgow had taken exception to a cartoon which linked the catholic church with the Soviet Union and Irish republicanism. It showed 'Fr O'Brezhnev, missionary to Ulster' alighting from an aircraft marked 'Irish Republican airlines' which was disgorging tanks with labels on them such as '250 samovars for Falls Rd'.[8] 350,000 copies of the paper were lost as a result of the action presumably of catholic print workers. The anti-catholicism of the cartoon rather than its Irish content may well have been the spur in this, an isolated incident. Catholic feelings towards the plight of their co-religionists remain ambivalent especially if they have relatives in Northern Ireland who have stories of police harassment to relate, but most are relieved that the conflict is not a complicating factor in their own lives and few want to tempt providence by being outspoken on it.

Whereas catholic immigrants to Scotland mainly came from counties now in the Irish Republic, their protestant counterparts largely hailed from what is now Northern Ireland. This may explain why feelings ran higher among Scottish protestants who cherished the Ulster link and why more active steps have been taken to reaffirm this link in the 1970s and 1980s.

The Grand Orange Lodge of Scotland remains the traditional point of contact between loyalists separated by the Irish Sea. It has avoided the fate of the Orange Order in Ulster which has tended to lose the initiative to paramilitary bodies like the UDA or to extremist politicians like Ian Paisley and his Democratic Unionist Party who criticise the order for temporising and for not providing bold leadership at times of crisis. Since protestant interests in Scotland are not seen as under threat, at least to the degree that they are in Northern Ireland, pressure on Grand Lodge from more extreme quarters is correspondingly weaker. However, in the early 1970s sizeable units of the UDA and the smaller paramilitary group, the UVF were being formed by sympathisers enraged by IRA terrorism and by Westminster's apparent willingness to sell out the Ulster protestant cause.

The Scottish Order usually kept the UDA and UVF at arms length, often forbidding them to take up collections in Orange halls and clubs. For a while, in 1975–76, a change of attitude could be discerned following a blatant sectarian attack on Tullyvallen Orange hall near the Irish border in south Armagh in which five Orangemen were killed. The south Armagh massacre had a traumatic effect in Scotland and brought home the sense of common identity between fellow Orangemen as nothing previously had done. Meeting soon afterwards Grand

Lodge suspended normal business and for hours talked only of Tullyvallen, security in Ulster, and what could be done to help. There was talk of organising a mass evacuation of Armagh protestants to loyalist homes all over Scotland. One district lodge, acting hastily, bankrupted itself by buying dozens of camp beds, blankets and other emergency supplies. But of much greater significance was Grand Lodge's decision to send a delegation to Belfast where it secretly met a joint committee of paramilitary groups.[9] One well-informed journalist reckoned that the Order planned to widen the scope of its charity work to include the welfare sections of these paramilitary groups as well as the Orange distress fund in order to help prisoners and their families.[10] David Bryce, the Grand Secretary who had handled public relations since 1975, stressed that the Order would not be giving money for the buying of arms.[11] But a hardening of its line had taken place in 1975 which boosted the confidence and visibility of militants in its ranks.

Attention came to be focused in particular on Roddy MacDonald, a foreman in the Edinburgh building trade who in a 1976 BBC Scotland programme televised in September envisaged a possibility of guns being shipped from Scotland to Ulster. MacDonald belonged to the Order and he also claimed that the UDA's membership in Scotland was 6,000 strong, an undoubted exaggeration, but it soon led to calls for its banning. Within the Order the leadership was alarmed that it had been indirectly linked with unlawful activities in such a public manner and it sought to regain the initiative in December 1976 by expelling Roddy MacDonald for defying the Order's constitution. However, the 300 delegates assembled at Grand Lodge refused to support the motion for his expulsion.[12] Faced with a looming split the ruling executive threatened to resign *en masse* unless delegates at the Order's AGM on 11 December endorsed a resolution which 'utterly rejected all support, be it active or tacit, of terrorist organisations, whose actions contravene the law of the land'.[13] The motion was approved overwhelmingly and the levelheaded leadership regained the initiative over grassroots militants which it has retained down to the mid-1980s.

In February 1977 *The Orange Torch*, the Order's monthly paper, promised to maintain continuous pressure on Westminster politicians to ensure that Ulster is never removed from the UK against the wishes of the majority and to provide 'massive humanitarian assistance' should the need arise, but flirtation with paramilitaries was firmly ruled out:

> Leaving aside . . . the question of the acceptability of members of a Christian association such as ours involving themselves in unlawful 'military' activity, how positive and effective has been the role of the Scottish wing of the UDA?
> They have been blunderingly ineffective . . . More serious still, they have endangered the credibility of the Orange institution in Scotland and have thus

imperilled the constitutional policies being pursued by Grand Lodge. In plain language, who in Scotland will want to listen to anything the Orange Order has to say about Northern Ireland when misguided men claiming the name of Orange are constantly in our newspapers on arms charges or flaunting themselves on television boasting about shotguns and flamethrowers.[14]

The Scottish paramilitaries had a smaller pool of talent and money to draw on in their arms smuggling activities than their Belfast counterparts and the police had no difficulty in apprehending most of those who committed criminal offences. By the end of 1977 Roddy MacDonald, 'the Supreme Commander' of the UDA was in prison beginning an eight-year sentence. One detective branded the Scottish UDA as 'the Union of Dumb Amateurs' because of its sheer incompetence.[15] However, scope continued to exist for a strong affirmation of loyalist views and, in 1979, the Young Scottish Loyalists were founded by ten young Glaswegians disenchanted by the Order's moderation. By 1982 they were claiming a paid-up membership of 1,500 and an ability to mobilise 5,000 supporters for street demonstrations.[16] Clashes took place with pro-Republicans who belonged to the Troops Out Movement and during the worst of these, at one rally in Glasgow on 14 February 1981, 152 people were arrested. At the time, such skirmishes have caused Scots to worry that their immunity to the contagion of Ulster sectarianism may be on the verge of disappearing, but they have turned out to be isolated incidents. The Orange Order has encouraged its members to stay away from pro-IRA demonstrations. Pastor Jack Glass has also spoken out against Glasgow becoming a battleground between Ulster-inspired factions and he is reluctant to see the Clydeside working-class split on the lines of Belfast.[17] Even a Glasgow Orange band member, interviewed on television in 1984, was prepared to speak reasonably about the rival Republican band: 'They've got their cause as well as we have got our cause. They came into the world the same way we did. It's just their religion, that's all it is. They go to their matches, we go to our's.'[18]

Scottish protestants may never be able to help their Ulster brethren in the way that Irish-Americans have backed the Republican cause, but many loyalists see them as the only friends they now have outside the province. They feel that their complex situation is better understood in Scotland than in the rest of Britain because of common circumstances: Scotland is a minority nation within the UK, like Ulster it has a double identity, looking to Westminster and to its own local institutions and traditions for a sense of purpose.

A poll carried out in 1978 showed that both protestants and catholics in Ulster felt a greater affinity with Scottish than with English people: 82% of protestants sampled felt that the Scots were about the same as themselves, only 43% being able to say the same about the English, 57% of the catholics sampled identified with the Scots in the same way, compared to only 33% who felt affinity with the English.[19]

At least one Ulster-based Scot has turned these bonds to his advantage in a way he would not have been able to do in his native land. George Seawright, a former Clydeside shipyard worker from the Drumchapel housing estate carved out a niche for himself in the 1980s as the most militant of Ulster's elected loyalist politicians. In 1984, at a meeting of Belfast city council, he suggested that an incinerator should be built by the council to burn catholics and their priests.[20] This outburst got him suspended from Paisley's DUP but he has prospered as an independent and was returned at the head of the poll in the 1985 local elections.

On no occasion have fringe protestant candidates standing in parliamentary or local elections in Scotland been able to win office by basing their campaign around Northern Ireland. The extreme right-wing National Front has likewise tried to gain a foothold in Glasgow by using Ireland but with a resounding lack of success. Turning to the major parties, it is an issue which they have been keen to downplay locally. For the Labour Party in Scotland it is a topic that rarely comes up at ward or public meetings or at the party conference. Helen Liddell, secretary of the party since 1977, could never remember being asked about it in any of these contexts in the last decade.[21] No Scottish Labour MPs have made it an issue, few if any have identified with the Troops Out movement and its campaign for British withdrawal and a united Ireland, none served as ministers in the Northern Ireland office during 1974-79 when Labour was in government. (Jock Stallard MP, a Hamilton-born catholic *was* vocal on violations of civil liberties that were brought to his notice in the 1970s resulting from the Northern Ireland emergency but he represented the London seat of St Pancras North.)

One Scottish Labour MP, Hugh Brown the member for Glasgow Provan, has monitored local opinion on the issue. In 1972, after visiting Ulster he made discreet enquiries about the strength of feeling in his own constituency by approaching a respected priest and the officers of a masonic club in his constituency which he had opened. He asked to be put in touch with 'some wild men': 'so I had conversations with two groups separately . . . I was appalled by the bigotry on both sides. Anybody who is complacent about the underlying tensions is making a big mistake; they are there without a shadow of a doubt.'[22]

1972, the year in which Brown took soundings was the worst in terms of violence and political upheaval that Northern Ireland has yet seen, so the depth of feeling he came across must be placed in that context, however, he continues to remain watchful and uncomplacent.

So are his Labour colleagues who tend to avoid the radical gestures on Ireland made by some English Labour MPs. Donald Dewar, the shadow Scottish secretary received an Orange delegation in October 1984 which found him to be 'much less adamant' about a conference resolution calling for a ban on the use of plastic bullets in Northern Ireland than the party's spokesman on Northern Ireland, Peter Archer, QC.[23] Several Labour MPs interviewed are prepared to recognise the moderating role played behind the scenes by the Orange Order. Ironically, its relations with the Tory Party in Scotland have been far stormier over the Irish issue.

Scottish Orangemen received a jolt in 1972 when William Whitelaw, grandson of a famous Glasgow Orange MP, was appointed Secretary of State for Northern Ireland after the imposition of Direct Rule from London, and given the task of forming a powersharing government which would bring catholic nationalists into the government of the province for the first time. He took to his task with alacrity and, although the powersharing bid failed as a result of a massive loyalist strike in 1974, relations between the Order and the Tory Party were never the same again. Grand Lodge showed its independence over the long-running debate in the late 1970s concerning whether Scotland should get its own elected assembly. It refused to line up with the Tories who branded it as a threat to the union. The grassroots membership was encouraged to make up its own mind after careful consideration and several leading officials were disappointed that the 1979 referendum on devolution failed to produce the conclusive majority needed for an assembly.

Relations between the Order and the Tory Party then reached an all-time low in 1986 following the British government's decision to give the Irish government a consultative role in the affairs of Northern Ireland. The Order claimed that the Anglo-Irish agreement led over one thousand people to resign or refuse to renew membership of the Tory Party in Scotland. In June 1986 the Order announced that it was sponsoring a new party, the Scottish Unionist Party which intended to fight nine Tory-held seats in the hope of exacting revenge for this 'capitulation to Dublin'. Never in recent times has the Order got so overtly involved in politics. A high-risk decision was being taken since most Orange support was concentrated in industrial Labour seats and the architects of the new departure had no way of knowing what control they could exercise over the Orange vote on polling day. The announcement that membership of the Scottish Unionist Party was to be open to all, including catholics 'who are on the same wavelengths as us' was also something of a novel departure.[24]

Those in charge of law and order were relieved that opposition to the Anglo-Irish agreement took a pragmatic form in Scotland unlike

Northern Ireland itself where the loyalist response was bitter and extremely violent. The police are well aware that if civil war breaks out there in earnest, the west of Scotland is still the part of the UK where it is most likely to spill over. In Glasgow when tension was briefly running high during 1981, the year of the IRA hunger strike in the Maze prison, the police were able to get permission from the Labour-controlled council for a three-month ban on marches. The strength of militant protestantism in Scotland has meant that, unlike the rest of the UK, the 1974 Prevention of Terrorism Act has been used by the Special Branch primarily against loyalist and not Republican suspects. This angered the Scottish Constitutional Defence Committee formed by David Cassells, an evangelical minister and friend of Ian Paisley which mounted a campaign against the Strathclyde force's chief constable who then was a catholic.

The Scottish police has enjoyed success in its drive against loyalist and republican paramilitaries. Over a hundred people have been convicted of arms and explosives offences. The only time when bombs were planted in a sectarian attack in Scotland occurred in 1979 when two crowded catholic bars in Glasgow were the target, few people being seriously hurt. Several dozen trials have taken place, the reporting of which by the media has been deliberately unsensational. James Gordon of Radio Clyde says that he is not alone in keeping a careful eye on reporting anything that could inflame the situation locally: 'these trials were not ignored but they were reported without eye-catching headlines'.[25]

Without the ritualised conflict involving supporters of the Old Firm teams Rangers and Celtic, it is likely that the Northern Ireland conflict would have had even less impact on Scotland. The age-old soccer rivalry which absorbed so much of the energy and free time of working-class Scottish males instead helped to bring it into sharper focus and threw up local recruits for rival Irish factions. Rangers–Celtic matches also continued to attract large numbers of Irish visitors. In 1980 Rangers had over thirty supporters clubs in Northern Ireland, Celtic had fourteen and many more in the Republic.[26]

Of the two clubs, Rangers continued to attract the most adverse publicity because it still insisted that every member of the team be of the one religion. The Club's board, as well as the hooligan element among its fans, was capable of generating intense controversy over this matter. In 1973 a new chairman was due to be appointed following the retirement of John Lawrence, a self-made man who had gone from being a joiner in the 1930s to head of a housing empire.[27] His designated successor, David Hope, by building up the Rangers Pools and social club, had done more for the club's off-the-field business success than any other individual, however an internal putsch ensured that he was chairman for only seventeen minutes and that two years later he was not even on the board. It was widely believed that the indiscretion of marrying a catholic, forty-three years previously, a woman who had been dead for fifteen years, had been enough to ruin his chances of succeeding Lawrence.[28]

The conflict in Ireland failed to be the catalyst which swept the religious cobwebs from the Ibrox-based club's terraces and boardroom. One of its managers even had no qualms in the 1970s about urging his players to roar out the loyalist battle-cry 'No surrender' as they ran up the tunnel at Ibrox.[29] But the club was finally stopped in its tracks in 1976 by the outrage which greeted the behaviour of its fans in Birmingham when a friendly match against Aston Villa had to be abandoned with only fifty-three minutes played after rioting that spread beyond the stadium. Next day *The Evening Times* in Glasgow declared that 'The Rangers bosses have to change their diehard, blue-nosed Protestant policy';[30] writing in *The Glasgow Herald*, columnist Ian Archer stated bluntly that 'as a Scottish football club, [Rangers] are a permanent embarrassment and an occasional disgrace. The country would be a better place if Rangers did not exist.'[31] Even the Orange Order, through its newspaper, waded in with notable criticism:

> How many of us saw the cruel irony in the fate of the *Tavern in the Town* public house—the one bombed three years ago by the IRA—smashed and devastated by the crazed minds who sang Orange songs! . . .
> Let us be perfectly blunt. The same examples of low animal life who force their support on Glasgow Rangers are one and the same with the foul-mouthed drunks who cause us great embarrassment every July when they turn up to 'support' our annual rallies.[32]

Shaken by this media storm, Willie Waddell, the team's general manager, announced a radical change of direction one week after Aston Villa: 'we are determined to end Rangers' image as a sectarian club. As far as humanly possible every possible measure will be taken to remove spectators from Ibrox who do not accept the policy'; while denying the existence of a 'no Catholic' policy, he went on to announce that 'no religious barriers will be put up by this club regarding the signing of players'.[33] The local media was jubilant at this breakthrough but it grew increasingly suspicious as the years passed and no catholic player materialised at Ibrox. At boardroom level the club was experiencing a series of power struggles which went on intermittently until 1985. In this volatile situation none of the aspirants for control seemed willing to risk censure or lose vital shareholders votes by initiating a signing policy that was unpopular with many supporters clubs and an indeterminate number of fans and which no large shareholder was enthusiastic about, perhaps understandably given their desire to be associated with this bastion of protestant working-class culture.

But the pressure on Rangers did not abate and in September 1978 the club faced ringing criticism from the national church itself. *The Bush*, monthly paper of the kirk's Glasgow presbytery, issued a scathing editorial, 'The Blue Barrier', part of which read:

> 'Are you a Catholic?' That's the big disqualifying question to an applicant for any job at Ibrox.
>
> Four years ago the Presbytery condemned that sectarianism. Rangers said it didn't exist. Two years later they changed their non-existent policy. 'We'll sign a Catholic', said their general manager. Two weeks ago, they still hadn't. Nor are they likely to. Blind prejudice is no respecter of football skills alone.
>
> Over the summer we investigated the Ibrox situation. We unearthed stories of people applying for advertised jobs who were asked their religion as almost the first question. We have a quote from a director that boldly states why Catholics should not play for Rangers. We looked at the careers of some players who were unfortunate enough to fall in love with Catholic girls . . . And we conclude that far from changing anything with a new policy, Rangers Football Club is more anti-Catholic than it ever was.[34]

Donald MacDonald, one of the ministers behind the editorial, later explained what had motivated him to speak out:

> The conviction grew within me over the years that to have an exclusively Protestant club in a sport that has nothing to do with religion or race was a sort of cancer in the heart of the city . . .
>
> When I found in my parish of Partick Protestant and Roman Catholic pubs that were exclusively so because one was where the Celtic bus left from on a Saturday and the other was where the Rangers bus left from, it appeared almost beyond belief in our day and age . . .
>
> But I think the thing that brought it to a head for me was the fact that people were making money . . . Remember, this was the time when the whole of Glasgow's industrial infrastructure was toppling just after the UCS [Upper Clyde Shipbuilding] work-in . . . and here was a football team, and not a particularly good one at the time, which could afford to spend millions of pounds on a new stadium.
>
> So I felt at that time that if we in the church were going to have any integrity at all, it should be made clear that segregated sport had nothing to do with us.[35]

However, *The Bush* proved out of step with many of its readers. An outcry ensued, some parishes cancelled their bulk orders forthwith, and before long its circulation had plunged from 13,000 to 8,000, making it uneconomic.[36] At the 1980 General Assembly of the Kirk a motion calling on Rangers to 'publicly disclaim a sectarian bias in management and team structure' was passed by a majority of 200 but it was an ambiguous result since 400 commissioners abstained. Taken along with the response to *The Bush* editorial from churchgoers, it slightly throws into question the view that nearly all hardliners on the Old Firm issue are people only lightly touched by religion who are instead motivated by tribal antagonisms. One critic argues that Rangers continued to be 'secure in the support of a silent majority that either does not see sectarianism in sport as a serious matter or which tacitly or openly supports it'.[37]

Up to the 1980s a large number of ministers were offered and accepted free stand tickets to Ibrox.[38] Celtic has similarly issued free passes to priests whose presence at Parkhead causes them to be dubbed 'The Black Watch'. The catholic archbishop is invited to official club functions but a non-catholic has still to be appointed to the Celtic board which shows how much the club's affairs are dominated by members of the west of Scotland catholic lower middle-class. However, Celtic regards itself as a Scottish club of Irish origin which is open to all members of the Scottish community. It has been more open and self-critical about disgraceful behaviour by a section of its fans than Rangers has been, as shown by the club's paper, *The Celtic View*, which publicises letters critical of management, players and supporters. Bill Murray considers that the Celtic management show a much greater willingness to abide by the guidelines suggested by outside bodies while Rangers are more inclined to dismiss this as unwarranted interference.[39]

Celtic has shown its abhorrence of political tyranny by severing all sporting contacts with South Africa and refusing, in 1986, to play against communist countries following the Soviet invasion of Czechoslovakia.[40] But the club has not been distressed by Rangers signing policy and for a very good reason: it means that its rival misses out on the chance to sign up good players who are catholics while Celtic is able to benefit from the skills of catholic and non-catholic players alike. This may partly account for why Celtic has a relatively good playing record while Rangers has been stuck in the doldrums for much of the 1970s and 1980s. Other teams, from the east coast, have ended the Old Firm's monopoly of Scottish soccer trophies which may have taken some of the sting out of the rivalry. Attendances at Rangers matches plunged in the early 1980s following the team's lack of success and matches between the two Glasgow rivals have lost the same degree of occasion and excitement, perhaps because they now meet more often under the new premier league.

By the mid-1980s it was the custom for the official Rangers supporters association to invite representatives from its Celtic counterpart to send guests along to its annual rally which is partly a fund-raising effort, and for Celtic to return the compliment. James Currie, the club chaplain and a doughty defender of Rangers, was impressed by the reception that the Celtic guests received at the 1986 rally: some booing by a small faction at the back was quickly drowned out by applause as the guests were introduced.[41]

Intimations of even more fundamental changes were provided by shake-ups in the Rangers power structure in 1986. After years of feuding a controlling interest was won in the club by Lawrence Marlborough, grandson of John Lawrence. The new chairman is based in America and the day-to-day running of the club was placed in the hands of chief executive David Holmes who, in July 1986 announced that Rangers would no longer be the prisoner of sectarian tradition:

> From now on Rangers will be run on lines that have nothing to do with religion. The club is part of the Govan community, and besides Protestants and Catholics, that includes Asians and others. I want the club to be part of the community as a whole.
>
> I have said before, and I will say it again, that if what we do alienates some people, I am sure it will be compensated by those who turn out to see a good football team. This is what we are determined to produce here.[42]

In 1986 the annual turnover of Rangers was a mere £1·5 million out of the Lawrence's group's total of £100 million, but the decision had been taken to allow Rangers 'to fly the flag for the entire group, realising its publicity value and the power of a favourable image when it comes to commercial advantage'.[43] None of the important signings of players made in the summer of 1986 in order to redesign the team were catholics but, in June 1986, the press announced that sixteen-year-old John Spencer, a roman catholic, had been taken on.[44] It remains to be seen whether he will play in a major game—and what the reception of the terraces will be—but an important psychological barrier has been breached. Graham Souness, the team's new player manager had made it clear that he would not be there if any religious restrictions had been imposed upon him. 'How could I refuse to sign Catholics and then go home to live with my wife, who is of the same religion?' he declared.[45]

The road away from an ultra-protestant image is unlikely to be a smooth one for Rangers but the new path may stand more chance of success because it was not dictated by external pressures but instead arose once internal forces voluntarily decided that it was commercially necessary for the health of the business that Rangers found itself part of. So it might just be that the capitalist imperative will manage to accomplish what the increasingly vocal disapproval of various Scottish institutions was unable to bring off.

The increasing self-confidence of catholics meant that a lot were able to laugh off Rangers' discriminatory ways and even feel a certain sympathy for the predicament that the club found itself in which would not have been the case before the 1970s. Frank McElhone, a Glasgow MP and a catholic even came to the club's assistance in a number of practical ways during the 1970s. He used to joke with parliamentary colleagues about being invited along to club dinners and he was fondly recalled by Rangers enthusiast, the Rev. James Currie as 'a man who transcended religious barriers'.[46]

By the 1980s there was no longer concern or even undue comment if a house in a middle-class area was bought by a catholic. However counter-productive it may have been in other respects, television had proved to be a great leveller by breaking down religious differences: the regular broadcasting of catholic services removed a lot of mystery about the Mass which ultra-protestants had previously played upon. Catholics in the public eye like media boss James Gordon encountered very little bigotry but a churchman like Archbishop Winning occasionally detected it still:

> Sometimes it is not difficult to read the animosity in people's features as you walk along the corridor of a hospital, for example, and somebody coming in the opposite direction obviously doesn't want to say hello: he will set his sights on a spot in the ceiling and make no effort to catch your eye. When people act like that it makes you feel sad.[47]

An important psychological hurdle was overcome when, in 1977, a catholic was appointed chief constable of Strathclyde, the largest British police force outside London taking in two-and-a-half million people. Patrick Hamill's headquarters were in Glasgow and the merger of small police authorities after Scottish local government was re-organised in 1974 seems to have allowed for greater mobility of catholics in an area where hitherto they had not made their mark, at least if they were of catholic Irish descent. Hitherto those catholics who had advanced in the force tended to be Highlanders. Sir David McNee, Glasgow's last chief constable before the 1974 reorganisation, has been credited with helping to sweep away much of any remaining bias that prevented other catholics attaining promotion—and Hamill was his *protege*.[48] McNee had served under an Asian, Clr Bashir Maan who was appointed chairman of Glasgow police committee in 1974 and, although a devout evangelical Christian, he was one of the few British chief constables not to be linked with the freemasons.

Hamill adopted a low profile but, just as he was taking charge, an unsettling incident occurred in Craigneuk, Lanarkshire which showed that the police were not immune from sectarian feeling in areas where it still prevailed. Tension had been higher than usual in this corner of Wishaw on the eve of the annual Orange walk because a catholic church on its route had been daubed with the slogan 'UDA'. Local catholics were so incensed that the march had to be switched to another part of town to avoid an angry crowd, but fighting did flare up outside a bar which reached such a pitch that policemen started fighting among themselves, two later being dismissed from the force.[49] However, this was a relatively isolated incident. In 1984, after complaining about police behaviour at a friendly match Celtic was playing in Northern Ireland, club chairman Desmond White did not hesitate to offer the following testimonial to the peace-keeping skills of the Glasgow police: 'if we could magically transport fifty Glasgow "bobbies" over here, there would be no problem'.[50]

Local government administration was proving an area where catholics increasingly came to the fore especially after the reorganisation of the 1970s. Most catholics were located in the Strathclyde region which encompassed Lanarkshire, Renfrewshire, Dumbartonshire, Ayrshire and part of the West Highlands as well as the city of Glasgow. Recruitment procedures had not always been free from religious interference or outright bias in some of the smaller authorities where informal criteria had sometimes come into play but the new system allowed less scope for local anomalies to flourish.

Recruitment procedure in council employment has become centralised. In Glasgow District Council, a new director of personnel saw to it in 1975 that an applicant for a council job was no longer required to put down the name of his or her school in the application form which has always been the question asked by a west of Scotland employer anxious to identify a person's religion. People still grade certain departments in Glasgow City Chambers (the town hall) such as the Lord Provost's office and the Clerk of the Court's office according to their religious colouring. One politician remarked that the Lord Provost's office had changed markedly in recent times thanks to one of the staff marrying a catholic and becoming a convert. One councillor has alleged discrimination against catholics in the parks department, another former councillor alleges it is practised by the council building department in the taking on of apprentices, but neither has been able to offer direct evidence according to a former head of Glasgow District Council.[51]

Sir Lawrence Boyle, Strathclyde Regional Council's first chief executive from 1974 to 1980, was a roman catholic, however he was careful not to identify with the 'catholic element' that some could identify on the Labour-dominated council; it would not have helped his image, that of being an impartial administrator who showed no special favour, not least to those who shared his creed. He even turned down an invitation to join the Catholic Union because he did not think membership was compatible with his position. But, since his retirement he has served on a government sponsored independent commission of enquiry into local government practices, a route followed by other catholics such as Sister Maire T. Gallagher, headteacher of Notre Dame School, Dumbarton, and James Gordon who both sat on the 1986 commission into the pay and condition of Scottish teachers, and Tom Carberry who served on the royal commission on gambling in 1975–77 and was a member of the Independent Broadcasting Authority from 1970 to 1979.

One priest based for some years in what is arguably the most prosperous middle-class parish in Glasgow, St Joseph's, Clarkston, considered that 'a catholic mafia' had grown up in Glasgow based on white-collar professionals who were in regular contact with one another but did not necessarily operate in an underhand manner. In talking to them the priest was anxious to 'inculcate the feeling that there is no point in having the ball at our feet and then behaving as previous generations did—excellence and competence have to be the yardsticks catholics in positions of influence adopt when making important decisions'.[52]

Archbishop Winning, by contrast, feels 'there is no established Catholic middle-class in Glasgow yet' and he emphasises that those professionals who do exist 'are still only a generation removed from the working-class'.[53] This assessment is partly reflected by Tom Carberry who is certain that the number of middle-class catholics is growing but that they are still drawn disproportionately from the 'ghetto professionals' (doctors, lawyers, teachers), from the public sector and from multinational firms, while being under-represented in local firms and in institutions like banking, accountancy, and insurance.[54] Dr Winning has still to meet a Scottish catholic banker, banking being an area where others perceive some lingering discrimination. One respected administrator, stung by this fact, took the opportunity of sharing a train compartment with a senior director of a premier Scottish bank to ask: 'Isn't it time you ceased to ask an applicant's religion? After all, a person opening an account with your bank doesn't have to say what his religion is.'[55]

Glasgow's archbishop feels that 'discrimination is subtle now, people would not get away with it if it was open'.[56] It is worth stressing that feeling was never strong enough in the west of Scotland for any calls to be made that the race relations legislation passed by parliament in the 1960s and 1970s be extended to cover religion, something which happened in Northern Ireland with the passing of the Fair Employment Act of 1976. The west of Scotland counterparts of the upwardly mobile Ulster catholics whose progress in the public white-collar sector was blocked by an insensitive Unionist regime, lacked the grievances which fuelled their protests in the 1960s. They retained a residual feeling of difference from the rest of the community but this was perhaps mainly instilled by the education system. Highly competitive catholic schools like Holyrood, St Mungo's, Notre Dame, and the fee-paying St Aloysius produced a flood of catholic graduates which by the

1980s were running at 650–850 a year in Glasgow University alone. By the 1980s Holyrood enjoyed a national reputation for debating which was confirmed by the school's success in winning the *Daily Express* and Conico public speaking competitions, it being the only Scottish school to win the latter twice.

Against this background more fluent and self-confident catholic students were now arriving at university. In 1984 they helped to elect their prototype, Michael Kelly, as Glasgow University's rector. This ambitious and energetic former lecturer had helped revive Glasgow's floundering image during his term as the city's Lord Provost from 1981 to 1984. He launched a public relations campaign entitled 'Glasgow's Miles Better', designed to banish the city's violent, unruly and run-down image by substituting a new one which stressed the warmth and wit of its inhabitants, the richness of its architectural heritage, and the open-air amenities and range of cultural events offered by the city. Some felt that Glasgow's image was beyond repair, others accused Kelly of self-promotion, but the campaign had an undeniable impact in the rest of Britain and further afield as shown by the sharp increase in tourism to the city, and far more people were prepared to praise Kelly for his enterprise and vision. (On retiring as Lord Provost he went into public relations and media work on a full-time basis.)

At Glasgow University in the 1980s, catholic students now virtually dominated union politics and took a full part in university life. Many still had time for the practice of their faith as shown by the attendance at daily Mass in Turnbull Hall, the catholic chaplaincy which, during 1986, was greater than in any other parish in the city.[57] A Catholic Society based in the chaplaincy existed until the mid-1970s. Increasingly dominated by 'cliques' from the top schools of St Aloysius and St Mungo's, it was wound up when it ceased to be a focal-point for a broad cross-section of students. Today the chaplaincy uses the resources of its own students to promote a full programme of activities during term time rather than relying on big name outside speakers to draw occasional audiences and it is concerned to encourage social commitment as well as devotion to the faith among its adherents. (The chaplaincy is situated nextdoor to the Scottish headquarters of the Orange Order with which relations have been neighbourly, a small ecumenical landmark it itself.)

The growth of self-confidence among younger catholics possessing strong social awareness, has already been demonstrated in a number of small but significant ways. West of Scotland parents and teachers have been to the fore in the UK pressure group STOPP which has campaigned against the continuation of corporal punishment in schools. Ian O. Bayne, a radically-minded catholic and college lecturer, has been its principal Scottish spokesman while it was Mrs Grace Campbell, with a son attending a catholic primary school in Bishopbriggs, who won a decision from the European Court of Human Rights in 1984 critical of the British government's refusal to outlaw corporal punishment in schools. The catholic religious authorities were reluctant to offer encouragement to STOPP but they looked with more sympathy towards Parents For Survival, a pressure group launched by Kay Caldwell, a young catholic mother and freelance journalist. Its aim is to increase awareness among the parents of young children of the danger to their future presented by nuclear weapons and the current escalation of the arms race. But the group did not have the official backing of the church and, along with the experience of STOPP, it perhaps illustrates a degree of impatience with clerical and hierarchical caution on some of the major moral and political issues of the time.

The time has gone when the committed laity automatically looks towards the clergy for leadership. This is validated, perhaps surprisingly, by the experience of SPUC (the Society for the Protection of the Unborn Child), the anti-abortion pressure group. It came too late to stop the passing of the 1967 Abortion Act which met surprisingly little opposition from the traditional lay catholic watchdog bodies, a sign of how moribund they had become by the 1960s. However, it has campaigned vigorously either for the complete repeal of the act or for its amendment to limit the opportunities for abortion. In Scotland its membership and especially its leadership is very strongly catholic in composition—some say almost exclusively so.

Several politicians I have talked to, including Helen Liddell who is opposed to abortion, feel that SPUC's allegedly inquisitorial and high-pressure tactics impede its cause. It and its sister organisation LIFE which aims to persuade women contemplating abortion to think again, provide an outlet for lay catholic action of a more traditional pre-Vatican II character. Their assertion of moral superiority in pursuit of their cause may reflect a triumphalist element that others in the Scottish catholic community are now less keen to project. However, SPUC is not directed by the clergy but is a secular body, despite the massive presence of west of Scotland catholics; some SPUC activists even criticise priests for being unwilling to publicise their activities from the pulpit.[58]

Clerical snubs of this kind more frequently come the way of local groups making up the national commission for Justice and Peace which 'advises the Scottish Bishops' Conference in matters relating to social justice, international peace, human rights and world development and promotes action in these areas'.[59] Some priests have hindered Justice and Peace activities by saying they want 'nothing political' in their church even though it has the approval of the archbishop.[60] Many are still uncomfortable about speaking out on topical questions and prefer to preach religious salvation from the pulpit admits Dr Thomas J. Winning. Until his appointment as Glasgow's archbishop in 1974 they had been encouraged by his predecessors not to attract attention by making controversial statements, and to keep away from the letter columns of the press. As a result priests found it difficult to shake off this conditioning, instilled in them from their seminary days, under a new archbishop who thinks it necessary for the church to show concern about whether gospel values are being applied in the present time by governments that now have the means to decide the fate of mankind.

During his dozen years at the helm of Scotland's largest arch-diocese Tom Winning has initiated more sweeping changes than any of his five predecessors. However, he is a fairly orthodox (some would even say traditional) churchman who has not rushed into any headlong desire for change purely for its own sake. In his willingness to more fully involve the laity in the essential work of the church and give it an outspoken voice on issues like nuclear weapons, political injustice, and economic hardship at home and abroad, he has been motivated partly by the need to preserve the church as a relevant force in the lives of Scotland's 823,000 catholics in the face of ominous signs that it is rapidly losing ground among the faithful. He has his critics who argue that his energy has largely gone into shoring up the institution for its own sake rather than into forging a more democratic and visionary church which can fully respond to the material and spiritual crisis people are facing in urban post-industrial Scotland; they note that a 'three-line whip' applies on questions like abortion and denomina-tional schools—where priests are required to toe the official line—one which is not imposed on the newer quasi-political concerns like un-employment, nuclear weapons, and Third World hunger which priests can choose to ignore. But at least these have been placed on the agenda in a very conservative church which has still to 'adopt the mind-set of Vatican II'.[61] Dr Winning today concedes that the Scottish Church may not have altogether understood the great implications of Vatican II:

> Vatican II was all about changing attitudes. It was not merely about changing vestments or externals . . . We've never really been told that till recently.[62]

Having grown up in a Lanarkshire mining community, the future archbishop studied for the priesthood in Rome and became a canon lawyer. Like most canon lawyers he is instincitively loyal to the Roman hierarchy of the church and most of his innovations have been in terms of organisation rather than doctrine. Stints of parish work culminated in two years spent in Clydebank (1972-74) where he won the respect of the trade unions for his defence of endangered shipyard workers jobs at the time of the famous UCS 'work-in': its leader Jimmy Reid, was tipped as the first Communist MP to be elected since 1945 when he stood for parliament in 1974 but Winning did not hesitate to remind his parishioners that the church's view about the Communist Party had not altered despite the merits of the individual candidate and Reid lost (soon after he joined the Labour Party).

Though not the best of speakers Archbishop Winning's accessability and charm made him popular among ordinary catholics who no longer felt they were in the presence of a remote potentate when their bishop moved among them. According to lay catholic, Patrick Reilly, 'he is representative of ordinary Catholics. His failings and virtues are those of ordinary Catholics. He fits Glasgow very well.'[63]

Visits to the USA and Australia where catholics 'often shout their faith from the rooftops' bring home to Dr Winning the contrast with Scottish catholics who, weighed down by their past, 'are sometimes almost ashamed of being a Catholic':[64]

> We form the working-class church in the country . . . We are very diffident about our faith. We are inclined to conceal it. We are afraid of making too much noise in case we disturb the tranquility of others . . .[65]

Dr Winning wishes to encourage a more self-confident laity and he is not afraid to be controversial in expressing his own point of view. This was shown in 1978 when he criticised Prince Charles, the heir to the throne who, on the day his cousin's divorced bride Princess Michael of Kent was refused permission to marry in a catholic church, made the public comment that 'it seems worse than folly that Christians should argue and bicker over doctrinal matters which only serve to bring needless unhappiness and distress to a considerable number of people'. Noting the context of the Prince's statement Dr Winning declared that:

> His remarks will cause annoyance and anger to millions of the Queen's loyal subjects who care deeply about truth, doctrine and principle and who also care deeply about relationships with fellow Christians in other Churches.
>
> Perhaps he might care to enlarge upon his remarks to cover other aspects of this case such as the law of the land which prohibits a Roman Catholic from becoming a monarch.[66]

To communicate with west of Scotland catholics on a regular basis, Winning founded *Flourish*, the archdiocese's own monthly newspaper. It is a lively and attractively-produced newspaper which has tended to eclipse the existing Scottish catholic weekly whose readership is now increasingly confined to the elderly and the pious. While conventional on questions of faith and morals, *Flourish* often adopts a radical pose on issues like nuclear weapons. Its August 1986 issue carried a sympathetic portrait of 'Peace Padre', Mgr Bruce Kent which was prepared to expose the sharp disagreement Kent's work for the Campaign for Nuclear Disarmament (CND) had produced between

Archbishop Heim, the former pro-nuncio to Britain and Victor Guazelli, Bishop in East London and a staunch defender of Kent. Having served in a Clydebank parish that is only a short distance away from the largest concentration of nuclear weapons in western Europe, Dr Winning has managed to pass on his own concern to other bishops and the Scottish hierarchy has been possibly the most outspoken anywhere in Europe on the question. At their 1982 annual meeting they concluded that 'if it is immoral to use such weapons, it is also immoral to threaten their use'. By 1986 *Flourish* was asking, 'is it not equally immoral to assist in the manufacture and installation of these weapons', perhaps a signal for any catholics working in US and British military bases in the west of Scotland to examine their consciences about their continued presence in them.[67]

Some conservative catholics are unhappy about the hierarchy's ringing condemnation of nuclear weapons, others feel that they have not gone far enough and that their rhetoric should be backed up by positive deeds. Radical teachers are unhappy that catholic headmasters still allow school visits by the army and navy at a time when record unemployment makes many impressionable youngsters 'fodder' for the military; they would like the Catholic Education Commission which is firmly under the hierarchy's influence to recommend that such visits be discouraged in future.

Justice and Peace groups have been formed in Glasgow catholic schools with the blessing of the archbishop. Pupils and teachers do valuable work outside their schools helping society's human casualties and offering practical assistance to groups in the Third World. But all too often, when a group exists in school, there is nothing at parish level where young people are rarely encouraged to think and question about the often unjust ways of the human world around them.[68] Justice and Peace groups also tend to be mainly active in middle-class not working-class parishes where the great bulk of catholics reside and where young people, trapped by unemployment and lulled by drugs often have the bleakest of perspectives on the world. Justice and Peace activists like Fr Willy Slavin, Ella Meechan, and Mary Cullen have been struggling to put this right and their work has added a vital new dimension to catholic life in Scotland.

During the Winning episcopate the Glasgow church has also seen important organisational changes. In 1987 the offices of the arch-diocese were transferred from the city's business quarter to the banks of the Clyde, next to the pro-cathedral where they will be more accessible to ordinary catholics.

Earlier it was decided to abandon plans for a new cathedral because of the expense and the feeling that the money could be better spent on more people-orientated projects.[69] Dr Winning's hand was also detected in the closure of the national junior seminar at Blairs, Aberdeenshire in 1986. The expense of maintaining an institution in which the roll had fallen from 240 boys in 1977 to just over 100 students in 1986 influenced the decision to close what was the oldest junior seminary in Britain. The hierarchy drew consolation from the fact that more young men were choosing to remain at home and attend local catholic schools before applying for senior seminary. Chesters College, an inter-diocesan major seminary, designed to take students from all over Scotland, was opened in Glasgow in 1985.[70] Glasgow still held the purse-strings and remained the largest diocese, but this form of rationalisation produced dissension within the hierarchy and revealed that east–west tensions had still not been banished from the Scottish church.

Perhaps understandably St Andrews and Edinburgh, the senior diocese in terms of ecclesiastical rank was made uneasy by these changes. Not only had Blairs been in one of its suffragan sees, but Edinburgh had already lost its catholic teacher-training college at Craiglockart which in the 1970s was amalgamated with Notre Dame college in Glasgow to become St Andrew's College with the site being in Glasgow. To restore a balance, Gillis college, a senior seminary for the east was opened in Edinburgh in 1986.[71] These developments also coincided with the retirement of Cardinal Gray in 1985 and although Dr Winning's commitment to a single national seminary in Scotland had not been realised, he was now widely seen as the most senior of the Scottish bishops in terms of authority if not status. The new Archbishop of St Andrew's and Edinburgh was Fr Keith O'Brien, the last rector of Blairs. It was encouraging that his being of northern Irish birth did not excite any controversy in Edinburgh and indeed passed virtually without notice, perhaps because his father had spent many years in the navy and the family had followed the path of integration taken by most Edinburgh catholics.

Proof of the Scottish church's greater openness in recent times was the decision of the bishops of Glasgow and Motherwell in 1979 to commission a Gallup poll which investigated the laity's attitude to its faith and the institutional church and then to publicise the findings. The poll was nationwide. A sample of 989 catholics was interviewed, of whom 88% were Scottish-born, 6% Irish-born and 3% English.

Ninety-five per cent of the sample emphasised the importance of being baptised and confirmed as against 78% on going to Sunday Mass. The poll indicated a weekly Mass attendance of 54%, only 22% saying it was a year since they had been. (This response led one bishop to declare that Scotland had the highest percentage of practising catholics in Europe after Poland and Ireland.)[72] A quarter of regular Mass goers did not believe in life after death while there was more belief in papal supremacy: 67% of all respondents expressed belief in papal infallibility whatever they understood it to mean, a sign of obedience to the prevailing authority structure. However, 54% of respondents did not oppose birth control and 58% did not object to divorce,[73] evidence of how everyday contact with an increasingly secular society had undermined the credibility of church doctrine on these most human of questions. Finally, the church could gain reassurance from the fact that 75% of the sample still felt it important to send their children to catholic schools.[74]

Only a small sample of findings have been taken from what was a massive report running into several large volumes. If the bishops were disturbed or shaken out of complacency about the health of the church and its relevance to their flock—only 20% of those in the fifteen to twenty-four age-group described the catholic faith as the most important thing in their lives—they did not show it and the survey's findings were given extensive coverage in the catholic press. Bishops like Joseph Devine, appointed to Motherwell in 1983, were now prepared to acknowledge 'the special or unique vocation of the lay person to penetrate the world of the home, community, marketplace and the workshop with the truth of Christ'.[75] He had been impressed by the effectiveness of the hundreds of parish committees set up to prepare for the 1982 papal visit to Scotland and he warned that 'it will be a missed opportunity of incalculable proportions if these committees are either dismembered or allowed to lapse into the void'.[76]

The episcopal vacancy in Motherwell was the first one in Scotland where priests, religious, and laity in the diocese were invited to submit names they considered suitable for a new appointment.[77] Bishop Devine has proven a popular and forward-looking choice but it is unclear to what extent the views of the laity or indeed local clergy carried the day. The whole process is conducted in secrecy and, through the pro-nuncio, the Pope still has sole competence in appointing bishops.

Few catholics in Scotland have been outspoken about the hierarchical and centralised character of the church. One exception is Fr Anthony Ross OP, a stimulating and respected advocate of institutional reform, but he was effectively silenced by a stroke in 1982 shortly after being appointed Prior Provincial (or head) of his order, the Dominicans. His ability to make the gospel relevant to the modern world as a preacher and an activist in numerous practical causes will be missed, especially by young people and the students of Edinburgh University showed their appreciation for Fr Ross by electing him their Rector in the early 1980s.

Rennie McOwan, a former editor of the SCO has also spoken out about the direction the church has been taking especially since the elevation of Pope John Paul II: newspaper articles by him on segregated schools and contraception, questions on which the church does not exactly encourage open debate, have appeared in the Scottish press. In 1985, while the implications of the Calvi–Marcinkus affair were still dogging the Vatican, which remained tight-lipped about the relationship between Archbishop Marcinkus, the director of the Vatican bank, and Calvi, an Italian financier with Mafia and Masonic connections found dead in London in 1982, McOwan warned in a letter to the *SCO* that:

> Church authorities cannot call on governments or local authorities or dictatorships . . . to be more open, honest, and more accountable unless its own life in this respect is a model for others to follow.[78]

James Coffey, the current editor of the *SCO*, had warned earlier in 1985 that:

> Many young adults want a strong active Pope who will condemn injustice, shame governments into helping the Third World, outlaw nuclear weapons and put pressure on repressive regimes in South Africa and Latin America. For them, these are the real sins of the modern world. Not the private, personal matters the Pope so often deals with in his speeches.[79]

This comment from the editor of a paper which normally reflects the official church position on important religious issues coincided with the publication of a fresh survey which broke the alarming news that attendance at weekly Mass had plummeted from 50% to under 40% in less than a decade.[80] The figures suggested that attendance among catholics was declining faster than among other Christian bodies in Scotland and Dr Winning conceded that if avoiding action was not taken, 'by the end of the first quarter of the 21st century, there will be very few committed Catholics in Scotland'.[81]

It was against this background that in 1985 Dr Winning launched a renewal programme in his archdiocese aiming to tap the enthusiasm and commitment of the laity and draw lapsed catholics back to the church. 'We are all lapsed, some are more lapsed than others' was the significant comment he made on television in 1985 which no bishop would have stated so openly ten years before. Winning was impressed by the diocesan renewal programmes adopted by the catholic church in the USA and with the effectiveness of co-operation between priests and people in parish work. Another model is Latin America which the archbishop visited for a month in 1985. Here many parishes have been broken down into networks of small groups known as basic communities, comprising perhaps twenty people meeting in houses rather than churches and through prayer and the study of the gospel reflecting on how to instil Christian values in their own community.

In his Pastoral Plan, the title of Glasgow's renewal programme,

Winning also places emphasis on forming groups in the neighbourhood and in the home which will give lay catholics more of a chance to shape the religious life of their parish than they have ever had before. The archbishop described his plan not as a leap into the unknown but as a long overdue attempt to put into practice some of the basic teachings and new insights that emerged from Vatican II. This was an acknowledgement that the institutions which could put into practice the principles enunciated in the council's documents on the role of the church in the world had simply not existed hitherto.

The decision to tilt the church in a new direction arose not from grass-roots pressure but as a result of a carefully arrived at decision which may have been strongly influenced by the crucial role the laity played at parish level in preparation for the 1982 papal visit. The Scottish situation can be contrasted with England where an active corps of lay people have long pressed for a share of responsibility in the work of the church and recognition that they are an integral part of its activity. The English hierarchy has gone some way towards satisfying these aspirations and permission was granted for a National Pastoral Conference which met in Liverpool during May 1980 attended by 2,100 lay and religious delegates. Detailed planning had gone into the congress and there was no sharp polarisation of opinion. Among other things it passed resolutions concerning ecumenism and the ordaining of women and married men to the priesthood, and urged the bishops to consider admitting the divorced and remarried to the sacraments. It also urged a fundamental re-examination of teaching on marriage, sexuality, and contraception, leaving open the possibility of change in the Church's teachings. The hierarchy did not stifle such views and while adopting some resolutions, it gave full and careful explanations why others could not be endorsed, it being only too aware that currents in the Vatican viewed the whole exercise as misconceived.[82]

It may well be that Glasgow's renewal programme will throw up a new generation of assertive lay people keen to make their mark in the affairs of the church. Unlike many of his priests Dr Winning does not seem daunted by this prospect and views the counter-prospect of a lifeless church of silence going through the motions of faith, with far more dread. On the question of the ordination of women he displays a very open mind and he is keen to promote a high-level of trust and co-operation between the church and its people; many have responded with enthusiasm to the invitation to form parish renewal groups in order to revitalise the life of the church. By mid-1986 these functioned in ninety-nine out of 109 parishes and over 1,300 people had received training at a specially formed Pastoral Centre about how to implement the renewal process. Dr Winning hopes that some of the leaders who emerge may play a positive role in the wider Scottish society;[83] by their defensiveness in the past Scottish catholics have contributed their full share to the inertia and pessimism that has characterised the corporate Scottish personality during much of this century.

Some critics consider that the Pastoral Plan is fifteen years too late and that those who could have done so much to revitalise the church have long ago opted for involvement in public affairs even if they still attend Mass. This is a view expressed by some middle-aged catholics whose idealism and energy were refused an outlet by the church in the 1960s and early 1970s. A more serious stumbling block is the role of many clergy who are still anxious to retain a veto over religious activities in their parishes and who do not relish a more participatory role where they consult with lay people over a range of questions they once decided on their own.

On being asked in 1986 how easy it had been to convince the clergy of the Plan's usefulness, Dr Winning replied only half jokingly 'how difficult is it you mean!'.[84] Many parish clergy, the bulk of whom are into late middle age or even older, have already been badly stretched creating new parishes in the newer housing estates or implementing the liturgical changes of Vatican II and they do not relish new challenges at their time of life. Unlike the English parish clergy they do not have to engage in the time-consuming task of raising funds for church schools, but their life is often gruelling and it is instructive that the average life-span of Scottish priests who died between 1966 and 1985 was just sixty-four years, rather below the male national average?[85] In large working-class parishes especially, home visits by clergy are increasingly a thing of the past as a parish which had three or more priests in the 1960s finds it has to make do with two in the 1980s. The death of priests is clearly outpacing ordinations (while the authorities are reluctant to provide information about how many priests have been laicised). The number of secular priests in Scotland fell from 927 in 1981 to 876 in 1984 and the curve still points downwards.[86]

Pointedly worded headlines like 'Why our priests must have the right attitude' have appeared in *Flourish* as part of Dr Winning's drive to transform the church into a partnership between committed laity and clergy.[87] Their resistance to change he puts down in large part to their seminary training and it may be no coincidence that the rectorship of the Scots College in Rome was entrusted in 1986 to Fr John Fitzsimmons, a Paisley priest strongly committed to the full implementation of the decisions of Vatican II.

Before his appointment Fitzsimmons played an important role in ecumenical dialogue, a feature which has not been lost sight of during Winning's episcopate. However, important obstacles still give rise to misunderstandings between the main churches. This was shown in 1982 when a document presented to the Pope by the Moderator of the General Assembly referred to 'widespread unease' about mixed marriage and separate catholic schools. At theological level a joint commission on doctrine and marriage had already done valuable work in trying to harmonise some of the practices and regulations of both the RC Church and the Church of Scotland, one important break-through being agreement on common baptism, whereby baptism in one church has validity in the other. But in the wake of the 1982 papal visit Dr Winning felt that closer links needed to be forged with those at the Presbytery level of the Church of Scotland. The Presbyteries of Glasgow and Dumbarton agreed that the Pope's senti-ments about the need for the churches to 'make our pilgrimage on earth hand in hand' was a worthy one that did not threaten the integrity of the Kirk and a series of meetings involving six representa-tives from each church were held, these giving way to intermediate meetings between ministers, church elders, priests and nuns who came together to study a theme of relevance to the mission of the churches in the west of Scotland.[88]

Perhaps owing to these regular grassroots contacts education is no longer the stumbling block that it once was in inter-church relations. Dr Winning thinks that in the mid-1980s Kirk ministers 'are less inclined to be envious' about RC state schools.[89] 'The fact that we have sold the pass in respect of religious education does not mean that you have to do the same' is a view commonly expressed by ministers today according to Fr Fitzsimmons.[90] The Right Rev Andrew Herron who has long been wary about ecumenism, feels that the Kirk's fight over religious education is not with the RC church but with the education authorities who should be prepared to offer the national church many of the rights that enable the catholic church to instil its faith in pupils attending denominational schools: placed in the hierarchy's shoes he would be just as tenacious in his bid to maintain the *status quo*.[91]

The question of mixed marriages remains a sore point even though the Vatican's Ne Temere decree was modified in 1970 by the apostolic letter Matrimonia Mixta. National hierarchies now have much greater autonomy in determining their attitude to a catholic who wishes to marry a non-catholic. In Holland and Switzerland, which like Scotland have a history of protestant–catholic rivalry, the bishops have long been happy to approve a marriage between a catholic and a Christian of any other denomination. In Scotland it took longer to edge towards this position, but a joint committee chaired by Archbishop Winning and the Rev George Balls of the Church of Scotland which met periodically after 1973, substantially narrowed some of the differences over marriage.[92]

The catholic church is now prepared to give its blessing to a wedding between an adherent and a committed Christian with the priest being ready to officiate at the service. However, it refuses to approve a wedding involving one of its members and a nominal protestant. The hierarchy and the Kirk's view of what constitutes a 'nominal' protestant is at variance and the Kirk does not go along with the hierarchy's hardline. There is little sign of a breakthrough especially since the catholic side is convinced that these disputed marriages are one of the prime causes of the steep decline in religious practice detected in the 1980s. By 1977 mixed marriages in the Glasgow archdiocese were running at 44% of all marriages involving a catholic and 48% in Paisley, the percentage having only been 28% respectively in both dioceses as recently as 1966.

The church sees itself making few gains from these unions (indeed the number of conversions to catholicism in Scotland has fallen markedly since the 1950s) and fears that these marriages will be the means by which it loses its presence in the working-class: nominal protestants are most commonly found in the urban working-class and, since the catholic community remains overwhelmingly working-class itself, a mixed marriage is highly likely to involve a couple where one partner does not share even the qualified religious conviction of the other.

Leaving aside such a tortuous issue, the post-1973 depression which has laid waste much of Scotland's manufacturing base, led many church leaders to recognise that the major contemporary problems besetting the west of Scotland transcended religious barriers:[93] the churches speak with an increasingly united voice on social issues like education, welfare and unemployment which have been at the forefront of political debate in the 1980s. The election of a Tory government in 1979 which only enjoyed minority support in Scotland and went on to pursue highly ideological policies which shattered the postwar consensus about the need to protect full unemployment and devolve a certain amount of wealth and opportunity to the regions and nations on the periphery of the United Kingdom, sharpened the social concern of the churches. Religious leaders have come together in the fight to save car plants, shipyards and steelworks on which the livelihoods of entire communities are dependent; local authorities and the trade union movement welcomed them as valuable allies prepared to travel to London to plead for a less unfeeling attitude from a government which, in 1983, derived its massive majority largely from the southern third of Britain.[94] Archbishop Winning has thrown his weight behind several campaigns in the 1980s to save jobs at a time when he fears that the poor in the catholic community are getting poorer and that many of the social advances secured after 1940 are in danger of being lost.[95] In 1983 the Scottish Bishops Conference adopted the report of an Inter-Denominational working-party looking at unemployment and issued it as a hierarchical statement with only minor alterations. It had been chaired by Tom Carberry, a lay catholic who remembered sharp differences of opinion among some of the participants but never along denominational lines.[96] To Fr Fitzsimmons such collaboration represents a second phase of the ecumenical movement in which scope exists for the catholic laity to be fully involved.[97]

Occasional setbacks occur as when the 1979 General Assembly expressed its overwhelming disapproval at the appointment of a laicized Irish catholic priest from an American university to the chair of theology at Edinburgh University named after the great nineteenth century Presbyterian Thomas Chalmers. By now Pope John Paul II was installed in the Vatican, one who gave the impression of preferring a more fundamentalist and even triumphalist brand of catholicism in which there is less emphasis than before about making common cause with other Christian faiths. Donald MacDonald is one minister who considers that the ecumenical movement has made 'little particular progress' under his papacy:

> People at my stage in the church regard the present Pope as a delightful man with a very warm personality. Then we go and read what he has to say and we are terrified out of our wits . . . The religious history of Poland is so different from that of other countries of Europe that I sometimes wonder if the present Pope really understands the western mentality.[98]

The 1980s have admittedly seen a series of ups and downs in ecumenical activity: the opening of a church centre at Bridge of Don, Aberdeenshire in 1983 which is the first building in Scotland to have under one roof a Catholic church and a Presbyterian church[99] was followed by the refusal of the minister of Glasgow Cathedral to allow a catholic service to be performed in 1986 on the occasion of its 750th anniversary; but, earlier in 1986, it had been the overwhelming decision of the General Assembly to repudiate the description of the Pope as anti-Christ and delete other anti-catholic statements in the 1647 Westminster confession, its principal subordinate standard of faith next to the Bible.[100]

Militant protestants opposed to the ecumenical movement tended to disregard these nuances and loudly accused the General Assembly of delivering the national church into the hands of Rome. They had their successes as when a sermon being given in St Giles Cathedral, Edinburgh by Edward Daly, the catholic bishop of Derry was successfully halted in 1975 by demonstrators.[101] In their eyes the administrators of the protestant cathedral operated a double-standard since three years earlier, permission had been withheld for the Orange Order in the east of Scotland to hold a service in St Giles on the 400th anniversary of Knox's death.[102]

But divisions among ultra-protestants in Scotland weakened the anti-ecumenical drive. Pastor Glass, the most visible of anti-papal clerics was often at loggerheads with some of his erstwhile allies. In 1976 he picketed the World Congress of Fundamentalists held in Edinburgh and organised by Ian Paisley and the American evangelist Bob Jones.[103] In turn the sale of his newspaper was banned by the Orange County Grand Lodges of Glasgow and Lanarkshire from its functions.[104] The Orange Order itself drew no encouragement from the rise of protestant fundamentalism in the USA and in 1985 its paper was denouncing the Moral Majority as 'an ecclesiastical Fifth Column' with 'Romanist overtones'.[105]

Such chronic internecine disputes reduced the effectiveness of the campaign mounted by local opponents of the visit to Britain made by Pope John Paul II between 28 May and 2 June 1982. They had been emboldened by Ian Paisley's success in pressurising the organisers of the 1979 papal visit to Ireland to scrap plans to bring him to Northern Ireland following the threat to create a protestant backlash in the province. For months in advance the press speculated that the thirty-six hours the Pope was scheduled to spend in Scotland would be the ones most likely to be marred by ugly protests. Opponents were not pacified by the hierarchy's insistence that the visit was a purely pastoral one designed to deepen the religious belief of catholics. If that was the case, they demanded, why were all Edinburgh children being give a day off school when the Pope came among them, a council decision which the Secretary of State overruled.[106] The Orange Order sent a telegram to the Queen warning her that she would be in breach of her coronation oath if she met the Pope.[107] Enoch Powell MP warned that the visit was an unwelcome intrusion into a basically protestant country which still had cause to remember that the Vatican had once been a deadly enemy of Britain's protestant constitution and religion. Powell's influence reached into government despite his absorption in Ulster politics and the government declined to support a proposal from a catholic MP that the Pope address both Houses of Parliament.[108]

The Orange Order's campaign against the visit was conceived mainly in theological and constitutional terms; it also had an ecological flavour since much indignation greeted the announcement that trees were to be felled so as to afford a better view of the Pope in Bella-houston Park, the venue of his Glasgow rally. After lively internal discussions the Order opted for peaceful and orderly protests and the 10% to 15% of the Glasgow membership who allegedly felt inclined to march on Bellahouston Park got no official backing.

But the 1982 visit, into which years of planning had gone, was almost cancelled at the last moment due to the outbreak of war in the spring of 1982 between Britain and Argentina following the Argentinian invasion of the disputed Falkland islands, a British possession in the South Atlantic. As pressure from Latin America for the Pope to cancel the visit mounted, Archbishop Winning stepped in, realising that because of the cost involved, it would be difficult to rearrange the visit for a later date and that cancellation would be a great blow to the morale of the Scottish Church.[109] After sending a telegram to the Pope urging him not to call off the visit, he sent private messages to the Argentinian cardinals and on 17 May, with the Archbishop of Liverpool, he flew to Rome, where he has been credited with saving the visit after a private meeting with the Pope.[110]

Earlier, Kirk leaders had reacted negatively on being informed by those drawing up the papal itinerary that the only time available for a meeting between the Pope and the Moderator would be in distant Canterbury where he would take his place in the queue with English protestant church leaders. For a time it looked as if no meeting would take place which would have been a severe blow to Scottish ecumenism. Then the Pope's crowded schedule was rearranged to allow for a meeting with the Moderator, Professor John McIntyre in the courtyard of New College on the Mound leading directly to the steps of the General Assembly Hall in Edinburgh. In the courtyard stands a statue of John Knox and the two church leaders were to meet in its shadow which infuriated militant protestants in Edinburgh. Eight hundred turned out to protest, the Pope blessing them as he passed by to meet the Moderator, their angry shouts remaining audible during the short meeting.[111] One of the organisers commented ruefully that if militant Orangemen in the west had congregated in Edinburgh rather than marching behind a band in Glasgow, the combined numbers could have stopped the Popemobile for several minutes which would have directed world attention on their action.[112]

Dr Winning was struck by the fact that in a generally incident-free Scottish visit what little trouble there was occurred in Edinburgh rather than in Glasgow.[113] Next day, on 1 June 1982, an estimated 300,000 people packed Bellahouston Park to greet the Pope, the largest turnout of any of the British rallies. In his homily John Paul II referred to Ninian, Mungo, and Margaret, the chief saints of Scotland, though significantly not to Patrick.[114] His speech-writers were keen to stress that roman catholicism was an authentic part of the life and traditions of Scotland and that the church had ceased to be an immigrant one. The novelist Allan Massie was not the only commentator to observe that 'John Paul has completed the rehabilitation of Scottish Catholicism and its reintegration into the Scottish nation'. He went on to observe that 'nothing could so clearly have demonstrated the changed position of Catholicism in Scotland . . . than the contrast between the huge, peaceful and happy crowds . . . and the tiny bands of demonstrators, outnumbered by the police'.[115] Many protestants packed into Bellahouston Park, one of them being the Rev. Donald MacDonald who felt that he must be among many co-religionists on noticing that in the enclosure in which he and his family was located, only 50% of people went to communion at the Mass being celebrated; it may also have been a sign that many catholics there did not feel themselves to be in sufficient state of grace to partake the communion host or that to many it was as much a carnival as a religious event. The failure of a spiritual revival to occur after the visit raises the question to what extent catholics were applauding the singer rather than the song, delighting in the presence among them of their religious champion rather than absorbing the serious religious message he elaborated in the homilies preached on Scottish soil, and then rearranging their personal lives accordingly.

The Pope went further than most politicians or royalty to emphasise Scotland's distinct nationhood and by kissing the soil of Scotland on his arrival at Turnhouse airport he allayed suspicions that the Vatican was going to commit the error of regarding Scotland as the northern extension of England.[116] In this context it is ironic that the only local politician to make a controversial pronouncement in the run-up to the visit was William Wolfe, president of the pro-independence SNP. In the spring of 1982 he expressed concern about mainly protestant Falkland islanders falling under the control of 'the cruel and ruthless fascist dictatorship of a Roman Catholic state' and he questioned the recent decision to raise the status of the papal envoy in Britain to ambassadorial level.[117] Wolfe was quickly relegated to obscurity by an angry SNP and Gordon Wilson, the party chairman was invited to attend the Bellahouston Mass by Cardinal Gray who, in his letter, reportedly assured the party leader that he was not at all worried by the Wolfe outburst and that catholics in the SNP should carry on regardless.[118]

In its quest for Scottish self-government the SNP had made impressive strides in the mid-1970s but further progress was effectively halted later in the decade as the bid to prise some legislative power back to Scotland from London failed and deepening economic recession eroded confidence in the belief that Scotland could manage its affairs by striking out successfully on its own.

The lower middle-class Presbyterian image which the SNP was firmly saddled with, hurt its prospects among catholic voters, many of whom were dimly aware that in the past their worst detractors had corresponded to that image or mind-set. This stereotype which the

Labour Party gleefully exploited, was unfair to the party: in the October 1974 general election, when it got 30% of the Scottish vote, its best result to date, ten of its seventy-one candidates had been catholics, two of whom were elected (George Thomson for Galloway, Iain MacCormick for Argyll). The party's national organiser in this windfall year was John McAteer, a Coatbridge catholic who died prematurely soon after; later in the decade several of the party's senior headquarters staff such as Steve Butler, Duncan McLaren, and Roseanna Cunningham were found to be catholics.[119] However, in its expansionary phase, the SNP had been unable to gather substantial backing from well educated or middle-class catholics. Upwardly mobile catholics remained attached to the Labour Party, an interesting psephological phenomenon occurring at a time when the new middle-classes were elsewhere deserting the party. Of course, materially successful Clydeside catholics were still disporportionately located in public sector posts and the new white-collar salariat tended to view Labour as the party best inclined to protect their pay and jobs. Many tended to be active at local level in the Labour Party, a trend that continued when the public sector came under threat after 1976 and it was only in the new towns that catholics in this social category gravitated to the SNP in any numbers.[120]

Even more discouraging was the SNP's total failure to break into the working-class catholic vote which ensured Labour dominance in the west of Scotland and helped give the party a clear majority of Scottish seats. In the February 1974 election it has been calculated that only 6·9% of catholics voted SNP compared to 48·4% of voters who were linked to protestant denominations.[121] In the second election of 1974, held in October, evidence has been gathered to show that, of a distinct selection of groups, it was catholics who showed the greatest resistance towards voting SNP.[122] The loyalty of the west of Scotland poor and disadvantaged, among whom many catholics were to be found, was in fact the one sure thing that stood between Labour's success and its collapse in an election where its nationalist rivals came within six percentage points of overtaking it.

The SNP bore its frustrations stoically and made no attempt to use religion to boost its credibility among one section of the working-class at the expense of the other. But neither did it seem to realise, at least sufficiently clearly, that sectarianism helped shore up a provincial mentality that was inimical to its plans. In a splintered working-class divided by small-scale religious rivalries the degree of mutual trust and self-confidence that could have fuelled the great Scottish leap forward towards statehood in a Scandinavian-style democracy was absent. In Scotland's biggest conurbations 1690, 1916 and other dramatic dates of Irish history still meant more than 1314 or 1320—famous landmarks in Scotland's past. Made complacent by its stunning breakthrough in

1974 the party seemed content to operate within these cramped confines, being careful not to give offence to rival Irish sensibilities in the west of Scotland rather than striking out and attempting to reforge the Scottish identity (the way Michael Kelly had attempted for the city of Glasgow?) so as to sweep away parochial rivalries.

Rather naively the SNP felt that the case for self-determination spoke for itself and that no Scottish cultural reawakening or assault on the provincial Scottish identity was needed to administer further shocks to the staid body politic. The Tory Party was ever more calculating; in a bid to shore up its crumbling base in Scotland it began to make overtures to groups which it had hitherto disdained. Teddy Taylor who held on to the predominantly working-class seat of Glasgow Cathcart for fifteen years (1964–79) by ventilating his constituents concerns with rising crime and changing moral standards was to the fore in giving the party a chameleon-like image. In his devolution diary, the journalist Neal Ascherson relates how, in 1977, he unveiled his master plan to rescue the party from the electoral doldrums, to the Glasgow press corps:

> He told us that he planned to inveigle two improbable groups towards the Conservative Party: the Pakistanis and the Catholics. His reasoning was cunning. The Pakistanis are small businessmen, deeply respectable, and anxious natural Tories who are only drawn towards Labour because of a vague impression that Labour are more concerned about racial tensions. (This is a brilliant and, I am sure, accurate perception . . .)
>
> As for the Catholics, in spite of their traditional loyalty to Labour in the west, their concern for sexual morality, social discipline and the family ought again to attract them towards the Tories. (This is also true, but here there exists a strong and institutional framework which through the hierarchy and lay associations binds the Catholics to Labour.) Teddy's brand of Cathcart plebeian Toryism is strongly Presbyterian . . . and it is hard to see him subverting priests. If Labour moved a long way to the Marxist left he might have a better chance. . .[123]

Ascherson's caution proved correct. Taylor's virtuoso performance in Glasgow politics ended at the 1979 general election when his was the only Tory seat in Britain to fall to Labour. However, at the same election two roman catholics were returned as Tory MPs in Scotland, Michael Ancram for Edinburgh South and Albert McQuarrie for Banffshire. Neither seat had many catholics and neither man was typical of the catholic community. McQuarrie was a Greenock businessman and Ancram was the son and heir of the twelfth Marquess of Lothian; in 1970 he had cut his teeth as a Tory candidate in West Lothian where he had been surprised at the depth of Orange feeling.[124] Ten years later Mrs Thatcher dismissed a few local objections arising from his religion and appointed Ancram chairman of the Conservative Party in

Scotland. A further sign that what remained of anti-catholic feeling was fast disappearing from the party's midst came in 1982 when Gerry Malone was nominated for the by-election in Hillhead, the party's only remaining Glasgow seat. He lost but few put this down to his religion and he was returned for Aberdeen South in 1983.

Awkwardness about giving top positions to catholics had vanished from the Labour Party by the 1970s. In 1976 Helen Liddell, the daughter of a Coatbridge bus driver who had been the first catholic in the town ever to reach the rank of inspector, was appointed secretary of the Labour Party in Scotland at the age of twenty-six. A journalist and economics graduate who married a non-catholic (her maiden name is Reilly) she has retained her faith while having the confidence to duel with SPUC over its hardline on abortion and under her firm steward-ship the party has avoided the internal convulsions faced by Labour in England.

By 1979 eight of Labour's forty Scottish MPs were catholics. They now included left-wingers like Dennis Canavan, Ernest Ross and Andy McMahon as well as Frank McElhone, the shrewd Gorbals green-grocer who had exploded a stereotype by moving steadily left after his election in 1969. But the equation between catholicism and con-servatism on social and moral issues was not yet dead as the political careers of James Hamilton and James Dempsey showed. They repre-sented parliamentary seats in Lanarkshire where a relatively low pro-portion of mixed marriages and pockets of sectarian tension produced a catholic community that was more inward-looking and socially con-servative than anywhere else in Scotland.

In local government old-fashioned catholic powerbrokers were also able to survive even as radicals began to disturb the complacency of local politics at the end of the 1970s. Pat Lally and Ken Fagan, local magnates in Glasgow and Dundee, whose style was reminiscent of Irish-American ward bosses, showed their tactical skill by arranging alliances with the left in order to stay in power. In 1968 and 1977 sharp swings to the SNP in Glasgow removed many of the self-serving or low calibre councillors whose misdemeanours had long bred widespread cynicism about the grubby character of Labour politics in Glasgow. With the growth of a small hard left faction in the 1980s that numbered several councillors whose background was RC, religion was no longer such a reliable means of identifying whether a Labour councillor was left or right; the fact that roman catholics (whether practising or lapsed) made up over half the elected Labour members on Glasgow District Council by the mid-1980s, meant that they were bound to be located at different points on the political spectrum. Strathclyde Regional Council which has responsibility for a wider range of services, tended to have fewer catholic members and its first convenor had been the radical minister, Geoff Shaw who was greatly mourned on his untimely death in 1978.

Between 1975 and 1987 four Glasgow Lord Provosts in a row were roman catholics which inevitably caused some eyebrows to be raised. Those who dismiss the idea that here is the 'catholic mafia' at work, put it down to sheer coincidence or to the fact that Labour has traditionally attracted 'oppressed minorities' with catholics being well to the fore in this category.[125] Conservatively minded older citizens who still took religious head-counts, were mollified by the pragmatic style of Labour rule in Glasgow. The administration did not use its runaway majority (in 1986 eighty-eight out of Strathclyde's 103 regional council seats were in Labour hands) to embark on confrontation with a right-wing government as happened in Edinburgh and Liverpool after 1981, nor were rates pushed up sharply in middle-class areas. Strathclyde Labour councillors also kept their heads down during the campaign for a devolved Scottish parliament which culminated in a referendum held on 1 March 1979.

The Labour government elected in 1974 had been panicked into drawing up plans for a Scottish assembly in Edinburgh by the success of the SNP. However, by 1978 the Nationalists had lost the initiative amidst a welter of claims skilfully put about by Tory and Labour opponents of devolution that it would be just another expensive tier of government or that it would lead to confrontation between Scotland and England. Another claim inserted into the debate was that sectarian strife was more likely to occur in a Scotland which enjoyed much the same measure of home rule as Northern Ireland, whose experiment with devolution failed disastrously earlier in the 1970s. Hugh Brown MP, a firm devolutionist with many RC constituents (who, in 1978, addressed several Orange conferences about what devolution would mean), found more apprehension among catholics than protestants.[126] Helen Liddell recalls hearing catholics express fears about how they would be treated in a separate or devolved Scotland. To her, it helped explain why the SNP vote in her native Coatbridge was always so derisory. Two of her cousins are SNP supporters because they feel that Scottish independence is the logical extension of Irish independence but, in her part of Lanarkshire, 'all it needs is for a couple of guys in the Orange lodge to wear SNP badges for feelings of unease to spread'.[127] The 'Labour Vote No' campaign headed by Brian Wilson, and Tam Dalyell (who is married into a well-known Labour catholic family), was accused of capitalising on these residual and atavistic fears about devolution in 1978–79.[128] Perhaps the SNP unwittingly gave it scope by backing away from the challenge instead of confidently proclaiming that Scotland was no mere extension of Northern Ireland but a nation with its own distinctive history and culture which had managed to absorb different waves of immigrants with ultimate success. In practice, wrote Owen Dudley Edwards in 1981 'the SNP has taken the utmost pains to avoid public debate and discussion of Northern Ireland over the last dozen years'.[129] When Gavin Kennedy, a maverick member, wrote in 1979 that Ireland *was* relevant because it 'represents the only case we have so far of a part of the UK breaking away from Britain', he was clearly out on a limb and was greeted with little enthusiasm; he went on to warn:

> It is a racialist delusion that somehow Scotland will be treated differently when the SNP approaches its goal of self-government. We will hve to begin to understand this when we demand the withdrawal of regiments from Northern Ireland and vote against legislation purporting to deal with terrorism but which, in reality, aims to preserve the power of the British state.[130]

The referendum campaign being fought out in the last months in office of a discredited Labour government was a dull affair. In Glasgow few constituency Labour parties felt inclined to mobilise their supporters on polling day. Perhaps more effective than Labour's feeble effort in helping RC voters to make up their minds was the intervention of Bishop Joseph Devine who campaigned on the 'Yes' side and declared in a speech that:

> As a Catholic, I belong to an international church, but internationalism flourishes best when rooted in a keen sense of one's nation, culture and identity. After all, you cannot have internationalism without nations and Scotland is a nation.[131]

In the referendum Strathclyde region returned a 54·0% 'Yes' vote in favour of a Scottish Assembly, the second highest in the country but on a low Scottish turnout of 63·8%. It is impossible to ascertain to what extent working-class catholics with reservations about devolution turned out to vote 'No' or merely stayed at home. But devolution was lost, since Parliament required 40% of the Scottish electorate (voters and non-voters alike) to vote 'Yes' and the low turn-out ensured that only 32·9% actually did so.

In the 1979 and 1983 general elections the Labour Party remained the largest party in Scotland in terms of votes and seats, but in 1983 sharp inroads were made into its vote by the breakaway Social Democratic Party (SDP). It fought the election in conjunction with the Liberals and together they pushed the SNP into fourth place. The SDP–Liberal Alliance does not threaten the institutional structure of Scottish politics in the way that the SNP does and it may, in the future, present an easier 'protest' option for disenchanted but conservative RC Labour voters.

The extent of catholic loyalty to Labour was particularly well illustrated in 1978 at the parliamentary by-election in Glasgow Garscadden when the Labour candidate was Donald Dewar, a keen supporter of the 1967 Abortion Act. SPUC forcefully intervened in the campaign but it focused as much on the 'discrepancies' of the SNP candidate's record on abortion as it did on Dewar's who retained the seat for Labour and confounded observers who felt that the SNP was likely to capture it.

Where possible, Labour has sought to accommodate special interest groups even if few votes are at stake, so as to boost the Glasgow administration's image as a left-wing but responsible one. *The Economist* praised 'the self-salesmanship . . . of a confident Labour leadership that keeps its heavies in check and its businessmen in partnership'.[132] The administration has displayed its pragmatism by refusing to crack down on masonic influences in local government in the way that the Greater London Council (GLC), under Ken Livingstone, had done. The GLC barred masons from using council premises and several left-wing London boroughs announced that proven masons would not be considered for sensitive managerial posts that fell vacant: freemasonry was perceived as a threat to egalitarian council policies owing to its secretive character and reputation for promoting the individual ambitions of its membership.

The municipal left in Glasgow has remained virtually silent about the freemasons even though in the west of Scotland they enjoy one of the highest levels of membership anywhere in the UK. This willing-ness to 'let sleeping dogs lie' is also illustrated by the Labour administra-tion's relationship with the Orange Order. Permission continues to be given for the use of Glasgow's public parks as the venue for Orange rallies and permits are still issued to allow frequent Orange processions in the city centre even though, in 1984, there were signs that business-men were beginning to resent the inconvenience to shoppers and the effect on their takings.[133] It is a good illustration of the Glasgow tendency to accommodate competing religious views that catholic politicians have not used their influence on the council to move against the Order. Peter McCann, a catholic Lord Provost laid on a civic reception for the Order in the mid-1970s and RC councillors prefer to smile when shown vitriolic articles in the Orange newspaper by an elderly contributor who describes them as part of 'the Pope's . . . "Scoto"-Eirish legion in Scotland . . . they constitute Romanmasonry . . . and Scotland is rotten with them'.[134] Despite such brickbats Labour MPs like David Lambie and Hugh Brown, both widely respected for their religious impartiality, still express admiration for the disciplined manner in which the Order seeks to organise its affairs and for the moderating influence of leading Orange officials. In 1979 Andy McMahon MP even attended the inaugural service of a new 'Orange Kirk' in Glasgow in his capacity as MP for Govan.[135]

The Labour Party is aware that perhaps the bulk of Orangemen now vote Labour—an impression shared by the Grand Secretary of the Order[136]—and that little is to be gained from forcing them to abandon their traditional religious attachments and marching routes against their will. The most vociferous members still tended to align with the Tories but an important exception was Sam Campbell, the Labour convenor of Midlothian District Council and a senior figure in the Convention of Scottish Local Authorities (COSLA) during the 1980s. His *Scottish Who's Who* entry listed 'supporting Glasgow Rangers' as one of his recreations and he rose in Labour circles despite his well-known Orange sympathies.[137] In 1978 he was almost nominated as the Labour candidate in the parliamentary seat of East Lothian now held by John Home Robertson, a catholic landowner and party colleague. Having spent a lifetime in the mining industry, his working-class credentials are unimpeachable and the fifty-six-year-old councillor was returned unopposed for a Midlothian mining seat in 1985. But his solid political reputation crumbled following a furious outburst he delivered against the roman catholic church and its allies which came in a speech at an open-air rally in Leith on 28 June 1986 at the annual parade of the County Grand Orange Lodge of the East. Even Orangemen among the platform party were taken aback by the stridency of his remarks which received wide coverage in the press. *The Scotsman* reported it as follows:

> Campbell, a Church of Scotland elder . . . said ministers should be told to 'stop fraternising with the Church of Rome . . .' Lord MacLeod of Fuinary, founder of the Iona Community, had 'betrayed the church and lived 90 years too long'.
>
> Priests who participated in radio counselling programmes had 'never been in a wedding bed, at least I think they haven't' but were advising on family life: 'let's get it stopped'. Protestants should withhold their TV licences until Roman Catholicism was 'cleared' off the screen . . .
>
> Campbell . . . said the best way to save money on education was to 'shut down the Papist schools' which were an insult and a memorial to Roman chains and darkness . . .
>
> After making more temperate points about resources for denominational education, he concluded: 'the moment that the Roman Catholic Church in this country loses its schools it is on the way down, so let's help it'.[138]

Campbell is a flamboyant personality and the violence of his language perhaps stems from an inability to articulate these views in Labour circles where discussion of contentious religious issues is frowned upon. Within a week Campbell had apologised for his views, which he claimed were 'out of character' and he had resigned both from the Orange Order and the convenorship.[139] Ironically the Order had lost one of its most influential members just as Robert Leitch, the County

Grand Master of the East, launched an appeal for greater interest in politics by Orangemen:

> We complain about our Politicians both local and national, but unless we ... spend more time at lodges discussing affairs of importance with relevance to the role of Orangeism in Politics, Religion, Education, etc., we will never be the force our principles dictate we should be. If all we do is talk about bands, buses and arrangements for demonstrations etc., our priorities are wrong and we will never have a fairer share of power in Councils, Churches and Schools. Come on, let us cast off the introvert complex and give more support to the Grand Lodge's committee for more public and political awareness.[140]

With Scottish politics having been remarkably little effected by the conflict in Northern Ireland, the one issue that seemed capable of generating the passions that Sam Campbell had given voice to, remained education. In theory the Labour Party supported the ideal of integration but was determined not to take any initiative which would make it a burning issue, so the status quo was maintained, albeit without conspicuous enthusiasm. (Much the same view is taken by the other parties, none of which show any desire, at least publicly, to withdraw the rights catholics have enjoyed by statute since 1918.) Catholics prominent in Labour politics like Helen Liddell and Jean McFadden see the day coming when an integrated system with provisions for religious education will be established and they are not greatly perturbed by the prospect.[141] Denominational schools were geared for the needs of a community at a specific phase in its evolution and now that the community is well on the way to integration, their role will be re-assessed, hopefully by mutual agreement, would seem to be the view of the majority of Labour officials who take an interest in education; there are no outspoken critics of the status quo among Labour politicians (Sam Campbell excepted). In the first half of the 1970s, at the annual Scottish conference of the party, anti-segregation motions were however submitted from the following branches:

1970 Glasgow Craigton, Post Office Engineering Workers' Union
1971 East Renfrewshire, Leith, Central Ayrshire, Glasgow Hillhead, West Edinburgh
1972 East Renfrewshire
1974 AUEW/TASS
1976 East Renfrewshire
1977 Kinross and East Perthshire

These motions came from working-class constituencies or from skilled trade unions likely to have relatively few catholics or from middle-class branches which regarded separate schools as an anachronism that needed to be replaced. The 1976 conference went as far as to pass a pro-integration resolution, one which suggested that there should be experiments in such a direction but, with Labour in office, it was nevertheless not acted upon.[142] Party managers succeeded in heading off the possibility of an internal row on the conference floor by providing little further space for discussion on segregated education. By now politicians of all parties were growing increasingly wary of the subject, given the recent volatility of the Scottish electorate and the issue fell from view thereafter in Scottish Labour circles.

However, if flared up dramatically at the 1979 conference of the EIS, the union which represents most of Scotland's teachers, when the longstanding policy of the EIS that no change can be brought about over religious segregation without the agreement of all parties, was rejected by 228 votes to 155. The debate had been a heated one and a large group of catholic teachers stormed out of the hall when the result was announced. John McKee, a retired headteacher, and church spokesman on education, warned that catholics would have to consider their place in the union and he reminded critics that the Catholic Teachers Federation had only agreed to enter the EIS after 1918 on being given a gentleman's agreement that its schools would be respected.[143]

Fears that catholic teachers would break away from the EIS proved unfounded but the 1979 vote showed that many teachers in the non-denominational sector opposed the dual system of schools. Some may have felt piqued that catholics enjoy untrammelled promotion prospects in both sectors (catholics have been headmasters of non-denominational schools) while non-catholics ambitious to advance in their careers, are effectively confined to one sector, or they may merely have been reflecting the views of the population at large. Polling surveys indicate that Scots continue to regard denominational schools as an anomaly even though they have been part of the state system since 1918. A 1984 survey commissioned by *The Glasgow Herald* produced a result not very different from ones reached in the past:[144] 72% of the sample polled were opposed to state-funded catholic schools, 20% in favour, and 8% didn't know; in addition, campaigns in favour of integration had recently been carried out by large circulation papers like *The Daily Record* and *The Sunday Mail* which may well have influenced popular attitudes on the subject.

The Catholic Education Committee, which represents the church's view on education questions, was faced with the fact that no fund of public goodwill existed for a state education system divided in two by religion. But consolation was to be gained from the 1979 Gallup survey into catholic attitudes which suggested that 81% of catholic children attended catholic schools, a proportion of the rest being located in areas where the catholic population was too scattered to justify having a school of its own.[145] Apparently, most working-class catholic parents who had ceased practising their faith, still automatically sent their children to the nearest denominational school, a sign that tribal loyalties had not been abandoned in the drift away from active religious belief. In a 1982 pastoral letter read out at all Masses, Dr Winning felt obliged to remind church-going parents that they were still required to send their children to catholic schools despite recent legislation establishing a 'parent's charter' that gave them greater freedom of choice.[146] Soon after, he remarked that 'eight years as archbishop have taught me that looming at the dawn of each day is a crisis in education'.[147] With demographic trends posing fresh question-marks over the viability of the denominational sector, the church stepped up its vigilance and Dr Winning showed no inclination to look again to see if a revised version of the 1918 settlement might not better serve catholic educational interests.

Official catholic sensitivity on the subject was highlighted in 1985 when Kenny McLachlan, the retiring president of the EIS, made an anti-segregation speech in his farewell conference address, part of which read:

> The segregation of children only five years old on religious grounds is wrong, grossly so . . . In this matter the law is not merely an ass but a assassin . . .
>
> The results . . . the tribalism of broken heads at Hampden and the broken hearts of couples whose plans to marry in good faith have been defeated by prejudice, are unacceptable to the majority of the Scottish people.
>
> It is a deliberate arrangement of our society—codified by statute, the law of the land—which dictates that our children do not enjoy socialisation and education together as they should . . .[148]

Although McLachlan was the only truly outspoken critic of the existence of catholic schools, within the EIS, Dr Winning responded angrily to his speech:

> Let Mr McLachlan put his own house in order and bring the strike to an end [a reference to the 1984-86 teacher's pay dispute]. He is talking utter rubbish and I have no time for him or the EIS.
>
> It shows what the Catholic community have to put up with from people who I believe have no time for religion in schools.[149]

Dr Winning soon patched up relations with the EIS and he was even awarded honorary membership of the union in 1986. Perhaps his indignation had been fuelled by cracks in the catholic edifice outside the Strathclyde region. In Edinburgh the last fee-paying catholic school had closed in the 1970s as middle-class catholics increasingly chose to send their children to selective schools attended by other incipient members of the Edinburgh bourgeoisie. (Unwilling to go down this path Brian Gill, the Edinburgh-based advocate and old

Aloysian, chose to send his children through to Glasgow to attend his old school in the absence of any equivalent selective RC school in Edinburgh.)

Catholic teachers in the east are now trained in Glasgow, owing to the closure of Craiglockart College, but growing room for doubt exists about the extent to which graduates from St Andrew's College, Glasgow—even those with a certificate to teach religious education— are able to instill that much-vaunted catholic ethos in pupils. The presence of many lapsed catholics in schools is bound to dent their image of being ' "holy islands of Catholicism" untouched by the "big bad world" beyond the school gates'.[150]

By the 1970s teachers wedded to the status quo were not being reproduced in the same numbers as before and some who still identified with it were mainly committed to ritual and respect for hierarchy as much as anything else. It was a sign of the times that the Catholic Teachers Guild in Glasgow was wound up by the archbishop in 1975 because the membership had largely dried up and the office-bearers were retired headmasters (however, it still manages to hang on in the Motherwell diocese).

In an age of growing uncertainty, Religious Education (RE) periods often proved the most boring part of the timetable due to the lack of genuine interest on the part of the pupils and teachers alike.[151] Fr Thomas Chambers, the episcopal vicar for RE in the Glasgow arch-diocese admitted as much in 1986:

> Quite frankly I know that much RE teaching is duff . . . We've been in something of a dark age in Catholic schools. Along came the 2nd Vatican Council and threw out the Catechism, putting very little in its place and teachers were left to flounder around.[152]

Younger RE teachers who were supposed to be offering catholicism not merely as a subject but as a guide for living were often half-hearted or evasive in their approach if their own lifestyle did not comply with catholic doctrine. Birth control was the issue where the discrepancy between catholic practice and teaching was most glaring and one orthodox catholic headmaster is able to appreciate that 'it is very difficult going into an RE discussion and being out of step on this issue'.[153]

At primary level, teachers are increasingly diffident about asking the question that used to be commonplace on a Monday morning: 'Hands up all pupils who were at Mass?' to be followed by supplementaries like 'Who was the priest?' 'What colour were his vestments?' in order to catch out those who stayed away. Especially in the peripheral housing estates like Easterhouse, where Mass attendance can be as low as 10%, asking this question is increasingly viewed as a waste of time.[154]

A more positive side to catholic religious education exists. Since the 1960s there has been a shift away from the dogmatism that stressed religious instruction and the necessity for pupils to memorise large portions of the catechism. In many schools RE has become more pupil-activity-based with pupils being given the opportunity to go out into the local community during RE periods to help the poor, the sick, and the elderly: less emphasis is placed on fire and brimstone and on learning by rote and more on creating opportunities for young people to show their Christian witness by positive deeds in the community. Schools such as Holyrood in Glasgow encourage the holding of inter-denominational services with nearby non-denominational ones and open their doors to Presbyterian ministers or rabbis who explain the tenets of their respective creeds to senior pupils.[155] Peter Mullen, Holyrood's energetic headmaster thinks in terms of providing Christian education rather than the disciplined catholic instruction that was offered in the old days. He rejects the view that an integrated and unitary system of education is automatically bound to produce a more cohesive society and notes with some satisfaction that some local protestants, concerned with the absence of a strong Christian perspective in non-denominational schools, have opted to send their children to Holyrood.

Under the 1918 Act catholic schools must remain open to all those who wish to make use of them in the local catchment area; non-catholics who place their children in denominational schools also have the statutory right to withhold them from RE classes, but Mr Mullen views the fact tht no non-catholic parent has so far insisted on using this right, as vindication of the school's policy of providing 'a Christian education for all those who want it'.[156] He considers that the catholic sector still harbours a strong vocational element that is not often reproduced elsewhere, that the sense of togetherness among the staff of all religions in catholic schools remains high and that the deeper social interaction combined with the sense of vocation, rubs off on pupils in their midst.[157] Opening a new catholic school in Glasgow in 1983, Malcolm Green, Strathclyde's convener of education, also praised the 'warmer atmosphere' and stronger discipline he had detected in catholic schools, a sentiment that did not go down well in some other sectors of the teaching profession since it reflected less well on them.[158]

In areas where Mass attendance has fallen below 20% Mullen sees teachers as playing a missionary role towards pupils 'whose faith has not been nurtured except by being taken to Parkhead to see Celtic!'[159] However, Ian O. Bayne, a catholic advocate of an integrated system, doubts whether this applies in practice. He argues that 'all the Catholic school can hope to do is *reinforce* the religious allegiance of young

Catholics; it cannot *create* a religious commitment which has not already been successfully fostered in the home'.[160]

The catholic teacher shortage which in the 1960s had seemed to pose a threat to the distinctiveness of the denominational sector had largely disappeared by the mid-1980s thanks to falling school rolls and the scarcity of alternative sources of professional employment that had been available to catholics in more prosperous times. The church drew solace from the ending of the shortage but it was alarmed that a new breed of teacher was emerging whose behaviour in relation to the faith left a lot to be desired. It still had the means to block the rise of un-satisfactory teachers but, until 1983, no catholic teacher had publicly challenged the grounds on which promotion had been withheld, those with grievances no doubt being constrained because it would bring their personal life under the spotlight of publicity. But in that year a catholic assistant headteacher at a primary school in Dundee who applied for the post of headteacher at another RC school in the city, decided to speak out about the way ecclesiastical vetting procedures had operated in her case.

Mrs Maureen Ruddy's application was blocked by the catholic representative on the local education committee on the grounds that she was unfit, having sent her children to Dundee high school, a non-denominational fee-paying school. She protested with the support of her union and the matter eventually reached the Secretary of State for Scotland who ruled in August 1984 that the catholic hierarchy had no right to veto her application for promotion since she had already been promoted in her existing job.[161] Mrs Ruddy was duly appointed head-teacher, the post having been kept vacant for a year. The church could have appealed to the Court of Session but it decided to let the matter rest. The Secretary of State had not withdrawn the church's right to decide the suitability of teachers but had ruled against it in this particular case. Soon after, in Glasgow, a catholic primary teacher whose promotion prospects were under threat because, like Mrs Ruddy, her children were attending a non-catholic school, threatened to go public but a confrontation was avoided when the relevant church official, declined after all to take action against her and she is now a headteacher in an RC primary school.[162] These cases show how a more assertive educated catholic laity is emerging within the teaching profession. This may also have increased the chances of a collision between the EIS and the hierarchy over ecclesiastical vetting.

In 1986 one EIS official was able to detect a trend whereby head-teachers in denominational schools were behaving in a more autocratic manner towards their staff. In previous decades when a teacher shortage had existed, conditions in catholic schools were more flexible, but RC teachers who got divorced or who married outside the church were now being called in and asked to give an account of themselves; sometimes they were told by the headteacher that they had effectively ruined their promotion prospects by their 'irregular' behaviour.[163] In 1986 the EIS was pursuing a number of cases in which it felt that its members had been thus victimised, a task which it had rarely been asked to pursue hitherto.

The union had emerged from a gruelling two-year battle with the government over pay and conditions with many of its members still in a militant mood. In the midst of the dispute, Dr Winning had expressed concern that the lightning stoppages organised by teachers might impede the sacramental training catholic pupils receive in school.[164] Catholic teachers from denominational schools (particularly young male RCs) were very much to the fore in the industrial action and the experience may have given some of them the confidence to resist demands to be available for extra-curricular work beyond school hours, some of which involves religious functions.[165] But it remains to be seen whether such militancy will propel more radically-minded teachers into union politics where hitherto it is orthodox catholics from the western, eastern, and northern catholic teachers associations who have been most conspicuous. Of the seventeen Glasgow members of the EIS national council in 1985, only six were roman catholics when the number of RC teachers suggested that at least half should have been.[166] However, two of the six did not identify themselves with the catholic schools lobby (they declined to join the Catholic national committee of the EIS) and, even in Lanarkshire, one of the three catholics on the EIS national council also held aloof; whether their numbers will be augmented in the future is still too early to say.

The industrial action of 1984-86 delayed the launch of a scheme drawn up by the education authority in Strathclyde designed to bring secondary school pupils from both sectors together in the one class-room for certain specialist subjects. Area planning curriculum groups or 'consortia' were devised by Strathclyde in order to pool teaching resources in subjects like business studies, music, or Spanish: local schools share a teacher in a scarce subject for which there is not a heavy demand and in order to keep class numbers at a realistic level, pupils from catholic and non-catholic schools are educated together. The education authority got the agreement of the Catholic Education Commission for this scheme by arguing that consortia had been forced upon it by financial constraints and that the scheme should not be interpreted as an attempt to introduce integration by stealth.

Falling pupil numbers in the 1980s forced even more drastic decisions on the Strathclyde education authority in 1986. The press speculated that up to eighty-four schools—sixty-nine primaries and fifteen secondaries—could face closure.[167] The Orange Order alleged that non-denominational schools were likely to suffer the greater cuts and that more favourable criteria would be adopted in assessing projected rolls at catholic schools.[168] It pointed to the example of Drumchapel in Glasgow where all three secondaries, one being catholic, operate well under capacity. The Grand Lodge believed that St Pius secondary school would survive while the non-denominational schools were likely to be amalgamated.[169] The local authority undoubtedly faced some tricky decisions, being aware that special lobbies are monitoring its every move for signs of favouritism to any specific group in the community. Where it is not possible to amalgamate a catholic school with another one because the distance separating them is too great, the local authority may be faced with the alternative of amalgamating it with the local non-denominational one. Over much of the east of Scotland, a single local state school has long been the norm since separate catholic secondaries do not make financial sense because of the low catholic population density. But it would be a traumatic moment for the church if catholics in the Strathclyde region, containing three-quarters of Scotland's catholics, had to follow this path.

Brian Meek, a Tory councillor in the Lothian region, which includes Edinburgh, inserted a new equation into the education debate in 1986 when he published figures that had convinced him the 1918 Act was in need of reform.[170] He was careful to insist that he did not think segregated schools promoted religious bigotry or that catholic schools had an inferior record, but he felt demographic changes were making them unviable. Between 1975 and 1984 the number of Scottish children in catholic secondary schools dropped by 16·5% compared with just 2·7% in the non-denominational sector. More alarming still were the primary school statistics. In 1975 there were 128,099 pupils in RC primary schools; by 1984 it was down to 76,313 (a drop of 40·4%, the non-denominational sector having fallen by 26·7%). Meek acknowledged that catholic schools were still generally well supported by the community they had been designed for, but the community's preference for much smaller families meant that the number of catholics in the younger age groups fell dramatically after 1970. The average catholic family size—previously well above the national average—now approached the Scottish norm and the sheer rapidity of the change, despite the hierarchy's firm stance on birth control, explained the plunge in pupil numbers after 1975.

The amount of heat or light generated in the debate over the future of the dual system of state education in Scotland will provide as good an indication as any of the current state of community relations between the major religious denominations in Scotland. If the issue is resolved without any of the major parties feeling that they have lost face or given way under stress, such a resolution will greatly reinforce the growth of toleration witnessed in previous decades. But an anti-climax may be too much to expect in a debate, the terms of which have changed relatively little since 1918.

In 1985 the power of religious education to cause political upsets was revealed in Canada where the Conservative Party fell from power in the state of Ontario after many years in office because it introduced state aid for denominational schools and triggered off a backlash among its Orange supporters. Today the Orange Order in Scotland views the existence of catholic schools financed from the public purse as an alien religious establishment in Scotland that needs to be cut down to size. Aware that it has resisted similar assaults on its schools in the past, the catholic church is inclined to haul up the drawbridge and prepare for a long seige. If it does fight a protracted rearguard action to maintain the status quo, this may well serve to confirm that, despite the confidence displayed at the time of the Pope's visit, it has still to shake off the defensive frame of mind which the long experience of being a 'ghetto church' instilled in it. Although denominational schools readily open their doors to visitors, the church is reluctant to engage in open debate about the future of its schools and articles like that by Brian Meek are greeted with a resounding silence. The hierarchy is also reluctant to pave the way for internal discussion on education in the catholic community and the Scottish religious press has been content to echo the official line on denominational schools.

Some radical catholics have argued in favour of integrated schooling at secondary level with primary schools remaining denominational because of their role in preparing children for the sacraments.[171] Bolder spirits think that both of the main Christian traditions in Scotland are capable of devising an RE syllabus which is broadly acceptable across the confessional barrier and throughout both primary and secondary education. W. J. McKechin, chairman of Renfrewshire education committee from 1973 to 1975 and vice-chairman of Strathclyde education committee from 1975 to 1978, adheres to this view.[172] Having taught in denominational schools early in his teaching career, he came around to the opinion that an integrated system was best from the point of view of educational standards, the personal development of pupils, religious amity, and cost, ideas he defended in a series of monographs and articles in the 1970s.[173] Ian O. Bayne, the other 'dissenting' catholic whose regular salvoes in the press demonstrate that not all catholics are prepared to close ranks on the schools issue, has argued publicly that a common RE syllabus in inter-denominational schools would be the most dramatic sign of ecumenical advance seen to date.[174]

These 'disloyal' catholics are not esteemed in church circles, but a sign that Dr Winning was prepared to consider Christian schools as a replacement for the existing denominational ones was provided in a

1985 interview in the education press which went unreported else-where; on being asked 'are Catholic schools here to stay?' he replied:

> Not necessarily. You see we are no longer talking about defence of the faith. We passed that point some time ago. Separate Catholic education is not a timeless truth. The only timeless truth is the Kingdom of God. Catholic schools have existed for the propagation of that truth. If there came a time we felt that truth would be better served in Christian schools—not non-denominational schools—then so be it.[175]

This statement may be a significant straw in the wind that reveals contingency plans have been prepared for a time when demographic factors or cash restraints make calls for a revision of the 1918 Act too insistent to ignore. But the problem with the creation of Christian schools is that little of a protestant character remains in the non-denominational ones: 'the once firmly defined Protestant ethos has dwindled almost to the point of extinction and has been replaced by a vaguely humanistic "comparative religion" atmosphere with occasional Christian overtones'.[176] Dr Winning believes this to be a matter of the utmost regret: 'I honestly believe that the absence of Church of Scotland schools has contributed more to the secularisation of our society than any other single factor in this century.'[177]

While the roman catholic church and its chief protestant counter-part have effectively buried their quarrel over schools, old allies may fall out as difficult decisions have to be made. In the Lothian region distinct signs of an impending clash between the ruling Labour group and the catholic church emerged in the autumn of 1986 over whether to build a catholic school in the new town of Livingstone or maintain existing ones in the nearby communities of Bathgate and Broxburn. The church accused the Labour administration of going back on its promise to build the Livingstone school;[178] the dispute spread to the Labour Party itself when the Livingstone and Linlithgow constituency parties clashed publicly over the matter.[179]

Lothian region's Labour convenor, John Mulvey, declared that he was in favour of amalgamating small secondary schools because it would help to break down religious barriers.[180] Long gone were the days when the holder of an Irish name like Mulvey could be expected to echo the church position in Labour circles. He spoke out in the week that angry Orangemen confronted an Irish republican band in Edin-burgh's Craigmiller housing estate whose front banner proclaimed 'Strip-search the Queen'.[181] The Labour Party was uneasy at seeing sectarian strife of this nature re-emerge in the east. But Harry Ewing MP, the party's parliamentary spokesman on Scottish education reiterated the official party line despite opposition to it among leading local government figures:

There will be no legislation by an incoming Labour government to impose integrated education . . . We have no intention of amending the 1918 Act unless the parents and the hierarchy approach us on the matter.[182]

However, the Labour Party has made little effort to discover what is catholic opinion on the schools question, how it may have changed, and whether the parents vocal on the issue are representative of catholics at large. Rennie McOwan considers it a major drawback that 'there is not a lively Catholic public opinion being openly expressed on the issue (and on many others)'.[183] He has argued in favour of a blueprint being prepared by the local authorities which would outline the Catholic stake in a shared system:

Catholic 'exclusiveness' would have to go but the gain in living and working with every other facet of the community would be immeasurable and only the most bigoted would deny that the Catholic schools have a contribution of significant worth to make to such plan. To say to parents, 'End Catholic schools,' is absurd. To say to Catholic parents, 'End Catholic schools because here is the proposed alternative plan,' is to provide a basis for discussion.

I don't think I am alone in believing that if no such moves are made over the next two decades or so, then separate Catholic schools will disappear anyway in time and in acrimony . . .[184]

It is a paradox that more dialogue may now be taking place between the catholic and major protestant churches on sensitive issues like education than within the catholic community itself. Rennie McOwan considers that 'the warmth and friendship that now exists between the mainstream churches' amounts 'in a very real sense' to 'a bloodless revolution . . . in Scottish life'.[185]

But the authority of the catholic church is not what it was owing to the decline of religious practice. In the large housing schemes on Glasgow's periphery up to one-third of the population was unemployed in the mid-1980s, perhaps half of the young people having no real work to go to. In such bleak circumstances there is now little scope for the economic rivalry which once caused workers to distinguish themselves from other workers by erecting racial and cultural barriers. But neither is there room for complacency: even in the absence of denominational and economic rivalry, sectarianism can still prove a menace to community peace.

In 1986, as the research for this book was being completed, reports began to circulate about the proliferation of republican bands in working-class areas. Where there had been just one in the early 1980s the existence of as many as seventeen was suspected by 1986.[186] They were composed of avowed supporters of Sinn Fein who were keen to put to music the graffiti and slogans peppered around Glasgow's housing schemes. Whether this amounts to a pro-republican youth movement is too early to say. It may be no coincidence that these bands have emerged in the wake of successful attempts by Sinn Fein in Northern Ireland to mobilise unemployed youth behind the Republican movement.

An outsider ignorant of the subtleties of Irish nationalist sub-culture, would find it difficult to tell the difference between these bands and their Orange counterparts. Both sets help keep alive the folk memories which have been such a powerful element in reinforcing a sense of religious or tribal difference in Scotland even as other divisions fade away.. If the Old Firm ceases in its turn to be an outlet for sectarianism the possibility cannot be ignored that some of Glasgow's housing schemes might become the focus for low-level sectarian warfare. Hugh Brown MP has warned that 'wherever you see graffiti proclaiming "FTP" or with reference to 1690 or 1916, you can bet your boots that there are a few "head bangers" around'.[187]

In Glasgow the catholic church no longer wields the communal influence in run-down areas like Castlemilk and Easterhouse which, in catholic areas of Belfast, has been the one sure thing that has slowed down the political advance of Sinn Fein. The blight of unemployment and its corrosive influence on a previously strong sense of community means that in the 1980s many young Glaswegians are prepared to rally behind rival Irish causes in a bid to give some meaning and importance to their cramped lives—just because Glasgow and other Scottish centres did not follow the English example and erupt into violence in the summer of 1981 does not mean that similar violence is out of the question in the future, perhaps of a more internecine kind.

Notes

1 Interviews with Right Rev Andrew Herron, 8 July 1986, and the Rev Donald MacDonald, 16 April 1986.
2 Sir David McNee, *McNee's Law*, Collins, 1983, p. 41.
3 Donald MacDonald.
4 Interview with David Lambie MP, 26 April 1984.
5 *Irish Post*, 3 May 1986.
6 *GH*, 11 March 1982.
7 Interview with Dr Thomas Winning, Archbishop of Glasgow, 4 July 1986.
8 Liz Curtis, *Ireland, the Propaganda War*, Pluto, 1983, p. 226.
9 For this and further details of Scottish Orangeism's reaction to the Tullyvallen killings see David McKittrick, *Irish Times*, 9 December 1975.
10 See note 9.
11 See note 9.
12 Bruce, *No Pope of Rome*, p. 175, for McDonald's television interview and its aftermath.
13 *GH*, 13 December 1976.
14 'The role of the Grand Orange Lodge of Scotland towards Ulster', *Orange Torch*, February 1977.
15 Bruce, *No Pope of Rome*, p. 184.
16 *Irish Times*, 20 April 1984.
17 *Guardian*, 10 April 1981.
18 'Green flutes', a documentary about republican and Orange flute bands in Glasgow broadcast on Channel 4 television, 3 March 1984.

19 E. Moxon-Browne, *Nation, Class and Creed in Northern Ireland*, Gower, Aldershot, 1984, p. 11.
20 *Scotsman*, 5 July 1984.
21 Interview with Helen Liddell, 20 February 1985.
22 Interview with Hugh Brown MP, 26 April 1984.
23 *Orange Torch*, November 1984.
24 *Observer*, 15 June 1986.
25 Interview with James Gordon, 25 March 1986.
26 *Credo*, London Weekend Television's series on religious affairs, broadcast a programme about the Old Firm in November 1980.
27 *GH*, 7 July 1986.
28 Murray, *The Old Firm*, p. 232.
29 Murray, *The Old Firm*, pp. 271-2.
30 *Evening Times*, 11 October 1976.
31 *GH*, 11 October 1976.
32 *Orange Torch*, November 1976.
33 *GH*, 16 October 1976.
34 *Bush*, September 1978.
35 Donald MacDonald.
36 Donald MacDonald.
37 Murray, *The Old Firm*, p. 240.
38 Murray, *The Old Firm*, p. 252.
39 Murray, *The Old Firm*, p. 201.
40 Murray, *The Old Firm*, p. 273.
41 Interview with the Rev James Currie, 26 March 1986.
42 *GH*, 2 July 1986.
43 *GH*, 7 July 1986.
44 *Observer*, 15 June 1986.
45 *Guardian*, 9 April 1986.
46 Talk with Willie Hamilton MP, 3 April 1984.
47 Interview with Archbishop Winning.
48 Interview with Sir Lawrence Boyle, 30 July 1986.
49 Information from a private source who witnessed the incident.
50 Desmond White, interviewed on Irish Radio news, 15 August 1984.
51 Interview with Jean McFadden, leader of Glasgow District Council, 1979-86, 31 July 1986.
52 Interview with Fr John Fitzsimmons, 1 August 1986.
53 Interview with Archbishop Winning.
54 Interview with Tom Carberry, 30 April 1984.
55 Private information.
56 Interview with Archbishop Winning.
57 Interview with Fr Michael Conway, 4 July 1986.
58 See letter from anonymous SPUC member published in the *Scottish Catholic Observer* (hereafter *SCO*), 29 June 1984.
59 *Justice and Peace, Mid-month Mailing*, June–July 1986.
60 Interview with a member of Justice and Peace.
61 Term used by Fr John Fitzsimmons.
62 Interview with Archbishop Winning.
63 Interview with Dr Patrick Reilly, 14 May 1982.
64 Interview with Archbishop Winning.
65 *Irish Times*, 17 May 1982.
66 *SCO*, 7 July 1978.
67 Editorial, 'The road to ruin', *Flourish*, August 1986.
68 Interview with a Roman Catholic secondary school teacher and member of Justice and Peace.
69 *SCO*, 30 September 1977.
70 *Flourish*, February 1986.
71 *Tablet*, 23 August 1986.
72 Bishop Joseph Devine in *SCO*, 28 May 1982.
73 James Coffey, *The Sunday Mail*, 19 May 1985.
74 A summary of the 1979 Gallup survey into Scottish catholic attitudes is provided in Cooney, *Scotland and the Papacy*, pp. 83-4, and Anthony Ross in *The Church Now*, pp. 31-3.
75 *SCO*, 28 May 1982.
76 See note 74.
77 *SCO*, 14 January 1983.
78 *SCO*, 18 October 1985: the letter specifically concerned the arrival of Opus Dei in Scotland but Mr McOwan saw his point as having wider application in the context of events in Rome.
79 James Coffey, *Sunday Mail*, 19 May 1985.
80 *Catholic Herald*, 17 May 1985.
81 Quoted in Bill Heaney, 'Winning's bid to make up for "lost" years', *GH*, 11 October 1985.
82 This short account of the Liverpool meeting is derived from 'Catholics in England and Wales, the present state of the Church', Catholic Information Service, London,

1982, pp. 16-17.

83 Interview with Archbishop Winning.

84 Interview with Archbishop Winning.

85 My own calculation based on the list of deceased priests in the 1985 CDS.

86 CDS, 1985, p. 452.

87 Flourish, June 1986.

88 Excerpt from one of the homilies delivered by Pope John Paul II on his visit to Scotland.

89 Interview with Archbishop Winning.

90 Interview with Fr John Fitzsimmons.

91 Interview with the Right Rev Andrew Herron.

92 SCO, 14 July 1978.

93 Interview with Fr John Fitzsimmons.

94 Interview with Alex Ferry, 23 November 1984.

95 Interview with Archbishop Winning.

96 Interview with Tom Carberry.

97 Interview with Fr John Fitzsimmons.

98 Interview with the Rev Donald MacDonald.

99 CDS, 1985, p. 461.

100 Tablet, 3 May 1986.

101 GH, 9 September 1975.

102 GH, 8 April 1972.

103 Scottish Protestant View, October 1975.

104 Scottish Protestant View, August 1975.

105 Orange Torch, February 1985.

106 GH, 15 April 1982.

107 GH, 28 February 1982.

108 Guardian, 2 April 1982.

109 Irish Times, 17 May 1982.

110 'How Glasgow may have saved the Pope's visit', Times, 29 May 1982.

111 Tablet, 5 June 1982.

112 View expressed to me by a prominent militant protestant from Edinburgh.

113 Interview with Archbishop Winning.

114 Willy Slavin, 'Roman in the gloamin', Cencrastus, No. 11, 1983.

115 Allan Massie, 'Vive l'Ecosse libre', Spectator, 5 June 1982.

116 See note 115.

117 GH, 16 April 1982.

118 Private information.

119 Information from Ian O. Bayne and Graeme Purves.

120 Interview with Helen Liddell.

121 Jack Brand, The National Movement in Scotland, p. 152.

122 Henry Drucker and Gordon Brown, The Politics of Nationalism and Devolution, Longmans, 1980, p. 50.

123 Neal Ascherson, 'Devolution diary', 16 September 1977, Cencrastus, No. 22, 1986, p. 52.

124 Interview with Michael Ancram, 7 May 1982.

125 Interview with Jean McFadden.

126 Interview with Hugh Brown MP.

127 Interview with Helen Liddell.

128 Interview with Ian O. Bayne, SNP member, 8 August 1986.

129 Irish Times, 1 June 1981.

130 Gavin Kennedy, 'Time for SNP to grasp Irish nettle', Scotsman, 23 January 1979.

131 SCO, 19 January 1979.

132 Economist, 7 December 1985.

133 E.g. letter from the managing director of Glasgow department store in GH, 6 July 1984.

134 'The Chiel' (an independent contributor), Orange Torch, July–August 1986, p. 9.

135 Orange Torch, July–August 1979.

136 Interview with David Bryce, Grand Secretary of the Orange Order.

137 Who's Who in Scotland, Carrick, 1986.

138 Simon Bain, 'Orange politician reveals his true colours', Scotsman, 3 July 1986.

139 GH, 5 July 1986.

140 'Souvenir Programme for the Annual Demonstration of the Loyal Orange Lodge of Scotland, County Grand Lodge of the East', 28 June 1986.

141 Interviews with Helen Liddell and Jean McFadden.

142 Scotsman, 29 March 1976.

143 Scotsman, 9 June 1979.

144 GH, 13 September 1984.

145 Annual General Meeting of the EIS, 4-6 June 1981, Minute No. 639.

146 Scotsman, 8 February 1982.

147 SCO, 20 May 1982.

148 Times Education Supplement for Scotland (hereafter referred to as TESS, 14 June 1985.

149 *Evening Times*, 6 June 1985.
150 Ian O Bayne, 'Time for second thoughts on Catholic schools', *Scotsman*, 9 March 1982.
151 The view of a practising catholic who teaches in the denominational sector.
152 *TESS*, 3 January 1986.
153 Interview with headmaster of RC secondary school.
154 Interview with RC primary school-teacher.
155 Interview with Peter Mullen, 5 August 1986.
156 Interview with Peter Mullen.
157 Interview with Peter Mullen.
158 *TESS*, 11 November 1983.
159 Interview with Peter Mullen.
160 See note 150.
161 *Scotsman*, 25 August 1984.
162 Private information (not from the teacher concerned).
163 Information from EIS official in the west of Scotland.
164 Interview with Archbishop Winning.
165 View of EIS official.
166 View of another EIS official.
167 *GH*, 7 July 1986.
168 *GH*, 7 July 1986.
169 *GH*, 7 July 1986.
170 Brian Meek, 'Two choices for Catholic education', *Scotsman*, 23 June 1986.
171 Fr Anthony Ross OP favoured this approach.
172 Talk with W. J. McKechin, 9 September 1986.
173 See *A School in Eastwood Park: a Case Study in Local Authority Decision-making and Public Participation*, Paisley College of Technology, 1979, and also *Plus or Minus: Problems affecting the Implementation of Positive Discrimination within Schools in Strathclyde*, Paisley College of Technology, 1976 (both in the Mitchell Library, Glasgow).
174 See note 150.
175 *TESS*, 22 February 1985.
176 Rennie McOwan, 'Unity movement in full swing', *GH*, 15 August 1985.
177 *TESS*, 22 February 1985.
178 *Flourish*, September 1986.
179 *Scotsman*, 8, 9 September 1986.
180 *Scotsman*, 9 September 1986.
181 James Freeman, 'Republicans marching to Scottish beat', *GH*, 15 September 1986.
182 *Scotsman*, 9 September 1986.
183 See note 176.
184 See note 176.
185 See note 176.
186 See note 181.
187 Interview with Hugh Brown MP.

Conclusion

The assimilation of the descendants of Irish catholic immigrants into Scottish life has been a very gradual process which is not yet complete. Early in the nineteenth century when the community took shape in industrial Scotland, it possessed a number of characteristics guaranteed to create difficulties with the host population and which were quite common among *diasporas* or minorities arriving in a new land. From the outset the Irish were located in certain types of economic activity which distorted the social structure of their community and made them a target for unfavourable stereotyping (and scapegoating in times of stress). For much of the nineteenth century they were overwhelmingly concentrated in the unskilled labour market of the west of Scotland. This brought down upon them the hostility of native Scots for reasons that fluctuated depending on the economic climate. In good economic times it confirmed their essential backwardness and inability to adopt the practical and achieving norms and values supposedly held in common by many Scots, irrespective of social class. To underline their inferiority, nineteenth century Scottish society branded the Irish as lazy, un-enterprising, superstitious, lawless, unclean, disloyal, and incapable of adapting their family size to their means; most proletarian minorities seeking their fortune abroad have been the targets of such labelling, though the stereotypes bestowed upon the Irish in Scotland were particularly negative and enduring.

Not all diaspora communities consisted of workers seeking employment abroad. Communities such as the Jews in Europe and America and the Chinese in east Asia became prominent in business, commerce, and the intellectual professions. In depressed economic times, their concentration in certain occupations often tended to look like a sinister monopoly and could bring down upon them the wrath of the indigenous population if it was roused by unscrupulous political forces. Just because the Irish and their descendants were located in low prestige jobs did not mean that they were immune from the scape-goating visited upon 'mobilised minorities'.[1] When work was scarce at all levels of the labour market, they came under suspicion and their ability to colonise jobs in the lower reaches of the public sector or as general labourers was treated with undisguised hostility. Perhaps this was demonstrated most clearly in Edinburgh during the 1930s when an anti-catholic movement was able to make alarming headway for several years by whipping up an unwarranted scare about the catholic penetration of the labour market.

Another feature that minorities on the move tend to have in common (whatever their material circumstances) is that they bring with them to the new land significant numbers of people expounding the religion that is essential to their culture or identity. Like the Jews wherever the diaspora extended, the Irish did this and for most of the nineteenth century the priest was viewed as a subversive element in Scottish society, an affront to the Presbyterian tradition which had been secured only after much upheaval and sacrifice and a danger to protestants as well as a superstitious drag on his own flock. Even though the Irish eventually became a familiar element in Scottish life who helped to bolster the self-esteem and sense of superiority of the Scots, their priests aroused unease and hostility because of their self-assurance and the hold they retained over their community. Only fairly recently have catholic bishops and priests begun to receive the same recognition in Scotland (honorary degrees, full obituaries in the press etc.) that other religious leaders have long been accustomed to.

The immigrants were fortunate that the established protestant church was preoccupied by an internal civil-war during the middle decades of the nineteenth century when their arrival was having its maximum impact on Scottish society. Evangelical churches which affirmed total opposition to 'Popery' were also enjoying a widening appeal, not least among Highlanders. Driven from the land like their fellow Gaels in Ireland by crop failure or eviction, they clung fiercely to their religion in the midst of economic calamity. The fact that they shared a common language and remnants of a common culture with the Irish counted for little in a Victorian age when religion was the key badge of identity in society.

Highlanders and Irish were locked in competition for unskilled jobs. If north America had not been such a magnet for the mainly protestant victims of the Highland Clearances and more had settled in and around Glasgow, then the conditions might have emerged for communal rivalry on the scale of that seen in Belfast after the 1850s. Common ethnic heritage is no antidote against internecine strife and the most searing of conflicts are often those involving members of the same tribe or broad ethnic group. After all, the northern Irish, protestants and catholics, have more in common with each other than with their respective patrons in Dublin and London, but this has not prevented them pursuing a fratricidal conflict which has brought their society to the brink of disaster.

It is easy to ascribe the consistently low social ranking of immigrants and their descendants from the 1820s to the 1950s to prejudice and organised discrimination and to leave it at that. Certainly, cultural and religious criteria such as membership of the freemasons, the Orange Order, or a respectable church were used to regulate entry into skilled trades and professions through nearly all of the period under discussion. But it needs to be kept in mind that a number of characteristics peculiar to the Irish community itself helped keep it near the bottom of the occupational structure for many generations. Scotland tended to attract many of those emigrants from Ireland who were least well-equipped to make their way in a new homeland: it was often the destination of those who lacked the passage money to travel to America, who were burdened with a great number of dependants, and who came from some of the poorest counties in Ireland such as Donegal or Mayo whose peasants were much less likely to have enjoyed land ownership or some other form of responsibility than those in other parts of Ireland. Thus, compared to an emigrant destined for America who often had no dependants to speak of and perhaps owned some money to cushion his arrival, the immigrant to Scotland was rather more likely to become locked into a culture of poverty which it could take a family generations to escape from.

Until recent decades, the immigrant community in Scotland lacked an 'upwardly mobile reference group' from among their own numbers that they could aspire to join: in the context of nineteenth century Scotland, craftsmen, tradesmen, professional types who might be viewed as community trend-setters. The Jews possessed such a reference group wherever they settled, long experience of persecution having instilled the belief that they needed to utilise their talents to the full in order for the Jewish race to endure in a hostile world. The religious leaders of the Irish in Scotland set a low value on achieving material success in a society they wished to prevent their flock assimilating with.

By the turn of the century, even the Irish-Americans had carved out an important niche for themselves in local politics and in the police forces of the large cities in which they settled: these were important bridgeheads which provided the basis for a significant middle-class. The Irish had a distinct advantage over other ethnic groups since usually they had no need to acquire the language spoken in the New World. They travelled a longer distance in both a physical and psychological sense than the Irish *en route* to Scotland and were less inclined to recreate a society in exile derived from their native hearth. Ethnic ghettoes were created but they were penetrated by a more fluid and less caste-like society than that found in Scotland.

In the 1840s the Irish in America faced greater organised hostility than the Irish did in Scotland and their desire to assimilate was resisted by the dominant Anglo-Saxon population, but soon other ethnic groups came along to distract attention from the Irish, something which did not happen in Glasgow until the formation of an Asian community in the 1960s. Generally, the Irish-Americans felt far more self-confident and less restricted than those in Scotland: they inhabited a land whose symbols of nationhood acquired by defeating the British made them feel at ease. They were able to remain loyal to Ireland while identifying themselves with the American nation and its institutions in a way their contemporaries in Scotland found it impossible to do even long after the great majority had become Scottish-born. The multi-ethnic character of the United States encouraged the Irish to compete for recognition and material rewards and throw off inhibitions about their status in their new homeland. Immigrant groups were not dissuaded from merging their European heritage with essentially American values so they felt far less inhibited about expressing themselves and demanding recognition than the Irish in Scotland. By contrast, they were unable to work out an acceptable identity to equip themselves for living in Scotland and establishing a discourse with its inhabitants.

The Scots were unsure of their own identity (did they owe loyalty to the Scottish or the British imperial nation?) and they viewed the Irish as a complicating force who did not fit in and had a worrying potential for trouble. Faced with such a reception, the immigrants never attempted to synthesise their Hibernian traditions with those of Scotland to produce a Celtic identity (except perhaps on the soccer field). Their religion being their main badge of identity, inevitably made them inward-looking: until after Queen Victoria's death roman catholicism was almost as un-British as Communism was later un-American.

A sense of ethnic identity is frequently the spur which prompts a minority group to assert the demand for the granting of full citizenship and favoured treatment from a dominant group that has hitherto neglected or exploited it. In the early twentieth century, the catholic sense of ethnic identity was never clearcut enough for them to demand greater justice for their community. (Arguably the willingness of catholic voters to support the Irish Home Rule ticket in the forty years up to 1918 was more a sign of their alienation from the Scottish social system than of any positive identification with Ireland as such.) Instead of mounting effective resistance, their dissatisfaction was expressed in the form of inter-personal violence and through outlets such as alcohol, syptoms often displayed by a community finding the transition to a new environment very difficult to adjust to. Scottish public opinion found the 'anti-social' behaviour of the group most at the mercy of a harsh and capricious economic order irritating and demeaning, but the Irish rarely posed a direct threat because they lacked the determination to assert an identity derived from their ancestral homeland and use it as a springboard to insist on equal citizenship.

Minority rights and the self-determination of ethnic groups were concepts that only acquired general recognition after the Second World War with the arrival of decolonisation and the United Nations. In previous decades, socialism or, in the British case, Labourism had possessed more attraction for an immigrant group like the Glasgow Irish whose position in the lower depths of the working-class meant that they were bound to benefit from some reforms, however, meagre.

Appropriately it was in 1922, the year in which Ireland ceased to be a disruptive issue in British politics, that an enduring partnership was struck up between the British Labour Party and the catholics of the west of Scotland when their co-religionists elsewhere in Europe were still encouraged to view socialism, however diluted, as worse than sin. For all its shortcomings, the Labour Party was crucially important to the catholics not for the material gains it brought them—which were pitiably few till the 1940s—but because it set them on the road to assimilation. Community leaders with political aspirations or skills became used to collaborating with other sections of the working-class in the pursuit of common ends. Labour's presence helped to break down the ghetto mentality and a growing number of catholics saw their horizons widen to the extent that loyalty to their class or their city became more important than loyalty to their parish.

The growth of the parliamentary and extra-parliamentary left (the CPGB) was psychologically liberating for a previously submerged minority, but it could still find itself dangerously exposed. The left was not able to do much for catholics when they were victimised by lower middle-class spokesmen and religious zealots looking for a scapegoat to blame for Scotland's decline after 1918. Animosity towards the religion and social standards of the immigrants sometimes even emanated from members of the labour movement.

Fortunately the dangerous tensions of the inter-war years—partly a result of the identity crisis facing many Scots as they tried to come to terms with the fact that their country was no longer a co-partner in British imperialism, more a peripheral corner of an island realm—did not flare up into a full-scale backlash. Scotland did not have a recent history of internal conflict and extreme forms of political behaviour enjoyed scant prestige (though Edinburgh in the mid-1930s briefly showed the depth of intolerance that respectable opinion was capable of permitting). It was perhaps fortunate for catholics and protestants alike that they inhabited a corner of Europe that was among the least disturbed by cataclysm in the last two centuries; if Scotland had been affected by foreign invasion or civil war, then undoubtedly they would have left their mark on community relations. There is also the fact that intellectuals and would-be professional people finding opportunities blocked off at home, have always found an outlet in the south or further afield. (It is no coincidence that the able journalist George Malcolm Thomson, considerably modified his views about the Irish in Scotland after rising in Fleet Street during the 1930s.) In the last 300 years, Scots settling in England have virtually colonised some of the professions and, by the 1970s, there may have been more people of Scottish origin living in England than in Scotland itself. This outward flow of talent was damaging to the cultural life of Scotland but the existence of an 'emigration ideology' may have prevented damaging tensions welling up which an exposed group like the catholics might have been on the receiving end of.

After the 1930s the 'us and them' syndrome, so noticeable before-hand, considerably diminished. Shared wartime experiences and the achievement of important social reforms broke down much of the religious rivalry within the working-class. It was fortuitous that catholic expectations were increasing at a time when the state was able to satisfy some of them. Many internal conflicts have flared up and turned into ethnic ones when rising expectations have met a negative response from power holders. The most relevant example in this context is Northern Ireland where catholic demands for better treatment were couched in explicitly nationalist terms only after pressure on the Unionist government for the granting of equal citizenship was rejected in the late 1960s.

After 1945 large numbers of catholics in Scotland gravitated towards the public sector and the service sector of the economy generally once it was clear that racial or religious criteria were not part of the entry qualifications as in many of the skilled trades. The income gap between the catholic minority and the rest of society began to close as the outline of a middle-class took shape in the 1960s. By now many catholics were ceasing to derive their basic identity from their religion, but even among new arrivals in the middle-class remnants of an enclave mentality could still persist. This residual feeling of difference was partly kept alive by the survival of ethnic friction in the fields of sport and education. State backing for separate catholic schools has never ceased to be controversial in the west of Scotland since it was granted in 1918, but it has remained an isolated source of discord since no other equivalent religious problem exists in a state that long ago settled its church-state differences.

The assimilation of separate ethnic groups living side by side stands the best chance of success if it is a gradual process that progresses almost without visibility. These conditions were available in the west of Scotland from the 1940s to the 1970s thanks to a global economic boom and the ability of major political parties to agree on basic norms.

The Labour Party remained an important vehicle allowing the catholic minority to emerge from 'civic anonymity'. In Scotland at least Labour remained well entrenched despite the collapse of industry and the relegation of much of the industrial proletariat to the history books. It continued to perform an assimilative function, being an arena where working-class Scots from varying religious backgrounds or none could interact to defend the interests of their class or community. On the whole the party kept sectarian tensions at arms length but it was content to operate alongside the existing social and political moulds within which religious antagonisms persisted (viz. its attitude to segregated schooling).

By the 1970s individuals of catholic extraction were to be found at all levels of the Labour Party in significant numbers. It is fairly exceptional for a minority group of humble economic status to enjoy such a degree of influence in a major political party. Like the Irish-Americans, west of Scotland catholics have been gifted in acquiring political power but they have been far less resourceful in applying it, another trait both groups have in common. Labour's record in coping with urban decay in Glasgow *after* the 1960s was better than that of many Irish-American city politicians but the point made by Daniel Patrick Moynihan, the Irish-American scholar-politician, about the leaders of his own community might well be applied to the political heirs of John Wheatley in Glasgow: 'they did not know what to do with political power once they got it. They never thought of politics as a system of social change'.[2]

In the 1980s Labour has done surprisingly little with its Scottish electoral majority to challenge the effects of English Conservative rule. If the party is unsure of itself it may partly be because of the presence of representatives of a minority which is still unsure of its own status. For a fuller explanation, one need only appraise Scottish life in general where inertia and defensiveness are pervasive, catholics having no monopoly of insecurity.

Those who feel that the only way Scottish vigour can be restored is through a form of self-government have received a cool response from the catholic community. Working-class catholics in particular find it difficult to relate to the symbols of Scottish nationhood. The custodians of Scottish national identity have tended to be bourgeois institutions like law, the Presbyterian religion, and education and these are alien entities to many working-class catholics. Those catholics who have utilised the law in the search for upward mobility or who are keen to stress their religious faith's authentically native roots have a far less hostile attitude to nationalism. But a great many catholics can display a fierce loyalty to their city or to local institutions like a denominational school or a soccer club which they find it hard to show for their country.

As a result Scottish catholics are unsure of whether to place their allegiance behind the Scottish nation or the British state. They are at the stage many Scots found themselves in during the 1960s when the disappearance of empire and the centralisation of wealth and opportunity in the south-east of England obliged them to question their status within the United Kingdom. Catholics have shown greater loyalty to the unitary state because it is associated in their own mind with the egalitarian and distributionist measures that raised their living standards and hopes after 1945. But a new philosophy of government has been emanating from London in the 1980s which explicitly rejects the 'One Nation' philosophy adhered to up to 1979 by the Conservative Party in favour of a more radical set of economic policies lacking in compassion for those in the regions badly hit by levels of unemployment that can be partly attributed to specific government policies. Catholics (still heavily located in the lower-income groups) are liable to be disproportionately affected by such policies, so a change in their outlook towards the British state may gradually occur. Scotland's difficulty in gaining proper recognition and access to economic opportunity within the UK may be a contributory factor in any shift of identity, since it parallels the experience of the catholic community locally over a long historical period. Both in different ways find themselves thinking and acting like minorities in a competitive and dangerous world: perhaps one result will be to cause catholics to subconsciously identify more with the fate of the Scottish nation whose image is more appealing to them than at any point in the last two hundred years.

Anxiety about their position in a self-governing Scotland also helps to explain catholic diffidence not only about full-scale independence but about a devolved Scotland existing within the UK. If either scenario takes shape, catholics will have to make psychological adjustments, but so will many other sections of the Scottish people. There is a chance that quarrels over education will emerge in a sharper form than before in a Scotland administered from Edinburgh, but in a Scotland managing its own affairs, catholics may stand a better chance of acquiring a coherent identity that does not put them at variance with the rest of the population. Whatever the outcome, Scotland's relationship with England was definitely on the political agenda in 1986, when opinion polls showed over three-quarters of all Scots giving support either to autonomy or outright statehood. Catholics will need to avoid being used in the way that the metropolitan heartland manipulated the Ulster protestants and before them the American loyalists in a bid to prevent Ireland and America slipping out of the imperial grip.

Britain has become so internally divided that such a parallel, laughable in the 1960s, now seems much less so in the 1980s. The first major example of internal instability was provided by Northern Ireland after 1968 and several years had to elapse before commentators felt confident enough that Scotland was not going to be devastated by the fall-out from this nearby inter-ethnic flare-up. If sectarianism is still capable of a last hurrah in Scotland, the evidence presented in these pages suggests that it will not be on the scale witnessed in Northern Ireland. Scotland does not face an identity crisis as sharp as that encountered in Ulster where religious differences buttress two rival nationalisms which between them have polarised the community in a thoroughgoing sense. Scotland is less isolated than Northern Ireland, a society that has proven fairly impervious to outside influence that stress common citizenship and secular values.

Of course the absence of ethnic strife in not conclusive evidence of the existence of a single community. Bilateral relations between groups like catholics and protestants in Ulster and the west of Scotland range along a continuum from a genocidal to a symbiotic one.[3] In the 1970s it became apparent that the Scots were more to one side of this spectrum whereas the peoples of divided Ulster were located perilously near the opposite edge. A calm Scotland undoubtedly has had a stabilising effect on Ulster and by not providing a fresh outlet for the conflict may even have been instrumental in preventing the province toppling into full-scale civil war. Perhaps greater awareness of the progress Scots have made in healing their religious differences may inspire some of those in Northern Ireland who seek peace, by showing that their aspirations are not altogether beyond reach.

Inter-ethnic strife represents the most important source of armed conflict in the world today and has made the planet an increasingly dangerous place to inhabit. By refusing to push their differences to the point of outright division, Scots have helped to make their corner of the world a more neighbourly and tolerant one. The historian Christopher Smout recently described the absorption of the Irish and their descendants as one of the triumphs of Scottish history. At a time when the bruised Scottish psyche badly needs some fresh self-confidence, this is a salutary reminder.

Notes

1 The distinction between mobilised and proletarian diasporas is made by John Armstrong in 'Mobilised and proletarian diasporas', *American Political Science Review*, 70, 1976.

2 Daniel Patrick Moynihan, 'The Irish', in D. P. Moynihan and N. Glazer (eds.), *Beyond the Melting Pot*, Cambridge, Mass., 1963, p. 229.

3 Walker Connor, 'Nation-building or nation-destroying?', *World Politics*, 23, 3, 1972, p. 348.

Appendix

(a) Roman catholic population of Scotland, 1878–1977, as a percentage of the Scottish population

	No.	%
1878	332,000	9·2
1901	446,000	10·0
1931	662,300	13·7
1951	750,000	14·7
1971	822,000	15·7
1977	823,500	15·9

(b) Roman catholic population of the Glasgow archdiocese, as a percentage of the population in the area covered by the archdiocese

	No.	%
1878	140,300	19·2
1901	186,100	17·6
1931	294,400	23·7
1951	321,300	25·6
1971	317,900	28·0
1977	293,400	

Source: James Darragh, 'The Catholic population of Scotland, 1878–1977', in David McRoberts (ed.), *Modern Scottish Catholicism, 1878–1978*, Burns, Glasgow, 1979, p. 230.

Bibliography

1. Public records

Scottish Record Office, HH1/777, 'Anti-Roman Catholic Demonstrations in Edinburgh, 1934–40'.

Scottish Record Office, HH/31/34, police reports of Irish political meetings gathered by the Prosecutor Fiscal's Office, Glasgow, 3 September 1920.

Scottish Record Office, HH/55/62, Report of the Chief Constable of Lanarkshire to the Scottish Office, 9 December 1920.

Scottish Record Office, HH/55/68, Report of the Chief Constable of Paisley to the Scottish Office, 10 July 1922.

Scottish Record Office, HH/55/71, '1923–24 Irish Disturbances'.

2. Other unpublished materials

The Broady Collection, Glasgow University Library.

Catholic Union Files, Glasgow Archdiocesan Archives.

'John Cormack, a book of Memories' (press cuttings and miscellaneous items assembled in 1978 by the Protestant Action Society).

Court of Session Scotland, 18 December 1936, 'Closed Record in Petition for Suspension and Interdict at the Instance of the Most Reverend Andrew Joseph McDonald Against (First), the Protestant Action Society and others; and (Second), John Cormack as an Individual'.

The Diaries of Fr Michael Condon (1807–1902), Glasgow Archdiocesan Archives.

P. J. Dollan, unpublished memoirs (two volumes), Glasgow Room, Mitchell Library, Glasgow.

Russell A. Fox, *Members of the Labour Party elected to Edinburgh Town Council, 1909–1971*, produced by author, Edinburgh, 1971.

Andrew Dewar Gibb Papers, National Library of Scotland.

Selected Papers of James Maxton, Strathclyde Region Archives.

Papers of Art O'Brien, National Library of Ireland, Dublin.

Papers of Ernest O'Malley, Manuscript Room, University College Dublin.

'Protestant Action, Election Literature', Edinburgh Central Library.

'Protestant Action' membership cards and election leaflets for South Leith Ward (1947–59), 1 Blenheim Place, Edinburgh.

Arthur Woodburn Papers, National Library of Scotland.

3. Interviews

Michael Ancram (1982), Conservative MP and roman catholic.

James Armstrong (1982), Glasgow solicitor.

T. C. Barry (1983), roman catholic businessman (retired).

John Bayne (1982), retired Glasgow Sheriff and founder of Glasgow University Distributist Society.

James Breen (1986), retired roman catholic headmaster.

Willie Brogan (1983), retired roman catholic teacher.

Hugh Brown (1984), Labour MP for Glasgow Provan since 1961.

David Bryce (1984), Grand Secretary of the Orange Order in Scotland.

Richard Buchanan (1986), former Labour MP for Glasgow Springburn.

Alan B. Cameron (1984), as Alan Hasson, Grand Master of the Orange Order in Scotland in 1958-59.

Dennis Canavan (1984), Labour MP and former deputy headmaster in a denominational school.

Fr Bernard Canning (1982), historian of the Irish catholic clergy in Scotland.

Tom Carberry (1984), Professor of Business Studies at Strathclyde University.

Neil Carmichael (1981), former Labour MP for Glasgow Kelvingrove.

Dr Patrick Connolly (1984), former general practitioner in the Gorbals district of Glasgow.

Fr Michael Conway (1986), roman catholic chaplain at Glasgow University.

James Cranston (1985), inhabitant of Leith.

The Rev. James Currie (1986), Church of Scotland minister.

Lionel Daiches (1984), Edinburgh advocate.

The Right Reverend Joseph Devine (1981), roman catholic Bishop of Motherwell.

James H. Dollan (1982) journalist and son of Sir Patrick Dollan.

John Durkan (1982), roman catholic historian.

Michael Fallon (1982), retired roman catholic journalist.

Alex Ferry (1984), Scottish trade union leader.

Russell Fox (1985), former Edinburgh city councillor and bailie.

George Galloway (1984), prospective Labour parliamentary candidate from Dundee.

James Gordon (1986), Managing Director of Radio Clyde and former television journalist.

James Hamilton (1984), roman catholic Labour MP.

Willie Hamilton (1984), Labour MP.

The Right Rev. Andrew Herron (1986), former Moderator of the General Assembly of the Church of Scotland.

Jack Kane (1985), former Lord Provost of Edinburgh.

Michael Kelly (1985), former Lord Provost of Glasgow.

David Lambie (1984), Labour MP for Central Ayrshire since 1970.

Archie Lamont (1981), Scottish nationalist writer.

Helen Liddell (1985), General Secretary of the Labour Party in Scotland.

The Rev. Donald MacDonald (1986), Church of Scotland minister.

Margo McDonald (1982), former SNP MP for Glasgow Govan.

McDonald Morris (1984), Scottish critic of the Roman Catholic Church.

J. G. MacLean (1984), Worthy District Master of the Orange Order's County Grand Lodge of the East in Scotland.

Jean McFadden (1986), former leader of the Labour group on Glasgow District Council and roman catholic convert.

Fr Henry McGinn (1986), roman catholic parish priest in Larkhall.

William McGuinness (1983), former SNP councillor in Glasgow.

W. J. McKechin (1986), former teacher and educational administrator from Renfrewshire.

William McKelvey (1984), Labour MP.

Kenny McLachlan (1986), former president of the Educational Institute of

Scotland.

John McLaughlin (1984), Edinburgh roman catholic and retired accountant.

Mr and Mrs J. McLay (1982), founder members of the Newman Association.

Harry McShane (1982), veteran Scottish Marxist.

James Morrell (1985), Scottish trade union official.

Peter Mullen (1986), Headmaster of Holyrood Roman Catholic school, Glasgow.

William Murphy (1982), former editor of the *Glasgow Observer*.

Mrs Molly Regan (1985), former official of the Union of Catholic Mothers.

Patrick Reilly (1982), lecturer in literature at Glasgow University.

Fr Anthony Ross OP (1981), former rector of Edinburgh University.

Ernest Ross (1984), Labour MP for Dundee West.

Fr Willy Slavin (1982), Justice and peace activist in Glasgow.

Lord Taylor of Gryfe (1983), former ILP councillor.

William Taylor (1982), former leader of the Labour group on Glasgow Corporation.

George Malcolm Thomson (1982), author and journalist.

Patrick Trainer (1986), Labour Party councillor in Glasgow.

Dora Wight (1983), sister of John Cormack, founder of Protestant Action.

The Right Reverend Thomas J. Winning (1986), Archbishop of Glasgow.

4. Unpublished theses consulted and used

Baxter, R., *The Liverpool Labour Party, 1918-1963*, Ph.D., 2 vols., Queens College Oxford, 1969.

Brand, Mary Vivian, *The Social Catholic Movement in England, 1920-1955*, Ph.D., Saint Louis University, 1963.

Brown, C. G., *Religion and the Development of an Urban Society, Glasgow, 1780-1914*, Ph.D., University of Glasgow, 1981.

Brown, Gordon, *The Labour Party and Political Change in Scotland, the Role of five Elections*, Ph.D., University of Edinburgh, 1982.

Butterworth, Ruth, *The Structure of some Catholic Lay Organisations in Australia and Great Britain: a Comparative Study*, Ph.D., University of Oxford, 1959.

Cooper, Samuel, *John Wheatley, a Study in Labour History*, Ph.D., University of Glasgow, 1973.

Elliot, R. D., *The Glasgow Novel*, Ph.D., University of Glasgow, 1979.

Ferns, Andrew, *Glasgow and the War in Spain, 1936-39*, B.A., University of Strathclyde, 1975.

Gunnin, G. C., *John Wheatley, Catholic Socialism and Irish Labour in the West of Scotland*, Ph.D., University of Chicago, 1973.

Harding, Keith, *The Irish Issue in the British Labour Movement*, Ph.D., University of Sussex, 1984.

Hutchinson, I. G. C., *Politics and Society in mid-Victorian Glasgow, 1846-1886*, Ph.D., University of Edinburgh, 1974.

Kellas, J. G., *The Liberal Party in Scotland, 1885-1895*, Ph.D., University College London, 1961.

Kirk, Neville, *Class and Fragmentation: some Aspects of Working-class life in North-east Cheshire and South-east Lancashire*, Ph.D., University of Pittsburgh, 1974.

O'Connor, Bernard J., *The Irish Nationalist Party in Liverpool, 1873-1922*, M.A., University of Liverpool, 1971.

Purdie, Bob, *Outside the Chapel Door: the Glasgow Catholic Socialist Society*, History diploma, Ruskin College, Oxford, 1975.

Ransome, Bernard, *James Connolly and the Scottish Left*, Ph.D., University of Edinburgh, 1975.

Reynolds, Brian A., *The Formation and Development of Fianna Fail*, Ph.D.,

Trinity College Dublin, 1976.

Roxburgh, J. M., *The School Board of Glasgow, 1873–1919*, B.Litt., University of Glasgow, 1968.

Savage, D. C., *The General Election of 1886 in Great Britain and Ireland*, Ph.D., King's College London, 1958.

Wollaston, E. P. M., *The Irish Nationalist Movement in Great Britain, 1886–1908*, M.A., King's College London, 1958.

5. Periodicals, journals, and newspapers consulted

The Bailie, The Bulletin, The Bulletin of The Scottish Labour History Society, The Bush, Catholic Herald, Cencrastus, The Daily Record, The Daily Telegraph, The Edinburgh Clarion, Edinburgh Evening Dispatch, Edinburgh Evening News, Edinburgh and Leith Observer, Evening Citizen, The Evening Times, Flourish, Forward, Glasgow Free Press, Glasgow Herald, Glasgow Observer, The Guardian, The Innes Review, The Irish News, The Irish Post, The Irish Press, The Irish Times, The Irish Weekly, Land For The People, The Motherwell Times, The Orange Torch, The Observer, Protestant Action, The Protestant Advocate, The Protestant Telegraph, The Protestant Times, St Peter's College Magazine, The Scotsman, The Scots Observer, Scottish Catholic Observer, Scottish Daily Express, Scottish Educational Journal, Scottish Historical Review, Scottish Protestant View, Sociological Review, Spectator, The Sunday Mail, The Sunday Standard, The Tablet, The Times, The Times Educational Supplement For Scotland, The Universe, The Vanguard, The Vigilant.

6. Works of reference

Catholic Directory for Scotland (directory published annually since 1829), published by J. S. Burns & Sons, Glasgow, since 1937.

Dictionary of National Biography, Oxford University Press, 1981.

Fasti Ecclesiae Scoticane, vol. 9 (1929–54), Oliver & Boyd, 1961.

Hansard.

Knox, William (ed.), *Scottish Labour Leaders, 1918–39, a Biographical Dictionary*, Mainstream, Edinburgh, 1984.

New Catholic Encyclopedia, McGraw-Hill, New York, 1967.

H. Stenton and J. Lees, *Who's who in Parliament* (4 vols.), Harvester Press, Brighton, last volume published in 1980.

Who's who in Scotland, Carrick 1985.

7. Books, articles and pamphlets cited and used

Alison, Sir Archibald, *Some Account of my Life and Writings*, II, Blackwood, Edinburgh and London, 1883.

Anson, P. F., *The Catholic Church in Modern Scotland*, Burns & Oates, London, 1937.

Armstrong, David, and Saunders, Hilary, *A Road too Wide*, Marshall Pickering, 1985.

Arnstein, W. L., 'The Murphy riots: a Victorian dilemma', *Victorian Studies*, 19, 1975.

Aspinwall, Bernard, 'David Urquhart, Robert Monteith and the Catholic Church: a search for justice and peace', *Innes Review*, 31, 2, 1980.

Aspinwall, Bernard, 'Half slave, half free: Patrick MacGill and the Catholic Church', *New Blackfriars*, LXV, 359–71.

Aspinwall, Bernard, *Portable Utopia: Glasgow and the United States*, Aberdeen

University Press, 1985.

Bayne, Ian O., 'A university institution with its own proud record', *Scottish Catholic Observer*, 9 May 1980.

Beck, George Andrew (ed.), *The English Catholics*, Burns & Oates, London, 1950.

Beltrami, Joseph, *The Defender*, Chambers, 1980.

Best, G. F. A., 'Popular Protestantism in Victorian Britain', in Robson, R. (ed.), *Ideas and Institutions in Victorian Britain*, Bell, London, 1967.

Bochel, J. M., and Denver, D. T., 'Religion and voting: a critical review and a new analysis', *Political Studies*, 18, 2, 1970.

Bogle, Albert, 'James Barr, B.D., M.P.', *Records of the Scottish Church History Society*, 21, 1983.

Bolster, Evelyn, *The Knights of St Columbanus*, Gill & Macmillan, Dublin, 1979.

Brady, L. W., *T. P. O'Connor and the Liverpool Irish*, Royal Historical Society, London, 1983.

Brennan, Niall, *Dr Mannix*, Angus & Robertson, London, 1965.

Brogan, Colm, *The Glasgow Story*, Muller, London, 1954.

Brown, Oliver, *The Extended Tongue*, n.d.

Bruce, Steve, *No Pope of Rome! Militant Protestantism In Modern Scotland*, Mainstream, Edinburgh, 1984.

Bruce, Steve, 'Popular Protestantism and politics in Scotland and Ulster', in Hadden, J. K., and Sharpe, A. D. (eds.), *Prophetic Religion and Politics*, (forthcoming).

Buckland, Patrick, *A History of Northern Ireland*, Gill & Macmillan, Dublin, 1980.

Burrowes, John, *Benny Lynch, the Life and Times of a Fighting Legend*, Mainstream, Edinburgh, 1983.

Byrne, Charles, *Hindrances to Catholic Organization, Education and Progress*, Glasgow, 1928.

Campbell, Alan B., *The Lanarkshire Miners, a Social History of their Trade Unions*, John Donald, Edinburgh, 1979.

Campbell, James, *Invisible Country*, Weidenfeld & Nicolson, London, 1984.

Campbell, John, *F. E. Smith, Lord Birkenhead*, Jonathan Cape, London, 1984.

Canning, Bernard J., *Adventure in Faith, St Ninian's, Gourock, 1880-1980*, Burns, Glasgow, 1980.

Canning, Bernard J., *Irish-born Secular Priests in Scotland, 1829-1979*, Bookmag, Inverness, 1979.

Catholics in England and Wales, the Present State of the Church, Catholic Information Service, London, 1982.

Centenary Brochure of John Barry & Sons Ltd, Mackenzie & Storrie, Leith, 1951.

Checkland, Sydney, *The Upas Tree, Glasgow 1875-1975*, Glasgow University Press, 1980.

Checkland, Sydney, and Olive, *Industry and Ethos, Scotland 1832-1914*, Edward Arnold, London, 1984.

Cooney, John, *Scotland and the Papacy*, Paul Harris, Edinburgh, 1982.

Crowley, D. W., 'The Crofters' Party, 1885-1892', *Scottish Historical Review*, 35, 1956.

Cunningham, John, 'Church administration and organisation', in McRoberts, David (ed.), *Modern Scottish Catholicism, 1878-1978*, Burns, Glasgow, 1979.

Curtis, Liz, *Ireland, the Propaganda War*, Pluto, London, 1983.

Darragh, James, 'The Catholic population of Scotland, 1878-1978', in McRoberts, David (ed.), *Modern Scottish Catholicism, 1878-1978*, Burns, Glasgow, 1978.

Davies, R. S. W., 'The Liverpool Labour Party and the Liverpool working-class, 1900-1939', *North West Labour History Society Bulletin*, 6, 1979-80.

Denvir, John, *The Irish in Britain, from the Earliest Times to the Fall of Parnell*, Kegan Paul, London, 1892.

Dewar Gibb, Andrew, *Scotland in Eclipse*, Toulmin, London, 1930.

Dewar Gibb, Andrew, *Scotland Resurgent*, Observer Press, Stirling, 1950.

Dollan, P. J., 'Memories of fifty years ago', *Mercat Cross*, July-October 1953.

Dowse, R. E., *Left in the Centre*, Hutchinson, London, 1966.

Drucker, Henry, and Brown, Gordon, *The Politics of Nationalism and Devolution*, Longmans, 1980.

Drummond, A. L., and Bullock, J., *The Church in Victorian Scotland, 1843-1874*, St Andrew Press, Edinburgh, 1974.

Dudley Edwards, Owen, *James Connolly, the Mind of an Activist*, Gill & Macmillan, Dublin, 1971.

Dudley Edwards, Owen, 'The Catholic press in Scotland since the restoration of the Hierarchy', in McRoberts, David (ed.), *Modern Scottish Catholicism*, Burns, Glasgow, 1979.

Dudley Edwards, Owen, *The Quest for Sherlock Holmes*, Mainstream, Edinburgh, 1983.

Dudley Edwards, Ruth, *James Connolly*, Gill & Macmillan, Dublin, 1982.

Ferguson, Ron, *Geoff, the Life of Geoffrey M. Shaw*, Famedram, 1979.

Ferguson, William, *Scotland: 1689 to the Present*, Oliver & Boyd, Edinburgh, 1968.

Fitzpatrick, Thomas J., *Catholic Secondary Education in South-west Scotland before 1972: its Contribution to the Change in Status of the Catholic Community*, Aberdeen University Press, 1986.

Forester, Marjory, *Michael Collins, the Lost Leader*, Sidgwick & Jackson, London, 1971.

Gallagher, Tom, 'Catholics and Scottish politics', *Bulletin of Scottish Politics*, 1, 2, 1981.

Gallagher, Tom, 'Scottish Catholics and the British left', *Innes Review*, 34, 1, 1983.

Gallagher, Tom, 'Red Clydeside's double anniversary', *Bulletin of the Scottish Labour History Society*, 1985.

Gilley, Sheridan, 'English attitudes to the Irish in England, 1780-1900', in Lunn, C. (ed.), *Immigrants, Hosts and Minorities in British Society*, Dawson, Folkestone, 1978.

Gilley, Sheridan, 'The Roman Catholic Church and the nineteenth-century Irish diaspora', *Journal of Ecclesiastical History*, 35, 2, 1984.

Gilley, Sheridan, and Swift, Roger, (eds.), *The Irish in the Victorian City*, Croom Helm, London, 1985.

Glasgow Observer and Scottish Catholic Herald, Scottish Survey 1878-1955, Burns, Glasgow, 1956.

Greacen, Robert, 'Taking the Derry boat: Patrick MacGill, novelist, an appreciation', *Eire-Ireland*, 16, 1, 1981.

Greaves, Desmond, *The Life and Times of James Connolly*, Lawrence & Wishart, London, 1961.

Greenall, R. W., 'Popular Conservatism in Salford, 1868-86', *Northern History*, 9, 1974.

Grieve, C. M. (alias Hugh McDiarmid), *Contemporary Scottish Studies*, Parsons, London, 1926.

Griffiths, Richard, *Fellow-travellers of the Right, British Enthusiasts for Nazi Germany, 1933-39*, Constable, London, 1980.

Haddow, William Martin, *My Seventy Years*, Gibson, Glasgow, 1943.

Handley, James E., *The Celtic Story, a History of Celtic Football Club*, Stanley Paul, London, 1960.

Handley, James E., *A History of St Mungo's Academy*, Aitken, Paisley, 1958.

Handley, James E., *The Irish in Modern Scotland*, Cork University Press,

1947.

Handley, James E., *The Navvy in Scotland*, Cork University Press, 1970.

Hanham, H. J., *Elections and Party Management*, Longmans, London, 1959.

Hanham, H. J., *Scottish Nationalism*, Harvard University Press, Cambridge, Mass., 1969.

Harvie, Christopher, 'Labour in Scotland during the Second World War', *Historical Journal*, 26, 4, 1983.

Harvie, Christopher, *No Gods and Precious Few Heroes, Scotland 1914-1980*, Edward Arnold, 1981.

Hastings, Adrian, 'Some reflexion of English catholicism of the late 1930s', in Hastings, Adrian (ed.), *Bishops and Writers, Aspects of the Evolution of Modern English Catholicism*, Clark, Wheathampstead, 1977.

Hay, Alice Ivy, *Valiant for Truth, Malcolm Hay of Seaton*, Spearman, London, 1971.

Hepburn, Anthony, *Communism in Scotland*, Burns, Glasgow, 1940.

Hickey, John, *Urban Catholics*, Chapman, London, 1967.

Hoehn, Matthew (ed.), *Catholic Authors: Contemporary Biographical Sketches*, St Mary's Abbey, USA, 1952.

Hollis, Christopher, *The Mind of Chesterton*, Hollis & Carter, London, 1972.

Howell, David, *British Workers and the Independent Labour Party, 1886-1906*, Manchester University Press, 1983.

Hunt, E. H., *British Labour History, 1815-1914*, Weidenfeld & Nicholson, London, 1981.

Hunter, James, 'The Gaelic connection: the Highlands, Ireland and nationalism, 1873-1922', *Scottish Historical Review*, 54, 1975.

Jamie, David, *John Hope, Philanthropist and Reformer*, Eliot, Edinburgh, 1900.

Johnson, Christine, *Developments in the Roman Catholic Church in Scotland, 1789-1929*, John Donald, Edinburgh, 1983.

Joyce, Patrick, *Work, Society and Politics, the Culture of the Factory in later Victorian England*, Harvester, Brighton, 1980.

Kellas, J. G., *Modern Scotland, the Nation since 1970*, Pall Mall, London, 1986.

Kellas, J. G., 'The Mid-Lanark by-election (1888) and the Scottish Labour Party (1888-1894)', *Parliamentary Studies*, 18, 1964-65.

Kellas, J. G., and Fotheringham, P., 'The political behaviour of the working-class', in MacLaren, A. Allan (ed.), *Social Class in Scotland Past and Present*, John Donald, Edinburgh, n.d.

Kendal, Walter, *The Revolutionary Movement in Britain, 1900-21, the Origins of British Communism*, Weidenfeld & Nicholson, London, 1969.

Kenneth, Brother, 'The Education (Scotland) Act, 1918, in the making', *Innes Review*, 19, 2, 1968.

Kiernan, Eoin, *Daniel Mannix and Ireland*, Gill & Macmillan, Dublin, 1984.

Lamont, Archie, *Small Nations*, Maclellan, Glasgow, 1944.

Larkin, Emmet, *James Larkin, Irish Labour Leader*, Routledge, London, 1965.

Lee, Jennie, *My Life with Nye*, Jonathan Cape, London, 1981.

Lobban, R. D., 'The Irish community in Greenock in the nineteenth century', *Irish Geography*, vi, 1971.

Lockart, J. G., *The Life of Sir Walter Scott*, Constable, Edinburgh, 1903.

Lunn, K., and Thurlow, R., *British Fascism, Essays on the Radical Right in Inter-war Britain*, Croom Helm, London, 1980.

Mackenzie, Compton, *Catholicism and Scotland*, Routledge, London, 1936.

Mackenzie, Compton, *My Life and Times, Octave X, 1953-1963*, Chatto & Windus, London, 1967.

MacEwan, Sydney, *On the High C's*, Burns, Glasgow, 1974.

McAllister, Gilbert, *James Maxton, Portrait of a Rebel*, John Murray, London, 1935.

McCaffrey, J., 'The Irish vote in Glasgow in the later nineteenth century', *Innes Review*, 21, 1, 1970.

McCaffrey, J., 'The origins of liberal Unionism in the west of Scotland', *Scottish Historical Review*, 50, 1, 1971.

McCaffrey, J., 'Roman Catholics in Scotland in the nineteenth and twentieth Centuries', *Records of the Scottish Church History Society*, 21, 2, 1983.

McCallum, R. B., and Readman, Allison, *The British General Election of 1945*, Frank Cass, London, 1964.

McClelland, V. A., 'A hierarchy for Scotland, 1868–1878', *Catholic Historical Review*, 56, 1970.

McClelland, V. A., 'The Irish clergy and Archbishop Manning's apostolic visitation of the western district of Scotland, 1867', *Catholic Historical Review*, 53, 1, 1967.

McCormick, John, *The Flag in the Wind*, Gollancz, London, 1955.

McEwan, Hugh G., *Bishop Grey Graham, 1874–1959, an Essay on his Life and Times*, Burns, Glasgow, 1973.

McGhee, Susan, 'Carfin and the Roman Catholic Relief Act of 1926', *Innes Review*, 16, 1, 1965.

McGhee, Susan, *Monsignor Taylor of Carfin*, Burns, Glasgow, 1972.

McGovern, John, *Neither Fear nor Favour*, Blandford Press, London, 1960.

McIntyre, Stewart, *Little Moscows, Communism and Working-class Militancy in Inter-war Britain*, Croom Helm, London, 1980.

McKechin, W. J., *Plus or Minus? Problems affecting the Implementation of Positive Discrimination within Schools in Strathclyde*, Paisley College of Technology, 1976.

McKechin, W. J., *A School in Eastwood Park: a Case Study in Local Authority Decision-making and Public Participation*, Paisley College of Technology, 1979.

McLaren, Moray, *The Scots*, Penguin, London, 1951.

McLeod, Hugh, *Religion and the Working Class in Nineteenth Century Britain*, Macmillan, London, 1984.

McLean, Iain, *The Legend of Red Clydeside*, John Donald, Edinburgh, 1983.

McMahon, Dierdrie, *Republicans and Imperialists, Anglo-Irish Relations in The 1930s*, Yale University Press, New Haven and London, 1984.

McMillan, James, *Anatomy of Scotland*, Leslie Frewin, London, 1969.

McNee, David, *McNee's Law*, Collins, London, 1983.

McNee, Gerald, *The Story of Celtic: an Official History, 1888–1978*, Stanley Paul, London, 1978.

McRoberts, David, (ed.), *Modern Scottish Catholicism, 1878–1978*, Burns, Glasgow, 1979.

McShane, Harry, and Smith, Joan, *Harry McShane, No Mean Fighter*, Pluto, London, 1973.

Machin, G. I. T., 'The last Victorian anti-ritualist campaign, 1895–1906', *Victorian Studies*, 25, 3, 1982.

Machin, G. I. T., *Politics and the Churches in Great Britain, 1832 to 1868*, Clarendon Press, Oxford, 1977.

Mann, Jean, *Woman in Parliament*, Odhams, London, 1962.

The Menace of The Irish Race to our Scottish Nationality, Bishop, Edinburgh, 1923.

Middlemas, R. K., *The Clydesiders: a Left-wing Struggle for Parliamentary Power*, Hutchinson, London, 1965.

Milton, Nan, *John Maclean*, Pluto, London, 1973.

Moody, T. W., 'Michael Davitt and the British Labour Movement, 1882–1906', in *Transactions of the Royal Historical Society*, 5th series, 3, 1953.

Moorhouse, H. F., 'Professional football and working-class culture: English thought and Scottish experience', *Sociological Review*, 32, 2, 1984.

Morris, R. J., 'Skilled workers and the politics of "Red Clyde"', *Bulletin of the Scottish History Society*, 1983.

Moxon-Browne, E., *Nation, Class and Creed in Northern Ireland*, Gower, Aldershot, 1984.

Muir, Edwin, *Scottish Journey*, Mainstream, Edinburgh, 1979 (first published 1935).

Muirhead, Ian A., 'Catholic emancipation: Scottish reactions in 1829', *Innes Review*, 24, 1, 1973.

Murray, Bill, *The Old Firm, Sectarianism, Sport and Society in Scotland*, John Donald, Edinburgh, 1984.

Neill, A. S., *Is Scotland Educated?*, Routledge, London, 1936.

Norman, E. R., *Anti-Catholicism in Victorian England*, Allen & Unwin, London, 1968.

Oakley, C. M., *The Second City*, Blackie, London, 1946.

O'Connor, Bernard, 'Irish nationalism in Liverpool, 1873-1923', *Eire-Ireland*, 10, 1, 1975.

O'Connor, Kevin, *The Irish In Britain*, Torc, Dublin, 1970.

O'Riordan, Michael, *The Connolly Column*, New Books, Dublin, 1979.

O'Tuathaigh, 'The Irish in nineteenth century Britain: problems of integration', in *Transactions of the Royal Historical Society*, 5th series, 31, 1981.

Paton, H. J., *The Claim of Scotland*, Allen & Unwin, London, 1968.

Paton, John, *Proletarian Pilgrimage*, Routledge, London, 1935.

Patrick, James, *A Glasgow Gang Observed*, Eyre Methuen, London, 1972.

Pelling, Henry, *The British Communist Party: a Historical Profile*, Black, London, 1958.

Pelling, Henry, *Social Geography of British Elections, 1885-1910*, Macmillan, London, 1967.

Power, William, *Should Auld Acquaintance . . .*, Harrap, London, 1937.

Primmer, J. Boyd, *Life and Work of Jacob Primmer, Minister of the Church of Scotland*, William Bishop, Edinburgh, 1916.

Pryde, G. S., 'The development of nationalism in Scotland', *Sociological Review*, 27, 3, 1935.

Purdie, Bob, 'The Friends of Ireland: British Labour and Irish nationalism, 1945-49', in Gallagher, T., and O'Connell, J., *Contemporary Irish Studies*, Manchester University Press, 1983.

Putnam, McEntee, Georgina, *The Social Catholic Movement in Great Britain*, Macmillan, London, 1927.

Quinn, James, 'Ecumenism and Scottish Catholics', in McRoberts, David (ed.), *Modern Scottish Catholicism, 1878-1978*, Burns, Glasgow, 1979.

Reilly, Patrick, 'Catholics in Scottish literature, 1878-1978', in McRoberts, David (ed.), *Modern Scottish Catholicism, 1878-1978*, Burns, Glasgow, 1979.

Reilly, Patrick, 'Demolition in Progress, Catholic education in Scotland today', *Forum*, 6, 4, 1980.

Rhodes, Anthony C., *The Power of Rome in the Twentieth Century, the Vatican in the Age of Liberal Democracies, 1873-1922*, Sidgwick & Jackson, London, 1983.

Rodgers, Murdoch, 'The Anglo-Russian military convention and the Lithuanian immigrant community in Lanarkshire, Scotland (1917-20)', *Immigrants and Minorities*, 1, 1, 1982.

Ross, Anthony, 'Resurrection', in Glen, Duncan (ed.), *Whither Scotland?*, Gollancz, London, 1971.

Ross, Anthony, 'The Church in Scotland', in Cummings, J., and Burns, P. (eds.), *The Church Now*, Gill & Macmillan, Dublin, 1980.

Ross, Anthony, 'Development of the Scottish Catholic Community, 1878-1978', in McRoberts, David (ed.), *Modern Scottish Catholicism, 1878-1978*, Burns, Glasgow, 1979.

Salvidge, Stanley, *Salvidge of Liverpool*, Hodder & Stoughton, London, 1934.

Scott, George, *The RCs*, Hutchinson, London, 1967.

Scott-Moncrieff, George, *The Mirror and the Cross, Scotland and the Catholic Faith*, Burns & Oates, London, 1960.

Shallice, A., 'Liverpool labourism and Irish nationalism in the 1920s and 1930', *North West Labour History Society Bulletin*, 8, 1982-83.

Sheed, Frank, *The Church and I*, Sheed & Ward, London, 1974.

Sillitoe, Sir Percy, *Cloak without Dagger*, Pan, London, 1955.

Skidelsky, Robert, *Sir Oswald Mosley*, Macmillan, London, 1981.

Slavin Willy, 'Roman in the Gloamin',' *Cencrastus*, 11, 1983.

Smith, Joan, 'Labour tradition in Glasgow and Liverpool', *History Workshop*, 17, spring 1984.

Smout, T. C., *A Century of the Scottish People, 1830-1950*, Collins, London, 1986.

Steele, E. D., 'The Irish presence in the north of England', *Northern History*, 12, 1976.

Stone, Norman, *Europe Transformed, 1878-1919*, Fontana, Glasgow, 1983.

Strachey, Lytton, *Five Victorians*, Reprint Society edition, London, 1942.

Strauss, Erich, *Irish Nationalism and British Democracy*, Methuen, London, 1951.

Taplin, Eric, 'Irish leaders and the Liverpool dockers: Richard McGhee and Edward McHugh', *North West Labour History Society Bulletin*, 9, 1983-4.

Taylor, A. J. P., *English History, 1914-45*, Oxford University Press, various editions.

Thompson, E. P., *The Making of the English Working Class*, Pelican edition, London, 1968.

Thomson, George Malcolm, *Caledonia, or the Future of the Scots*, Kegan Paul, London, 1927.

Thomson, George Malcolm, *The Re-discovery of Scotland*, Routledge, London, 1928.

Torrance, John, *Scotland's Dilemma, Province or Nation?*, Oliver & Boyd, Edinburgh, 1939.

Treble, J. H., 'The working of the 1918 Education Act in the Glasgow archdiocese', *Innes Review*, 31, 1, 1980.

Turner, Bryan S., 'State, civil society and national development: the Scottish problem', *Australia and New Zealand Journal of Sociology*, 20, 2, 1974.

Urwin, D., 'The development of the Conservative Party organisation in Scotland until 1912', *Scottish Historical Review*, 44, 2, 1965.

Walker, William, 'Dundee's disenchantment with Churchill: a comment on the fall of the Liberal Party', *Scottish Historical Review*, 49, 1, 1970.

Walker, William, 'Irish immigrants in Scotland: their priests, politics and parochial life', *Historical Journal*, xv, 4, 1972.

Walker, William, *Juteopolis: Dundee and its Textile Workers*, Scottish Academic Press, Edinburgh, 1979.

Walkinshaw, Colin, *The Scots Tragedy*, Routledge, London, 1935.

Waller, P. J., *Democracy and Sectarianism, a Political and Social History of Liverpool, 1868-1939*, Liverpool University Press, 1981.

Walshe, James, 'Archbishop Manning's visitation of the western district of Scotland in 1867', *Innes Review*, 18, 1, 1967.

Whitley, Henry C., *Laughter in Heaven*, Hutchinson, London, 1962.

Wilson, Gordon M., *Alexander McDonald, Leader of the Miners*, Aberdeen University Press, 1982.

Wood, Ian S., 'Irish immigrants and Scottish radicalism, 1880-1906', in Ian McDougall (ed.), *Essays in Scottish Labour History*, John Donald, Edinburgh, 1979.

Wood, Ian S., 'Scotland and the Spanish Civil War', *Cencrastus*, autumn 1984.

Wood, Ian, S., 'John Wheatley, the Irish and the Labour Movement in Scotland', *Innes Review*, 21, 1980.

Index